A SHORT HISTORY
OF
GERMANY

To

GEORGE P. GOOCH
C.H., D.LITT., F.B.A.

and

T. S. R. BOASE
DIRECTOR OF THE COURTAULD INSTITUTE
UNIVERSITY OF LONDON

in gratitude and
friendship

A SHORT HISTORY
OF
GERMANY

BY

S. H. STEINBERG

εἴ τις αὐτοὺς ξυνελὼν φαίη πε-
φυκέναι ἐπὶ τῷ μήτε αὐτοὺς
ἔχειν ἡσυχίαν μήτε τοὺς ἄλλους
ἀνθρώπους ἐᾶν, ὀρθῶς ἂν εἴποι.

THUCYDIDES I, 70

The sober teaching of history is
the foundation of sound politics.

H. A. L. FISHER

NEW YORK: THE MACMILLAN COMPANY
CAMBRIDGE, ENGLAND: AT THE UNIVERSITY PRESS

1945

943
S819

COPYRIGHT, 1945, BY THE MACMILLAN COMPANY

All rights reserved — no part of this book may be reproduced in any form without permission in writing from the publisher, except by a reviewer who wishes to quote brief passages in connection with a review written for inclusion in magazine or newspaper.

PRINTED IN THE UNITED STATES OF AMERICA

CONTENTS

Prefatory Note		*page* vi
Introduction: Centralism and Federalism in German History		vii
Chap. I.	The Empire as champion of the Christian world (900–1050)	1
II.	The contest between Empire and Papacy (1056–1250)	27
III.	The disintegration of the Empire (1250–1493)	52
IV.	The contest between Empire and Territories (1493–1648)	76
V.	The Empire in decay (1648–1786)	117
VI.	The collapse of the Empire (1786–1815)	156
VII.	The German Confederation (1815–1866)	177
VIII.	The Bismarck Empire (1867–1890)	223
IX.	The Empire of William II (1890–1918)	241
X.	The Weimar Republic (1918–1933)	264
Epilogue: The Nazi Dictatorship		278
Index		286

Maps

1.	Germany in the Tenth and Eleventh Centuries	*page* 2
2.	Europe about 1180	43
3.	Germany in 1378	65
4.	Germany in 1546	88
5.	Europe in 1555	89
6.	Germany in the second half of the 17th century	116
7.	Germany in 1793	155
8.	Germany in 1815	176
9.	German Customs Union	193
10.	Germany, 1867–1918	222
11.	Bismarck's system of alliances	238
12.	Germany, 1919–38	263

PREFATORY NOTE

This book aims at giving the English public a narrative, on a modest scale, which is, in fact, a history of Germany and not a history of Brandenburg-Prussia's expansion into Greater Prussia.

For a detailed study of events the reader is referred to the relevant chapters of the *Cambridge Medieval* and *Modern Histories*, and their comprehensive bibliographies. The present author's *Historical Tables* (Macmillan, 1939) may be found useful as a synoptic conspectus of facts and dates.

I am grateful to those friends who were good enough to read and criticise my manuscript and, in particular, to

Mr W. T. Gairdner, Mr J. D. Higham, Mr Stanley Morison, Mr R. H. Samuel, Mr I. Scotland and Mr H. Thistlethwaite.

Mr D.E. Mende permitted me to make liberal use of his unpublished history of Germany from the accession of William II, and Mr R. M. Spencer helped me in drawing the maps.

S. H. S.

INTRODUCTION

CENTRALISM AND FEDERALISM IN GERMAN HISTORY

The outstanding fact in the history of Germany is the non-existence, up to 1871, of any political unit called Germany. When the Frankish Empire was partitioned among the grandsons of Charlemagne in 843, the parts east of the Rhine were called the East Frankish Kingdom as distinct from the West Frankish Kingdom, which was soon to be known as France. From 962, when Otto I was crowned emperor in Rome, the official title of his dominions was 'Holy Roman Empire'. At its head was the 'King of the Romans', who was elevated to the dignity of 'Roman Emperor' after his coronation by the Pope; when the coronation in Rome was discontinued the 'Roman King' assumed the title of 'Roman Emperor Elect' (from 1508). These titles remained in use until the dissolution of the Empire in 1806. The term 'German Lands', first used in an official document in 1442, occurs hereafter only at wide intervals. From 1486 it became the custom to speak of the 'German section of the Roman Empire' (*Römisches Reich deutscher Nation*) when referring to the regions north of the Alps. It was only after the Napoleonic wars that a 'German Confederation' was established (1815); and the empire of the Hohenzollerns was the first to be called officially the 'German Empire' (1871).

There was no 'Germany' for a thousand years because there was no German nation to which the term could be applied. The term 'Germans' comprises the West Teutonic tribes on the continent (the Anglo-Saxons forming the remaining part), just as the term 'Scandinavians' comprises the North Teutonic peoples. Saxons, Bavarians, Franks, Hessians, Swabians and Thuringians are not regional subdivisions of one nation, they are nations themselves. They stand in the same racial relation one to another as do the Danes, Swedes, Norwegians and Icelanders. The description of early nineteenth-century Italy as a 'merely geographical expression' may be applied even more aptly to Germany. The Scandinavian peoples have been allowed to develop as independent nations throughout the centuries, apart from one or two short-lived attempts at a Scandinavian union under German princes. The

German nations, on the other hand, were forcibly welded together by the Frankish kings from Clovis (481–511) to Charlemagne (768–814), before they could fully develop their own institutions by themselves. Despite this handicap the racial, political and cultural differences remained strong enough to enable the Alemanni of Switzerland and Alsace, the Bavarians of Austria, and the Low Franks of the Netherlands and Luxemburg to establish and maintain their political independence with comparative ease.

The Frankish overlordship was established by brute force of arms; but it was given a spiritual justification when Charlemagne was crowned Roman Emperor on Christmas Day, 800. As the anointed protector and defender of the Christian Church, the Emperor was in theory the overlord of the *res publica Christiana*. As this Christian world was composed of various national units, none of which was willing to abandon the whole of its independence, the Roman Emperor may be described as the titular head of a worldwide Christian federation. Successive Emperors tried to extend their powers and thereby to transform the commonwealth of nations into a centralized monarchy. The Carolingians failed to amalgamate the whole of the Teutonic and Romance nations, which broke apart fifty years after Charlemagne's death. Would it be possible to establish a central power limited to the German tribes? Would the German tribes each go their own way, and thus further disintegrate the West? Or might a compromise be found on a federal basis? These were the questions with which German rulers and peoples of each successive generation were confronted. Upon their solution depended the future of the Germanies, indeed of Central Europe.

Writing under the influence of the idea of the Nation State, one of the products of the French Revolution, German historians of the nineteenth and twentieth centuries rashly considered the centralized monarchy (or republic) to be the only natural solution, and condemned the opposition of the tribes as an obstinate deviation from the predestined course of German history. In actual fact, the German tribes were far from wishing to obstruct a reasonable federal union. What they resented was the imposition of a centralized rule that would have stifled their natural growth. The strength, and, one may add, the justification of the tribal spirit can be gauged by the fact that it has survived the break-up of the old tribal organizations. From the twelfth century onward, these gave way to the growth of territorial states which were based on merely dynastic principles. Even then, the rulers of Bavaria and Hesse retained the old tribal names, and those of Hanover and Württemberg kept the tribal arms and colours, although their territories were no longer identical with those of the medieval Bavarians, Hessians, Saxons and Swabians respectively. It is noteworthy that the one state which pursued the scheme of forcibly subduing the other German territories, and eventually succeeded in doing so, was Prussia, i.e. the only German territory of importance that has grown up outside the old tribal boundaries. The march of Brandenburg and the dukedoms of Prussia and Pomerania, the strongholds of the Prussian monarchy and Prussian spirit, were originally inhabited by Slavs and Balts. German settlers from every tribe poured in from the twelfth century onward, and mixed with the aboriginal population. This mixture of every German, West Slavonic and Baltic tribe developed into a new race whose mentality was entirely different from that of any of its components. It was this Prussia that scorned the idea of a free federal union of the German tribes, and did not rest until it had forced upon Germany that unity which was the reverse of a thousand years of German history.

The way for the unification of Germany has been prepared by two men who were certainly far from envisaging the results of their exertions: Luther and Napoleon; the former, by creating the national language; the latter, by creating the national consciousness. Luther's translation of the Bible bridged the gulf which up to that time separated the High and Low German languages, by choosing a vocabulary and syntax derived from and intelligible to both regions. Even the section of Germany that remained faithful to the Roman creed adopted the 'Lutheran German' because of its obvious advantages; and the 'classical' writers and poets—Lessing, Klopstock, Wieland, Herder, Goethe and Schiller—finally based German literature on Luther's vocabulary and grammar. It is, however, remarkable that up to the present day, the German 'dialects' have preserved the main features of 'languages', namely that they are spoken by every national regardless of social position; and 'pure' German is in fact relegated to the stage. There is no standard German comparable with the King's English and considered the natural mode of expression by every German from whatever district he may hail.

Napoleon I, Emperor of the French, was the man who instilled the vision of a free, great and united Germany in the hearts of nations so different in their political and intellectual outlook as were the Prussians, Saxons, Austrians and all the other Germans of his age. He did away with literally hundreds of petty states, arbitrarily altered the frontiers of the remaining ones without regard to historical and racial boundaries, and thus forced the peoples of the newly created states to forget their age-old differences. Moreover, the pitiful and subservient role which the monarchs of the Rhenish Confederation played in the Emperor's wake was hardly calculated to satisfy the spirit of a generation which had learned from the French Revolutionaries the value of nationhood, if nothing else. Thus Napoleon, by radically destroying the historical bonds, became the involuntary promoter of German nationalism.

The 'German Confederation' as created by the Congress of Vienna (1815) was a half-hearted attempt at a solution of the German question on federal lines. The rivalry of the two great powers, Austria and Prussia, was the main obstacle to its development. Prussia was not interested in being *primus*, much less *secundus inter pares*, but aimed at a hegemony over the middle and small states, and at the exclusion of Austria. Nor were liberalism and nationalism, the two great intellectual and political movements of the nineteenth century, willing to compromise with an institution which was conservative and supra-national in its very structure. Thus Bismarck might feel in accord with the spirit of the age when he overthrew the German Confederation (1866) and established the Hohenzollern Empire (1871). It was a skilful blend of the Prussian blood-and-iron creed with the national-liberal ideology of the middle classes. But right from the beginning Bismarck had to wage bitter feuds against the 'enemies of the Empire' as he chose to describe the adversaries of Prussian hegemony. He also called 'peevish grumpiness' (*Reichsverdrossenheit*) what was, in fact, mere unwillingness to acquiesce in his solution of the German question; and this dissatisfaction was, though for different reasons, to be found amongst the Prussian Junkers, the Bavarian, Rhenish and Silesian Catholics, the adherents of the dethroned Guelph and Hessian dynasties, not less than amongst progressive and socialist politicians in every part of the Empire. Bismarck's solution was not the final one; so much was clear even before its downfall in 1918.

The creators of the Weimar Constitution envisaged a federal organization of the Republic: Prussia was to be dismembered and the other states reshaped according to their historical, racial, economic and cultural needs. This tendency found its expression in the preamble of the Weimar Constitution, which referred to 'the German people, united in its tribes, and animated by the desire to renew and consolidate its Empire in freedom and justice'. These words remained, however, a dead letter. No serious attempt was ever made to develop the constitution on federal lines, for Prussia remained an insuperable stumbling-block. When Hitler came to power in 1933, he proclaimed himself the fulfiller of German unity, and made some violent efforts to eradicate traditional divisions, the most curious among them being the introduction of a uniform German passport. (Up to 1935 there had in fact been no German passport nationality; the individual German had continued to be described as a Saxon, Badener, or Hamburger.) On the other hand, the National Socialists have created further confusion by establishing their party districts as additional administrative units. They frequently overlap other frontiers; the very word 'Gaue' has a medieval ring to German ears: in view of the avowed centralism of the Nazi administration, it is an indirect proof of the underlying strength of the old federal divisions. In short, the structure of Germany has remained what it appeared to a seventeenth-century political theorist, namely 'a rather irregular body, like unto a monster' (*irregulare aliquod corpus et monstro simile*).

The history of the Germanies is the history of the unending struggle of the continental Teutons for a working compromise between uniformity and disruption. Uniformity was and is contrary to the racial, cultural and political divergency of the Germanic tribes; the complete independence of each part would have been and will be contrary to the economic, cultural and political interests of those very parts. At no time was one central power strong enough to crush the centrifugal tendencies of the component elements. At no time were the component sections weak enough to let themselves be merged into one body politic. The main problem of German history is very similar to that with which the League of Nations was confronted, namely, to find a working compromise between centralism and anarchy. What the League failed to achieve in twenty years, the Germanies have not been able to achieve in a millennium.

CHAPTER I

THE EMPIRE AS CHAMPION OF THE CHRISTIAN WORLD (900–1050)

ALMOST every German historian makes German history begin with the inroad into the Roman orbit of the Cimbri and Teutones (112 B.C.). The history of any Germanic tribe which at one time or another settled within the boundaries of present Germany is considered part and parcel of German history, without further questioning. Now, every Germanic tribe, with the exception of the Scandinavian peoples, has, in fact, migrated through, and stayed for some period in, the country between the Meuse and Memel. German history becomes thus identified with Germanic history; and the claim to the leadership of all Germanic peoples put forth by German nationalists receives thereby a seemingly historical justification.

The origin of this identification of German with Germanic history can be traced back to the humanistic historiographers of the time of the Emperor Maximilian I (1493–1519). It was these forefathers of our contemporary journalists who supplied the 'copy' for Maximilian's anti-French propaganda. The French and, in fact, every other nation were, so they argued, inferior to the Germans because of the latter's pride of place in the pedigree of the Western nations: had they not for ancestors the Cimbri who made Rome tremble, the Cherusci who annihilated three Augustan legions, the Ostrogoths who conquered Italy, the Visigoths who subdued Spain, and the Vandals who ruled North Africa and the Mediterranean? Were the Germans of Maximilian not the sons and heirs of the Lombards who gave their name to Upper Italy, the Franks who established their rule over Gaul, the Angles and Saxons who made themselves masters of Britain?

It is not surprising that German nationalists should have accepted this noble pedigree which implied the inherited claim to the dominion of the then known world. What is amazing is that this German nationalistic conception, born of political propaganda, has not only survived the feeble French counter-propaganda of the time, but has been taken ever since for an historical truth inside and outside Germany.

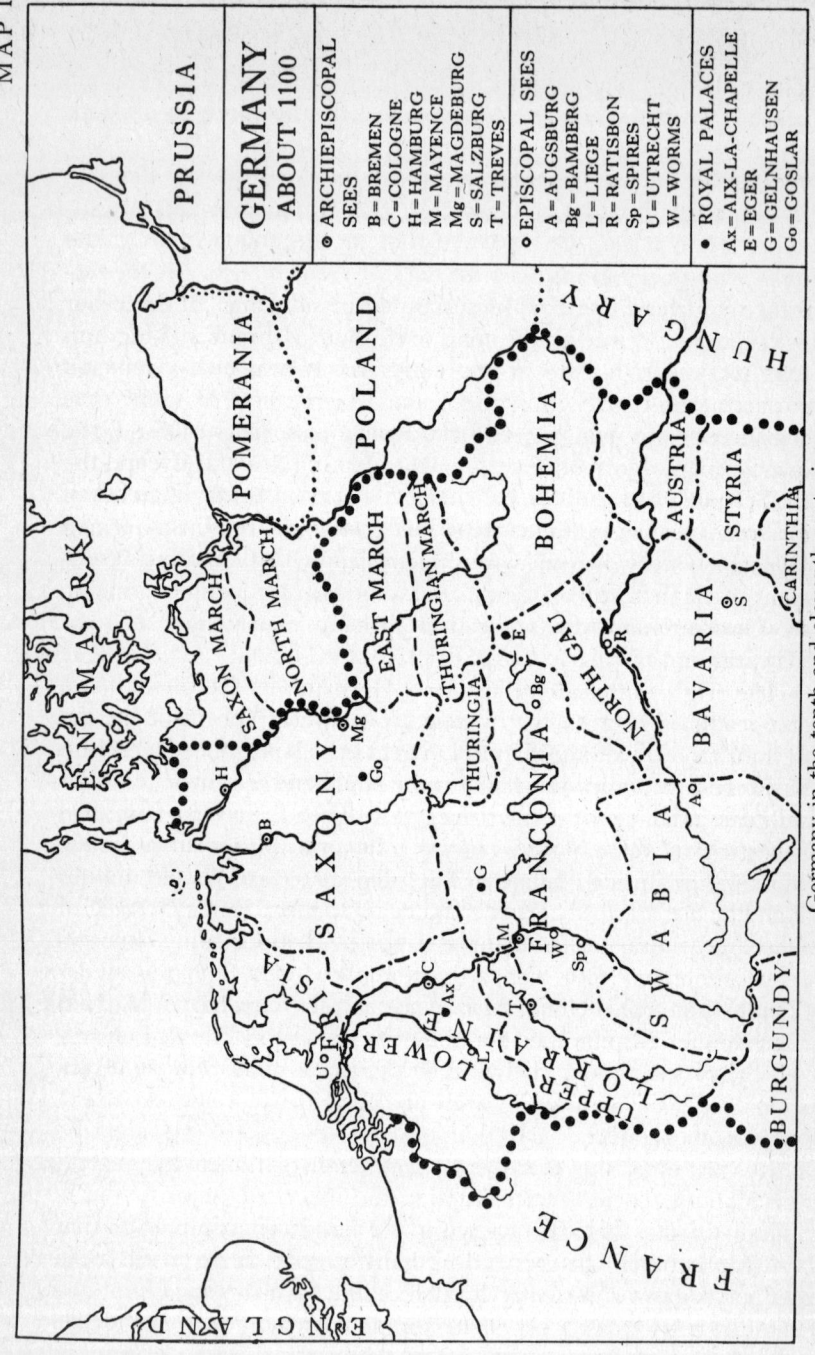

Germany in the tenth and eleventh centuries

There should be no doubt that the history of the East Teutonic tribes, i.e. Goths, Vandals, Burgundians, has no more to do with the history of Germany than with that of England or Norway. Nor is the history of the West Germanic tribes in any way identical with the early history of Germany. The Lombards and Anglo-Saxons, for instance, were part of that racial group: so were the Franks who made themselves masters of Gaul in 486. In the following centuries these Franks succeeded in subduing all the other West Germanic tribes on the continent. But the Frankish kingdom of the Merovingian and Carolingian dynasties was not 'German'. Its centre was Northern France, and it comprised not only the German tribes proper, but also the Romanized Kelts of Gaul, the West Germanic Lombards and the Romanic Italians of Italy, and the East Germanic Visigoths and Romanized Iberians of Spain north of the Ebro. It was a conglomerate of many races and regions: German it was not. Only when the Carolingian Empire broke into its component parts, the German tribes, as distinguished from the Germanic tribes, made their entry into European history.

The attempt of Charlemagne to unite the Teutonic and Romanic nations of Western Europe in one body politic finally broke down in the reign of his grandson. After the treaty of Verdun (843) the three main parts of the Empire began to shape themselves into what were later to be known as France, Italy and Germany. A hundred years after the death of the great Charles their separation had become irrevocable. Not so, however, the principles of unity underlying the Carolingian Empire. The idea that there should always be one flock and one shepherd was one of the fundamental tenets of Christianity; that the *civitas terrena* was to be the earthly counterpart of the *civitas Dei* had been established once and for all by St Augustine; that the final form of the earthly monarchy was given in the Roman Empire and its legitimate successor followed clearly from the prophecies of Daniel. The theocratic monarchy as established by Charlemagne was based on the identity of interest of the heads of the spiritual and temporal powers, the Pope and the Emperor; it was thus the utmost perfection that Christians could expect in this world of imperfection.

The weakness of this conception is evident; it presupposed that there would be no change in the conditions prevailing at the time when an all-powerful monarch wielded the secular sword over the undivided *res publica Christiana* in complete harmony with, or rather in hardly disputed ascendancy over, the spiritual forces of Papacy and Church. The history of the following centuries took an exactly opposite course: the unity of the Western nations gave way to a number of independent national states sharply divided against one another; and the harmonious co-operation of Empire and Papacy was replaced by a life-and-death struggle which eventually resulted in the utter ruin of both.

When in 911 the East Frankish line of the Carolingian dynasty died out, the political situation was widely different in the various parts of the former Empire. In Italy, a number of petty princes had established feeble sovereignties over all those parts of the peninsula not in the possession of the Byzantines or the Arabs, the latter having just finished the conquest of Sicily (902). The kings of Burgundy and the dukes of Swabia and Bavaria made frequent inroads into the Lombardic plain. The empty title of king of Italy, sometimes combined with the even emptier one of emperor, fell to the rulers of Friuli, Spoleto and Lower Burgundy without giving any of them the power to consolidate Italy. The Papacy had sunk into that 'era of pornocracy', when an unscrupulous Roman noblewoman and her daughters freely handed the keys of St Peter to their paramours and sons as an appendage to the rule over the Eternal City.

In France, the degenerate descendants of Charlemagne still held nominal sway over the whole of the country from the mouth of the Scheldt to the Pyrenees. In fact, however, the great vassals of the crown had become independent rulers in their own right. The Midi went its own way which, for three centuries, led it farther and farther from the Île de France. In 911, Hrolf, a Norman chieftain, forced the weak French king to cede the mouth of the Seine and the territory adjacent to the English Channel, and to recognize him as duke of Normandy. The counts of Paris, or dukes of Francia, were the true regents of the country as far as it still obeyed the shadow king; before the close of the tenth century they were even to become the legitimate occupants of the throne.

The old Teutonic tribes east of the Meuse had preserved their tribal constitution even under the centralistic system of Charlemagne. The weakness of the central administration under the later Carolingians freed the dukes of Bavaria, Swabia, Franconia, Saxony and Lorraine of the fetters imposed upon their independence. These dukedoms constituted as many independent states; they were held loosely together by the political reminiscence of the Carolingian monarchy and the racial bond of their common Teutonic descent.

Whilst the French kingdom was opposed by the centrifugal forces of regionalism, any bearer of the German crown was confronted by the double hostility of regionalism and tribalism; which, moreover, found much common ground and were therefore the more formidable. As the king had perforce to be chosen from one tribe, he had invariably to face the opposition of all the others.

When the East Frankish line of the Carolingians died out in 911, the German tribes had regained enough of their old spirit of independence to scorn the idea of returning into the old fold. They set up a king of their own choice without regard to the still existing Carolingian kingdom of France. Conrad I, formerly duke of Franconia, was, however, unable to master the problem of tribalism. The first effect of his election was the defection of Lorraine, comprising the territories between the rivers Rhine, Scheldt and Meuse. The Lorrainers, half-German and half-French, transferred their allegiance to Charles the Simple, king of France. Nor did the other German tribes submit to the Franconian duke. Their principal leader, Duke Henry of Saxony, openly defied the king, who proved powerless against him. Faced by the open hostility of the entire nobility, Conrad tried to support his tottering authority by leaning on the ecclesiastical powers; he even conceded the presidency of an imperial synod to a papal legate. That was of no avail, however, and Germany continued to be a prey to civil strife and lawlessness.

Conrad was fully alive to this impossible state of affairs. On his death-bed he designated his strongest adversary, Henry of Saxony, as his successor, and sent him the regalia by the hand of his brother, who had been his heir apparent.

Henry's dukedom of Saxony comprised the territories between the lower Elbe and the lower Rhine, the North Sea and the Hartz mountains. The country had never formed part of the Roman Empire; it was the last to accept the Frankish rule and the Christian religion. It was the homeland of the strongest, most ferocious and least civilized German tribe. The Saxons boasted of their undiluted Nordic blood and their near kinship with the Scandinavians and with the Anglo-Saxons who had emigrated from those very parts which had now become the core of the German kingdom. Henry I, learning from his own past and the mistakes of Conrad, judiciously refrained from imposing the royal prerogatives upon the unwilling dukes, and thus secured at least their tacit compliance with his nominal overlordship. Sober, cautious and realistic, he devoted his reign to laying the foundations on which his more brilliant and ambitious son afterwards revived the splendour of the imperial edifice.

At the beginning of his reign Henry was confronted with the recurrent invasions of the Magyars, Asiatic horsemen whose plundering expeditions into Germany and Italy succeeded those of the Vikings of the ninth century. Favoured by an unexpected stroke of good fortune, Henry concluded a nine-year truce with these raiders (924); when it expired he was strong enough to meet them in battle. He crushed the Magyars near the river Saale, so that they never again extended their forays to Northern Germany. Henry used the respite gained by that truce to consolidate his power. He took advantage of the internal troubles of France, where one pretender after another opposed the weak Charles the Simple, and recovered Lorraine (925). By marrying his eldest son Otto to Edith, sister of King Aethelstan of England, in 929, he gained an ally across the sea who was labouring for the consolidation of the English monarchy on similar lines and with similar success as himself. King Edward the Elder had introduced a system of fortified and self-supporting boroughs to secure England against the Danes and Kelts: Henry took over the scheme in order to combat the recurring raids of Magyars and Slavs, and a number of these fortified camps developed afterwards into flourishing towns.

It was the Western Slav tribes on the right banks of the rivers Saale and Elbe which were the main obstacles to the expansion of the Saxons. Now space and expansion were of vital necessity to every nation in the Middle Ages. The agricultural structure of society, the exhaustion of the overworked soil and the lack of settled industry resulted in a comparative over-population of each country. The scarcity of precious metal made enfeoffment with arable land the only possible reward for military and civil services. All these motives made necessary the acquisition of more and more territory, even if a nation and its ruler only wished to maintain their standard of living; much more so if they desired to improve it.

The fight against the pagan Slavs was moreover a missionary task imposed upon every Christian people. For centuries, the German expansion eastward was deemed necessary from religious as well as political and economic motives. Nationalistic conceptions were, however, absent, as nationalism was altogether alien to the medieval way of thinking. On many occasions German settlers were called in by Slav princes themselves to populate the wide and empty spaces and make them yield better crops. For the iron plough of the German peasants was infinitely superior to the primitive wooden plough of the Slavs and it had a greater and certainly more honourable share than the sword in Germanizing the East Elbian and Baltic countries.

During the truce with the Magyars Henry led a successful expedition across the middle Elbe and took Brandenburg, the central encampment of the Slavs of the Havel district (928-9), which was afterwards to become the cradle of the Prussian state. Farther south he forced his overlordship upon the recently Christianized Bohemia, whose duke, Wenceslaus I, was, however, speedily overthrown by a pagan reaction; he was murdered and became the first of the Czech martyrs (929).

At the end of his reign Henry seems to have felt secure enough to think of even more far-reaching schemes. He acquired the march of Slesvig from a petty Danish ruler. The port of Slesvig was the main emporium of the Baltic trade in the ninth and tenth centuries; and the territory across the Cimbric peninsula was then as afterwards a suitable jumping-off ground for a ruler wishing to interfere in Nordic affairs. Henry also made a treaty with the king of Upper Burgundy who, in exchange for some territorial acquisitions near Basle, gave the German king the Holy Lance of St Constantine, thereby bestowing on him a symbolic claim to the crown of Italy. Possibilities of further expansion north, east and south were thus left at his death to his son and successor, Otto I (936).

Otto (936-73) showed at the outset of his reign the course he meant to pursue. He had himself crowned by the archbishop of Mayence as 'King of the Franks' on the model of Charlemagne in the minster of Aix-la-Chapelle, Charlemagne's favourite foundation. He thus added a spiritual consecration to the popular election, and raised the kingship above tribal disputes. The coronation at Aix-la-Chapelle by the primate of the German Church was henceforth essential: only after it did the elected king become entitled to the homage and fealty of the tribes. At the coronation banquet Otto made the tribal dukes attend him as chamberlain, steward, or marshal, with intent to reduce them to the status of officers of the crown. Their independence, however, was not to be overcome so easily. It is characteristic that even the Saxon court historiographer, Widukind of Corvey, did not accept the official version of a united Germany: to him Otto remained the Saxon duke who had subdued the Frankish, Bavarian and other nations by force of arms. With the greatest misgivings the Franks saw themselves ousted from their old position as the royal tribe; the Lorrainers still cherished the memory of their virtual independence between the Eastern and Western parts of the Carolingian Empire; and the Bavarians, from time immemorial to the present day the most self-willed and refractory of all the Germans, did not yield without struggle to the Saxon dominion. The combination of all the non-Saxon tribes against Otto's centralizing policy was the more formidable as it was headed by his younger brother Henry, who pretended to have better claims to the crown as being born after their father's accession to the throne. It took Otto almost four years (938–41) to master these opponents, by which time his power was sufficiently established to allow him to tackle several problems left unsolved by Henry I. The Christianization of the East was a matter of real concern to the king, deeply conscious as he was of the obligation his coronation had laid upon him as a Christian ruler. The Bavarian bishopric of Passau undertook the hard task of converting the savage Magyars, who by this time had settled in the central plain of the Danube basin, yet without entirely abandoning their pillaging raids. Adaldag, archbishop of Hamburg, one of the closest political advisers of Otto, set up the ecclesiastical organization of Jutland, while Otto himself consolidated the march of Slesvig. At the same time the bishoprics of Brandenburg and Havelberg were established; they gave the 'North March', the eastern outpost of Saxony, a glacis across the middle Elbe, and secured the safety of Magdeburg, which soon afterwards became the see of a new metropolitan organization.

The unstable conditions still prevailing in France gave Otto an opportunity to interfere in the West. A French invasion of Lorraine, arranged and coinciding with the rebellion of 938, was repelled without difficulty. When a few years later King Louis IV fell into the hands of his most powerful vassal, Duke Hugo of Francia, Otto sided with the king as the weaker party, and advanced as far as Rouen and the outskirts of Paris (946). The peace he mediated between the rivals in 950 left him enough influence over France to render her incapable of interfering with his own designs upon Italy.

The fates of Germany and Italy were interwoven in a very strange pattern, from the moment when Berengar of Ivrea, one of the contesting princelings of Upper Italy, having taken temporary refuge at the German court (941), turned the eyes of the German king to the unsettled conditions of Italy, up to the occupation of Rome by the dynasty of Savoy in 1870, which was made possible by the German victory over Napoleon III. Nominally the two countries formed part of the Holy Roman Empire, the secular lordship of which soon became almost an appurtenance of the German crown, whereas the spiritual guidance of the West was fixed at the Italian capital even when the Vicar of Christ was not of Italian nationality. The overthrow of the theocratical dyarchy, brought about by the downfall of the Hohenstaufen dynasty through papal agency (1250), and the humiliation of the Papacy at the hands of Philip le Bel of France (1303), resulted in the political ruin of both nations. Their lands became the battle-grounds of European armies and diplomatists for many centuries. Both eventually gained political unity through the exertions of their least centrally situated and least genuinely national parts, namely the half-Slavonic Prussia and the half-French Savoy. In concerted actions Prussia and Savoy defeated the lawful heirs of the Holy Empire, namely the house of Austria and the Papacy (1866–70).

A fierce controversy has raged among German historians over the Italian policy of the German kings from Otto I onward. Instead of pursuing idealistic dreams of a theocratical world monarchy, one school of thought argues, the kings should have concentrated on *Realpolitik* nearer home, i.e. the consolidation of the royal power over the great vassals of the crown. Instead of trying to subjugate the Italians, who never willingly suffered the foreign yoke, they should have directed their efforts towards the thinly populated Eastern regions; the Slav tribes, lacking political organization, economic power and an historic tradition, would have fallen an easy prey to a resolute conqueror. A compact German empire might thus have been established as far as the gulf of Bothnia and the waters of the Dnieper. An impartial study of Central Europe in the middle of the tenth century, and of the motives which led Otto to his Italian expeditions and the revival of the Roman Empire (962), will, however, lead to conclusions very different from those inspired by the ideology of nineteenth-century nationalism.

When, in 951, Otto set out against his former protégé Berengar, now king of Italy, he was still following the established policy of the Bavarians and Swabians, who had seized every opportunity to advance their tribal frontiers across the Alps into the region of the Upper Italian lakes. Italy, torn between rival pretenders who lacked the power necessary to support their ambitions, was a political vacuum which necessarily attracted every powerful neighbour. The physical law that does not allow vacant spaces has an exact counterpart in politics; a political vacuum has the same tendency to be filled as has an air-pocket. It was not a question whether Otto should make himself predominant in Italy or no; but whether he himself should tackle the task or leave it to somebody else—the French, the Byzantines, or the Arabs. Otto, who considered himself the lawful heir of Charlemagne and the champion of Western and Christian civilization, could not well abandon the head of the Church to schismatics and infidels, nor leave the tempting spoils to an inept ruler of France. He easily reduced the tyrannical rule of Berengar, assumed, again on the model of Charlemagne, the title of 'King of the Franks and Lombards', and legalized his rule over Italy by marrying Adelaide of Burgundy, the widow of Berengar's predecessor. The eastern approaches to Upper Italy were given to Duke Henry of Bavaria, Otto's youngest brother, who had become his firm supporter. This increase of the Bavarian power, however, stirred up the old antagonism of Swabia. Its duke was Otto's eldest son, Liudolf; and personal feelings exacerbated the issue. Soon Otto had to face a fresh rebellion, headed by Liudolf and the king's son-in-law, Conrad of Lorraine. The Magyars were not slow to take advantage of the civil war that raged for three years, and invaded South Germany as far as Augsburg. The onslaught of this foreign enemy, however, retrieved Otto's almost hopeless situation. The rebels joined the royal standard to combat the Magyars, and a united German army crushed their hordes near Augsburg so effectively that the Mongol horsemen never again crossed the frontier of the Empire (955). It was a victory of Western and Christian civilization over Asiatic barbarism that may be compared with the victory over the Turks before Vienna, in 1683. A general rising of the Slavs came too late to imperil Otto's position; a few weeks afterwards he inflicted a major defeat on them in Mecklenburg.

Otto's position and reputation were now firmly established throughout the Western world and beyond it. Envoys not only of France and England, but of Byzantium, Kiev and Cordoba, appeared at his court. It became the custom to call him 'the Great'. It was only a natural consequence that he followed his venerated model in obeying the call for aid which Pope John XII sent to him in 962. Berengar, wholly unaware of his precarious position after the first expedition of Otto, continued to pursue his independent policy and even encroached upon the Patrimonium Petri. John XII, one of the most worthless successors of St Peter and remarkable only as the first Pope to change his name (Octavian) on his accession, promised Otto the imperial crown as reward. Otto did not hesitate. He overthrew the rule of Berengar once and for all, and was crowned emperor immediately after his entry into Rome (2 Feb. 962). The 'Ottonian Privilege' (13 Feb.) regulated the relations between the Emperor and the Papacy on a basis of mutual concessions; their vagueness and ambiguity were such as to render them afterwards an incessant source of disputed claims. For the moment, Otto was undoubtedly the superior partner. He remained in Italy for several years and interfered vigorously in the affairs of the peninsula. He soon had John XII deposed by a Roman synod; an anti-pope who was put up against the imperial candidate was carried off to Germany and died at Hamburg, a prisoner of Archbishop Adaldag. During a short return of the Emperor to Germany (965), Harald Bluetooth of Denmark was baptized, and had to recognize the temporal and spiritual overlordship of the Empire and the Hamburg archiepiscopate alike. From 966 to 972 Otto was again busy strengthening his rule in Italy. He marched against the Byzantines, whom he confined to Apulia and Calabria, had his son, Otto II, crowned emperor in 967, thus securing an undisputed succession, and gained for him eventually a Byzantine bride, Theophano (972). This meant the formal recognition of his imperial status by the oldest surviving heir of the original Roman Empire, comparable in its political and ceremonial significance to the marriage with a Hapsburg princess of the upstart Napoleon I in 1810.

While Otto thus gained a supreme position in international politics, he did not neglect to strengthen the royal prerogatives at home. The acquisition of the imperial crown and his close collaboration with the papal see could not but have the strongest repercussions upon his position as German king; the solid foundations upon which he erected the royal supremacy remained unshaken for a century and continued a distinct feature of the German body politic until the dissolution of the Empire in 1806.

The main object of any central power in Germany was the elimination of the political independence of the tribal dukedoms and the establishment of a firm central administration. The imperial crown gave Otto a status which set him above tribal jealousies: the Lord's Anointed stood too high to be drawn into quarrels over the rival claims of Saxons and Franks to which Conrad I owed his failure, which Henry I had contrived to evade, and which had harassed Otto himself more than once. The close co-operation of the two supreme powers in Christendom further provided the Emperor with those assistants who, by virtue of their allegiance to the Church, were independent of the intermediate secular powers, but willing and able to make the theocratical union of Empire and Papacy succeed in practical politics. Thus Otto based the central administration almost exclusively upon the bishops and abbots of the Empire. Their interests did not coincide with those of the secular princes; their sees and jurisdictional power overlapped the frontiers of the secular rulers; being celibate, they had not to provide for the needs and greeds of their progeny; being princes of the Church as well as of the Empire, they united happily in themselves those very tendencies of which the Holy Roman Empire was the supreme expression. The scheme adopted by Otto had been designed by Charlemagne, but Otto went farther than Charlemagne had intended in bestowing secular privileges upon the high clergy. He gave away the rights of coining, of levying duties, of holding markets, and other prerogatives which Charlemagne had, more wisely, reserved to the crown. Under Otto's successors those privileges assumed an even larger proportion; to give one example, the bishops of Würzburg and the archbishops of Cologne eventually obtained the ducal rights of Franconia and Westphalia respectively. Otto was so sure of his ascendancy over the Church that he seems to have given no thought to the inherent dangers of this system. Could the German king trust the allegiance of the clergy if a pope should choose to upset the balance of power and turn against the imperial overlordship? In that case, the king, having bound himself to co-operation with the Papacy, could not well defy the executive organs of the Church. On the other hand, might not the clergy, vested with an abundance of worldly goods, one day throw in their lot with the secular princes in defending their common secular interests against their secular overlord? Having deprived himself of the greater part of the means of sustaining the royal power, the king would be helpless against a confederacy of both his lay and ecclesiastical vassals. These were exactly the dilemmas with which the kings of the following centuries were confronted. During the Investiture Struggle, the better elements among the clergy, who therefore held the greater sway over the lay world, decided that they must obey God rather than men, and thus brought about the downfall of Henry IV. And when at the beginning of the thirteenth century the German princes definitely established their own rights in defiance of the central administration, the ecclesiastics had become territorial princes of the same pattern as the secular dynasts and consequently claimed and received analogous privileges on an entirely worldly basis. The ecclesiastical principalities which loom so largely on the maps of Germany from the thirteenth to the eighteenth century and were one of the main obstacles to a political consolidation had their origin in the Ottonian administration.

Otto himself could not be aware of these consequences. In fact during his reign and for a century to come the advantages of his system far outweighed its defects. A brilliant combination of the old Saxon administrative policy with the opportunities which his newly acquired position as the worldly head of the Christian commonwealth gave him led to his most lasting success. Immediately after the coronation (962) he broached the plan of the possible establishment of the archbishopric of Magdeburg as the centre of Christian missionary activities and a stronghold of German influence amongst the Slavs. It took him, however, several years to overcome the resistance of the German bishops and the Pope before the foundation became a reality (968). The Pope wished to exempt the Polish Church from the jurisdiction of Magdeburg and succeeded in placing it immediately under the Roman obedience. On the other hand, Otto had his way when the Bohemian bishopric of Prague was placed under the jurisdiction of Mayence. The significance of that step becomes clear when we see the duke of Bohemia appear as a German vassal at Otto's last court at Quedlinburg. On that occasion, envoys from Poland, Russia, Byzantium, Hungary, Bulgaria, Denmark and Rome demonstrated the world-wide relations Otto had established, and which at his death shortly afterwards he left to his son, Otto II (973–83).

Public life in the Middle Ages was determined by the personal bonds between lord and liege, from the king down to the last holder of a fief. The modern conception of the state as a permanent institution independent of the qualities of its temporary ruler was utterly alien to the medieval mind, and the smooth working of an administration which was based only on personal loyalty required an unbroken succession of powerful rulers. It was one of the weakest points of the feudal system that an incapable leader at once endangered the whole edifice, and that even a strong prince had to vindicate his claims again and again by manifestations of personal valour.

Thus Otto II had to deal with almost the same problems which had troubled his father and grandfather before him. His cousin, Henry of Bavaria, tried to gain a greater independence if not actually the royal crown; he was defeated, imprisoned, and deprived of Carinthia, which was established as a dukedom of its own. Danes,

Poles and Bohemians suffered defeats when they tried to loosen their ties with Germany. King Lothair of France took advantage of the Bavarian rebellion to make a sudden attack and sacked Aix-la-Chapelle (978). But Otto swiftly returned the blow, and advancing as far as Paris, compelled Lothair to renounce Lorraine for good. An agreement with Hugo Capet, the French pretender, secured the western frontier of Germany (981). Otto was less fortunate in his attempt to pacify Italy after the Arabs had crossed the straits of Messina (976) and advanced into the Greek and Longobardic possessions of Southern Italy. The preoccupation of the Byzantines with the powerful Bulgarian empire made Otto the natural defender of Christendom against the infidels, but he was heavily defeated and nearly killed near Rossano (982). The report of this catastrophe led to a violent reaction in the North: the Danes and Wends cast off the German and Christian yoke, and within a few days the German rule and the Christian Church were wiped out east of the Elbe. Given time, Otto might have retrieved the double disaster. Certainly his power was not broken: without encountering opposition, he had his three-year-old son elected and crowned king and was again on the march against the Arabs when he died suddenly in Rome (983).

The dangers of a minority reign made themselves immediately felt. The guardianship of the boy king was claimed by his senior relatives on the paternal and maternal sides: they were Duke Henry of Bavaria and King Lothair of France, potentially the worst enemies of the little king. Henry went as far as to claim the crown for himself and for that purpose allied himself with the Slavs. He was, however, placated and reinstated in his hereditary Bavaria, of which he had been deprived in 976. Hugo Capet was played off against the French king once more; shortly afterwards (987) he succeeded the last Carolingian and established the long rule of the Capetian kings of France (987–1792, 1814–48).

It was mainly due to the firm foundations laid by Otto I that the Empire was able to stand this extraordinary strain. The clergy, ably led by Archbishop Willigis of Mayence, stood firmly by the young king. Moreover, Otto had two guardians by his side, his mother and grandmother, who proved exceptionally gifted and capable. Theophano maintained a strong régime, especially in Italy, until her death in 991; Adelaide then continued the guardianship until 995 (died in 999). Nevertheless, the royal power was inevitably weakened, and the structure of the Empire had to be overhauled when Otto attained his majority and was crowned emperor in 996.

During his minority the eastern neighbours of Germany, Bohemia, Poland and Hungary reached their political unification under strong rulers. They broke the resistance of the pagan nobility with the help of the Roman Church and gained for their countries a recognized place in the comity of Western nations. Boleslav II of Bohemia (967–99) and Misica I of Poland (960–92) had been the allies of Henry of Bavaria in the latter's abortive attempt on the German crown. They had soon parted company, however, and Misica assisted the Germans to recover their losses from the Wends, and to regain their overlordship over Bohemia, thereby securing for Poland the eastern fringe of Silesia. Taught by the political consequences of the subordination of the bishoprics of Prague and Olomuc under the metropolitan see of Mayence, Misica placed the Polish Church immediately under the papal obedience (990–2). His successor, Boleslav Chrobry (992–1025), completed the task of unifying Poland by ruthlessly assassinating all his male relatives and possible rivals; keeping on friendly terms with the Germans, he extended the Polish rule over the greater part of Silesia and Slovakia and subdued Pomeranians and Prussians, thus gaining access on a wide front to the Baltic Sea.

Hungary took a course similar to that of Poland. Duke Geza (972–97) had his son Stephen baptized according to the Roman rite. He, too, supported Henry of Bavaria, whose daughter married Stephen, and he organized Hungary on the model of Western feudalism. Disregarding the claims of the bishop of Passau, Stephen followed the Polish example and placed the Hungarian Church directly under Rome; in return he received the royal crown from the Pope (1001).

The violent reaction in Denmark against Harald Bluetooth, who had favoured a close collaboration with Germany and the Christian Church, was of less consequence than might have been expected. Although the Jutland bishoprics were wiped out, Danish attacks on Saxony were warded off, and the Danes directed their attention to England, an easy prey which they, in alliance with the Norwegians, ravaged systematically year after year and finally occupied (1017).

That was the international situation which confronted the young Emperor Otto III. In view of the consolidated Slav, Hungarian and Scandinavian monarchies, it was impossible to continue the expansionist policy of the earlier Ottonians. Otto III was, in fact, far from envisaging such a course. Brought up under the care of his Greek mother and Burgundian grandmother, educated by Bishop Bernward of Hildesheim, the greatest contemporary patron of art and learning, Otto was from his infancy imbued with the loftiest ideals with regard to his future task as the secular head of the Christian commonwealth. In Gerbert of Aurillac, one of the greatest theologians, philosophers and scientists of the Middle Ages, Otto found a congenial collaborator. Gerbert, elevated to the papal see in 999, styled himself Silvester II in remembrance of the first Pope of that name, and thereby implied that Otto would reign as a second Constantine for the welfare of the Christian universe. The co-operation of the Emperor and Pope was, in fact, ideal. Otto's device, as it appears on his seals, *Renovatio Imperii Romanorum*, was carefully chosen in order to efface the German origin of that Empire. National and regional peculiarities vanished before the one conception of the universal Empire and the universal Church. Otto styled himself *Servus Jesu Christi*, or *Servus Apostolorum*, thus almost wiping out any difference between himself and the Pope. As the imperial and papal interests were regarded as identical, Otto supported the establishment of independent churches in Poland and Hungary, despite the violation of the older claims of the metropolitans of Magdeburg and Salzburg. Germany meant to Otto III nothing more than one of his many dominions. His heart was certainly with Rome, his 'imperial city', and with 'his Romans'—although he used this expression chiefly when he scolded them for their 'ingratitude'.

It remains open to serious doubt whether the perfect harmony existing between Otto III and Silvester II would have outlasted any serious tension between even such intimate friends. It did not, however, come to the test, as Otto III died in 1002, not yet twenty-two years old, and Silvester followed him within a year.

As the young emperor died unmarried, the direct line of Otto the Great had become extinct. Saxon and Bavarian nobles and the archbishops of Mayence and Magdeburg had made no secret of their growing disapproval of Otto's imperial policy. Signs of opposition had appeared throughout Germany during the last years of his life. Now, a dissolution of the Ottonian creation seemed to be imminent. Under great difficulties Henry of Bavaria, the last male descendant of Henry I, eventually succeeded in obtaining recognition as king; but his power outside his native dukedom was little more than nominal and had to be bought by considerable concessions. Henry was in a position similar to that of his great-grandfather Henry I, and his cautious and slow progress ran on parallel lines. He had, however, the greater advantage of the Ottonian administrative system; and he even extended the power and possessions of the Church. Henry II, although he was afterwards canonized, had little of the idealistic character of Otto III, but he was a devout Christian and in full agreement with the great movement of the age that aimed at a thorough reformation of the Church. It had originated at the Burgundian abbey of Cluny, in the middle of the tenth century, and by Henry's reign had been adopted by the majority of the clergy, at least by those who tried to make Christianity the leaven of life. In compliance with the wishes of the Cluniac reformers Henry issued the decrees of the synod of Pavia (1022) as an imperial law; it enforced the celibacy of the higher clergy and deprived the children of priests borne by bondwomen of certain claims to their paternal inheritance. Henry did not, however, mean to relax his hold over the Church. He rather enhanced the services and obligations of the clergy, arguing sarcastically that 'unto whomsoever much is given, of him can be much required'. He exercised to the full the royal prerogative in appointing bishops and abbots; although it was certainly done in the interest of a homogeneous administration, it was little short of simony in the eyes of the strict reformers.

In his foreign policy, Henry had to reckon with the strength of Denmark and Poland. The power of Denmark, which under Svein and Canute had annexed England, made the recovering of the Slesvig march impossible; it was fortunate for the Empire in these circumstances that Canute eventually refrained from placing the Danish episcopate under the obedience of Canterbury and acknowledged the metropolitan claims of Bremen. Poland, however, under the empire-builder Boleslav, could not be checked with the scanty powers at Henry's disposal. Boleslav, taking advantage of Henry's unstable position, invaded and annexed Lusatia, Misnia and Bohemia. Despite the protests of the Saxons and the clergy Henry allied himself with the heathenish Slav tribe of the Liutitzi against the Poles; but, after more than ten years of border warfare, he had finally to renounce Lusatia (1018), whereas Bohemia had freed herself very soon (1004) and Misnia could be recovered.

Henry's policy in Italy contrasted sharply with his predecessor's. Here he had to contest the kingdom of Ardoin, margrave of Ivrea, who resumed the policy of his grandfather, Berengar. As in Germany, Henry overcame his adversary with the help of the bishops, whom he treated in the same way as their German brethren in respect both of their rights and their duties. By supporting Benedict VIII who, although a layman, had been raised to the Papacy by a Roman faction against a rival Pope, Henry achieved his coronation as emperor without difficulty (1014). The Polish war, however, did not allow him to pay much attention to Italian affairs, and he left the country to his trusted friend Benedict and the host of German bishops whom he appointed. It was the Pope who organized the sea power of Pisa and Genoa to combat the Arabs (1016); it was he who, in the same year, engaged five brothers of the Norman house of Hauteville to stem the rising tide of the Byzantines, and thereby become the founders of the Norman kingdom of Sicily. Henry could not be aware of the far-reaching consequences which these events would have for the German dominion over Italy.

After the peace with the Poles, Benedict VIII came to Germany and consecrated the cathedral of Bamberg (1020). This bishopric was founded by Henry in 1007, ostensibly to Christianize the Slavs of the upper Main district. The place held a key position between Bavaria, Bohemia, Franconia, Thuringia and Saxony. The semi-independent status of the bishop with respect to the metropolitan see of Mayence, and the lavish gifts which Henry bestowed upon the cathedral, indicate his intention to create a stronghold of the royal power in the heart of Germany. Bamberg well fulfilled the expectations of its founder. For more than two hundred years a steady flow of young ecclesiastics came from it to the 'royal chapel', where they were initiated into the problems of the imperial administration and policy. They were afterwards endowed with bishoprics and abbeys, where they were expected to practise the ideas with which they had been imbued at the court. There were other places which similarly served as nurseries for the diplomatists and administrators of the Empire, but none of them outrivalled Bamberg.

Benedict's chief concern while at Bamberg was, however, the renewed danger which threatened the papal state from the advancing Greeks. Henry granted the aid which the Pope requested, and led a strong expedition to Southern Italy (1022). Yet he failed to weaken seriously the Byzantine position, as an epidemic forced him to a premature retreat—not the last time that a German army had to capitulate to the Italian climate. But the Greek advance was definitely checked, and the Normans soon swept their armies back.

The relations between the Emperor and the Pope were most cordial. Although Henry II did not think of imitating the policy of Otto III, events had lately set him on a road not altogether different from that of his predecessor. Already the same forces of opposition raised their heads: the archbishops of Mayence, Cologne and Treves were on the point of forcibly claiming certain rights which they thought had been infringed by the Pope and the Emperor —when Benedict VIII and Henry II died unexpectedly within three months of each other (1024).

The archbishop of Mayence, who headed the opposition against Henry II, secured the election to the throne of Conrad, duke of Franconia. He was the great-grandson of Conrad of Lorraine, son-in-law of Otto the Great, so that the connection with the Saxon dynasty was not altogether severed. Cunigonda of Luxemburg, the widow of Henry II, eased the transition by immediately sending the regalia to the king elect. Conrad came of a family, afterwards known as the Salian house, which was far from wealthy. That helped him to understand the situation and needs of two classes which had hitherto been neglected, namely the small barons and the inhabitants of the cities. They slowly began to play their part in the economic and political life of the Empire, especially in the Rhineland. It was of vital importance for the crown to decide whether to meet or oppose the demands of these rising classes. The Salian kings favoured them; and it was largely due to the support of the lower nobility and the citizens that Henry IV and Henry V survived the contest with the Papacy. The Hohenstaufen dynasty, which succeeded the Salians, took a different course as far as the towns were concerned. The result was that from the thirteenth century onward the German citizens were thrown back on their own resources, to the great detriment of crown and cities alike.

Conrad II was a shrewd and energetic statesman who coolly calculated his own strength and limitations and those of his adversaries. Without much learning and with no religious proclivities, he played the game of power politics with consistency and clear-sightedness. In direct contrast to the ideals of the Cluniac reformers, he wholly abandoned the theocratic ideas of the Ottonian dynasty, treating the clergy as state officials, and appointing and deposing bishops and abbots as political considerations required. His attitude towards the Papacy was one of utter indifference. The contemporary Popes, John XIX (1024–32) and Benedict IX (1032–48), brother and nephew of Benedict VIII, were regarded by Conrad as petty Italian princes; he either accepted or annulled their decisions in Church affairs as it suited him best.

The secessionist tendencies always fighting the central power in Germany found their expression in the great rebellion of Conrad's stepson, Duke Ernest of Swabia (1025–30). Conrad overcame it by calling up counts, barons and other minor liegemen. He fully succeeded in gaining their loyal support against the intermediary power of the duke. He even felt strong enough to take the duchies of Bavaria and Swabia under the direct administration of the crown. His son and heir, Henry III, was invested with both duchies—in addition to which he seized that of Carinthia later on (1039)—and elected and crowned king (1028).

In the West, Conrad reaped the fruits of his predecessor's assiduous labours. Henry II had been appointed the heir of the childless King Rudolf III of Burgundy; when the latter died (1032), Conrad claimed the inheritance and succeeded in uniting Burgundy with the Empire. Odo, count of Champagne, the most powerful French vassal, put forward rival claims; he had previously supported Ernest of Swabia. Conrad continued cultivating the alliance into which Henry II had entered with King Robert II of France, and also continued it with his successor Henry I. He was thus able to checkmate Odo and, by uniting the duchies of Upper and Lower Lorraine (1033), to fortify the barrier against possible French expansion eastward.

The acquisition of Burgundy rounded off the territorial gains of the Holy Roman Empire, which henceforth consisted of the three kingdoms of Germany, Italy and Burgundy; the archbishops of Mayence, Cologne and Treves were the nominal heads of the respective chanceries and administrations. The kingdom of Burgundy comprised the western half of Switzerland and the eastern departments of France, stretching from Basle and Belfort in the north to Arles, Marseille and Nice in the south, and Besançon, Lyons and Avignon in the west. Its incorporation with the Roman Empire severed France from Italy and gave the western Alpine passes into the hands of the Germans, thus doubly strengthening their hold over Italy. At the beginning of his reign, Conrad had, in fact, been confronted with a French invasion of Italy: the Italians offered the vacant throne to King Robert, Count Odo, and Count William V of Aquitaine; the latter accepted for his son, and it took all Conrad's diplomatic skill to break the coalition of the three French princes before he could overcome the pretender, with the support of the German bishops whom Henry II had installed in the Italian bishoprics. Henceforth France was effectually barred from Italy until the famous expedition of Charles VIII in 1494.

On the occasion of his last expedition across the Alps, Conrad issued the famous *Constitutio de feudis* (1037). It made the fiefs of the small vassals (here called valvassors) hereditary and strengthened thereby the economic and political power of a rising class which was to make a brilliant display of its abilities in the later history of Italy. Subsequently Conrad satisfied himself with protecting the southern frontier against Greeks and Arabs. He refrained from advancing it farther and left the frontier defences to the care of local princes. One of them, the Norman knight Rainulf, received Conrad's recognition as count of Aversa; he became the ancestor of the Norman kings of Sicily.

The same policy of securing rather than extending the frontiers was followed by Conrad in the north and east. The great power of Poland vanished with the death of its founder, Boleslav Chrobry (1025). Conrad recovered Lusatia and forced the rival occupants of the Polish throne to recognize his overlordship (1033). He ceded a frontier district to Stephen of Hungary (1031) and gave up the march of Slesvig to Denmark. The river Eider was fixed as the northern frontier of the Empire, an arrangement which held good until the conquest by Prussia of the Elbe duchies in 1864. Conrad's friendship with Canute, the self-styled 'emperor' of the united Scandinavian and English domains, was further cemented by the marriage of Henry III to the daughter of Canute. The young queen died in 1038 of the plague, which compelled Conrad also to a hasty retreat from Italy.

In the following summer Conrad died. He left the Empire at the peak of its power, secure on all its frontiers and strong in its internal administration. The opposition of the princes of the laity and the Church had ceased, for Conrad respected their legitimate rights as scrupulously as he guarded his own. The minor vassals and the citizens were ardent supporters of the crown that administered justice impartially and effectively. The Nordic Empire of Canute broke apart after his death (1035). Poland and Hungary, after the death of Stephen (1038), were engaged in internecine strife, and various pretenders solicited German intervention. The Papacy was an obedient tool in the hands of the Emperor. The heir to the throne was fully trained for his task, and his succession took place without opposition.

The weak spot in Conrad's system was his utter disregard for, and lack of comprehension of, spiritual forces. His contemptuous dealing with the head and representatives of the Church was incompatible with his position as its anointed protector; it was bound to break up the harmonious co-operation of State and Church. That meant, however, that the Empire would lose its spiritual justification, and hence the very reason of its existence.

The new king, Henry III (1039–56), was the right man to retrieve his father's mistake. He had been carefully brought up by learned and pious ecclesiastics and was permeated with the ideals of the reform party. He had openly disapproved of Conrad's encroachments upon ecclesiastical privileges, and at once righted some of the wrongs which had been committed. His second marriage with Agnes of Poitou bound him more closely to the Cluniac movement, as she was the daughter of William V of Aquitaine, the chief secular supporter of the reformers (1043). Henry soon found the opportunity to practise his ideas on the co-operation of Empire and Papacy. The latter, wholly secularized, was at its lowest spiritual level. John XIX had scarcely been prevented from selling the primacy of the Roman see to the patriarch of Constantinople; Benedict IX sold his sacred office without scruples to the highest bidder when he had become weary of it (1045). It was bought by John Gratianus, the son of a baptized Jew, who styled himself Gregory VI. He was an adherent of the reformers and obviously hoped to achieve their ends even by such doubtful means. Against him a hostile faction of the Roman nobility elevated Silvester III as an anti-pope, so that there were actually three occupants of St Peter's chair. The situation called loudly for the intervention of the protector of the Church. It was the supreme moment of the co-operation of Empire and Church when the synod of Sutri under the presidency of Henry III deposed Gregory VI and Silvester III (20 Dec. 1046), and a synod held at Rome four days later elected the bishop of Bamberg as Pope Clement II. The Emperor (for Henry was crowned on Christmas Day) had delivered the Church from the scandal of schism and simony; and the elevation of a man of his own choice, reared in the best tradition of the Ottonian scheme, seemed to guarantee the smooth co-operation of the supreme powers of Christianity. When Clement died in the following autumn and Benedict IX usurped the papal throne once more, Henry again showed his strong hand, enforced the election of the bishop of Brixen as Pope Damasus II, and obliged Benedict definitely to resign. Damasus died only ten months after his election, and again Henry secured the elevation of a German bishop who was, moreover, his second cousin. Leo IX (1048–54), formerly Bruno, count of Egisheim, bishop of Toul, had, however, a strong personality, and held his own against the Emperor. In his person one of the energetic reformers acceded to the

Papacy; it is characteristic that from this time the papal chancery ceased to date papal documents by the years of the reign of the Emperor, as had been the custom from the time of Charlemagne. The radical reformers gained a majority in the college of cardinals; and among the advisers of Leo the subdeacon Hildebrand, a relative of Gregory VI, began to play a role of ever-increasing importance. The final break with the Greek Church (1054) was chiefly due to the rigid attitude of the Roman reformers who would not, and could not, tolerate the Caesaropapism that had established itself at Constantinople. The majority of the German bishops were, however, far from sympathizing with the stern tenets of the reform party, which favoured asceticism and monachism, and looked askance at the combination of priesthood and state-officialdom. When Leo IX died in 1054, Henry had to yield to their opposition and nominated as Pope the champion of the German episcopate, Gebhard of Eichstätt, who assumed the name of Victor II.

The most brilliant representative of the German episcopate was Adalbert, archbishop of Bremen. This Thuringian count, who took his best collaborators from the chapter of Bamberg, wholeheartedly supported the central government in defiance of the strong opposition of the Saxon nobility. Adalbert cherished the most far-reaching schemes: he wished to establish a Nordic patriarchate that would have included the whole of Scandinavia and given him a rank above other archbishops. His exertions induced King Svein of Denmark to seek the alliance of the Emperor, and led to the conversion of the people of Mecklenburg, whose prince became a German vassal and the ancestor of the only ruling house of Slav origin in Western Europe. So important did the Nordic mission seem to Adalbert that he declined Henry's first offer of the papal see in 1046. He sent his missionaries as far as Finland, Greenland, Iceland and the Orkneys in competition with missionaries from Canterbury, and at the same time spread the power of the Empire and the teaching of Christianity.

The unsuccessful attempt of Duke Bretislav of Bohemia to establish a greater Bohemia at the expenses of Germany and Poland led to the final submission of Bohemia (1041); and as Poland under Duke Casimir I pursued a policy of co-operation with the Empire, Henry transferred Silesia from Bohemia to his Eastern ally (1046). Henry's decision to support Stephen of Hungary's lawful heir against a heathen pretender made Hungary a tributary vassal state of the Empire, and advanced the Austrian frontier to the river Leitha, which remained the Austro-Hungarian frontier until 1919.

On the other hand, Henry loosened the bonds with which Conrad II had yoked the tribal dukedoms to the central government, and he even gave away the duchies of Carinthia, Bavaria and Swabia which Conrad had brought under the crown. For these actions Henry has been blamed by German historians; but it was apparently impossible to keep those divergent territories together in view of the difficulties of communication and the lack of a permanent bureaucracy. Henry tried to make amends for the loss of immediate power by bestowing the dukedoms upon foreigners. A duke of Bavaria of Saxon origin, for instance, would be in greater need of the royal protection than a native ruler, and upon such men the king might still exercise an indirect influence of sufficient weight. Furthermore, he again divided Lorraine in order to prevent the duke from becoming too powerful. France, the natural ally of a hostile Lorraine, was at the same time held in effective check by Henry's father-in-law, the duke of Aquitaine.

In a short war against Flanders, another ally of France, Henry had, however, to rely upon the support of English and Danish men-of-war. This need reveals one of the weaknesses in the organization of the Empire: the Emperor had no navy at his disposal, either in the northern waters or in the Mediterranean. The lack of a fleet greatly hampered the Sicilian expeditions and the crusades of the Hohenstaufen kings in the twelfth and thirteenth centuries; it allowed second-rate powers with a maritime tradition, such as Denmark and Sweden, to interfere in German affairs from the thirteenth to the nineteenth century. The complete misunderstanding of British mentality and institutions is the most remarkable result of the German isolation from world affairs in general, which has its origin in the lack of seamanship. Only a few representatives of the Empire seem to have been alive to this great need: the Emperor Charles IV (1346–78) was the only German emperor before William II who ever saw the sea; and Wallenstein, the generalissimo of Ferdinand II, urged in vain the building of an imperial navy (1628).

Henry III was as unsuccessful in suppressing the anti-centralistic tendencies of the tribes as were all his predecessors and successors. Geoffrey of Lorraine never acknowledged the loss of half his inheritance in 1044, much less his complete dispossession in 1047. He became the most formidable adversary of the imperial power when he married Matilda, marchioness of Tuscany, and thus acquired the most important part of Central Italy (1054). Nor were the other dukedoms pacified. On the contrary, Bavaria and Carinthia were in open rebellion towards the end of Henry's reign; and the little disguised animosity of the Saxons was hardly less dangerous to the central administration.

Henry seems to have thought of mitigating or quelling the Saxon opposition by a bold step. The German king had so far no permanent residence comparable with the Paris of the Capetian or the Winchester of the Anglo-Saxon kings. In theory, the capital of the Roman Empire was, of course, Rome. The jealousy of the German tribes would not suffer that the seat of a Saxon, Frankish, Bavarian or Swabian duke should become automatically the residence of the king when that duke was raised to the royal throne. The problem of a central seat of government has indeed remained unsolved up to the present. In the last centuries of the Holy Empire Frankfort was the city where the king was elected and crowned, Ratisbon the seat of the imperial diet, Wetzlar that of the imperial Court of Chancery; the regalia were kept at Nuremberg, whilst the Emperor himself and the greater part of the administrative bodies had their abode at Vienna. The Weimar Republic had its National Assembly at Weimar, its Supreme Court at Leipzig, and its administrative centre at Berlin. In Hitler's Germany, Munich and Nuremberg rival Berlin as the permanent seats of the Party headquarters and the annual Party meetings, and Goslar has been made the centre of the agricultural administration. Henry III is said to have planned to settle the imperial court permanently at Goslar in the Hartz mountains. Its silver mines were of paramount value to the revenues of the crown, of tenfold importance in an era notorious for its lack of precious metals. At Goslar Henry built a spacious palace and a magnificent cathedral, the chapter of which was intended to emulate the Bamberg foundation of Henry II. It indeed produced a great many leaders of the Church and of the imperial administration. Near Goslar, Henry III died in October 1056, when only thirty-eight years old. Pope Victor II was at his death-bed and promised the Emperor to take over the guardianship of his six-year-old boy who two years before had been elected king. Neither could foresee that the Pope would follow his friend to the grave within less than a year.

In the light of following events, the death of Henry III appears as an irrevocable breach with the achievements of the past hundred and fifty years. The position of the Emperor as a joint leader of the Christian universe was lost irretrievably when soon afterwards the Papacy, in the person of its greatest representative, put forth its exclusive claim to leadership in affairs temporal and spiritual alike.

In the great struggle that ensued the Emperor lost that peculiar sanctity that had given his predecessors their unique position above all other rulers of the Christian world, and especially his ascendancy over the German tribes. After having lost the spiritual justification of the imperial office, the king-emperor could no longer claim the homage of the nations as a divine right, and his policy would henceforth be directed, like that of every other monarch, by national and dynastic considerations. The opposition of the princes would now no longer be directed against the secular leader of the Church, but against an earthly monarch like themselves; his title to supremacy was no whit better than their own; and his authority would depend on fear or favour rather than on divine sanction. The age of theocracy had closed.

CHAPTER II

THE CONTEST BETWEEN EMPIRE AND PAPACY (1056–1250)

THE minority of Henry IV would in any case have created a critical situation for the Empire, but the harm it did was the greater as it coincided with one of the decisive revolutions in the political and spiritual history of Western Europe. Strong and determined monarchs, such as William the Conqueror and Robert Guiscard, consolidated France, England, Spain and Southern Italy; they were the last to accept even the nominal overlordship of the Roman Emperor. The general drift of the age towards the creation of powerful national cells could not fail to inspire the rulers of the German tribes, who duly recaptured a great part of their independence which had been wrested from them by the Ottonian and Salian kings. In Italy it was the cities which not only defied the Emperor as an alien ruler, but at the same time challenged the feudal system as a whole. Enriched and enlightened by their flourishing trade all over the then known world, the population of the North Italian cities were no longer willing to submit tamely to their feudal lords, whose rule ill suited the needs of bankers, merchants and artisans. Milan, the ancient capital of Lombardy, took the lead; and, by the end of the eleventh century, autonomous town government had become the rule throughout Northern Italy; the free election of 'consuls' was the most cherished outward sign of civic independence.

While the political and economic forces of the Western states and free cities were to determine the distant course of European history, the immediate present was dominated by the power of the Papacy and the Church. While the supreme secular authority lay dormant, the supreme spiritual power wielded an autocratic rule. The man who inspired and guided papal diplomacy in these fateful years was Hildebrand, from 1059 archdeacon of the Roman Church, and in 1073 elected Pope, with the name of Gregory VII. After the death of the last German Pope, Stephen IX (1057–58), Hildebrand secured the successive elections of Italian popes who were devoted to the programme of Church reform and hostile to the imperial prerogative. Hildebrand also prompted the decree which made the cardinals the sole electors of a pope and thus legally freed the Papacy from imperial interference (1059). In the same year Robert Guiscard and his brother swore fealty to St Peter for their South Italian possessions, deliberately ignoring the imperial suzerainty, and thus establishing a precedent for papal claims to secular overlordship. Finally Gregory outlined a scheme of papal world domination in his *Dictatus Papae* (1075). The 'holy' Pope, he asserted, is equivalent to the Church Universal; he alone is entitled to issue laws, and to appoint and dismiss bishops; all secular princes are subject to his bidding; he may dethrone emperors and release subjects from their allegiance. These principles were bound to rouse the opposition of all secular authorities. The clergy was everywhere closely bound up with the feudal system, exercising feudal rights and acknowledging feudal obligations. When therefore the Pope forbade priests to take the oath of fealty to laymen, the whole fabric of the feudal state was endangered, and because of this the Investiture Struggle was fought out in every country. It affected Germany more deeply and universally than any other country, as the German Church had from the time of Otto the Great become an integral part of the secular administration. The state no less than the Church would be shaken to its foundations if their mutual ties were severed as completely as the Pope demanded.

The Empress Agnes, who acted as regent for the boy king Henry IV, with her councillors failed altogether to realize the implications of the tremendous changes which were taking place in the political, social and spiritual life of Europe. They committed their worst blunders in their dealings with the Papacy, for they were too weak to retain the influence which Henry III had wielded at Rome, and too biased to co-operate wholeheartedly with the reform party. Driven from defeat to defeat on the spiritual battle-field, they hoped to retrieve their losses by political expedients, and set up an imperial anti-pope (1061). Even this reversal of the policy of Henry III miscarried, as the regents failed to give their candidate effectual support. Six years after the death of Henry III, Germany and Italy were in a state of anarchy.

The German aristocracy, secular and ecclesiastic, were deeply mortified by the disasters which the regency had brought upon the Empire. Dissatisfaction ripened into conspiracy, and conspiracy into a *coup d'état*. The young king was kidnapped and placed under the tutelage of the archbishops Anno of Cologne and Adalbert of Bremen (April 1062). Unfortunately the two regents soon fell foul of each other, and their rivalry did as much harm as the incompetence of the dowager empress had done before. Anno worked for a balance of power between the crown and princes. His main supporter was Duke Geoffrey of Upper Lorraine (1044-69), who had married the marchioness of Tuscany and thus become the most powerful ruler in Central Italy (1054); in 1065 he was also invested with Lower Lorraine. Anno and Geoffrey composed the schism by dropping the anti-pope. Anno, in his capacity as arch-chancellor of Italy, now wanted Henry IV to go to Rome and be crowned as emperor, but this sound plan was wrecked by Adalbert of Bremen. Adalbert's dream of a Nordic patriarchate required a strong central power at home. He therefore thwarted Anno's policy of appeasing the Pope and the secular princes, and encouraged the autocratic tendencies of the young king. Most unfortunate of all, he passed on to Henry his violent antipathy for the duke and nobles of Saxony, who resented Adalbert's vast territorial additions to the archbishopric and opposed him as the representative of centralized government.

In 1066, the princes removed Adalbert from the regency, and Henry IV took the reins of government into his own hands. The bitter experiences of his untutored youth had taught him the arts of cunning and dissimulation; his pride, often and deeply hurt, reasserted itself in deeds of violence and licence. Lacking a sense of proportion, he was overbearing in success, and never great but in adversity. Nevertheless, his home policy was not unsuccessful, as he, following the example set by Conrad II, sought his supporters chiefly among the gentry, i.e. the *ministeriales* and citizens. Common antagonism to the princes and bishops brought the king and these rising classes together: for the secular lords who opposed the centralizing tendencies of the royal administration also blocked the way to full freedom and equality of status demanded by the lesser vassals; and the episcopal lords of the towns who deprived the royal exchequer of the revenue accruing from the intensified commercial activities of the townsfolk at the same time excluded the citizens from the government of their towns. Henry chose his councillors almost exclusively from the ranks of the lesser nobility; and the charter of liberties which he granted to the citizens of Worms in 1074 paved the way to the growth of civic freedom. He also adopted the French method of policing and pacifying the country by means of the 'truce of God'. This *treuga Dei* decreed the cessation of hostilities during the Passion days of the week and on all high feast days. It was designed to promote political as well as economic security, and was therefore welcome to the peasantry and townsfolk.

Henry extended it over the whole Empire in 1085, and renewed it in 1103 for four whole years.

Henry's first intention was to check the increase of power which the princes had obtained during his minority at the expense of the royal government. He soon recalled Adalbert of Bremen, and, guided by him, recovered and extended the royal demesnes in Saxony and Thuringia. The Saxons promptly rose in arms (1073) under the leadership of Count Otto of Nordheim, who had been appointed duke of Bavaria by the empress regent, but deprived of his dukedom by Henry. Duke Rudolf of Swabia, the king's brother-in-law, defeated the Saxons (1075), and they surrendered unconditionally. Otto of Nordheim went over to Henry, and was rewarded with the dukedom of Saxony.

Henry, however, overestimated his success and light-heartedly took up a challenge which came from a more formidable quarter. Pope Gregory VII seized the moment when Henry was embarrassed by the Saxon war to advance the programme of the ecclesiastical reform party. He openly contested the royal right to the investiture of bishops, and excommunicated a number of Henry's councillors for simony. At the lenten synod of 1075 Gregory directly appealed to the laity and bade them reject the services of married and simoniacal priests. At the same time he again enjoined the prohibition of lay investiture.

Henry unwisely ignored the Pope's warnings, kept the excommunicated councillors, and continued to invest bishops before their consecration. Gregory, bent on carrying out the reform of the Church, reprimanded the king and threatened him with excommunication and deposition. Thereupon Henry summoned a national council at Worms. The king and bishops, however, were totally blind to the spiritual power of the Papacy and ignorant of the moral forces of the reform movement; not a few of the bishops were prompted by motives of personal greed and hatred. On 24 Jan. 1076, a passionate letter of defiance was issued. It was addressed to 'Hildebrand, no longer pope, but a false monk', declared him 'damned in eternity' by the judgments of St Peter and St Paul (I Peter ii. 17; Gal. i. 8) and the verdict of the bishops and the king, and bade him 'descend from the usurped apostolic see'. Gregory struck a deadly counterblow. At the lenten synod of 1076, he excommunicated Henry, suspended him from government, and released his subjects from their oath of allegiance.

It became at once obvious that Henry's position was built upon sand. The spiritual and intellectual forces of the age were almost without exception arrayed against him. The ranks of his corrupt ecclesiastical supporters were soon thinned: for no high moral ideals fortified these worldly clerics against the rewards and threats of the Church. The secular aristocracy realized that the Church's cause and their own interests coincided: their struggle for political independence was elevated to a higher moral plane when it became aligned with the Church's fight for spiritual freedom. Otto of Nordheim and the South German dukes quickly agreed upon a meeting of the princes at which the constitutional problems of Germany should be reviewed; and they invited Gregory to appear in person and judge between them and their king.

Gregory accepted this invitation and was on his way to Germany when Henry surprised his opponents and upset their plans. The Pope was his most formidable foe, and by placating him Henry reckoned that the princes would simultaneously be overcome or, at least, that they would lose their spiritual backing. He therefore hurried to Italy and intercepted Gregory at Canossa, a castle of the Marchioness Matilda of Tuscany (Jan. 1077). Henry approached Gregory in penitential garments, asked for his absolution, and recognized the Pope as arbiter between himself and the German princes. Henry's 'going to Canossa' has become proverbial for the utter submission of the secular to the spiritual power, but for the time it was a tactical victory for the king. For this unheard-of act of humiliation had the success on which Henry had speculated: Gregory absolved him from excommunication; and though his restitution as king was postponed to the general meeting of Pope, king and princes, Gregory was prevented by internal unrest in Lombardy and Rome from going to Germany. He refrained from committing himself for or against Henry, and concentrated on carrying out the ecclesiastical reform work in Germany, England and France. This sufficed to give Henry a breathing space and at the same time to alienate the princes from the Pope. Despite the provisional agreement of Canossa, they elected Rudolf of Swabia, Henry's brother-in-law, king (15 March 1077). Rudolf found his main support in Saxony, whereas South Germany was recovered for the royal cause by Count Frederick of Hohenstaufen, whom Henry appointed duke of Swabia and to whom he married his daughter. The Babenberg dukes of Austria and the citizens of the Rhineland, too, were his faithful supporters.

Faced by Henry's progress and alarmed by the dissensions in

Rudolf's camp, Gregory at last abandoned his restraint. He once more excommunicated Henry, declared him dethroned, and even prophesied his complete ruin within five months (7 March 1080). Moreover, he recognized Rudolf as the lawful king. This time, however, Gregory had overreached himself. His insistent demands upon clergy and laity drove them into the king's camp: the nobles were afraid of losing the disposition and usufruct of Church estates, and bishops and abbots preferred their status of princes of the Empire to that of servants of the Pope. Henry set up Wibert, archbishop of Ravenna, as Pope Clement III (1080–1100), and the new pontiff won over large portions of Italy and a great part of the clergy to Henry's cause. When, moreover, King Rudolf was killed in battle (15 Oct. 1080), his death was generally considered a judgment of God. The opposition could not bring themselves to submit to Otto of Nordheim, their most determined leader. They preferred the insignificant Count Hermann of Salm (1081), whose mock royalty relapsed into nothingness after Otto's death (1085).

Henry's power in Germany was sufficiently consolidated to allow him to lead an expedition across the Alps. As Gregory's only reliable allies were the marchioness of Tuscany, who had just put her vast possessions under the overlordship of the Roman see, and Robert Guiscard, the sovereign of South Italy and Sicily, Henry allied himself with the Emperor of Byzantium against the Normans. Byzantine money and an increasing dissatisfaction with Gregory's obduracy made thirteen cardinals desert the Pope; and the Romans themselves opened the gates of their city to Henry. A synod deposed and excommunicated Gregory, and formally enthroned Clement III, who then crowned Henry IV emperor (31 March 1084). Shortly afterwards the Normans forced Henry to retreat; but Gregory had to leave Rome with his liberators in order to escape the fury of the people. He died a broken man under Norman protection at Salerno (1085).

While the imperial Pope reigned undisturbed at Rome, the Emperor was supreme in Germany. He reconciled the Saxons and obliged the duke of Bohemia by bestowing royal dignity upon him (1085). Conrad, Henry's eldest son, was crowned king (1087), and when Hermann of Salm ingloriously perished in a private feud (1088), no other anti-king was raised. All the same, the fundamental issues of the struggle were not composed. Gregory's second successor, Urban II (1088–99), resumed the fight, and again the spirit of the age was with the Papacy. Urban, a Frenchman, was intimately familiar with German affairs, for he had been papal legate for Germany; he surpassed Gregory both in breadth of vision and in diplomatic skill, though he was less fervently religious and a less original thinker. The king of Aragon and the count of Barcelona did homage as papal vassals; the Cluniac reform reached its peak when Urban, as the first Pope to visit Cluny, went there in 1095; and the Orders of Chartreuse and Citeaux (founded in 1086 and 1098) put two more armies of zealous soldiers of Christ into the field.

Urban scored his first great success against Henry when he arranged the purely political marriage between the old marchioness of Tuscany and the youthful son of Duke Guelph IV of Bavaria. Henry's adversaries in Germany and Italy thus gained a formidable rallying centre, and Henry at once hurried to Italy to forestall their joining hands (1090). After some years of successful warfare, he was suddenly flung into abject misery by a masterstroke of unscrupulous papal diplomacy. In 1093, young King Conrad raised the standard of rebellion against his father, had himself crowned king of the Lombards, and showed his subservience to the Pope by performing the marshal's office. Henry's second queen, a Russian princess of Kiev, also went over into the papal camp and laid the vilest accusations against her husband, which a papal synod, without examination, declared proved. Urban himself recovered Rome from Clement III; and Henry, cut off from Germany, spent the following years in Upper Italy, everywhere surrounded by enemies and almost a prisoner. Thus it came about that the Emperor, the secular sword of the Church, took no part in the greatest enterprise ever undertaken by the united Western nations under the leadership of the Church, the first crusade and the conquest of the Holy Land (1095–99).

Henry's position took an unexpected turn for the better when the marriage of Guelph V and Matilda proved a failure. The king, having reconciled himself with the duke of Bavaria, could at last return to Germany, and had his second son, Henry, elected king (1099). Two years later the anti-king Conrad died in misery. Henry successfully pacified Germany, and promoted the interests of trade and commerce. But the support which the mercantile classes gave him did not balance the loss of prestige which he suffered with the bellicose nobles; and the Church struggle dragged on under Urban's successor, Paschal II (1099–1118), a timid doctrinaire. The heir to the throne realized that another combination of Papacy and nobility would spell final disaster. Henry V was a cold-hearted, cunning and ruthless egoist. In order to forestall the enemies of his house, he placed himself at the head of the Bavarians and Saxons (1104), seduced the royal troops, and took his father prisoner Henry IV was compelled, under penalty of death, to surrender the regalia, and the Curia recognized the new king without demanding any guarantee on the question of investiture. Once more Henry IV showed his ability to restore a hopeless situation. He escaped from prison, rallied his Rhenish adherents, and set about stirring up the kings of France, England and Denmark on his behalf. The fate of the rebels was in suspense when Henry IV suddenly died (7 Aug 1106).

Henry V found himself the undisputed ruler of the Empire. The new king did not intend to sacrifice one tittle of the royal prerogative. Untroubled by moral scruples, he pursued his father's policy more ruthlessly, more coldly, and more successfully. He continued to lean upon the lesser nobility and bestowed most valuable privileges upon the citizens of Spires and Worms. These and the foundation of Freiburg (1120) mark the beginning of the glorious growth of the German towns which during the next two centuries monopolized the commerce of Northern Europe and became one of the most potent forces in German politics. Henry's marriage with Matilda, daughter of Henry I of England, brought two experienced statesmen into close contact. Henry I's great charter of liberties, the establishment of the Curia Regis, and the organization of the Royal Exchequer, appealed to his son-in-law's shrewd instinct. He planned to reorganize the fiscal and legal systems of Germany on the lines of the enlightened absolutism of Norman England. The shipwreck of Prince William (1120) made Matilda the heiress of England and Normandy. A joint Anglo-German campaign against France (1124) was the firstfruits of a political combination which opened up the widest prospects. Unfortunately, Henry V died prematurely in 1125 leaving no issue, and Matilda returned to England to become the ancestress of the house of Plantagenet, 'retaining, however, the title of empress all her life', as the chronicler says.

The compromise which Henry I and Anselm of Canterbury reached in the investiture question (1107) may have inspired Henry V to take a similar course. For years he held out to the Curia vain hopes of a settlement, all the while exercising the traditional rights of the crown. While in Rome for his coronation, the king came to an agreement with the Pope. The Church was to hand back all privileges and possessions acquired since the days of Charlemagne; in return the king was to refrain from influencing ecclesiastical elections and to give up the investiture. The papal promise raised an outcry of indignation amongst the clergy, which was exactly what Henry had intended. He seized the Pope and the cardinals in St Peter's Church, and compelled Paschal to grant him unconditionally the right of investiture (12 April 1111) and to crown him emperor on the following day.

As had happened before, a success gained by worldly cunning only strengthened the spiritual opposition. Two synods declared the agreement null and void and excommunicated the Emperor. Paschal was threatened with a trial for heresy until he finally revoked the privilege (1116). Nor did Henry enjoy his triumph very long. With increasing ruthlessness he expanded the royal demesnes at the expense of local nobles. Archbishop Adalbert of Mayence, the king's former chancellor, and Lothair of Supplinburg, duke of Saxony, became the leaders of a strong opposition, and Henry suffered a major defeat at Lothair's hand (1115). Nevertheless, when he learned of the death of Matilda of Tuscany, he felt secure enough to hurry unarmed to Italy. By a secret treaty, she had made him the heir of her vast possessions, and Henry at one stroke became the biggest liege lord of Italy. A faction of the Roman nobility persuaded him to set up an imperial pope. The inevitable consequence was that the canonically elected Gelasius II excommunicated Henry (1118). There seemed to be no end to the Investiture Struggle, especially when Gelasius was succeeded by Calixtus II (1119–24), who, as archbishop of Vienne, had been the chief opponent of Paschal's policy of appeasement. However, the German princes now took the matter into their own hands and appointed a committee of twelve to meet an equal number of papal delegates.

After long bargaining, a compromise was achieved and promulgated as the concordat of Worms (23 Sept. 1122). Henry abandoned the canonical investiture by ring and crosier, but retained the secular investiture by the sceptre which entailed the rendering of homage and feudal service; this form of investiture was to precede the consecration of the invested cleric in Germany and was thereby tantamount to the royal consent; in Italy and Burgundy the prelates had to apply for the investiture within six months of their consecration, which thus fell into a mere formality. There was realized none of the extravagant expectations with which both parties had started the struggle fifty years earlier. The Curia had not reduced the Emperor to a vassal and the German bishops to humble servants; nor had the Salians restored the supreme control which Otto the

Great and Henry III had exerted over the Roman see and the German episcopate. It was the German princes, temporal and spiritual, who gained most: courted by the Pope and Emperor, they had forgotten their former quarrels and consolidated their position at the expense of both. The dukes, margraves, counts, archbishops, bishops and abbots began to array themselves in a solid phalanx of territorial lords who scorned to receive orders from any overlord, whether king or pope.

Their influence at once made itself felt at the election of a successor to the childless Henry V. The claims of Frederick II of Swabia, Henry's nephew, were passed over and Archbishop Adalbert of Mayence contrived to get Duke Lothair of Saxony elected king (30 Aug. 1125). As the trusted champion of the rights of the tribal magnates, Lothair commanded the respect of the aristocracy; and as he immediately asked for the papal approval of his election, he was also assured of the good will of the hierarchy. Only the Hohenstaufens remained hostile. When Lothair commanded them to sunder the crown lands from the private estates of the Salian house and restore the former to him, they set up Conrad, Duke Frederick's younger brother, as anti-king (1127). For a while Conrad put up a good fight and was even crowned king of the Lombards at Milan, but in the end the brothers had to submit to Lothair, whose position was never seriously threatened (1135).

Lothair refrained from making capital out of the schism which rent the Church from 1130 to 1138. He followed the lead given by St Bernard of Clairvaux and unhesitatingly supported Innocent II against Anacletus II. Nor did he object to performing the marshal's office and being described as the Pope's liegeman (*homo papae*). In return he obtained not only the imperial crown but also the investiture with the estates of the Marchioness Matilda (1133). On the other hand he refused to commit himself too deeply in Italian affairs and conducted two campaigns against the Normans, the supporters of Anacletus, with very little zeal. In Germany, too, he abstained from interfering with his fellow-princes. He allied himself with the powerful Guelph dynasty of Bavaria by marrying his only child to Duke Henry the Proud. Through him, Lothair exercised an indirect influence upon the South, while his main concern was with his patrimonial dukedom of Saxony.

From 1105 onward, wave after wave of settlers migrated from the overpopulated districts of Western Germany and Flanders into the marshy and wooded regions of Eastern Germany, and, when these were filled to capacity, farther eastward into the thinly populated and poorly cultivated lands of the West Slavonic tribes. Lothair gave the support of the royal authority to this eastward drive. He invested the farseeing Count Adolf of Schauenburg with Holstein, where he founded the city of Lübeck (1143); the energetic Ascanian, Albert the Bear, was given the Northern march, which he soon enlarged into the margraviate of Brandenburg; and the Wettin margraves of Misnia gained Lower Lusatia as an eastern outpost. At the same time, Bishop Otto of Bamberg was invited by the duke of Pomerania to convert his country to Christianity. The duke himself, as well as the king of Denmark, did homage to Lothair; and Bohemia, the most important link between the northern and southern pincers of the recent eastward drive, was again reduced to vassalage.

When Lothair died on the return from his second Italian expedition, the princes, instigated by the Roman Curia, passed over Duke Henry the Proud and elected Conrad III of Hohenstaufen king (7 March 1138). His very weakness recommended him, as the Curia and princes were opposed to the concentration in one hand of the two most powerful dukedoms, Bavaria and Saxony, together with the imperial crown. Thus began the feud between the Hohenstaufen and Guelph dynasties, which rent Germany for a hundred years, and survived in Italy in the factions of Ghibellines and Guelphs for two more centuries. Civil war ensued at once when Conrad refused to invest Henry with Saxony and even dispossessed him of Bavaria. Albert the Bear and the duke of Austria, upon whom these duchies were conferred, were no match for Henry, and Conrad's cause was on the verge of ruin when Henry suddenly died in his prime, leaving a ten-year-old boy his heir (1139). His next of kin, however, successfully upheld his rights, and in 1142 Conrad was compelled to restore Saxony to young Henry the Lion while Bavaria went to Duke Henry Jasomirgott ('So-help-me-God') of Austria, together with the hand of Henry the Proud's widow. Despite this settlement, civil war continued throughout the reign of Conrad. It very much resembled the nineteen long winters' of King Stephen's rule in England, when 'men said that Christ and his saints slept'. Bishop Otto of Freising, the king's half-brother, expected the imminent appearance of the anti-Christ and the end of the world. The severe losses which the Christians sustained in the Holy Land at the hands of the Moslems deepened the gloom. The Pope proclaimed a crusade (1145) and St Bernard became its passionate preacher. He inflamed with enthusiasm the French and German peoples together with their kings. He also brought about the pacification of Germany. Conrad had his son Henry elected king, while Henry the Lion promised to postpone his claims to Bavaria and to undertake a crusade of his own against the heathen Slavs of Mecklenburg. The conquest of Mecklenburg by Henry the Lion, and that of Lisbon by a fleet of German and Nordic crusaders (1147), were the only tangible results of the whole enterprise; for the main armies of Conrad and Louis VII were annihilated by the Seljuks in Asia Minor, and the survivors met their final doom before Damascus and Ascalon. Conrad returned to Germany, broken in body and spirit; the country was again plunged into civil war, and Henry the Lion again outmatched the king. Conrad was deeply aggrieved by the death of his son, King Henry; and on his death-bed he designated Duke Frederick of Swabia, his nephew, as his successor (1152), passing over his younger son, Frederick of Rothenburg.

Frederick, whom the Italians nicknamed Barbarossa because of his auburn beard, was the embodied spirit of feudal chivalry. Throughout his life he championed the cause of the aristocracy and gave final shape to the feudal caste system by which the knights were sharply separated from the citizens and peasants. This happened at the same time when the right of primogeniture began to take root in England, with the result that (in Dr A. F. Pollard's words) the absence of impassable barriers between class and class enabled the younger sons of the nobility to adapt themselves to commercial and maritime enterprises, whereas in Germany they wrapt themselves up in their noble exclusiveness and turbulence, grew prouder and poorer than ever, and consoled themselves for their poverty by attaching an inordinate value to their birth and to the customs of their class. Frederick also revived the supra-national and Christian ideals of Charlemagne whom he had canonized, and blended them with the political and legal theories of imperial Rome, which the jurists of Bologna University were adapting to the needs of the sovereigns of medieval Europe. Untouched by the spiritual pangs of the age of St Bernard, Frederick conceived the world and his own task in terms of a naïve secularism, such as found its expression in contemporary literature, art and philosophy. The Latin poetry of Walter Map and the Archipoeta, the vernacular lyrics of the troubadours and minnesingers, the logicality of Aristotelean philosophy and Gothic architecture, and Richard Fitznigel's system of political economics, show the same spirit of enlightened, though by no means anti-clerical, worldliness.

Frederick's claims to overlordship over Christian Europe could not fail to resuscitate the struggle between the Empire and the Papacy, but it was a struggle for the rule over Italy rather than for spiritual issues, though both parties used the old weapons: antipopes were set up, the Emperor was excommunicated, and episcopal synods were appealed to. During the eighteen years of ecclesiastical warfare (1159-77) Frederick enjoyed the almost unanimous support of the German nobles and bishops. As he was careful to respect their rights, the papal sentence of excommunication was ineffective. When the archbishop of Mayence deserted him (1165), he had no difficulty in replacing him by a faithful adherent. The imperial cause was weakened by excess of zeal on the part of Frederick's ecclesiastical followers rather than by their lack of enthusiasm. His chief adviser was Rainald of Dassel, who was appointed imperial chancellor and archbishop of Cologne. Rainald was an ambitious schemer, who directed the imperial policy in a spirit of ruthless aggressiveness. From the beginning he steered towards a rupture with the Curia. He accomplished it by giving an ambiguous Latin term in a papal note an offensive German translation (1159). The Pope called the imperial crown a papal *beneficium*, which might mean 'benefit' or 'fief'. Rainald chose the latter interpretation and thereby succeeded in provoking the wrath of all Germany. When the Lombards were overcome and Milan razed to the ground (1162), Rainald felt sure of final victory. He arrogantly declared that the election of the bishop of the imperial city of Rome was no concern of 'petty princes', to wit Louis VII of France and Henry II of England. He thus wrecked the imperial cause at the very moment when there was a fair prospect of composing the quarrel in favour of the imperial pope. Rainald was more successful when he exploited the natural rivalry between Henry II and his nominal liege-lord of France. This, and the antagonism to the Curia which resulted from Henry's feud with Thomas Becket, drove the Plantagenet on to the side of the Emperor. An alliance was concluded, and Henry's daughter, Matilda, was married to Henry the Lion, the Emperor's cousin (1165). Frederick's fourth expedition to Italy, however, ended in complete disaster. Within a few days a terrible plague annihilated the greater part of the German army (Aug. 1167); Frederick himself only just escaped to Germany.

This judgment of God, as it appeared to contemporaries, was a turning point in Frederick's career. Rainald of Dassel was amongst the victims of the plague, and his ruthless ambitions were interred with him. Frederick used the following years to consolidate his position at home. From the beginning of his reign, his home policy was directed towards a general appeasement of the conflicting interests which had wrecked the life of his predecessor. Barbarossa, a son of a sister of Henry the Proud, was the very man to reconcile the Hohenstaufen and Guelph families. He at once restored Bavaria to Henry the Lion, and acknowledged his cousin's unlimited sovereignty over the conquered Slav territories beyond the Elbe. Henry Jasomirgott was compensated for the loss of Bavaria by extraordinary privileges: his margraviate of Austria was raised to an autonomous dukedom (1156), which in time was to become an independent Austrian state. Duke Guelph VI, Henry the Proud's brother, was invested with the imperial fiefs in Italy, which comprised Tuscany, Spoleto, Sardinia and Corsica. The Guelphs thus satisfied, Frederick concentrated on strengthening his position in South-West and Central Germany. With his first wife he gained the Vogtland, i.e. the strategically important triangle between Thuringia, Misnia and Bohemia, which included the palatine castles of Eger and Altenburg. The king of Bohemia, the margraves of Misnia and Brandenburg, and the archbishop of Magdeburg thus came under his direct influence and remained his faithful adherents throughout his reign. From this base Frederick undertook several campaigns against Poland, which resulted in establishing a Germanophil dynasty in Silesia, and prepared the Germanization and incorporation of this province.

Frederick's second queen (1156) was Beatrice, the heiress of Upper Burgundy, by marrying whom he acquired a firm foothold in the Western Alps. The deaths in the Roman plague of hundreds of liegemen allowed him to seize a great number of fiefs. The most important was Swabia whose duke, Frederick of Rothenburg, was amongst its victims. Barbarossa created his eldest son duke of Swabia and had at the same time his younger son, Henry, elected king (1169)—a division of power which effectively allayed possible misgivings on the part of the princes. Thus the Hohenstaufen possessions stretched in an uninterrupted chain from Arles and Nice to Nuremberg and Eger, from the Rhone and Meuse to the Lech and Mulde. In his later years Frederick I, like Henry III before him, thought of setting up a permanent residence. His choice was Gelnhausen near Frankfort-on-Main, situated right in the heart of Germany and easily accessible from every province.

Even in Italy, Barbarossa's position took a turn for the better.

Guelph VI, whose only son had died in the disaster of 1167, sold him his large possessions in Central Italy, where Archbishop Christian of Mayence, the imperial legate, successfully restored the authority of the Emperor. In 1175, Frederick crossed the Alps once more. But a reverse at the hands of the Lombard League at Legnano (29 May 1176) speedily convinced him of the hopelessness of further military adventures. No longer under the spell of Rainald, he acknowledged defeat; and at Venice, on 23 July 1177, the Emperor bowed his knee before Pope Alexander III. Frederick abandoned the imperial suzerainty over the pontifical state, but was conceded the usufruct of Matilda's domains until a court of arbitration should have settled this intricate problem. A truce of six years with the Lombards, and of fifteen years with the Normans, secured peace throughout Italy. The Papacy gained full spiritual independence, but the German Church remained an organ of the state, and the imperial rule over Italy was left unimpaired.

The defeat of Legnano—to this day the only battle in which Italians unaided by foreign allies were victorious over soldiers of a European country—had been brought about by the defection of Henry the Lion. For more than twenty years, Frederick had based his policy on co-operation with his cousin. Again and again he had silenced the growing dissatisfaction of the princes and nobles with Henry's high-handed demeanour. Henry was left a free hand to organize his conquests in Mecklenburg, Holstein and Pomerania on the absolutist lines of his English father-in-law. As the founder of Munich, re-founder of Lübeck, and shrewd supporter of German commerce in the Baltic, Henry showed himself fully alive to future possibilities. He wielded a power in no way inferior to that of the Emperor, but he failed to recognize that the imperial shield was indispensable for the protection of his own achievements and his own safety. When Frederick asked his help for the first time, Henry demanded the imperial city of Goslar with its rich silver mines as recompense. Frederick rejected this bargain, and Henry thereupon refused to succour the Emperor in his hour of need.

On his return from Italy, Frederick took action against the Lion, based first on common, then on feudal law. As Henry, presuming on his power, flouted two summonses, Frederick sentenced him by default, deprived him of his imperial fiefs and put him under the ban of the Empire, which involved also the loss of his allodia (1180). Deserted by his liegemen and forsaken by his father-in-law, Henry on his knees implored Frederick's mercy. He was given back his allodia on the condition of a three-year exile, which he spent at Henry II's court.

As a result of Henry the Lion's fall from power, numerous bishoprics, abbeys, counties and cities passed under the immediate rule of the Emperor; but, faithful to his general policy, Frederick let the princes share in the fruits of his success. Westphalia was severed from Saxony and given to the archbishop of Cologne as a secular duchy; Styria was separated from Bavaria and made an independent duchy. The ducal dignity of the remaining part of Saxony was conferred on the youngest son of Albert the Bear, that of Bavaria on Count Palatine Otto of Wittelsbach, one of Frederick's most trusted adherents. The settlement of 1180 did away with the old tribal dukedoms; their place was taken by the territories of the 'princes of the Empire', who now began to form an order of their own. Their position in the feudal hierarchy was soon legally defined, and it was the princes of the Empire who henceforth shaped the destiny of Germany.

Having settled the affairs of Germany, Frederick again turned his attention to Italy. The peace of Constance (1183) liquidated the struggle with the Lombards. Frederick acknowledged the Lombard League and conceded the free election of consuls. The cities paid him a huge war indemnity and pledged themselves to restore and respect the imperial rights and possessions in Lombardy. It was a compromise which satisfied both parties. Frederick underlined this state of friendship when he celebrated the gorgeous wedding-feast of King Henry at Milan (1186). The bride was Constance, a posthumous daughter of King Roger II of Sicily, and the marriage was meant to seal the peace between the Empire and the Normans. It opened the prospect of South Italy and Sicily being added to the Empire, for Constance was the heir presumptive of her childless nephew, William II; and the significant title of 'Caesar' was bestowed upon Henry. The marriage was arranged by Pope Lucius III, a mild and peaceable old man, who, aided by English mediation, also prevailed upon Barbarossa to let Henry the Lion return to Brunswick (1184).

Urban III (1185–87), however, renewed the quarrel with the Emperor. As a former archbishop of Milan, he disapproved of the Lombardic settlement; as a pope, he clearly recognized the danger of encirclement which the union of Sicily and the Empire would entail. But the German bishops, with the sole exception of the archbishop of Cologne, stood firmly behind the Emperor; King

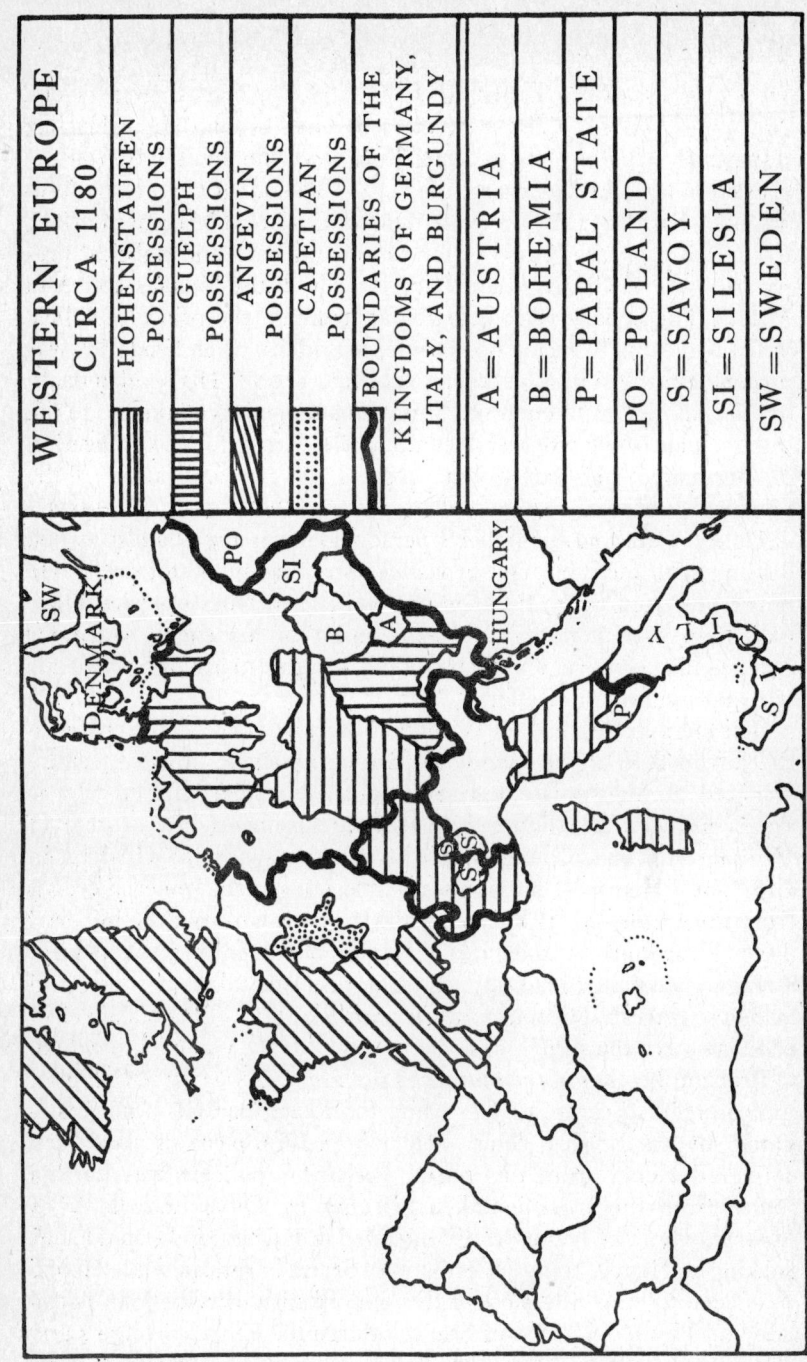

Europe about 1180

Henry occupied the pontifical state, and the Pope had to yield. Moreover, public opinion demanded unity among the Christian potentates when reports reached Europe of the annihilation of the crusaders at Lake Genezareth and the subsequent capture of Jerusalem by Saladin (1187). At the 'Diet of Christ' at Mayence (1188), Frederick took the cross. After careful military and political preparations he led a magnificent army through the Balkans and Asia Minor. The Seljuks were defeated at Iconium, the prince of Cilicia did homage and Syria lay open to the crusaders, when Frederick was drowned in the streamlet Saleph (10 June 1190). His sudden death in the remote Orient endowed him with a legendary glamour; to the intellectuals of the nineteenth century who strove for the unification of Germany, 'old Barbarossa' became the personification of the powerful medieval empire and the hero of their own aspirations.

Henry VI lacked his father's personal charm and affability when dealing with men, but far surpassed him in cunning statecraft. He never hesitated to go back on his word if treachery proved more expedient than honour. No weak point in his enemy's armour escaped his keen eye, and he was a past-master in attaining his ends with the minimum of effort.

The unexpected death of William II of Sicily (1189) left Constance the lawful heir of the kingdom. The nationalists, however, chose Tancred, an illegitimate descendant of the Norman dynasty, who at once concluded an alliance with Richard Lionheart, the brother of William II's queen, and established contact with the Guelphs in Germany. Henry VI hurried south and bought the imperial crown from Pope Celestin III by letting the Romans wipe out the imperial city of Tusculum. At the gates of Naples, however, he was repulsed, a plague decimated his army, the Empress was taken prisoner, and he had to retreat. The murder by imperial knights of the bishop elect of Liége gave the signal for a rising in which the Guelphs, the duke of Brabant, brother of the murdered prelate, and the city of Cologne, the commercial centre of Germany, took part, backed, if not instigated, by the English court. An unhoped-for piece of good luck delivered Henry from this peril. Richard Lionheart was, on his return from the crusade, taken prisoner by Duke Leopold V of Austria, whom he had mortally offended in Palestine. Leopold sold the king to Henry, being invested with Styria in return, while Henry proceeded to make the most of this opportunity. Prince John Lackland and Philip Augustus of France offered the Emperor huge sums if he would keep Richard imprisoned. Richard was constrained to exert his influence with the Guelphs to make them submit to Henry, and eventually bought his freedom for 150,000 marks, besides doing homage for England and promising an annual tribute of £5000 (1194). Henry, provided with the money and auxiliary troops of his English vassal, resumed his campaign against Sicily. The sudden deaths of Tancred and his eldest son were another timely piece of good fortune for him. On Christmas Day, 1194, Henry was crowned king of Sicily in Palermo Cathedral, and on the following day Constance gave birth to an heir to the crowns of Germany, Burgundy, Lombardy and Sicily.

The death of Henry the Lion (1195) freed Henry from his most formidable adversary; and the Guelph's successor was drawn into the Hohenstaufen orbit by his marriage with a niece of the Emperor. On the death of the margrave of Misnia Henry appropriated that country as a vacated fief of the Empire, and thereby made his position in Central Germany impregnable. In order to secure the greatest possible stability for his achievements, he suggested to the German princes that the elective empire should be transformed into a hereditary monarchy. A majority of the princes agreed to this scheme, which promised them, among other privileges, a guarantee of their own right of succession, even on the distaff side, to the fiefs held from the Empire. But when Henry tried to obtain the papal sanction for this plan, he failed and had eventually to be content with having his son unanimously elected king (25 Dec. 1196). After he had crushed a conspiracy of the Sicilian barons to which the Empress was said to be privy, Henry combined the aggressive tendencies of the former Norman princes in the Mediterranean with the Hohenstaufen claims to European leadership. His youngest brother, Philip, had become duke of Swabia after the death of Barbarossa's eldest son in Palestine (1191), and had married the Byzantine princess Irene, widow of Tancred's son. When Irene's father was dethroned by his brother (1195), Henry compelled the usurper to redeem himself by a huge annual tribute. With this Greek money he financed a campaign against Saladin's sons, who were divided against themselves. The kings of Cilicia, Cyprus and Jerusalem acknowledged Henry as their overlord, and a German army conquered the Syrian coast as far south as Beirut and Sidon. It was in full advance when it was brought to a sudden standstill. Henry VI had died at Palermo on 28 Sept. 1197, only thirty-two years old.

Most of the German princes were alarmed at the prospect of a minority reign. They therefore disregarded the claims of Frederick II, the three-year-old king elect, and a great assembly persuaded Duke Philip of Swabia to accept the crown (8 March 1198). Richard Lionheart at once shed the yoke of vassalage. He easily induced the Guelph party and their Rhenish followers led by the archbishop and the city of Cologne to put up a rival king, and his persuasion and money made them elect Otto IV (9 June), a younger son of Henry the Lion, who had been brought up at the Anglo-Norman court, and created duke of Aquitaine and count of Poitou by his devoted uncle, Richard. Ten years of civil war followed. The German princes sold themselves again and again to the highest bidder and changed sides with mercenary regularity. Foremost amongst them was the landgrave of Thuringia, who exploited the key position of his country to amass a huge fortune by means of which he raised the Wartburg, his residence, to the centre of German art and poetry. Philip and Otto vied with one another in squandering the royal demesnes and throwing away one royal prerogative after another. Otto cast himself on the mercy of Pope Innocent III (1198–1216), the greatest statesman in the succession of St Peter. He acknowledged the papal suzerainty over Sicily and abandoned the imperial rights and possessions in Italy. Thereupon the Pope excommunicated Philip and drew many of his adherents to Otto's side. However, the defeat of King John, Otto's chief supporter, at the hand of Philip Augustus of France, Philip's faithful ally, changed the situation (1204). Otto's eldest brother and the archbishop of Cologne were the first to desert him, and after the loss of Cologne he had to flee to England. Pope Innocent, roused against King John over the latter's quarrel with Archbishop Stephen Langton, made his peace with Philip. Otto's cause was lost, when the victorious Philip was suddenly murdered for personal reasons by Count Palatine Otto of Wittelsbach (21 June 1208)

The German princes now displayed a remarkable sense of statesmanship. As early as 1199, they had issued the declaration of Spires in which they proclaimed their right of electing the king without foreign, i.e. papal, approval. Now the Hohenstaufen party unanimously supported Otto IV who, moreover, married Philip's daughter. Otto pledged himself to defend the Church's every right and possession. He resigned the last privileges which the concordat of Worms had conceded to the king and thereby terminated the Ottonian system of collaboration between king and bishops (22 March 1209). But no sooner was he crowned emperor (4 Oct. 1209), than he took up the very policy of the Hohenstaufens. He seized the former imperial demesnes and revenues in Italy and advanced southward to conquer Naples and Sicily.

There was only one pretender whom Innocent could set against the perjured Guelph, namely the young Hohenstaufen king of Sicily. Frederick was, after Constance's death (1198), brought up as the Pope's ward, and Innocent hoped to find him a pliable tool. Frederick pledged himself to keep Sicily independent from the Empire, had his son Henry crowned king of Sicily, and hurried to Germany. Otto was deserted by the majority of his followers, who formally elected Frederick II king (5 Dec. 1212). Philip Augustus's victory over Otto and his English allies at Bouvines (27 July 1214) decided the issue. The victor sent the captured golden eagle of the imperial standard to Frederick. A few years later (1218) Otto died lonely and half-forgotten.

Circumstances had made Frederick II a German king; but by birth and inclination he was an Italian, and he valued the German crown only as a means of furthering his Italian interests. The greatest personality of the medieval emperors, whom his contemporaries called 'the wonder of the world', therefore cuts only a minor figure in German history proper. After 1220, in which year he had his son Henry (VII) elected German king, he never crossed the Alps except for the briefest visits. He bought the consent of the German princes by appointing the archbishop Engelbert of Cologne governor of the Empire and guardian of the young king. The ecclesiastical princes had some misgivings because Frederick had broken his promise to the Pope that the crowns of Germany and Sicily should not be united. He allayed them by the *Confoederatio cum principibus ecclesiasticis* (26 April 1220), which released the prelates from their last obligations as servants of the crown and secured their position as territorial rulers.

For Frederick's preoccupation with Italian affairs and the renewal of the conflict with the Papacy made him very dependent on the German princes and therefore wary of interfering with their interests. He was consequently mortified when King Henry pursued a different course. Archbishop Engelbert was murdered by a personal enemy (1225), and Henry soon rid himself of the tutelage of Duke Lewis of Bavaria, Engelbert's successor. He surrounded himself with a council of lesser barons, and championed their cause and that of the cities in the teeth of the princes' opposition. The latter, however, were in a strong position. They supported Frederick II in his struggle with the Papacy and mediated the peace of

Ceprano (1230), which absolved Frederick from excommunication and restored his full sovereignty in Sicily. At two successive diets at Worms (Jan. and May 1231) the princes forced Henry to grant them two important privileges which the Emperor subsequently confirmed at Cividale (May 1232). The first of these statutes checked the growth of civic liberties and established more firmly the authority of the episcopal lords of the towns. The second document, called *Statutum in favorem principum*, extended to all secular princes the privileges granted to the bishops in 1220; it reduced the royal prerogative to a shadow, and legally established the sovereignty of the princes. Sixteen years earlier, the English barons had obtained similar guarantees against the absolutism of their monarch. What distinguishes the charter of Runnymede from the statute of Cividale is that Magna Carta was granted to the commonalty of the realm as a whole, nobles, clergy and citizens joining hands, whereas in Germany each estate tried to obtain privileges for itself to the exclusion of the others; king, princes, lesser nobles, prelates and citizens, each pursued their own way regardless of the common weal, and 'every man's hand was against every man'.

Henry (VII) tried to play the role of Henry V and prepared a rebellion in conjunction with the Lombards. But Frederick had only to appear in Germany to scatter his hopes (1235). Henry disappeared into a dungeon in Apulia. Frederick's second queen had been the heiress of the kingdom of Jerusalem, and Frederick had recovered the Holy Land from the infidels and crowned himself king in the Church of the Holy Sepulchre (1229). Widowed again he now married Isabel, sister of Henry III of England, and thereby brought about a reconciliation with the Guelphs. A grandson of Henry the Lion was invested with the Saxon domains under the title of duke of Brunswick-Lüneburg (1235). On the same occasion, Frederick issued the Public Peace of Mayence (15 Aug. 1235). It was the first imperial law in the German language, and set up a legal machinery and a penal code which made it the model of all subsequent peace regulations. So secure was Frederick's authority that he had his son, Conrad IV, elected 'Roman king and future emperor' without any bargaining, in 1237.

Frederick was by no means oblivious of the possibilities by which the royal power might still be extended despite the irretrievable losses it had sustained since 1198. In 1226 he granted a charter to the imperial city of Lübeck, which enabled it to carry on its far-reaching commercial policy under the protection of the imperial eagle. The treaty which German merchants concluded with the grand duke of Smolensk in 1229 secured the abundant raw materials of Russia for the German market; and the alliance of 1241 between Lübeck and Hamburg extended the growing commercial hegemony of the Hanse towns from the Baltic to the North Sea.

In the same year in which Lübeck was made an imperial city Frederick raised the grand-master of the Teutonic Order to the dignity of a prince of the Empire. The Order was founded on the shore of Acre by citizens from Lübeck and Bremen during Barbarossa's crusade (1190) with the object of caring for sick pilgrims. Henry VI transformed it into an Order of Knights on the model of the Templars and Hospitallers (1198). Andrew II of Hungary, the father of St Elizabeth, called the Teutonic Knights to aid him against the Bulgars; and the Order ruled over Transylvania for fifteen years (1211–25), colonizing the country with German peasants and citizens. When, however, the Magyar nobles murdered Andrew's German queen and forced him to desist from his pro-German policy, the Order was glad to receive an invitation from the Polish duke Conrad of Masovia (1226). Conrad wanted their support against the heathen Prussians, and granted them the district of Kulm on the Vistula. Hermann of Salza, the grand-master, however, wanted to become neither a Polish vassal nor a papal missionary nor yet the governor of a province of the Empire. He established an autonomous state which soon comprised the whole region between the rivers Vistula and Memel. In 1237 the Teutonic Order absorbed the Order of the Brethren of the Sword which was founded at Riga in 1202 and had subjugated Courland and Livonia. The Teutonic Order profited very much from the experience which Hermann of Salza had collected as one of the most trusted councillors of Frederick II. The efficient bureaucratic machinery of the Norman administration of Sicily was added to the military readiness and missionary zeal of the Knights. By the time the grand-master fixed his residence at Marienburg (1309) Prussia gave Europe the first example of a thoroughly organized community in which foreign affairs and internal administration, commerce and industry, army and church were perfectly co-ordinated, and all personal interests and ambitions were put at the sole service of the state.

In South Germany Frederick also tried to reassert and increase his rights. The opening of the pass over St Gotthard (1226) gave a new importance to the districts round the lakes of Zurich and Lucerne. Frederick hastened to bind them more closely to the

Empire, and Swiss troops fought under his banner in Italy when the struggle with the Papacy was renewed (1239). More important was the seizure of the duchies of Austria and Styria (1246). Frederick had married his son, Henry (VII), to the sister of the last duke of the house of Babenberg so as to establish a legal claim on his possessions; but that marriage was dissolved by Henry's death. On the duke's death Frederick therefore treated the duchies as vacated fiefs of the Empire, despite the pledges given in the statute of 1231 that the feudal right of succession should be observed in such cases. Frederick here showed his successors how to build up a strong royal power in South Germany. For the Hapsburgs were only following his example when they acquired Austria and her dependencies (1282) and when, from 1298 to 1499, they tried again and again to annex the Swiss cantons, though they were unsuccessful in this latter direction.

The struggle between Frederick II and Pope Gregory IX (1227–41) which filled the beginning and end of the latter's reign was concerned exclusively with the political status of Italy. Germany was therefore immune against interdicts, excommunications, and bulls releasing subjects from their allegiance—spiritual weapons which the Pope used for very worldly purposes. The German princes found it advantageous to make and keep agreements with the Emperor rather than to run the risk of a civil war at the Pope's bidding. In vain Gregory sounded French, English, Danish and German princes, hoping to find amongst them a possible pretender. Indeed, Frederick succeeded in assuming the role of the champion of the Christian world in defiance of the Vicar of Christ. Richard, earl of Cornwall, his brother-in-law, went to Palestine as an imperial plenipotentiary and, for the last time before Allenby, recovered Jerusalem from the Moslems (1240–42). At the same time, the king of Hungary offered the overlordship of his country to Frederick if the Emperor would assist him against the Mongol hordes which were advancing into Central Europe. They had conquered Russia, and even devastated Silesia, whose duke, Henry, a son of St Hedwig, was defeated and killed at Liegnitz (1241). Papal machinations in Italy prevented the Emperor from coming to the succour of these Christian princes.

Pope Innocent IV (1243–54), the cold, calculating descendant of a Genoese banking-house, succeeded where the passionate Gregory had failed. A general council of the Western Church excommunicated and deposed the Emperor at Lyons on 17 July 1245, and now the German prelates deserted Frederick almost to a man. Henry Raspe, landgrave of Thuringia and imperial governor for King Conrad IV, was persuaded by Innocent to accept the German crown (22 May 1246). He died, however, in the following winter without having gained wide recognition. His patrimony went to the Wettin margraves of Misnia, who henceforth ruled the greater part of Central Germany. Innocent now prevailed upon some Rhenish princes to set up William, count of Holland, as king (3 Oct. 1247). William allied himself with the Guelph party by marrying a daughter of Otto IV, and thus secured the adherence of Saxony, the Lower Rhineland, with the powerful commercial centre of Cologne, and incidentally the goodwill of England. He was beginning to establish his rule over North and West Germany when he was killed in an unimportant skirmish in Frisia (28 Jan. 1256).

Before that, Frederick II died, only fifty-six years old (13 Dec. 1250). His death marked an epoch in European history. Papal propaganda had depicted him as the anti-Christ of the Book of Revelation, his adherents had looked upon him as the Emperor-Messiah of the sibylline prophecies. He had fought to the last the supreme fight between Empire and Papacy. The Empire lost, but the Papacy did not win. The dominating place which the Empire had held in the Christian commonwealth for three hundred years was henceforth taken by the national states of the West; first by France, later by Spain, then again by France and finally by England. The Papacy, now thoroughly secularized, could maintain itself only by leaning on one of these powers. It recovered its moral ascendancy only when it underwent a complete spiritual rebirth after one half of Europe had forsaken the Roman obedience for ever.

In the history of Germany, it was the death of Henry VI (1197) rather than that of his son which ushered in a new era. From that date onward her political destiny was irrevocably bound up with the territorial states which by this time had superseded the original tribal dukedoms. The main problem of German history, however, remained unchanged amidst the changing constitutional forms of its component parts, namely, the problem of how to correlate co-operation between the member states of the Empire with their self-determination.

CHAPTER III

THE DISINTEGRATION OF THE EMPIRE
(1250–1493)

THE deposition of Emperor Frederick II by Pope Innocent IV (1245) marks the beginning of a new phase in the constitutional history of Germany. The union with Italy was terminated; the last Hohenstaufen rulers—Frederick II (d. 1250), Conrad IV (1250–54), Manfred (1254–66) and Conradin (1267–68)—took little interest in German affairs and cared chiefly for their Sicilian kingdom. The popes desired the German crown to be permanently in their gift; but the era of papal supremacy in European politics drew to its close. The 'Babylonian Captivity' of Avignon (1305–77) deprived the popes of freedom of action and reduced them almost to French vassals. The Great Schism (1378–1417) deprived them of their role as arbitrators between the secular princes, making it necessary for them to court the latter's good pleasure. Once or twice the popes succeeded in having their candidates elected as kings. It was, however, one of these 'Church kings' who eventually put an end for good to papal interference in German politics: Charles IV deliberately omitted any reference to the Pope from the constitution which he issued in 1356. Henceforth the Pope had nothing more than the honorary privilege of crowning the Roman Emperor, and Maximilian I even assumed that title without coronation (1508).

The right of electing the king was in theory the privilege of every free-born man. In practice, it was always limited to the higher nobility. By the middle of the thirteenth century the privilege was confined to seven princes, the 'Electors'. They were the archbishops of Mayence, Cologne and Treves; and four secular rulers, the king of Bohemia, the Count Palatine, the duke of Saxony, and the margrave of Brandenburg. Why these seven princes should have become the sole agents of the German aristocracy is still a matter of controversy. Their exclusive right was, in fact, disputed for a long time; and their number, precedence and privileges were fixed only by the Golden Bull of 1356. The growth of this College of Electors made it certain that Germany would not become an hereditary and centralized monarchy. Centralism had become impossible since Frederick II had bestowed his great privileges upon the secular and spiritual princes (1220, 1231) and thereby made them virtually independent. The Electors, being themselves such princes, were jealous of their privileges and those of their peers: they used their prerogatives to weigh the balance in favour of their order, by stipulations or 'capitulations' which they pledged the candidates for the throne to observe. Also, their position as independent princes made it impossible to reduce them to the status of a royal Privy Council, in which capacity they might have increased the efficiency and authority of the sovereign. An hereditary monarchy would have been against the natural interests of the Electors, who obviously would not wish to lose their electoral rights; moreover, the weaker the elected king, the surer they could be of their continued influence upon the affairs of the Empire. The result of this state of affairs was a wearisome monotony in the history of the German kingship: the Electors elect a powerless princeling; once made king, he tries to acquire a sufficient personal territory to make him independent of the goodwill of the princes; this rouses their opposition; an anti-king is set up for whose complaisance the Electors obtain previous safeguards; or, if they do not go to such lengths, they at least prevent the crown from becoming hereditary by electing a successor from a different dynasty. No political stability could be achieved in these circumstances.

It has sometimes been suggested that a stable political order might have been built up by the king in co-operation with the towns. The king and citizens—so runs the argument especially of Hanseatic historians—might well have crushed the nobles in the way they did in England under the Yorks and Tudors. It is certain that from the thirteenth to the fifteenth centuries the German towns were the most powerful and stable components of the German body politic: at least, as regards economic strength, military organization and diplomatic skill. The old tribal dukedoms broke up at the end of the twelfth and the beginning of the thirteenth centuries: Bavaria and Saxony were carved up after the downfall of Henry the Lion (1180); Swabia, Franconia and the Rhineland were parcelled out to buy adherents for the rival kings after the double election of 1198. The new territorial states which rose out of the ruins of the old tribal dukedoms were only in the making during the following centuries. They had yet to build up an internal organization, to secure the allegiance of their subjects, and, most important of all, to find their proper place in relation to one another, within the Empire and in

Europe. It was about three hundred years before this task was completed; and it was not until 1648 that the national and international position of these states was fully established. During this interval, i.e. from the thirteenth to the sixteenth centuries, the towns were able to play a political as well as an economic role, which is without parallel in the history of France and England and has its counterpart only in Renaissance Italy.

German towns may be divided into two groups according to their origin. Those which grew from Roman foundations led a precarious life through the dark centuries when the Teutonic barbarians flooded Western Europe, but were the first to recover when peace and order were restored. The most notable of these towns were situated along the Rhine and Danube. Constance, Basle, Strasbourg, Spires, Worms, Mayence and Cologne on the Rhine: Augsburg on the Lech; and Ratisbon and Passau on the Danube were such Roman foundations that had weathered the vicissitudes of many centuries. Nearly all of them were episcopal sees; and it was against the episcopal overlord that the townspeople directed their struggle for autonomy from the end of the eleventh century. By the middle of the thirteenth century that struggle was everywhere decided in favour of the citizens: by force or agreement the citizens had wrested the municipal government and nearly all the administrative and financial rights from their feudal overlords.

A second group of towns grew up during the twelfth and thirteenth centuries to satisfy an imperative economic need. Overpopulation caused the peasantry to clear the forests and drain the swamps, and to colonize the regions east of the Elbe. Overpopulation also led to the foundation of many towns which were meant to absorb the surplus population of the rural districts and to create fresh centres for expanding industry and commerce. The margraves of Baden founded Freiburg in the Breisgau and Fribourg in Switzerland (c. 1120). The merchants of Ratisbon, at the time the most flourishing emporium in South Germany, suggested the revival of the deserted Roman site of Vienna as a halting-place on the route to Kiev and Constantinople. Munich owes its existence to Henry the Lion, who also helped the growth of Brunswick and Lübeck. Lübeck, founded in 1158 by the count of Holstein, at once became more important than all the others; and from it soon sprang other new foundations on the southern fringe of the Baltic Sea: Rostock, Danzig, Riga, Reval and Dorpat are the most important of these colonies. Inland, Leipzig, Berlin and Breslau were to become the most prominent of the towns founded during this wave of expansion. Not all were a success; many hundreds remained modest country-towns of merely local importance; some of them, however, attained wealth, power, and international reputation.

The common characteristic of the old and new towns was their political autonomy, i.e. their independence of the feudal system. The town councils were controlled by the aristocratic wholesale-merchants and industrialists. They wielded supreme power in the internal affairs of the towns, and represented their communities abroad. They dealt with the princes of the Empire and the rulers of Northern and Western Europe on terms of equality and often of superiority. The overlordship of the Emperor was gladly recognized as long as his financial demands were reasonable and he did not interfere with self-government. It was indeed the ambition of every town to attain the legal status of an 'imperial city' so as to be safe from the plots of the princes against its freedom. This danger increased with the growing stabilization of the territorial states. For two centuries the towns held out successfully. From the middle of the fifteenth century, however, they succumbed one after another to the power of the princes. The Hohenzollerns destroyed the autonomy of the Brandenburg towns: Berlin was subjected in 1448; by 1488 the last town of the Electorate had lost its privileges. The last stronghold of the 'free cities' was proud and mighty Brunswick: in the end it, too, had to submit (1671) and became the residence of the Guelph dukes. Only those towns which had secured their recognition as 'imperial cities' survived the advance of the territorial powers. Three of them—Hamburg, Bremen and Lübeck—have even preserved their semi-sovereignty to the present day.

The golden age of the German municipalities was from c. 1240 to 1480. The spirit of freedom, however, that made them fight against subordination to the princes prevented them from forming any binding and permanent organization for mutual defence. They could never be induced to pool their formidable resources for more than a short time and a limited purpose. Thus it happened that in the end the towns were overpowered piecemeal. The free cities lost their independence altogether, and the imperial cities sank into political impotence.

In addition to the mutual petty jealousies—a characteristic of political life in Germany from the earliest times—the real interests of the various groups of cities were too diverse to weld them permanently together. Just as Swabia, the Rhineland, and Saxony, for instance, never abandoned their essential independence in favour of a centralized German monarchy, so the Swabian, Rhenish and Saxon towns only reflected the general tendency of German history when they refused to abandon their racial peculiarities and serve the ends of imperial centralism.

An external factor contributed a good deal to the different courses which the South and North German towns took. In the South, the great majority were imperial cities and therefore comparatively immune from interference by territorial princes. In North Germany, only Lübeck, Goslar and Dortmund were imperial cities; all the others were only 'free cities' and therefore at least nominally subject to a princely overlord, who in any case could proceed in law, if not by force, against his towns should they push their semi-independence too far. It thus happened that the North German towns nearly always subordinated political considerations to commercial ones: the protection of their economic and trade interests was uppermost in their minds. That is apparent in the first treaty between Lübeck and Hamburg, whose object was to suppress highway robbery and to safeguard common trade interests (1241). The towns of the German Hanse were later on always anxious to stress the fact that they were not a political 'corpus', but only a loose association whose interests were strictly confined to commerce and trade.

The South German towns, on the other hand, whose main trade routes opened on to the Mediterranean, had before their eyes the example of the Italian communes, such as Venice, Florence and Genoa. They, too, were intent on making their weight felt in the political sphere. The first memorable event in their history is therefore the foundation of the Rhenish Town League (1254). This was followed during the following centuries by a number of similar alliances in South and West Germany which all had political rather than economic aims, although naturally political stability was of paramount importance for the growth of commerce. For some decades the Rhenish Town League was the most powerful organization in South and West Germany; and its political and financial backing of any candidate for the royal throne was of greater weight than that of all the princes of those regions. It was the cities which decided the rival claims of Lewis of Bavaria and Frederick of Austria in favour of the former; and it was again due to the loyalty of the citizens that Lewis could hold his own in the twenty-five-year struggle with the Roman Curia.

The history of the Hanse towns, on the other hand, is part of the economic history of Europe rather than of the political history of Germany. When they agreed to recognize Lübeck as their head (1295), they had already established their economic supremacy over the whole of Northern Europe, from Novgorod to Bergen and Bruges; the Steelyard in London was the chief of a number of permanent trading stations in England. In the fourteenth century the Hanse towns tightened their grip on the Scandinavian kingdoms. As a rule they preferred the weapons of diplomacy, economic warfare and naval blockade to open warfare. When, however, Valdemar IV of Denmark (1340–75) seized Estonia, Schonen and Gotland, and thus threatened the very substance of Hanseatic life, the towns took up arms, and utterly defeated Valdemar and his Norse ally. The peace of Stralsund (1370) which followed marked the zenith of the Hanse's international power. In 1377 Richard II of England confirmed their privileges to the exclusion of all other foreign merchants. A hundred years later, a victorious naval war (1471–73) prolonged their privileges in England for one more century, until Queen Elizabeth, in pursuance of Walsingham's protectionist policy, closed the Steelyard in 1598.

By this time the political role of the German towns was a thing of the past. The political aspirations of the South German cities, united in the Swabian and Rhenish Town Leagues, were crushed by the princes (1388). Henceforth they concentrated on industry and commerce, and the fifteenth and sixteenth centuries saw their greatest prosperity. The merchandise of Nuremberg, Augsburg and Ulm was in demand all over Europe. But it was individual merchants, and no longer the towns as a whole, who now meddled in national and international politics. And they gained fame and fortune as the agents and bankers of those dynasties which their forefathers had tried to oust from the political stage.

In North Germany, the inland cities were absorbed by the territorial states in the second half of the fifteenth century, as has been said before. The maritime cities were able to keep their power somewhat longer. They could, however, no longer compete with the national states of Northern and Western Europe. Lübeck's foolish attempt to impose its power upon Denmark and Sweden ended in disaster: its defeat meant the end of the Hanse in international affairs (1535).

Little can here be said of the cultural importance of the towns in the age of their splendour. Suffice it to mention one or two outstanding facts. The poet of the epic of Tristan and Isolde, Gottfrid of Strasbourg, was the first of the long line of writers and poets of bourgeois origin, at the end of which stands Goethe, a son of the imperial city of Frankfort. In the field of art, the painters Stephen Lochner of Cologne, Albert Dürer of Nuremberg, and Hans Holbein of Augsburg; the sculptors Veit Stoss and Peter Vischer of Nuremberg, Bernt Notke and Claus Berg of Lübeck; and the architects of the cathedrals of Strasbourg, Ulm, Cologne and Freiburg, bear comparison with the best European artists of the Gothic period. No historical abstract, however brief, must leave unnoticed the cities' greatest contribution to civilization and progress—the invention of printing with movable type. Johann Gutenberg, the son of a patrician family of Mayence, invented the art at Strasbourg and perfected it at Mayence (c. 1450); and before the end of the century printing presses had been established in every town of the Empire, and printers from Augsburg, Spires, Cologne and Lübeck spread the new invention all over Europe. These cultural attainments contrast oddly with the petty quarrels which fill the greater part of the political history of those centuries.

At King William's death (1256) the Electors (who appear for the first time on this occasion) were divided between Richard of Cornwall, nephew of Otto IV and brother-in-law of Frederick II, and Alfonso X of Castile, grandson on the distaff side of King Philip of Swabia. Civil war was averted, as Alfonso never left Spain. King Richard established his ascendancy over West and North Germany and was recognized nominally also in the East and South. He was prevented, however, from giving his undivided attention to his German realm by the troubles of his brother, Henry III of England, whose chief adviser he was. His heir, Henry of Almaine, was murdered by the hostile Montfort party (1271), so that Richard's death (1272) left Germany as unsettled as before.

The Electors raised to the throne an insignificant and aged Swiss count whom they thought unlikely to interfere with their authority. They had underrated, however, the political skill and tenacity of their candidate. Rudolf of Hapsburg was to become the ancestor of a dynasty which would be supreme not only in Germany, but in Europe for many centuries, and outlive the College of Electors and the Holy Empire itself. The new king gained the papal approval by renouncing all claims to the Italian possessions of the Hohenstaufens. He then set out to break the power of the strongest of the princes of the Empire, the Czech king Ottokar II of Bohemia.

Ottokar, the son of a Hohenstaufen princess, had for more than twenty years laboured to establish a dominion that ranged from the Baltic to the Adriatic seas. After the extinction of the Austrian and Carinthian dynasties he acquired their dukedoms, and wrested Styria from the king of Hungary. He aided the Teutonic Knights in their fight against the pagan Prussians and Lithuanians; and the capital of Prussia was named Königsberg (Mount Royal) in his honour. By his support of Richard of Cornwall he secured recognition of his acquisitions and the goodwill of the North and West German followers of Richard. Thus Ottokar entertained justifiable hopes of becoming German king himself after Richard's death, and was mortified when he found that his powerful position was the very reason for his exclusion from the throne. He trusted he might defy Rudolf with impunity, but the latter rallied all the lesser princes of the Empire against him. Ottokar was outlawed; he submitted to the unexpected, and was allowed to keep only Bohemia and Moravia (1276). When he took up arms again, Rudolf allied himself with the Magyars and defeated him at Dürnkrut near Vienna: Ottokar was killed in the battle (1278). In order to avoid the jealousy of the princes, Rudolf did not himself take over Ottokar's Austrian possessions; he invested his sons with them (1282) and thus laid the foundations of the future Austrian empire of the Hapsburg dynasty.

Ottokar's failure was a major tragedy for Germany. He would have been strong enough to uphold the royal prerogative. His dominion was half-Slavonic and half-German, and the German portion was not part of the old tribal territories, and therefore sufficiently detached from tribal interests. Most important of all, Bohemia had become, as a consequence of the German colonial movement eastward, the geographical centre of the German orbit: Prague, the capital of Bohemia, would have been the best situated capital of Germany. There was as yet no racial antagonism between Czechs and Germans, and Ottokar's brilliant administration did everything to amalgamate the two races for the benefit of the whole community. The fact that Charles IV (1346–78), the shrewdest and most far-seeing of the German kings, pursued exactly the same policy as Ottokar, is full proof of Ottokar's statesmanlike gifts. In fact, the union of Bohemia and Austria seems to be necessary both for political and economic reasons; for whoever has ruled at either Prague or Vienna has always endeavoured to make himself also master of the other: Albert I, Rudolf's successor, seized Bohemia after the death of Ottokar's childless son (1306–7); Charles IV and his son-in-law, Rudolf IV of Austria, concluded a family pact of mutual succession (1364), in fulfilment of which Albert V of Austria became king of Bohemia (1437-39). After many vicissitudes, the Hapsburgs eventually established their rule over both countries in 1526 and held them together for four centuries, until 1918. After the rape of Austria in March 1938, it was only to be expected that the conqueror would extend his grasp to Bohemia and Moravia.

When the throne fell vacant (1291), the Electors, frightened by the prodigious rise to power of the Hapsburgs, passed over Rudolf's eldest son, Albert I. They agreed at last upon Adolf, count of Nassau, who was as impotent as Rudolf had once been and gave them every promise of circumspect behaviour (1292). Adolf was, however, most unscrupulous. He obtained large subsidies from Edward I of England, whom he was to support in his war against France (1294); and immediately let himself be bought off by France for a greater sum. He used the English and French money for an expedition against the landgraves of Thuringia and Misnia, seized their countries and thus put himself well on the way to establish a formidable territory in Central Germany. The Electors took alarm, deposed Adolf and reluctantly elected Albert of Austria as king; Adolf was killed in battle (1298). Albert pursued his aims with ruthless force; and the Rhenish Electors were the first to smart under his iron fist. He seized Bohemia for his son and, after the latter's death (1307), fought the king whom the Bohemians had elected. Nor did he restore Misnia, whose unlawful seizure had been one of the pretexts for deposing his predecessor; he was, however, defeated near Leipzig and had to renounce that claim. He then advanced against the Swiss cantons which separated his hereditary possessions between Zurich and Basle from the lately acquired Austria. On the way there he was assassinated by his nephew, from whom he had withheld his paternal inheritance (1308). This event freed the 'Everlasting League' of 1291 from its most dangerous enemy and opened the way to the glorious history of the Swiss Confederation. The importance of Albert's premature death was fully recognized in later legends, which made the original foundation of the League coincide with Albert's reign and added the figure of William Tell as one of the principal heroes of the story.

Again the choice of the Electors fell on an insignificant candidate, Henry, count of Luxemburg. His election was promoted by his younger brother Baldwin, archbishop of Treves (1307-54). A serious rival was Charles of Valois, brother of Philip IV of France;

but Pope Clement V, although pressed hard by the French king, frustrated the plan. The brilliant diplomacy of Baldwin secured for his family the powerful bastion of Bohemia, where John, Henry's eldest son, was elected king (1310). Henry tried to revive the imperialistic policy of the Hohenstaufen emperors. In 1311 he went to Italy, fervently acclaimed by Dante as the heaven-sent liberator from internal strife and French tyranny, and was crowned emperor at Rome by a papal delegate (1312). Immediately afterwards he found himself opposed by the Papacy and Naples, both influenced by the French. As he advanced southwards, he died suddenly (1313). His fervent desire had been to re-establish the imperial dignity and imperial rule over Italy. By this time, however, the imperial ideology had become unreal, although Dante devoted to it the immortal splendour of his poetry and prose. Only the institution of 'imperial vicars' in Italy was of lasting importance; Matteo Visconti was raised to that office at Milan, and Can Grande della Scala at Verona. In favourable circumstances these places could always become starting-points of fresh intervention in Italy without encumbering the Emperor with their permanent defence and administration.

Baldwin of Treves tried to secure the election of his nephew, John of Bohemia, as successor to Henry VII, but the majority of the Electors were against such an attempt at making the crown hereditary. The French king made a fresh effort to have a French prince elected, while the Hapsburgs put forward Frederick of Austria as a candidate. In order to exclude both the French and the Hapsburgs, five Electors agreed upon the election of Duke Lewis IV of Upper Bavaria; but the two dissentients elected Frederick of Austria. As there was as yet no definite regulation of the procedure, and unanimity could not be achieved, the double election of 19-20 Oct. 1314 resulted in a civil war of eight years' duration. At last, Frederick was defeated and taken prisoner by Lewis (1322). Peace would have been ensured, had not Lewis chosen this moment to hurl defiance at another and more formidable adversary.

Pope John XXII, a great scholar, a brilliant administrator, and an unscrupulous business man, had used the struggle between Lewis and Frederick to re-establish papal authority in Italy. He claimed the right to decide between the rival kings and declared the throne vacant until he should make his judgment known. Lewis, elated by his victory over Frederick, dispatched an imperial governor to Italy who speedily raised the siege of Milan by papal and Neapolitan troops. The Pope did not hesitate to use his spiritual authority: he summoned Lewis, on pain of excommunication, to renounce the usurped title of king and to annul his past acts of government; Lewis's subjects were ordered to refuse him obedience. Lewis reacted as rashly as Henry IV in 1076. Instead of taking his stand upon constitutional grounds, he introduced ecclesiastical issues, pronounced the Pope a heretic, and appealed from him to an oecumenic council. A reconciliation became altogether impossible when Lewis adopted the doctrines of Marsilius of Padua, one of the acutest political writers of the Middle Ages. Marsilius, in his *Defender of the Peace*, had denied the authority of the Church in secular matters and repudiated the claim to primacy of the bishop of Rome; he advocated the sovereignty of the people to whom, he declared, rulers are responsible. On the strength of this theory, Lewis had himself crowned emperor by the representatives of the people of Rome (1328). John XXII pronounced him a heretic, deposed him, and preached the cross against him. Lewis replied by setting up an anti-pope, Nicholas V; and Emperor and Pope crowned each other. It was an empty gesture. Lewis's rule in Italy collapsed at the first show of opposition, and he returned ingloriously to Germany (1329).

Here Lewis had so far operated with fair success. His rival, Frederick of Austria, was placated: Lewis had taken the unprecedented step of appointing him co-regent (1325). At the extinction of the Anhaltine margraves of Brandenburg, descendants of Albert the Bear, Lewis invested his son with the Electorate and humoured the neighbouring princes by apportioning to them large frontier districts. At the same time the king married the heiress of Holland and thus became the brother-in-law of Edward III of England. The struggle with the Papacy upset all these hopeful beginnings. At first the great majority of the secular and ecclesiastical princes, all the imperial cities, and the influential Order of the Minorite Friars, stood by Lewis; but the long duration of the struggle, the prospects offered to the ambitious, the sincere anxieties of the devout, and the lack of real statesmanship in Lewis himself, gradually thinned the ranks of his followers. Though Frederick of Austria died as early as 1330, Lewis and the Hapsburg family maintained their good relations and divided Carinthia, Carniola and the Tyrol peacefully amongst themselves. This friendship, however, cost Lewis the allegiance of the powerful John of Bohemia and the latter's brother, Baldwin of Treves, the greatest German statesman of the time. Consequently, Lewis and John took different sides when the outbreak of the Hundred Years War between England and France stirred the comity of Europe (1337). The Bohemian king took the field with the French and was eventually killed in the battle of Crécy (1346); the three ostrich-feathers and the motto *Ich dien* of John's coat of arms were adopted by the victorious Prince of Wales. King Lewis, as was to be expected, made an alliance with Edward III, his brother-in-law. Edward appeared at a court which Lewis convened at Coblentz, and Lewis, in concurrence with the princes and magnates of the Empire, gave a solemn judgment to the effect that Edward was the lawful king of France. At the same time Edward was appointed imperial vicar of the German territories left of the Rhine (1338).

The Anglo-German alliance might have led to the most momentous consequences for Germany. In the years 1338–39, representatives of the high aristocracy, the lesser nobility, and the cities assembled no fewer than six times in order to deliberate the affairs of the Empire. There is no doubt that a kind of parliament was forming, as naturally as it had grown in England a century earlier. Even the division into two houses was foreshadowed when on one occasion the 'gentry', i.e. the lesser nobility and the cities, assembled separately, as had recently (1332) become the usage in England. The English influence upon the development in Germany cannot be mistaken, and yet nothing came of it. Lewis, inconstant as ever, tried again and again to come to an agreement with the Curia, ready to sacrifice every ally and every principle, except the 'honour of the Empire', i.e. his royal dignity. He was supported by some of the most subtle political philosophers of his age: in addition to Marsilius of Padua, there was William of Ockham, who, expelled from Oxford on the accusation of heresy, spent the last twenty years of his life in his service. But Lewis was incapable of understanding the soaring thoughts of his propagandists: the aggrandisement of his family possessions was of greater importance to his narrow mind than the problems of national and international policy.

His desire to be reconciled with the Church may have been more sincere than his provocative boasts made believe, for when there appeared a hope that the French king might bring about a mediation, Lewis abandoned his English brother-in-law and made an alliance with France (1341). This vacillation was, however, as useless as all his former ones. The Pope—it was now Clement VI (1342–52)— was determined to bring the unending strife to a close, for the Curia, too, had suffered great damage during the twenty years of open warfare. None was more harmful than the declaration issued by the Electors at Rense in 1338: in it the representatives of the Empire stated expressly that a legally elected king did not need the papal confirmation. It is easily comprehensible that the cardinals at Avignon read the declaration *vehementi cordium stupore nec absque displicencia multa* (with a very heavy oppression of their hearts and not without great displeasure); for it undid with one stroke all the endeavours of three hundred years of papal diplomacy. It was only a temporary gain when the Curia eventually succeeded in having Charles, margrave of Moravia and son of John of Bohemia, elected anti-king (1346) and generally recognized after Lewis's death (1347); for it was this same Charles who, a few years after, issued the constitution of the Golden Bull which excluded once and for all any papal influence upon the election of the German king.

Charles had been brought up at the French court, where he exchanged his baptismal name Wenceslaus for that of his godfather, King Charles IV. He had the mind of a scholar and lawyer, was a liberal and discriminating patron of the arts, and an accomplished man of business. There was nothing about him to stir the imagination of his contemporaries or of posterity. When he went to Rome to be crowned emperor (1355), he fought his way through Italy with bribes instead of arms. Military glory meant nothing to him; he was content to pursue his aims by the least obtrusive means, and usually obtained what he wanted. He carefully avoided challenging the hostility of the princes, which had been fatal to his predecessors, and increased his power by legal procedure rather than by force. He brought about a complete reconciliation with the Wittelsbachs and Hapsburgs, bestowing the margraviate of Brandenburg upon the former, and the Tyrol upon the latter. In the end, however, the Wittelsbachs were obliged to sell him Brandenburg; and a family pact of succession with the Hapsburgs opened the prospect of a later reversion of the whole of their possessions to the house of Luxemburg. From his brother-in-law he bought part of the Upper Palatinate; and thanks to his good economy he was always able to take in pawn castles, fiefs and other feudal rights of needy nobles.

His matrimonial policy was a marvel of statesmanship. Through his third wife he obtained the last independent Silesian dukedoms; his fourth brought him the friendship of the dukes of Pomerania. One of his daughters was married to Rudolf IV of Austria, the first Hapsburg to style himself archduke; another to King Richard II of England. His son Sigismund married the heiress of Hungary and

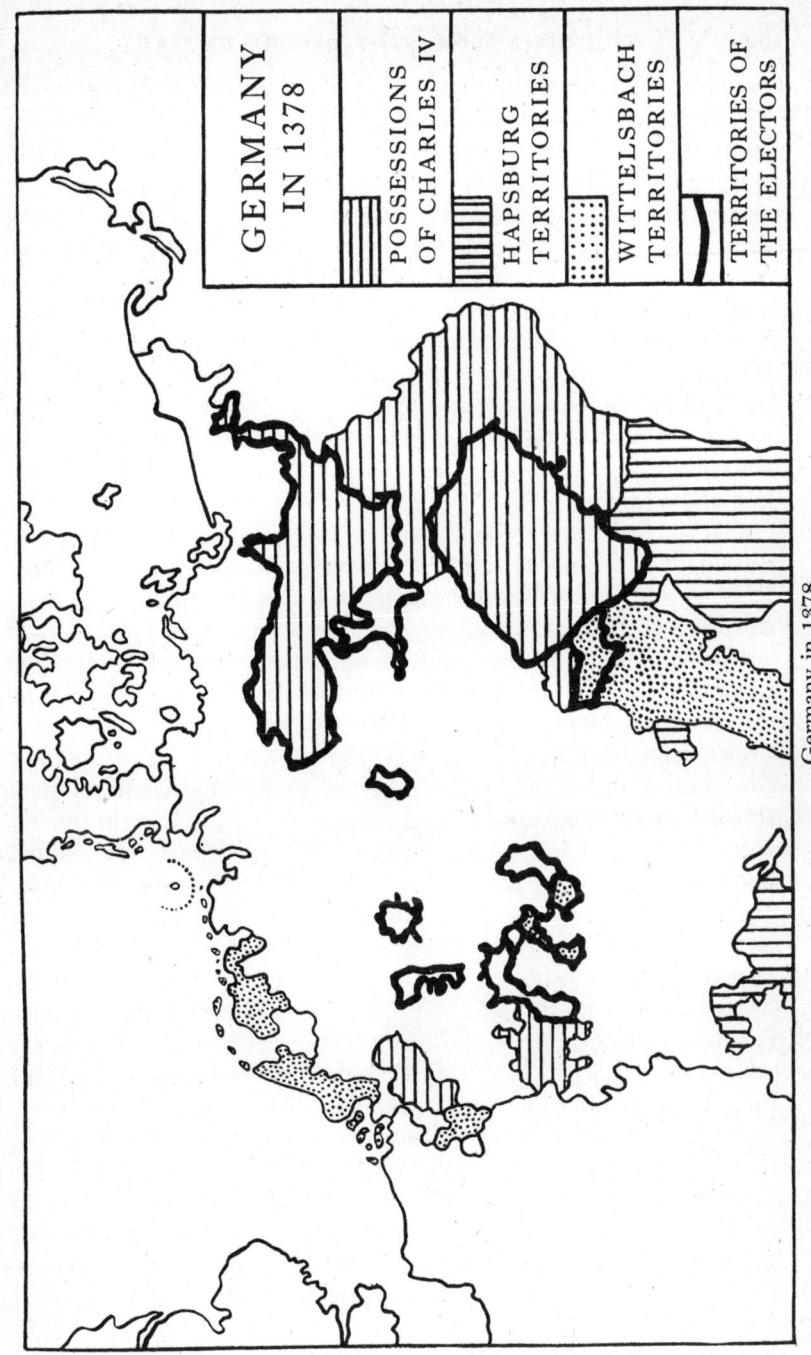

Germany in 1378

Poland. In brief, Charles would have combined the power and territories of Frederick the Great of Prussia and Maria Theresa of Austria, if he had been granted a longer life and an heir capable of continuing his policy. Moreover, Charles extended his following among the secular princes without cost to himself, when he granted ducal rank to the princes of Mecklenburg and Jülich; and he used his considerable influence with the papal see to have every important episcopal vacancy filled with his own faithful adherents. All these acquisitions and political combinations were means to the realization of one great scheme—the creation of a solid political and economic bloc with Prague as its centre. The traffic from the Mediterranean to Scandinavia was to be directed across the Brenner and Semmering passes, through Austria and Bohemia, and down the river Elbe, until it met the great west to east sea route at Hamburg and Lübeck. Similarly, the inland trade from Western to Eastern Europe was to follow the route from London and Bruges to Cologne, up the Rhine to Frankfort, up the Main through the Upper Palatinate to Prague, and from there through Silesia to Cracow and other Polish cities.

Charles did everything in his power to make Prague not only the economic, but also the cultural centre of the Empire. In 1348 he founded here the first university north of the Alps, which was soon to be imitated in Poland (Cracow, 1364) and Austria (Vienna, 1365). Although Charles IV himself was an essentially medieval personality, as is borne out by his 'Autobiography', he was in contact with Petrarch and Rienzo, who represented the literary and political Renaissance; and the masters of Prague University strove for an elegant Latin style as well as a purified literary German which later on became the basis of Luther's language. The see of Prague was raised to an archbishopric, and the cathedral was made one of the finest Gothic buildings by French and South German masons. The Prague guild of painters achieved an international reputation; its influence is apparent, for instance, in the famous Wilton triptych of Richard II (now in the National Gallery).

These economic and cultural activities required peace and order, and Charles was therefore most anxious to remove those political and constitutional disputes that had disquieted the Empire for so long. His original plan was to settle the affairs of the Empire in free deliberation with princes, nobles and cities, that is, on the model of the English parliament; but he soon found it more advantageous to transact the most important items only with the Electors. Their power consequently so much outweighed that of the other Estates that the parliamentary development, which began under Lewis IV, was nipped in the bud. The Golden Bull issued on 10 Jan. 1356 became the final constitution of the Holy Empire It settled first of all the election of the 'King of the Romans' by the seven Electors under the presidency of the archbishop of Mayence. The majority of votes should be decisive; the papal claim to the right of approval was passed over in silence. The Electors received a number of special privileges, such as the rights of exploiting metal and salt mines, of minting currency, of administering customs and markets, the lucrative protection of the Jews, and the exclusive jurisdiction over their subjects. A yearly meeting was contemplated when the Electors should discuss the imperial affairs with the Emperor; but this plan never came into effect.

The place assigned to the cities was less favourable than might have been expected from Charles's economic policy. He deliberately barred them from participation in imperial politics and confined them to the economic sphere. Contrary to Lewis IV, who had gained valuable assistance from the wealthy, self-assertive, and warlike citizens, Charles preferred to deal with the princes, whom he found more manageable and readier to submit to his hard-cash arguments. In one respect only he gladly availed himself of the co-operation of the cities, namely in enforcing public peace, which was of common interest to both parties. The Emperor was indefatigable in encouraging the conclusion of regional associations of princes and cities with a view to pacifying the country. When he paid a visit to Lübeck in 1375, he treated the burgomasters like sovereign princes, contrary to his usual policy. The Hanse was recognized as a mandatory of the Empire to protect and preserve the public peace on land and sea.

The realization of Charles's far-sighted plans had hardly begun when he died in 1378. Two years before, he had had his son, Wenzel, elected and crowned king, and the Luxemburg dynasty seemed to be secure. Wenzel, however, abandoned the corner-stone of his father's policy. Barons, knights and citizens whom Charles had excluded from the government of the Empire tried to assert their rights against the privileged princes. Town leagues and associations of knights sprang up throughout the Empire, and Wenzel favoured them. He may have hoped to strengthen the royal authority with the military prowess of the knights and the financial backing of the towns, but his hot temper, of which the murder of St John of Nepomuk is but an instance, his dissipation and his indolence made him unfit to become a popular leader. The heavy defeat which the princes inflicted upon the Rhenish and Swabian town leagues (1388) weakened Wenzel's position; quarrels within the Luxemburg family made it even more unstable. Thus he could offer no resistance when, in 1400, the Electors proclaimed a state of emergency and deposed him.

They chose as his successor one of their number, Rupert, Count Palatine, who, in 1388, had quelled the Rhenish towns. The majority of the towns remained faithful to Wenzel; an expedition to Italy which Rupert undertook at the instigation and expense of the Florentines had to be abandoned at Venice; the South-Western princes and towns under the leadership of the archbishop of Mayence organized themselves in open defiance of Rupert. Wenzel had more than one opportunity to re-establish himself; but the continued quarrels with his brother Sigismund of Brandenburg and his cousin Jobst of Moravia, and his own inertia, prevented him from carrying out any such scheme. Yet he did not abandon his claims, so that there were in fact three rival kings when, after Rupert's death, Sigismund and Jobst were elected by the divided Electors (1410). The Elector of Cologne had mooted the election of Henry IV of England, but met with no response. The situation was the more complicated as the triad of kings coincided with a triad of popes. In 1378 the great schism had broken out, and its repercussions were felt in the political affairs of Europe. The Council of Pisa, summoned to end the schism, had only increased the confusion by setting up a third pope without having the power to remove the other two. The rift which rent the Empire was healed more speedily than the schism.

Sigismund, who had inherited much of the political sagacity of Charles IV, carried the day: Jobst of Moravia died three months after the election; and Wenzel was compensated for renouncing his claims by the prospect of obtaining the imperial crown, and meanwhile retaining the title of Roman king.

Sigismund tackled the major issue of the schism first. He convened a general council at Constance (1414). In three years and a half the three main items of union, reform and faith were dealt with: the union of the Church was restored by the elevation of Pope Martin V (1417); a dozen decrees did away with the worst abuses of the financial policy of the Curia; and the Catholic faith seemed to be restored when the arch-heretic, John Hus of Prague, was burnt at the stake (1415). Sigismund had promised him safe conduct, but pretended afterwards that this had not included Hus's safe return to Prague. The flagrant breach of the royal pledge had to be paid for more dearly than either the king or the council could have anticipated. The Hussite movement which rose from the ashes of its protomartyr was profoundly to disturb the peace of the Empire and the Church, to antagonize for ever the Czechs and Germans, and to prepare the permanent split of Western Christianity.

The Hussite movement is, in its social, religious and racial aspects, part of a process which, from the end of the fourteenth century, was spreading all over Europe. The risings of the cloth-weavers at Florence (1378) and the rebellion of the Kentish and East Anglian peasantry under Wat Tyler (1381) were the first large-scale outbreaks of social discontent. They have their counterparts in every district of Germany; and the grievances and the attempts to abolish them were the same everywhere. The artisans in the towns revolted against the capitalistic exploitation of the big industrialists, who at the same time monopolized the town councils and thus united economic, legislative and executive power to the exclusion of the working class. The peasantry began to raise their voices and arms against the lords of the manors, who arbitrarily increased the burdens in kind and service and tried to reduce the peasant to a state of virtual or even legal bondage. These latent subversive tendencies in town and country broke into open rebellions throughout the fifteenth century; in the end they flamed up in the great Peasants' War of 1525, in which the artisans of the South and Central German towns sided with the peasants. The crushing of that rebellion by the princes and nobles meant the end of the free yeomanry in Germany.

The beginnings of this social upheaval in England were accompanied by the preaching of John Wycliffe and his followers. In Bohemia, Militch of Kremsier (d. 1374) played a similar role to Wycliffe, and John Hus, a professor of Prague University, was his greatest disciple. Hus attacked a number of basic doctrines of the Church, advocated social justice, and opposed the preponderance of Germans in the Church and administration of Bohemia. He was inspired by religious, social and national conceptions whose relative importance it is often difficult to estimate. Undoubtedly national feeling was awakening everywhere at the time, and it was a momentous and significant step when the Council of Constance abandoned the figment of the one and indivisible Christian commonwealth and acknowledged the diverse nations as independent units. A decade later, France was roused to a supreme effort against the English invaders by the national propaganda of the Maid of Orleans. Nowhere, however, did nationalism run higher than in the West Slavonic peoples. They had been the victims of German aggression and penetration for many centuries: as early as 1285, the archbishop of Gnesen bitterly complained in a letter to Rome that his nation was brutally oppressed by the Germans and robbed of its traditional rights and usages. In 1410, the combined forces of the Poles and Lithuanians crushed the Teutonic Order in the battle of Tannenberg, and thus finally stopped the German movement eastward. The German towns and nobles of Prussia, it is true, left the standards of the Teutonic Order during the battle and hailed the Poles as their liberators from the harsh yoke of the Order; but on the Polish side, nationalistic impulses cannot be overlooked. The rise of Czech nationalism is even more unmistakable. The expulsion of the German masters and students of Prague University, who thereupon went to Misnia and founded Leipzig University (1409), was a deliberate step towards a national and cultural revival; while the martyrdom of Hus stirred the national and religious feelings of the Czechs to the highest pitch. The death of Wenzel and the succession of the perjured Sigismund gave the signal for the outbreak of a war of religion and nationalism (1419). One German army after another was defeated; and even the internecine strife between the radical and conciliatory sections of the Hussites did not wholly paralyse the Czech superiority. In the end, Sigismund had to concede the main requests of the Hussites before he was acknowledged king of Bohemia (1436); and the Council of Basle, convened to advance the reform of the Church, had to grant to the Hussites the sacrament in both kinds and other doctrinal deviations which, in fact, constituted an independent Czech Church.

The war with the Hussites clearly revealed the weakness of the organization of the Empire. The king could dispose only of the military or financial powers of his own territories; the unwieldy machinery of the diet was more or less controlled by the Electors; and the Electors and the other Estates had not yet found a common ground, being united only in their endeavour to curb any increase of the royal prerogative. A working order might nevertheless have been feasible if the Electors had had a clear conception of a federal structure of the Empire to set against the centralizing tendencies of the sovereign; but they were too much engrossed in the immediate tasks of their own territories to see them in proper relation to the commonwealth. The antagonism between the princes who held the political power, and the cities who held the financial power, further prevented any decisive step towards the necessary changes. Yet, reform of the political structure of the Empire was the slogan which was raised again and again during the fifteenth century. Sigismund tried to make himself the head of a great town league which would have been capable of facing the opposition of the princes. He tried to impose a uniform taxation and currency; he suggested the division of the Empire into four districts, each under its own 'captain', for the preservation of the public peace. All his schemes, however, came to nothing, as none of the Estates was willing to sacrifice a jot of its rights.

Sigismund therefore resorted to the usual expedients of strengthening his patrimonial possessions, and of gaining the goodwill of individual princes. By his marriage to the heiress of Hungary he had become king of that country. The virtual union of Germany and Hungary from 1387 to 1866 brought the problems of the Near East on to the horizon of the rulers of the Empire; and that meant, for some centuries to come, the task of defending the West against the onslaught of the Turks. On St Vitus's Day, 1389, the Serbian empire collapsed before the scimitar; henceforth, the Turks never ceased pressing westward until they appeared before Vienna in 1529. Sigismund did his best to provide for future emergencies. He married his only child to Duke Albert of Austria who, as the future lord of Austria, Hungary and Bohemia, would be capable of protecting the eastern frontier. Following the example of Charles IV, he raised the counts of Savoy and Cleves to dukes, and thereby secured potent allies in the south-west and north-west. He even forged his way into the College of Electors. His most trusted counsellor, who had done most to bring about his election as king, was invested with the Electorate of Brandenburg: it was Frederick of Hohenzollern, burgrave of Nuremberg (1415). A second Electorate was drawn into the orbit of Sigismund, when the dynasty of the Electors of Saxony died out; Sigismund conferred the dignity upon the margrave of Misnia (1425). From that time Misnia has been known as Saxony, a name which originally denoted the country at present called Hanover. Looking back, one must regard the raising to power of the Hohenzollern and Wettin dynasties as the most far-reaching results of Sigismund's reign. They were certainly the most stable ones; for Albert of Austria, his son-in-law and successor, died after a reign of less than two years, only forty-two years old (1438–39), so that Sigismund's far-seeing dynastic policy was frustrated prematurely and unexpectedly.

The majority of the Electors gave their votes to the senior member of the Hapsburg dynasty, Duke Frederick of Styria (1440-93). The new king realized that the vindication of the royal prerogative was beyond his power; peaceable and chary of clear decisions, he preferred to leave the Empire to fend for itself. The separate conclusion of concordats with the Holy See by a number of German princes, including Frederick himself (1447-48), was a momentous sign of the fact that the Empire had ceased to act as a corporate body. The contracting princes gained a full supervision of the Church within their respective territories: it was the formal termination of the Investiture Struggle and an important step towards the establishment of national churches in the age of Reformation. The concordats also meant the end of the conciliar movement by which Sigismund had set so great a store. Henceforth, the papal supremacy was firmly established; opposition against it became impossible within the pale of the Roman Church.

Frederick's policy in imperial and Church affairs was conducted largely by the chancellor, Kaspar Schlick, and the secretary, Enea Silvio Piccolomini. Schlick had received his training in the chancery of Sigismund; he is the first of a long line of Austrian statesmen whose diplomatic skill and administrative efficiency steered the ship of the Hapsburg monarchy through deep and shallow waters until it was abandoned by its own crew in 1918. Enea Silvio, one of the shining lights of the humanist movement, was to become Pope Pius II (1458-64); Schlick is the hero of this young ecclesiastic's lascivious novel *Euryalus and Lucretia* (1444). After Schlick's death, Frederick III retired almost completely from the affairs of the Empire and concentrated on the internal administration of his Austrian possessions. For thirty years he did not once attend a diet in person. As guardian of the posthumous son of King Albert II, he ought of necessity to have made permanent the union with Hungary and Bohemia. But Frederick alienated the allegiance of both countries by his double-dealing, and eventually each country chose a native king: Bohemia, George Podiebrad (1452-71); Hungary, Matthias Corvinus (1458-90). After their deaths Polish princes succeeded in both Bohemia and Hungary (until 1526). Under Casimir IV (1447-92) Poland was by far the most important power of Eastern Europe. Casimir reduced the Teutonic Order to complete submission: the Order lost the western half of its territory (what is now called the Corridor), and the rest (the present East Prussia) was made a Polish fief (1466). The territory of the Teutonic Order was never part of the Roman Empire or of the later German Confederation; it was made a constitutional part of Germany as late as 1871. Therefore neither Frederick nor the German princes had a legal title to interfere with the Polish expansion. In the north and west, however, the inertia of the Emperor and the princes paved the way for the loss of large parts of the Empire. In 1459, the counts of Holstein who, from 1326, were also dukes of Slesvig, died out, and in the following year the estates of Slesvig and Holstein elected the king of Denmark as their duke, with the proviso that the duchies should 'remain undivided for ever'. Thus the Danish kings became members of the Empire, as dukes of Holstein, and were able to use their Danish resources to interfere in imperial affairs—as they did in the seventeenth and eighteenth centuries. On the other hand, this clause gave the Empire a handle to interfere in Danish affairs when the interests of Holstein were concerned. The administrative separation of Slesvig and Holstein in 1863 was, in fact, the reason for the German Confederation, and the pretext for Prussia to declare war upon Denmark and deprive her of both duchies.

In the south-west corner of the Empire, the Swiss League was steadily drifting away from the Empire. Originally, the feud of the Swiss cantons was directed only against the Hapsburgs. Kings who were themselves opposed to that dynasty, as Henry VII and Lewis IV, maintained good relations with the League and even extended its privileges. By 1353, Lucerne, Zurich and Berne had joined it; and it defeated the Austrians during the years when the Rhenish and Swabian towns, since 1385 allies of the Swiss, succumbed to the onslaught of Rupert of the Palatinate and other princes (1386–88). In 1415 the Swiss annexed the Aargau, the county from which the Hapsburg dynasty originally came. When the German crown became vested in the Hapsburgs, the Swiss League was bound sooner or later to turn against the Empire; and this development became irrevocable during the reign of Frederick III. When Maximilian I tried to retrieve the losses of two centuries, he not only most ingloriously lost the great 'Swabian War', but he had also to acknowledge the final separation from the Empire of the Swiss League (1499).

The increasing estrangement of the Swiss from the Empire was closely connected with the growth and fall of the Burgundian monarchy. In 1363 the French dukedom of Burgundy was given to

Philip, younger son of King John II of France. Philip added to it not only Flanders and Artois, but also Franche-Comté, which was still part of the Empire. His grandson, Philip II (1419–67), obtained Holland, Zeeland, Friesland and Hainault as the inheritance of his Bavarian mother (1433), Brabant and Limburg from his childless brother (1430), and Namur and Luxemburg by purchase from the heirs of Jobst of Moravia (1441). His defection from the English brought him further French territories as reward (1435). His son, Charles the Bold (1467–77), was undoubtedly one of the most powerful and perhaps the wealthiest prince in Christendom. The wool industry of Flanders, the grain crops of Holland, the vineyards of Burgundy lay within his dominions; Dijon and Arras, Bruges and Brussels, the chief centres of international trade, equalled Paris, London and Cologne in opulence and splendour. Charles set to work to round off his vast possessions; by fair means and foul, he acquired within a few years Liége, Ghent, the Alsace and Breisgau, Gelderland and Zutphen, and, the most coveted prize of all, the dukedom of Lorraine (1475). The exiled duke of Lorraine and King Louis XI of France, now thoroughly alarmed, gained the assistance of the Swiss, who felt themselves threatened by Charles's ever-expanding might. The Swiss levy defeated and annihilated the Burgundian knights in two battles (1476–77); in the second, at Nancy, Charles was killed.

The growth of the Burgundian monarchy took place mainly at the expense of the Empire and some way had to be found to compose Burgundian and imperial interests. Charles suggested his own election as Roman king by the side of Frederick III, who in 1453 had been crowned emperor—the last emperor to be crowned in Rome. As the prize he offered the marriage of his only child, Mary, to the Emperor's son, Maximilian. But the deliberate Hapsburg was slow to commit himself to the impetuous Valois. He deferred his decision until the death of Charles made it imperative to act lest the whole Burgundian inheritance should devolve to Louis XI of France. Maximilian, Frederick's fiery son, acted spontaneously. He hurried to the Netherlands, married Mary, and defeated the French, who had occupied a large portion of her possessions, in the brilliant victory of Guinegate (1479). After the premature death of Mary (1482), the partition of Burgundy took place. Maximilian regained all the territories which had formerly belonged to the Empire, apart from the restored duchy of Lorraine; and, in addition, Flanders and Artois. All at once, the Hapsburg dynasty had become the paramount power in the western part of Germany. Further successes fell to Maximilian in the south-east. Matthias Corvinus of Hungary had been tempted by Frederick III's sloth to extend his power westward, and succeeded in subduing Austria, Styria and Carinthia; from 1485 he resided at Vienna. His death (1490) allowed Maximilian, who had been elected Roman king in 1486, to recover these countries; in the same year he also acquired the Tyrol from a collateral line of the Hapsburgs. When Frederick III died in 1493, after a reign of fifty-three years, he left the Empire more unsettled than he had found it at his accession; but the greatness of the house of Austria was firmly established.

CHAPTER IV

THE CONTEST BETWEEN EMPIRE AND TERRITORIES (1493-1648)

WHEN Frederick III died in 1493, two generations of men had become used to seeing an Austrian archduke on the throne of Charlemagne. The connection between the imperial crown and the house of Hapsburg was so firmly established that henceforth no serious attempt was ever made to transfer the imperial dignity to another dynasty. With the exception of the hapless Bavarian, Charles VII (1742-45), all the subsequent emperors were chosen from the house of Hapsburg. In fact, after 1519 the election became a mere matter of form, and the succession to the Empire of the Hapsburg heir apparent was always taken for granted.

On the other hand, the territorial states had definitely asserted their virtual independence from the central administration. The 'Emperor' and the 'Empire' were no longer identical, but had become conflicting, political forces. The history of the Empire became more and more the history of its member states; and the title of Emperor was little more than a cloak to the territorial interests and ambitions of the rulers of Austria, itself the most powerful of the member states.

Three Hapsburg emperors tried to overthrow this balance of power in favour of the imperial side.

Maximilian I (1493-1519) was too weak and too cunning to subdue the Estates by force, while the federal party was in his time farther-sighted, more reasonable, and better led than ever before or after. So he resorted to evasion and obstruction, in which practices he was a past master. Although he failed to extend the imperial power, the opposition failed likewise to reorganize the administration on federal lines.

His grandson, Charles V (1519-56), had to tread very cautiously for about twenty-five years, but he bided his time and at last felt powerful enough to make short work of his opponents. He skilfully exploited the religious cleavage between the Protestant and Catholic Estates, and the dynastic rivalries within the Wettin and Guelph houses, and thus overcame with comparative ease the armed resistance of princes and cities (1547). For five years he wielded a power over the whole of Germany more absolute than that of almost all his predecessors or successors—when suddenly his former allies combined with the opposition. They overthrew the imperial power within a couple of weeks and turned the balance of 'Emperor' and 'Empire' again in favour of the latter.

Several times during the so-called Thirty Years War, the Emperor Ferdinand II (1619–37) was almost as near final success as Charles V had been from 1547 to 1552. Again, however, his allies forsook him at the decisive moment and sided with their peers against the Emperor. The peace of Westphalia (1648) finally turned Germany into a commonwealth of independent states under the nominal presidency of the Roman Emperor.

The reign of Maximilian I began with great hopes for an improvement in the internal situation. The young king enjoyed a popularity as widespread and unmerited as Richard Lion-heart in the popular imagination of the English. He skilfully increased it by clever propaganda. He took a great interest in literature, learning and art; and his genuine taste and widely distributed largesse secured him the support of the foremost scholars, poets and artists of his age. The educationalist and publicist, Jacob Wimpheling, wrote some historico-political pamphlets in which he supplied the historical justification for Maximilian's anti-French policy; his arguments have remained the stock-in-trade of nationalistic German historians ever since. Humanistic poets contrived masterpieces of adulation on Maximilian and his house. Albert Dürer, the greatest German painter and graphic artist, and many more craftsmen and sculptors, glorified and popularized by their art Maximilian's real and imaginary achievements.

The Estates realized that the virtual independence they had gained during the past forty years must be supplemented by a fresh delimitation of their functions within the framework of the Empire. The Electors were willing to make concessions to those princes who equalled them in actual power without sharing in their historic privileges. It was admitted that the larger towns which had weathered the advance of the territorial princes must be given a recognized status. The economic and social position of the lesser nobles and the peasants, which was rapidly deteriorating, demanded a solution. Such problems as regulating coinage and customs, unifying police and justice, and organizing the finances and defence of the Empire, had to be dealt with on broad lines. A co-ordination of the territorial powers on the principle of federalism was the goal towards which the Estates of the Empire steered. Their leader was Bertold of Henneberg, archbishop of Mayence (1484–1504), one of the most gifted and far-sighted statesmen Germany ever produced.

During his father's lifetime, Maximilian had pledged himself to set up an imperial high court of justice, one of the most urgent demands of the reform party. In fact, the *Reichskammergericht* was created at the first diet which Maximilian summoned at Worms in 1495; but it was to be the only lasting success of Maximilian's reign. For the king was very far from sharing the reformers' views on the government of the Empire. He used to sneer at Charles IV and call him 'the father of Bohemia and the arch-stepfather of the Empire'; with far greater truth one might apply that epithet to Maximilian, only replacing Bohemia by Austria. For Austria, or rather the Hapsburg possessions, formed the chief, almost the only object upon which he bestowed his care. The Empire, in his view, existed only to furnish him with the means of consolidating, defending and expanding his own domains.

In dealing with the Hapsburg countries Maximilian's labours were crowned with complete success. He established the administrative organization which up to 1918 held together the various regions and races of which the Hapsburg monarchy was composed. The bureaucracy of Vienna was for some centuries the most efficient body of civil servants Europe had ever known. Even when the machinery lost its adaptability and its wheels creaked with the rust and dust of centuries, its original driving power was still strong enough to survive the revolutionary tendencies of the nineteenth century. The Hapsburg bureaucracy as organized by Maximilian ended only with the Hapsburg dynasty itself.

In the lustrum from the Diet of Worms in 1495 to that of Augsburg in 1500 the political reform movement was at its zenith. The failures and vicissitudes of his foreign policy, of which something will be said presently, made Maximilian largely dependent upon the goodwill and assistance of the Estates. Both parties drove a hard bargain. The king demanded first of all a military reorganization of the Empire, permanently if possible, or at least for the next ten or twelve years. In this way he expected, rather too hopefully, to get a force of 30,000 men at his disposal. He further aimed at a uniform system of taxation, the revenues of which were to flow into the imperial treasury. The Estates acknowledged the basic soundness of these proposals, but wished to keep the control of the army and the finances in their own hands. They therefore put forward their counterproposals: a Council of Regency (*Reichsregiment*) which should fix and supervise the general policy of the Empire; a Perpetual Peace to safeguard public and private affairs; and an independent High Court of Justice to administer a uniform and impartial justice.

The Diet of Worms proclaimed the Perpetual Peace, set up the High Court of Justice, and granted a general tax, the Common Penny, a complicated blend of property and poll taxes. They could not, however, induce Maximilian to accept the Council of Regency, the most important of their proposals. It was only when the Estates deliberately obstructed the collection of the Common Penny that the king yielded. At the Diet of Augsburg (1500) a compromise was achieved. The Estates consented to the levy of an imperial army, and Maximilian agreed to the institution of the Council of Regency. It consisted of twenty members, under the presidency of the Emperor, and included, beside the Electors, representatives of the other princes, prelates, counts and towns. The Empire, with the exception of the Hapsburg possessions, was at the same time divided into six Circles (*Kreise*); they had to provide members of the Regency Council, to guarantee the Public Peace, and to carry out the sentences of the High Court of Justice.

The Council of Regency was in theory vested with legislative, executive and administrative powers. It might well have developed into something similar to the original Privy Council of the English constitution, if only Maximilian had had the slightest intention of giving it a fair trial. Its beginnings, first at Nuremberg, then at Frankfort, were promising. The regents started negotiations with France in order to settle the Italian question which Maximilian had hopelessly bungled; but they were no match for the prevaricating king. He foiled, obstructed and eventually paralysed the Council to such a degree that it terminated its activities after two years (1502). The Electors, as the perpetual representatives of the Estates, took alarm, and considered dethroning the fickle monarch, who would not keep his word; but before any decision had been reached, Archbishop Bertold, the leader of the reform party, died (1504). His death meant the failure of the reform movement, as none of his fellow-princes possessed his tenacity, prudence and vision. The stage was left to Maximilian on the one side and the short-sighted and narrow-minded representatives of an egotistical particularism on the other. The opportunity for a constructive and organic readjustment of the German constitution was irretrievably lost.

Maximilian would have avoided even the scanty concessions which he had been forced to make, if the international situation had given him a free hand. His foreign policy, however, compelled him again and again to ask for the military and financial support of the Empire; and he could gain it only by complying with a modicum of the wishes of the reform party. The inheritance of the greater part of the Burgundian dukedom of Charles the Bold added fresh complications to the policy of the house of Hapsburg. The gain of the most populous and wealthy territories of Western Europe was dearly bought at the price of the implacable antagonism of France. The peace of Senlis (1493), in which Charles VIII of France ceded the Netherlands and Burgundy to Maximilian, marks the beginning of the age-long enmity between the German and French nations.

Prior to that, Maximilian had tried to checkmate the French king by marrying the heiress of Brittany and thereby putting himself at the head of the unruly French aristocracy. Charles, however, outwitted him and gained both the bride and Brittany (1491). Matters came to a head when Charles VIII entered upon his famous expedition into Italy (1494). The year before, Maximilian had married a Sforza princess of Milan and thereby gained the alliance of one of the most powerful Italian dynasties. The international conflagration which followed the French attack on Italy was exploited by Maximilian to secure further portions of the Burgundian inheritance and to gain a firm foothold in Italy. In the end both projects failed.

In turn, he supported Perkin Warbeck against Henry VII of England (1494) and allied himself with Henry against France (1496). In 1495, he joined the Holy League, of which Venice was a principal member, and in 1508 the League of Cambrai, which was directed against Venice. From 1504 to 1512 he even abandoned his hostility to France and recognized her conquests in Upper Italy. In 1513, however, he made a treaty with Spain and England against France and, together with Henry VIII, defeated the French in the famous Battle of Spurs at Guinegate.

This one victory, however, could not retrieve his losses. In the peace of Brussels (1516) he had to abandon Milan to France, and Verona to Venice; and a recovery of the French portion of Burgundy had become plainly impossible. Moreover, his ill-advised attempt to force the Swiss back into submission sealed their final separation from the Empire and drove them into the arms of France: the 'Swabian War' of 1499 ended in the recognition of the virtual independence of the League, which henceforth was exempt from appeals to the imperial Court of Justice and from paying imperial taxes.

All these failures, however, were more than counterbalanced by the marriage of Maximilian's only son, Philip, to the heiress of Spain. In 1479, Ferdinand of Aragon had married Isabella of Castile and thus founded the 'catholic' Spanish monarchy. Their troops conquered Granada, the last stronghold of the Arabs, in 1492. In the same year, Christopher Columbus discovered the New World; and the treaty of Tordesillas (1494) secured the greater part of the Americas and the Pacific for Spain, leaving the rest to Portugal. In 1504, Ferdinand compelled the French to cede Naples and Sicily to him; they remained united with Spain until 1713. The heir of this vast accumulation of territories, indeed, of whole continents, was Joan, Ferdinand and Isabella's only child. She was married to Philip in 1496, and she and her husband acceded to the throne of Castile after Isabella's death (1504). Joan was seized with madness, and Philip died in 1506: but their progeny fulfilled the most extravagant hopes which Maximilian could ever have cherished for his son. Charles, Philip's eldest son, succeeded Ferdinand in Spain (1516) and Maximilian in the Empire (1519); the second, Ferdinand, followed his brother as Emperor (1556-64). The Spanish and Austrian branches of the Hapsburgs dominated the European scene for two centuries. Even the name of the last-discovered continent bears witness to that family union: the Spanish discoverer of Australia named it 'New-Austria' in honour of a cousin of his royal house. Philip's daughters opened further prospects for the aggrandizement of the Hapsburg dynasty; two of them married kings of Portugal, which led to the union of Spain and Portugal from 1580 to 1640; one married the last Jagellon king of Hungary, after whose death (1526) the country fell to Ferdinand of Austria; and two other daughters married the kings of France and Denmark respectively. It was not without foundation when the word spread about that

Bella gerant alii; tu, felix Austria, nube.

Seen from the Austrian point of view, even the unsatisfactory state of imperial affairs was not wholly disadvantageous; for the reform movement was definitely killed by the obstructionist tactics of Maximilian. Although he failed to increase the imperial power, he successfully prevented the Estates from imposing their will upon him; and the creation of two separate Circles for the Austrian and Burgundian possessions of the Hapsburgs (1512) made his internal administration entirely free from any interference on the part of the Empire.

When, in 1555, Charles V separated Belgium and the Netherlands from the Empire and bequeathed them to his son, Philip II of Spain, it was a purely inter-Hapsburg arrangement, and the Empire had no say in the loss of two of its richest provinces. From Maximilian onwards, Austria ceased to be merely part of the Empire; she was an independent European power pursuing her own policy regardless of, and sometimes in opposition to, the interests of the Empire of which the Austrian monarch continued to be the nominal head.

The Estates of the Empire drew the natural inference; they no longer regarded the affairs of Austria as their own concern, and began to consider the Emperor a foreign monarch rather than their overlord. When looking round for assistance against the increasing power of Austria, their eyes were directed towards the natural enemy of the Hapsburgs: France, encircled by the Hapsburg possessions on each of her frontiers, now became the natural ally of the German princes.

Very soon the princes got a clear proof of the significance of the united power of the Austro-Spanish monarchy. When Maximilian I died in January 1519, the Electors looked round for a suitable candidate. Charles I of Spain, Maximilian's grandson, put up the first claim to the imperial crown. Henry VIII of England, for whom Wolsey had secured a resounding triumph in the peace of London (1518), soon withdrew from the competition as he did not think it worth while to pay the excessive sums with which the Electors expected to be bribed. The Elector of Saxony, Frederick surnamed the Wise, would have had a fair prospect, but he was too cautious to stake his fortune on a game in which other Electors had been the losers before him. Francis I of France (1515–47) was the most serious rival of Charles of Spain; three Electors—Brandenburg, Treves and the Palatinate—were won over by him as early as 1517. Finally the balance was cast in favour of the king of Spain. The unheard-of wealth of the greatest bankers of Europe, especially of the Fuggers of Augsburg, was lavished upon the Electors; bands of adventurers under the unscrupulous Franz of Sickingen were assembled in and near Frankfort and intimidated those who were not yet cajoled into compliance. Moreover, the election of Francis was strongly favoured by the Pope, and the popular aversion to the Papacy greatly contributed to the failure of his candidate. In the end, Charles was elected unanimously (28 June 1519). The Electors did their best to secure 'German liberty', as the rights of the members of the Empire were called from that time onward, by imposing upon Charles a number of conditions. The Emperor pledged himself not to employ foreign, i.e. Spanish, troops within the Empire, not to summon a diet outside the Empire, and to use the German language in his deliberations—Charles's native tongue was French. The old demands of constitutional reform, especially the establishment of a Council of Regency, were also put forth, but half-heartedly and without any real hope of fulfilment, as was to be expected.

The world-wide empire of Charles V 'upon which the sun never set' was teeming with difficult problems. All of them, from the organization of the New World to the amalgamation of the Iberian kingdoms, from the pacification of the Western Mediterranean to the affairs of Italy and Hungary, had their repercussions on German affairs. For Charles was seldom at liberty to direct his undivided attention to German affairs. Again and again he had to make concessions to the German princes in order to keep them quiet while he was engaged elsewhere. Germany meant little to him. As early as 1531 he had his brother Ferdinand elected king of the Romans; and it was Ferdinand upon whom devolved the main functions of the Emperor as far as Germany was concerned.

From the first to the last day of his reign the inherited antagonism to France was the decisive factor in Charles's European policy. The first phase of the war led to the crushing of the French at Pavia (1525) and the sack of Rome (1527). For a hundred years, France was reduced to a second-rate power in international affairs; and the sack of Rome gave a deadly blow to the Italian Renaissance and all it stood for. When Francis I resumed the war in alliance with a number of German princes (1532) and with the Sublime Porte (1535), Charles was unsuccessful by land and sea and had to agree to a patched-up truce for ten years (1538), which left the issue in suspense.

During these first twenty years of his reign a spiritual revolution took place in Germany which Charles was impotent either to hinder or to influence, and unwilling to adopt for his own purposes. In 1517, a young professor of Wittenberg University entered upon a learned dispute on the true meaning of sin, repentance and redemption according to St Paul and St Augustine, which he contrasted with the Roman practice of selling indulgences. The academic controversy at once spread like wildfire throughout Germany. The failure of the reform councils, the upheaval of the Hussite movement, the glaring worldliness of the Church and priesthood, and the general disposition towards a spiritualization of life had made the minds of the people sensitive to the shortcomings of the Church, and inclined to take its reform into their own hands. In Martin Luther all those vague hopes and expectations found a focus, while the buoyancy of his personality, the sincerity of his purpose, and the complete concord of his pronouncements with the general feeling made him the inspiration and natural leader of the nation. Within a few years about nine-tenths of the German people accepted the Lutheran doctrine of the 'pure Gospel'.

The matter was dealt with summarily at Charles's first diet, at Worms, 1521. Luther here roused the enthusiasm of his adherents and even the unwilling admiration of his adversaries, by his intrepid courage. As he refused to recant his doctrines, the Edict of Worms put him and his followers under the ban of the Empire. However, such was the impotence of the executive that Frederick of Saxony, Luther's sovereign, dared to take the banned heretic under his protection. Frederick, who had taken a leading part in Archbishop Bertold's reform movement, and had made Saxony the most powerful German principality next to Austria, maintained that his subjects were exempt from imperial jurisdiction; nor did he want to lose one of the pillars of his university, whose religious tenets moreover agreed with his own inclinations. Held in a kind of protective custody at Wartburg castle, Luther was given the opportunity to complete his German translation of the New Testament (1522). It was one of the greatest literary and publishing successes of all times and became the foundation of the New High German literary language; Tyndale's English translation (1525), the principal source of the Authorized Version, was based on Luther's German version rather than the original Greek text.

Together with the majority of the population, the majority of the secular Estates of the Empire embraced the Reformation during the next decades. It was therefore impossible to carry out the Edict of Worms, and the Lutheran affair occupied every successive diet. In 1529, the Reformers gained a great constitutional victory at the Diet of Spires when they formally protested against the validity of majority resolutions in religious matters; from that time onward they were called Protestants. They presented their doctrine to the Diet of Augsburg in the following year in the form of the 'Augsburg Confession', which has remained the basis of the Lutheran Church ever since.

The war with France compelled Charles to turn a blind eye to the open violation of the Edict of Worms. No sooner had the peace of Cambrai been signed (1529) than a greater danger in the East caused him to make even greater concessions to the Protestants. In September 1529 the Turks appeared for the first time before the walls of Vienna, and the assistance of the evangelical Estates was indispensable to ward them off. The imperial cities, for instance, nearly all of which adhered to the new doctrine, owned not only the best artillery of the time, but were the only places where gunpowder and ammunition were produced and ready for sale. When therefore the Turks, beaten off in October 1529, advanced again towards Austria in 1532, Charles hastily concluded the religious peace of Nuremberg. It laid down that all the Estates should keep the peace until an oecumenic council could decide the religious controversy. Charles was then in a position to raise the greatest army Germany had mustered so far—some 80,000 men—and compel the Sultan to withdraw from Hungary.

The chief effect of the Reformation upon the political and constitutional development of the Empire was the further consolidation of the power of the princes. It is true, the break-up of the Estates into two hostile religious factions definitely ruined the slender prospects of their harmonious co-operation, as the Catholic party was often willing to side with the Catholic Emperor against their Protestant peers. Constitutional reform became almost an exclusive interest of the Protestant princes and therefore lost its general attraction for the whole body of the Estates. Nevertheless, the Catholics were as eager as the Protestants to make the most of the new situation. Both of them extended to the full the ascendancy over the churches of their territories which the concordats of 1447–48 had granted them in part: the Protestant Estates, by openly appropriating the movable and immovable possessions of the Church; the Roman Catholics, by extorting from the intimidated Pope practically the same rights and liberties, although they made some pretence of keeping up appearances. The effect was a very considerable increase in the power of the territorial administrations. Hitherto the Church had managed what we call nowadays the social services, in the widest sense of the term, including elementary and higher education, care for the sick, old and unemployed, and the like. The state now took away the financial means by which the Church had maintained schools, infirmaries and asylums; it became therefore inevitable that the state should take charge of the respective responsibilities as well. The bureaucracy, which during the last generations had everywhere taken control of public administration, eagerly seized this opportunity to extend the sphere of state interference. The officials, who had been brought up on the revived Roman law, fully endorsed its conception of the omnipotence of the state. The Protestant rulers were even able to cloak their sovereignty with the semblance of divine right. They made themselves the supreme heads of the newly established churches of their respective territories and thus represented both God and the state to their subjects. This co-ordination, almost identification, of 'throne and altar' has remained a characteristic feature of German public life ever since. Once the Christian justification (or its pretext) was thrown overboard, the naked deification of the state as proclaimed by the National Socialists was the inevitable result.

The Catholic princes were no less well served by the Reformation in establishing their absolute power. The majority of the nobles and cities within their territories had embraced the Lutheran creed. Their suppression by force therefore fulfilled a double purpose: on the one hand, the extermination of the heretics ingratiated the sovereign with the Roman authorities and made the latter comply with the prince's encroachments upon ecclesiastical privileges; on the other hand, the abolition of the political prerogatives of the heretic Estates effectively freed the sovereign from their awkward control of the public finances. Charles V extirpated the liberties of the Flemish towns and gave the Protestant Church its first martyrs in the Netherlands. A faked conspiracy of the Bavarian nobility furnished Duke Albert V with the pretext for reducing the Bavarian Estates to complete submission. The consolidation of absolutism which was to become the general form of government in the late seventeenth century was ahead in Catholic countries by a hundred years.

Catholic and Protestant rulers were of one opinion when their sovereign rights were at stake, whether they were threatened by the centralizing tendencies of the Emperor, or the democratic aspirations of their own subjects. The bureaucratic organization intensified taxation in cash and kind, and the heaviest burdens fell upon the weakest shoulders; the rising absolutism abolished the privileges of the Estates and classes, and the poorest lost most. From 1476 onwards revolts of the peasantry, chiefly in Franconia and Swabia, followed one another with increasing intensity. The Reformation kindled the peasants' hopes for an improvement of their social status by adding a religious fervour, and often chiliastic expectations, to their economic demands. They looked for the Emperor to defend their rights, which were fast vanishing in the melting-pot of territorial sovereignty: the best thought-out programme of social reform, Eberlin of Günzburg's *Fifteen Allies*, was dedicated to Charles V (1521). In 1524, the great Peasants' War broke out in Swabia and soon spread over the whole of South, West and Central Germany. Artisans, miners, knights, even some imperial towns and one or two petty princes, joined the standard of the rebels. The princes acted with unwonted speed. Within a few weeks the rising was drowned in a sea of blood: the political, social and economic conditions of the peasantry were reduced to an even lower standard than before: the proud yeomen of old were brought into a state of virtual, and in many places even legal, serfdom.

Ten years later (1534-35) Protestant and Catholic princes combined again to ward off a peril common to them both. Religious enthusiasts from the Netherlands had seized power in the Westphalian capital of Münster, where they put into practice communistic ideals. The anabaptist heresy and political utopianism were simultaneously crushed when the town was subdued after heroic resistance.

Meanwhile the Protestant Estates, under the able leadership of the energetic Landgrave Philip of Hesse, had taken a decisive step towards the full federalization of the Empire. They proclaimed that logical interpretation of the constitution of the Empire and the rights of the Estates, the lack of which had formerly impeded most of the attempts at a thorough constitutional reform. The theory of non-resistance, their argument ran, was valid only as far as the subjects of hereditary princes were concerned. The Emperor, however, was not an hereditary monarch, but an elected *primus inter pares*; and the constitution of the Empire was aristocratic, not monarchic. The princes, they concluded, were therefore entitled to resist the Emperor even by force, if he should encroach upon their liberties; and the subjects owed allegiance only to their hereditary princes.

That was the programme upon which Saxony, Hesse, Lüneburg, the towns of Bremen and Magdeburg, and some counts, concluded the League of Schmalkalden (31 Dec. 1530). First, it was joined by the Protestant imperial and free cities of North and Central Germany. The South German cities followed suit when the defeat of Zurich at the hands of the Catholic Swiss cantons, in which the reformer Zwingli was killed (11 Oct. 1531), taught them a grave lesson. At the same time, Catholic princes, too, approached the League, which thus became the rallying centre of all anti-Hapsburg

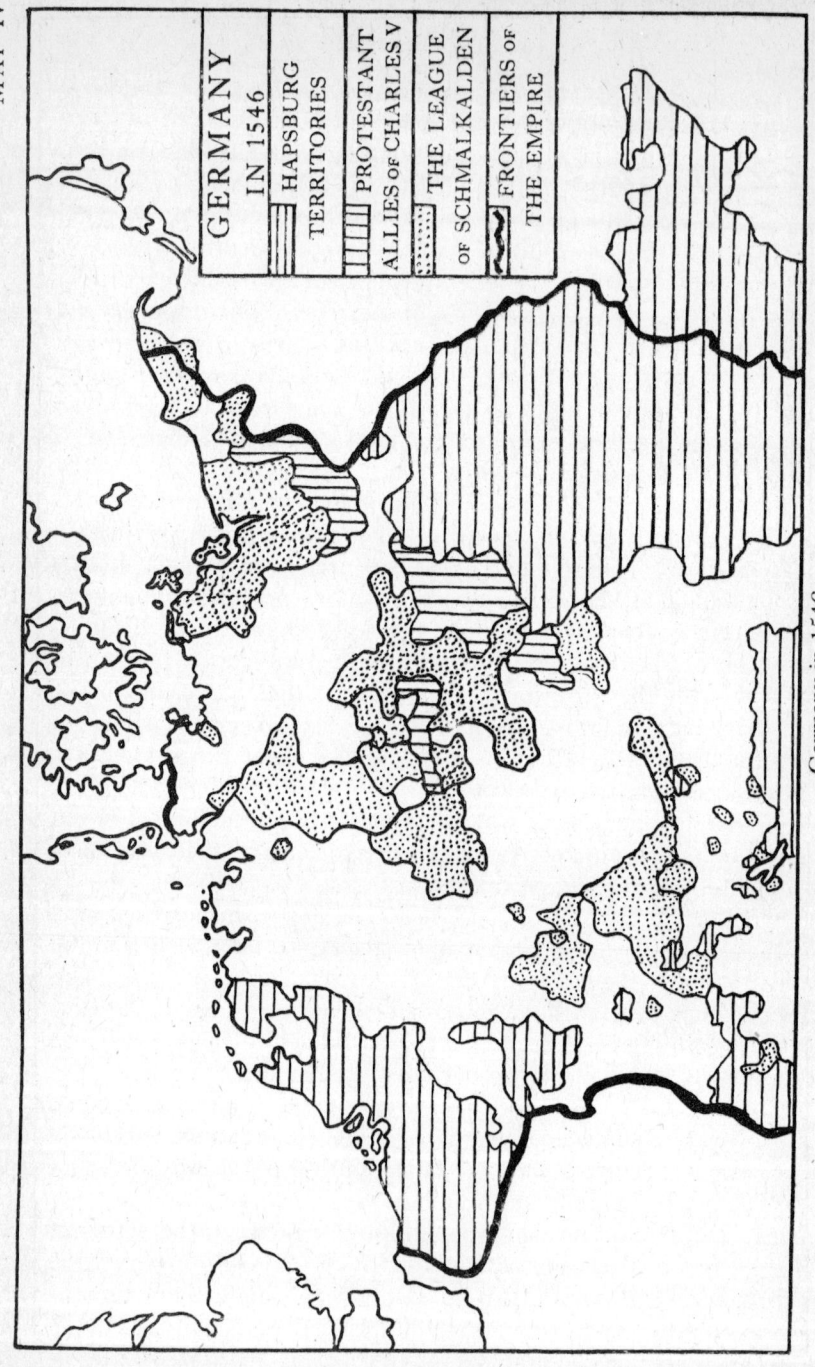
Germany in 1546

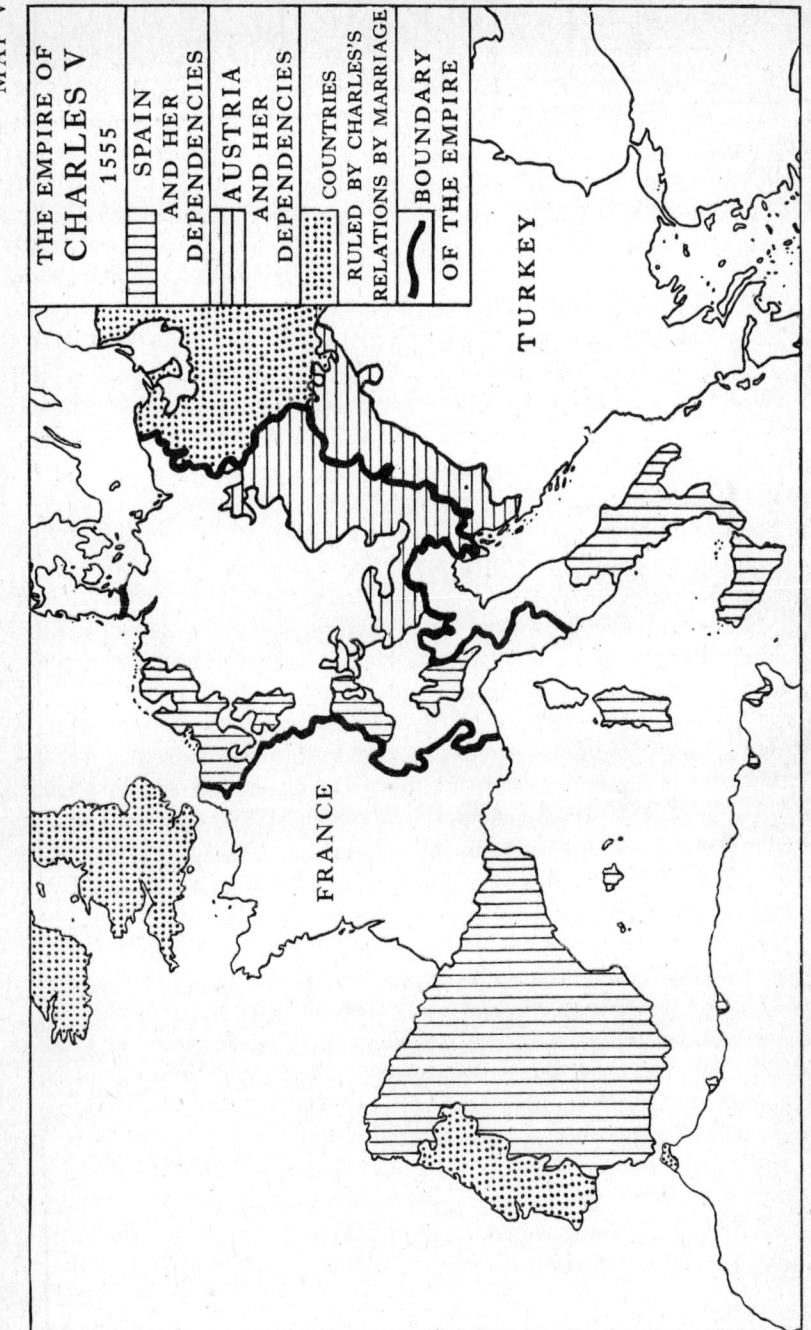

Europe in 1555

forces in the Empire. The League of Schmalkalden also secured the support of the most powerful enemy of the Hapsburgs outside the Empire: Saxony, Hesse and Bavaria made an alliance with France for their mutual aid against Ferdinand, the recently elected king of the Romans (26 May 1532). The League soon included practically every Estate of the Empire, although the Protestant tendencies outweighed the federalistic aims. It was therefore a grave matter when the imperial vice-chancellor succeeded in setting up the counter-league of Nuremberg (10 June 1538), which was composed of the principal Catholic Estates only. Henceforward the antagonism between Protestants and Catholics was deepened, and the pursuit of their common anti-centralistic programme became almost impossible, for King Ferdinand himself was the most powerful member of the Nuremberg League. The Schmalkalden confederates achieved a great triumph when they overcame the leader of the North German Catholics, Duke Henry of Brunswick, whose country immediately turned Protestant (1542).

Charles, however, was no longer willing to endure the ascendancy of the League. His alliance with Henry VIII of England and their victorious campaign in France put the foreign ally of the Schmalkaldeners out of action (1543–44). The truce of Adrianople secured the eastern frontier against the Turks (1545). Moreover, Duke Maurice of Saxony, next to Philip of Hesse the best statesman and general of the Protestants, was won over to the Emperor. Thus, in two short and brilliant campaigns (1546–47), Charles was able to overthrow the League of Schmalkalden, divided against itself and badly led in the field. Maurice, the 'Judas of Misnia' as public opinion in Protestant countries nicknamed him, got his full reward and was given the Electorate of Saxony. Yet, when Charles tried to exploit his victory to the full and re-establish the imperial authority throughout the Empire, he saw himself faced at once by the old opposition. The Estates quickly restored their common front, regardless of their religious differences. Duke Albert V of Bavaria, an ardent supporter of the Counter-Reformation, was foremost in urging the maintenance of 'German liberty' and tying the hands of the Emperor. While John Frederick, ex-Elector of Saxony, and Philip of Hesse languished in prison, Maurice of Saxony became the leader of the anti-imperial opposition. He suddenly attacked the unsuspecting Emperor and all but captured him at Innsbruck. The Catholic princes did not stir hand or foot on his behalf, and Charles had to agree to the treaty of Passau (2 Aug. 1552).

This defeat destroyed at once the supreme position which Charles had occupied during the last five years, and restored the uneasy balance between the Emperor on the one hand, and the Estates, Protestant and Catholic alike, on the other. At the same time, the Protestants renewed their alliance with France. They paid the price for it out of Charles's pockets, ceding the imperial cities of Metz, Toul and Verdun. Those places were inhabited by a French-speaking population, but had formed part of the Empire ever since the reversion of Lorraine in 925; they were at the time the pivot of the Burgundian territory, linking up Franche-Comté and Alsace with Belgium and the Netherlands. Their loss therefore was a serious blow for Charles, and he immediately set out to retrieve them. He failed, however, to take Metz and had to retreat ignominiously (Jan. 1553). Charles's plight might have opened fresh avenues to the scheming Maurice of Saxony, had he not become involved in a quarrel with Albert of Brandenburg-Kulmbach, his most serious rival for the leadership of the Protestant party. When his victory over Albert would have made him the undisputed champion of the anti-imperial Estates, he was killed in the hour of triumph (July 1553).

The decrees of the Diet of Augsburg (Sept. 1555) therefore bear every sign of a compromise. The Public Peace of 1495 was made the basis of the permanent organization of the Empire as laid down in the *Exekutionsordnung* (executive ordinance). The ten Circles were charged with the maintenance of Public Peace and the execution of the sentences of the imperial Court of Justice. The office of a Supreme Circle Commissar (*Kreisoberster*) was created; he was to be the senior secular Estate of the respective Circle, and would in wartime be the commander of the imperial troops raised in it. The Circles were moreover entitled to collect a military fund. The Religious Peace of Augsburg extended the terms of the Public Peace to the sphere of religion. The Public Peace secured the secular possessions of the Estates against forcible seizure, and referred the settlement of all claims and disputes to legal arbitration: similarly, the Religious Peace protected the free exercise of the Roman and Lutheran religions—the Calvinists were excluded; and the secular ownership of those ecclesiastical domains and rights which had been expropriated at the time of the treaty of Passau, of 1552, was ratified. The High Court of Justice was to be composed equally of Protestant and Catholic judges.

The Golden Bull of 1356, the Public Peace of 1495, and the

Executive Ordinance and the Religious Peace of 1555, were henceforth the four organic statutes of the imperial constitution. To them may be added the *Constitutio Criminalis Carolina*, the criminal law code, which was put into operation in 1532; it was the supreme effort of the imperial jurists to adapt the Roman law to the needs of their own time, and it remained in force throughout Germany until the second half of the eighteenth century, and in some German states even until 1871.

The events of 1552–53 wore out Charles's strength and filled him with an inexorable disgust for his Sisyphean task. He had one more triumph in the diplomatic field when his eldest son, Philip, married Mary, queen of England (1554); the encirclement of France was thereby completed and Charles might well hope that Philip would succeed where he himself had failed. He therefore took the unprecedented step of resigning to Philip first the Netherlands and his Italian possessions (1555), then Spain and her colonies oversea (1556); and lastly he abdicated from the Empire in favour of his brother, Ferdinand (1556). Charles himself retired into a Spanish monastery, where he died two years later.

Ferdinand I was very unlike his elder brother. Ever since he took over the administration of the Austrian dominions of the Hapsburgs (1521), he had concentrated on developing them into a self-contained monarchy. Not heeding the lure of the imperial tradition, he acted in exactly the same way as the other territorial princes; except that he, being the heir presumptive of the imperial crown, was naturally opposed to federalistic and Protestant tendencies. In 1526, his brother-in-law, King Louis II of Bohemia and Hungary, was defeated and killed by the Turks in the battle of Mohacs. Ferdinand immediately secured his election as king of Bohemia, and henceforth Bohemia was one of the most illustrious Hapsburg territories. It was Bohemia against which every enemy of the Hapsburgs directed his main effort, from the beginning of the Thirty Years War (1618) to the Austro-Prussian war of 1866; and the final collapse of the Hapsburg monarchy followed immediately after the proclamation of Bohemian independence on 30 Oct. 1918.

Great, however, were the difficulties Ferdinand had to overcome in his succession in Hungary. Here he encountered the advancing Turks, who in 1521 had taken Belgrade and were now approaching the eastern fringe of Austria. Moreover, the Magyar magnates were violently opposed to the rule of foreign monarchs, under whom they had smarted since 1301. In 1505, they expressly excluded any foreigner from the succession; and now, in 1526, they elected a native nobleman, John Zapolya, voivod of Transylvania, as their king. Ferdinand, however, favoured by his widowed sister and her followers, was set up as a rival king. Zapolya made alliances with the Sultan and the king of France (1528); but when the latter made his peace with the Emperor and the former was repelled from the walls of Vienna (1529), Zapolya had to accept a truce (1531) and finally a peace treaty (1538) in which he recognized Ferdinand's claim to the Hungarian throne. However, for a hundred and fifty years to come Hungary was a liability rather than an asset to the Hapsburgs. The acquisition of Burgundy had burdened them with the implacable hostility of France: the claim to Hungary made them the defenders of the West against the Turks. The Most Christian King and the ruler of the Moslems were always willing to ally themselves against the common enemy; whenever a Hapsburg had to wage war in the East, he had to envisage a concerted attack in the West, and vice versa.

A year after the death of John Zapolya, the Turks took Buda, the capital of Hungary (1541), and the country was reduced to a Turkish province until 1699. It was of little avail that Zapolya's widow ceded it formally to Ferdinand. It had to be won back before it could be incorporated in the Hapsburg possessions. A campaign in 1542 failed; and in 1545 the Emperor had to conclude the truce of Adrianople which left Hungary to the Turks. Charles was on the eve of his campaign against the League of Schmalkalden and wanted to protect his rear. The truce was subsequently extended and kept more or less faithfully until 1593.

With Charles V, the mystical splendour of the imperial crown finally died away. He was the last emperor to be crowned by a pope, and even that ceremony took place only at Bologna instead of within the sacred precincts of St Peter's (1530). Ferdinand I discarded the coronation altogether and simply assumed the title of emperor (1558), as did henceforth all his successors. It was an outward sign of the fact that the age of feudalism had drawn to its close.

The progressive secularization of Europe, of which the Reformation was another aspect, did not take place without violent revulsions in the economic sphere. The rulers of all European states had to cope with the problem of adjusting the machinery of government to the fresh requirements of a changed age. The general increase of bureaucratic state-interference, already mentioned, was one of its results. In the economic field this intensified state-supervision led to what was afterwards called 'mercantilism', an economic system of which William Strafford's *Examination of Certain Complaints* (1581) was the first theoretical summary. The internal history of almost every German state shows the administration's genuine care for the welfare of its subjects as well as unnecessary and annoying interference with the details of their everyday life. Some of these measures were passed on the lines of the famous Elizabethan acts for the relief of the poor, the organization of apprentices, and the fixing of wages in trade and industry. Foremost amongst the princes of his age who paid attention to the economic improvement of their countries was Augustus of Saxony, brother of the Elector Maurice. He set up model farms for the instruction of the peasantry; had fruit trees planted along the highways which themselves were well looked after; and instituted a medical service for the needy, which included the free distribution of medicines. An attempt was made to introduce the breeding of silkworms so as to open new markets for the textile industry of Saxony; with greater success the population of the Erzgebirge, where the silver mines had become exhausted, was persuaded to take up the manufacture of lace and hosiery. Leipzig's half-yearly fairs were given additional privileges and facilities; the city soon became the international centre of the book and fur trades. From that time onward, the Saxons have kept their reputation for industry, enterprise and adaptability; and Saxony ranked amongst the richest, best cultivated and most civilized parts of Europe.

Similarly, other German princes tried to increase the economic and intellectual resources of their countries. The school regulations issued by Duke Christopher of Württemberg, for instance, were instrumental in keeping the intellectual life of the small country far above the general level. For this reason, perhaps, Württemberg remained almost the only German territory where the Estates did not succumb to the rising tide of absolutism: the deputies of the Württemberg Diet were able to safeguard their independence right down to the general destruction of the old forms of government in the Napoleonic era.

The age of mercantilism completed in the economic sphere what, a generation before, had been accomplished in the constitutional sphere, namely the consolidation of the territorial states and, incidentally, the further break-up of the fictitious unity of the Empire. This process showed itself clearly in the failure to reorganize the currency of the Empire: a sphere far enough removed from religious arguments that in it Catholics and Protestants could and did work hand in hand. The change from the agricultural age of feudalism to the industrial age of mercantilism, a complicated issue in itself, was aggravated by the influx into Europe of the gold and silver from the Central and South American mines, which flooded the Old World in the second half of the sixteenth century. The Elizabethan currency reform of 1560 is one of the few examples of a successful attempt at coping with that crucial problem which affected all European nations alike. Spain herself experienced the curse of Mammon rather than its benefit: from 1557 national bankruptcies occurred with an alarming regularity.

Ferdinand I was very much alive to the dangers which resulted from the chaotic monetary conditions: in 1559 he made a bold attempt to standardize the coinage throughout the Empire. His failure was due to the fact that 'the Empire' was no cohesive institution in itself, and that the rivalries of its various components were stronger than the theoretical unity as personified by the Emperor. The fruitless attempts at regularizing the monetary system of the Empire, if anything, worsened the situation. The cities which, for centuries, had been the mainstay of German economic life rapidly lost their international markets. The bankruptcy of the Welsers, the leading Augsburg banking house, in 1614, was only the most glaring instance of the general decline which took place in the second half of the sixteenth century and is often, though erroneously, attributed to the effect of the so-called Thirty Years War. It was only after the devastating experience of a general inflation (1619–23) that the political and economic leaders found the remedy: a number of monetary conventions, based on regional principles. These conventions worked very satisfactorily in the Rhinelands, Austria, Lower Saxony, and elsewhere. The 'Mark Banko' created at Hamburg in 1622 became a currency of international reputation; the monetary convention of Zinna (1667), comprising Brandenburg, Saxony, and the Guelph territories of Hanover and Brunswick, gave an economic stability to the greater part of Northern Germany.

Even common commercial interests were no longer strong enough to bridge the gulf between the diverging policies of the Emperor, the Empire and the individual member states. This became evident when the English advanced into a sphere of interests which for centuries had been monopolized by the German Hanse. The Hanse itself, it is true, had been defunct since the catastrophe of Lübeck which followed the wanton attack upon Denmark (1535). The individual maritime towns kept up their position notwithstanding; and

Hamburg rose to fill the place of Lübeck as the chief trading centre, followed by Bremen and, to a lesser degree, Emden. It was therefore a heavy blow at the monopolistic tendencies of the Hanse towns when the English Merchant Adventurers established factories first at Emden (1564), and shortly afterwards at Hamburg (1567). They enjoyed the full backing of the English government. In 1579, the privileges formerly granted to the Hanse merchants in England were withdrawn and simultaneously a charter was given to the Fellowship of Eastland Merchants, whose commercial activities were directed towards Scandinavia and the Baltic Sea, i.e. the very centre of the Hanse trade. The situation grew worse during the Dutch war of independence. The trade war between England and Spain, which began in 1564, led to the embargo against England by the Spanish Netherlands in 1571: it meant the economic ruin of Flanders, the western centre of the Hanseatic commerce. The sack of Antwerp by the Spaniards in 1585 meant the transfer of almost all international business to Amsterdam: and Amsterdam was now the capital of an independent Holland, out of the reach of Hanseatic pressure. In the face of these serious threats to German oversea trade it seemed for a while as if something like an imperial trade policy would gain shape. In 1597 the Hanse secured an imperial act banishing English merchants and goods from the Empire. Queen Elizabeth answered by closing the Hanseatic Steelyard near London Bridge, which meant the practical exclusion of Germans from English commerce. Moreover, the temporary unity of the German front did not last long. The Emperor Rudolf II was induced to confirm an English factory at Stade on the mouth of the river Elbe opposite Hamburg (1607). Hamburg, thus abandoned by the Empire, made its peace with the English regardless of the interests of other members of the Empire, and admitted the Merchant Adventurers on a permanent footing (1611). It was of little avail that in 1630 the three towns of Hamburg, Bremen and Lübeck concluded a federation as the assigns of the Hanse, for the peace of Westphalia (1648) brought the mouths of all rivers flowing into the North and Baltic Seas under foreign jurisdiction and thereby excluded German commerce from international competition for two hundred years.

Meanwhile the religious cleavage deepened the political dissensions of the Estates. It was the Roman Catholic party which, after having lost nine-tenths of Germany, took up the offensive, while the split between Lutherans and Calvinists paralysed the Protestant cause at the time when the Catholic Church increased its power of resistance and attack. The ecclesiastical reform, long overdue, was at last taken in hand with vigour and success. The Council of Trent (1545–63), which the Protestants refused to attend, brought about a complete revision of the organization and doctrine of the Church; the Jesuit Order, confirmed in 1540, carried out its ambitious programme of restoring the unity of the Church. At the Diet of Worms, of 1557, a last official attempt to reconcile the dissenting parties was made; it failed, as was to be expected. In the following year, an attempt to unite the Protestant groups was equally fruitless. Indeed, very often the Lutherans professed a greater abhorrence of their Calvinist co-religionists than of their common Catholic adversaries. In these circumstances, the Protestant cause suffered one setback after another. The archbishop of Cologne's failure to introduce the reformation in his country (1542) ought to have warned the Protestant rulers of the growing power of the Catholic counter-reformation. The followers of Zwingli and Calvin, it is true, reached an agreement (Zürich Consensus, 1549), but the Lutherans held aloof and did nothing to prevent the exclusion of the Calvinists from the religious peace of Augsburg (1555). For the antagonism between the two reformed denominations was political as well as religious. The Calvinists stood for a form of ecclesiastical government which, expressed in political terms, meant self-government of the people. It is therefore not surprising that Calvinism should be strongest in the republics of Switzerland and the Netherlands and in the imperial towns. On the whole, the Calvinists were more enterprising and energetic, and the command of the Protestant party naturally fell to their leader. When the 'Heidelberg Catechism' of 1563 established Calvinism in the Palatinate, the Elector Palatine became the head of the progressive party in the Empire almost as a matter of course.

In the following year the Emperor Ferdinand I died and was succeeded by his eldest son, Maximilian II (1564–76). Ferdinand had divided the Austrian possessions amongst his sons, and it was not until 1665 that the last of these collateral lines died out. Maximilian had already been elected king of Bohemia (1562) and Hungary (1563) when he became Emperor. The loss of the greater part of Austria proper which had been his father's chief interest made him inclined to pay greater attention to the imperial prerogative. Whilst his predecessors had openly supported the Catholic faction, Maximilian II tried to come to terms with the Protestants. His personal proclivities were certainly evangelical, and Ferdinand I had even had to force him to renounce his heretical inclinations (1561). In 1571, he issued the 'Religious Assurance', which gave the Austrian nobility the right of free exercise of the Lutheran cult; and the 'Monastery Council' which he established in 1567-68 was intended to enforce state control on the Catholic clergy. It is doubtful whether Maximilian's policy of religious toleration would in the course of time have reconciled the contesting parties, and even more whether it would have given the Emperor the role of an umpire trusted by both sides. Much as the princes were divided against one another they certainly did not want to submit their quarrels to the Emperor. The chief result of the neutral religious attitude of Maximilian II and his two successors on the imperial throne was that the Catholic party of the Empire now regarded the Spanish monarch as their principal ally, just as the Protestant princes had become fain to rely on the French king.

Maximilian's policy was, however, not allowed to mature. His brother and successor, Rudolf II (1576-1612), was a misanthropist and subject to fits of melancholia which bordered upon madness. He alternated between brutality and indifference, leniency and obstinacy, in political as well as religious dealings. The other Hapsburg princes took alarm at the rapid deterioration of their common interests as a result of Rudolf's misrule. They forced him to resign all his possessions, except Bohemia and the imperial dignity, to his brother Matthias (1606 and 1608), and eventually to acknowledge Matthias as king of Bohemia also (1611). One of the last and most fateful acts of the unfortunate Rudolf was the issue of a charter granting freedom of conscience in Bohemia (1609); its breach in 1618 was the cause of the Bohemian war which began that sequence of conflagrations commonly called the Thirty Years War.

Neither religious group was as yet prepared to grant toleration to the heterodox, for the medieval abhorrence of the heretic was still a vital force. The restoration of universal unity, it is true, was becoming less and less probable despite some spectacular successes of the Roman Church, and the principle of *Cuius regio, eius religio* was therefore the nearest approach to complete religious unity; it meant that within the boundaries of one state the subjects had to conform to the religion of the ruler. Bavaria and Fulda were the first countries to be completely re-catholicized; a second attempt to gain the archbishopric of Cologne for Protestantism failed (1583-84); and a similar struggle in the chapter of Strasbourg also ended in the victory of the Roman Catholic party (1584-1602). When, in 1590, the

Archduke Ferdinand succeeded in Inner Austria, he vowed that he would rule an uninhabited desert rather than a country peopled by heretics; and by 1603 the re-catholicization of the whole of Austria was completed. On the other hand, the Protestant party firmly consolidated their doctrinal position, and thereby definitely rendered a full reconciliation with Rome impossible. In 1577, the Lutherans agreed upon the *Formula Concordiae,* and in 1580 the Calvinists issued the *Harmonia Confessionum Fidei*; the Elector Augustus of Saxony suppressed the Calvinists and 'Crypto-Calvinists' with no less cruelty than his Lutheran co-religionists underwent in Roman Catholic countries; and the population of the Palatinate had to change their religion six times according to the changing opinions of five successive rulers. A map showing the distribution of religious denominations in present-day Germany reproduces exactly the political frontiers of the first half of the seventeenth century.

It was a curious coincidence that the leadership of the Protestant and Catholic parties fell to the rival branches of the house of Wittelsbach. After the death of King Lewis IV (1347) the Bavarian line had lapsed into obscurity, and repeated partitions weakened its influence still further. Its rise to power began in 1504, when Albert IV defeated his cousin Rupert of the Palatinate and secured for himself the succession in the re-united Bavarian dukedoms. His successor, William IV (1508–50), followed the wise counsels of his chancellor, Leonhard Eck, and kept faithfully to the Roman Church when almost every other secular prince of consequence went over to Protestantism. As a reward for his adherence to a cause which seemed almost lost the Church granted him an influence upon religious matters equal to that usurped by the Protestant rulers. Albert V (1550–79) made Catholicism his tool in establishing his absolutism over the Protestant nobility. William V (1579–97) accomplished the work of his predecessors: he gave the Jesuits a free hand, and their consummate skill as organizers, coupled with the careful planning of the ducal administration, made Bavaria one of the most prosperous countries despite its lack of natural resources.

The grateful Church did even more to reward its most unswerving adherents north of the Alps: younger princes of the house of Bavaria were given important bishoprics throughout the Empire whenever they fell vacant. The Church of Rome thus secured territories which otherwise might have become Protestant; and the Wittelsbachs thereby gained reliable support in regions where they could not have exercised any direct influence. Thus not only was the bishopric of Freising in the immediate vicinity of Munich, the Bavarian capital, incorporated, as it were, in the dukedom of Bavaria; but Bavarian princes also occupied for centuries the sees of Cologne, Münster, Hildesheim, and other bishoprics, as if by hereditary right. It must therefore not be overlooked that, from the sixteenth to the eighteenth century, the Wittelsbach dynasty was in direct or indirect control not only of Bavaria, but also of large tracts of the Rhineland, Westphalia and Lower Saxony.

When Maximilian I (1597-1651) came to the throne, he enjoyed an inherited wealth and reputation that would have made him the champion of the Catholic party, even if he had not been the exceptionally gifted statesman and general he was, and even if the internecine struggle of the Emperor and his brothers and nephews had not paralysed the house of Hapsburg at that juncture.

The elder branch of the Wittelsbach had acquired the Palatinate in the family compact of Pavia (1329). The Palatinate surpassed Bavaria in natural wealth, industry and population, in commercial and strategical importance and, above all, in political influence, since the Count Palatine was one of the Electors and the only secular one of the Rhenish group. At Heidelberg, the Palatine capital, the first German university was founded (1386), and the new learning of the Renaissance was looked upon with favour by the court. The new wing of Heidelberg castle, erected by the Elector Otto Heinrich (1556), was at the time considered the most magnificent palace on the continent. On the other hand, the Counts Palatine impaired their power even more than the other German princes by repeated partitions of their country; and the chief of the house could never be sure whether he would or would not receive the support of his cousins at Neuburg, Simmern, Zweibrücken, and elsewhere. Moreover, there was a strain of recklessness and extravagance, coupled with personal temerity and political shortsightedness, in most of the Palatine Electors which made their leadership of the Protestants a doubtful blessing to their cause, even if the Lutheran Electors of Saxony and Brandenburg had not felt it a slight that a Calvinist should have assumed precedence. In consequence, Saxony and Brandenburg took up a lukewarm attitude and thereby damaged the Protestant cause when it needed the greatest unity amongst its adherents.

It was the two Wittelsbach cousins who eventually unleashed the furies of war, after the tension between the rival camps and the inertia of the consecutive emperors made a peaceful settlement more and more impossible. In December 1607, Maximilian of Bavaria occupied the imperial city of Donauwörth without provocation or pretext. The place gave Maximilian control over the palsgraviate of Neuburg and a bridgehead from which to open communications into Franconia; its Protestant population was forcibly brought back to the Roman obedience. Rudolf II did nothing to vindicate the imperial rights; but the Protestants at last realized how imminent was their danger. They formed the Union of Auhausen (May 1608), and put themselves into a state of military preparedness. However, their usual slackness prevailed, due to the usual lack of cash. Before anything was done to recover Donauwörth, an event of even greater importance occurred, and Donauwörth remained Bavarian and Catholic for good. This event was the death of the last duke of Jülich, Cleves, Berg and Mark. For the last two centuries, the dukes had ruled the largest territory in the lower Rhineland and Westphalia; the country had also rendered them the wealthiest potentates in Western Europe, as it included the textile industry of Krefeld and Gladbach, the coal mines of the Ruhr district, and the cutlery manufacture of Solingen and Remscheid. (Thomas Cromwell's scheme of harnessing the 'Flanders mare' and her immense dowry to the English statecoach (1540) had been very sound, and its repudiation by Henry VIII a major blunder, since it drove the duke of Cleves into the French camp.) As the last duke left no issue, the husbands of his sisters had the greatest claim to the highly desirable inheritance. They were the Elector of Brandenburg and the heir to the County Palatine of Neuburg, both of them Lutherans and members of the Protestant Union.

The danger that the richest part of Germany and the bridgehead to the powerful republic of the Netherlands should strengthen the opposite faction quickly rallied the Catholic princes. Three months after the demise of Jülich, a Catholic League was formed at Munich under the leadership of Maximilian of Bavaria. Austria was excluded from the League: religious zeal did not make the Catholic princes oblivious of their political interests, which were very similar to those of the Union. The Emperor made a feeble attempt to seize the disputed dukedom and reserve the ultimate decision to himself, but his troops were quickly driven out of Jülich by the common exertions of Brandenburg and Neuburg, supported by English and Dutch detachments. The rival pretenders could hope for a settlement of their claims only if they got the wholehearted support either of the Union or of the League. They therefore changed their Lutheran creed for that of the leaders of these groups: John Sigmund of Brandenburg turned Calvinist, and Wolfgang William of Neuburg went over to Rome and married a daughter of Maximilian of Bavaria (1613). Both factions, however, were anxious to keep out the Emperor and therefore arranged some kind of condominium. In the end (1666), the country was partitioned: Cleves, Mark and Ravensberg fell to Brandenburg, which thus got its first foothold in Western Germany; whereas Jülich and Berg came to Bavaria, the loot of the splendid palace of Düsseldorf providing Munich with the best picture gallery of Germany.

In 1613 it seemed as if the Protestant Union would carry the day. It concluded an alliance with the Netherlands and thereby gained the support of the only state of the time which always disposed of ready cash and unlimited credit. In an age when there were as yet neither regular budgets nor standing armies, the well-filled coffers of the Dutch corporations wielded an influence upon international affairs comparable with, and even superior to, the loans and credits granted or refused by the Rothschilds and Barings of the nineteenth century. In addition to the Dutch alliance the Protestant Union gained a further success of international consequence when its leader, the young Elector Frederick V of the Palatinate (1610–32), married Elizabeth, daughter of James I of England (1613). This union seemed to checkmate the Spanish-Catholic party throughout Europe, especially as Denmark, the greatest Scandinavian power, was closely allied to the Union, King Christian IV being the brother-in-law of James and uncle of the Electress Palatine.

The steady decline of the Hapsburg power drove the archdukes once more into action. When the days of the aged Emperor Matthias drew to a close, his brothers and cousins agreed to waive their claims of seniority in favour of Ferdinand of Styria, a young nephew of theirs. Ferdinand had succeeded his father in the government of Inner Austria in 1590 and displayed a stern energy and relentless fervour in stamping out the political and religious privileges of the Austrian nobility and citizens. Moreover, he was a first cousin and brother-in-law of Maximilian of Bavaria, so that he might well count upon the support of the League. Matthias consented to have him crowned king of Bohemia (1617) and Hungary (1618), and after Matthias's death (1619) Ferdinand was duly elected emperor, the Elector Palatine alone voting against him. For in the meantime the head of the Union had openly challenged the head of the Hapsburg dynasty, and attacked him where he was most vulnerable, namely in Bohemia.

In 1609, the Emperor Rudolf II, deprived by his brothers of all his possessions except Bohemia, had issued a Royal Charter which granted a great measure of religious freedom to the Bohemians. It was one of the first acts of Ferdinand as king of Bohemia to break this charter in the spirit if not in the letter, by condoning and encouraging Catholic outrages against Protestant churches and believers. The Bohemians, jealous of their privileges and still inflamed by the spirit of John Hus, punished the royal commissioners in the traditional way by throwing them out of the windows of the Hračin, the royal palace of Prague. This 'defenestration' (23 May 1618) was followed by the formal deposition of the perjured king, in whose stead the Bohemian nobles elected Frederick of the Palatinate (26 Aug. 1619). The young king and his beautiful queen Elizabeth were not allowed to enjoy very long their royal dignity; and Frederick has gone down in history as the 'Winter King' whose power melted away with the snows in spring. He was cruelly disappointed in his expectations of foreign assistance. For Frederick's father-in-law, James, was firmly set on close collaboration with Spain: Sir Walter Raleigh, the last representative of the Elizabethan policy, was beheaded while Frederick negotiated for the throne of Bohemia (1618); and James looked on complacently at the ruin of his daughter and grandchildren. The Protestant Union, too, forsook its leader in the hour of danger, pretending that the fight between Frederick and Ferdinand was not a *casus belli* concerning the interests of the Union. This feeble and, as it turned out, disastrous policy was prompted by France, which feared an increase of the power of the Anglo-Palatine combination.

On the other hand, Maximilian of Bavaria quickly saw his opportunity. He forced upon Ferdinand the support of the League. His generalissimo, Tilly, took Frederick entirely by surprise. The Bohemians met the enemy only at the gates of Prague, and in an hour their army was beaten, the royal family in headlong flight, and Ferdinand the undisputed master of Bohemia (Battle of the White Hill, 8 Nov. 1620). The victor took a harsh revenge. Ferdinand tore up the Royal Charter with his own hands; the country was re-catholicized with brutal force; thousands of families left their homes, carrying their industrial skill and technical experience to Saxony; a great number of nobles were beheaded or attainted; fortune-hunters bought up their estates, and one Albrecht of Wallenstein, who had just married an elderly heiress of immense wealth, bought up a number of towns, villages and landed property which surpassed a good many principalities of the Empire.

After the self-dissolution of the Protestant Union (1621) a number of isolated Protestant princes tried in vain to continue the struggle with insufficient subsidies from Holland. Tilly defeated them one after another (1622). Frederick of the Palatinate was outlawed immediately after the conquest of Bohemia and the Palatinate (Jan. 1621). He spent the last decade of his life as a pensioner of the Dutch government; and his patrimony remained in Bavarian occupation for almost thirty years. He could not have divined that one of his younger sons, Rupert, who was born at Prague during the short splendour of his Bohemian kingship, was to become one of the most brilliant generals of the age; nor that the descendants of his youngest daughter would ascend the throne of his wife's native country and become the sovereigns of the greatest empire the world has ever seen.

Maximilian of Bavaria got his full reward. In 1623 the electoral dignity of the Palatinate was conferred upon him, and he was now undoubtedly the most influential prince of the Empire. After the sack of Heidelberg, he sent the valuable library of the old university to Rome as a thank-offering; and the codices of the 'Palatina' still form the most precious part of the Vatican collections. Maximilian continued to be sure of the favour of the head of the Church. Would his friendly relations with the head of the Empire stand the test of further co-operation?

Ferdinand was by no means happy about owing his restitution in Bohemia to the exertions of the Catholic League. He therefore strove to create an independent imperial army which would carry out his designs and his only, so that he might rid himself of the embarrassing dependence upon Maximilian and Tilly. In Wallenstein he found the man who was prepared to serve his purposes, capable of raising money and organizing an army, and able to lead military operations as well as diplomatic negotiations. In many respects Wallenstein might have become a German counterpart of Oliver Cromwell. He was no professional soldier; war was to him but a means to an end. Supreme as an organizer of victory, he was indifferent as a leader of battles. Though quick in realizing the value of military innovations and ingenious in perfecting them, he is not to be classed among the military geniuses. His real talent lay in the organization of great masses; his commissariat was a model; care for feeding and housing his troops, and for balancing their needs with those of the civil population meant to him more than the drawing up of battle lines. The industrial development of Bohemia originated to a large extent in the model husbandry and economic improvements which Wallenstein organized in his titular duchy of Friedland. Measured by the standards of his time, he was tolerant in religious matters: Protestant and Catholic generals and soldiers were equally acceptable to him. His broadmindedness, however, was not the outcome of a deeply religious spirit, but of a superstitious belief in astrology. This unshakable confidence in the stars was instrumental in his eventual downfall, as it led him to cling to his most dangerous enemies as trusted friends.

The sudden catastrophe that befell Wallenstein makes it difficult to form a definite opinion on his ulterior aims. He seems to have had in mind a reorganization of the Empire and the exclusion of foreign influence, whether Spanish, French, or Swedish; the position of the Emperor would have been overwhelming and the princes reduced to a very moderate status. After that, Wallenstein would have directed the power of Austria and the Empire against the Turks, and shifted the weight of the Hapsburg influence to the Balkans, thus anticipating the policy of Prince Eugene by almost a hundred years.

When Wallenstein was appointed imperial generalissimo and created duke of Friedland (1625), a fresh war threatened in the North. Charles I of England, who succeeded his father in that year, reversed the latter's pro-Spanish policy, and approached the anti-Hapsburg group of powers. After the disasters that had overcome the minor Protestant princes of the Empire, and considering the reluctance of France to complicate her internal difficulties by a foreign war, Denmark was the only power left that might counteract the spreading influence of the Roman and Hapsburg combination. Moreover, the Danish king was, as duke of Holstein, a prince of the Empire and the director of the Circle of Lower Saxony. He had therefore a legitimate right, or could at least find an ostensible pretext, to interfere on behalf of his co-religionists and co-Estates. England and the Netherlands therefore concluded a treaty with Christian and subsidized him for his campaign (Dec. 1625).

Wallenstein and Tilly at the head of the imperial and League troops respectively lost no time in carrying the war into North Germany. At Dessau, on 25 April 1626, Wallenstein crushed the last remnants of the mercenaries whom the Dutch had hired in support of Frederick of Bohemia; Tilly took the Danes unawares at Lutter near Goslar and carried the day as quickly as at the White

Hill (27 Aug.). Lower Saxony, Mecklenburg and Pomerania were occupied in quick succession, and the allied armies soon advanced through Holstein to the northernmost point of Jutland (1627). Since the days of Otto the Great (947) no German army had appeared on Danish soil. Christian was compelled to sign the treaty of Lübeck (22 May 1629), in which he renounced any further intervention in the Empire. It was the virtual end of the Danish aspirations to the status of a European great power.

The position of the Emperor was even stronger than had been that of Charles V after the victory of Mühlberg (1547). Never since the days of the Saxon emperors had an imperial force set eyes on the shores of the North and Baltic Seas. Wallenstein, who was not slow in realizing the potentialities of this situation, conceived the great scheme of creating an imperial navy which, in combination with Spain, would indeed have given world dominion to the house of Hapsburg. The Emperor created him duke of Mecklenburg after outlawing the dukes, stout supporters of the Protestant Union and Denmark; and in the shortest possible time Mecklenburg, one of the most backward regions of the Empire, enjoyed prosperity as never before or after. Furthermore, Wallenstein was appointed 'Admiral of the Baltic and North Seas', thus clearly indicating the next steps he proposed to take. However, he suffered a serious setback when he failed to take Stralsund, the most important seaport of the Pomeranian coast, which he intended to make the main base of the imperial navy (Aug. 1628). Before he could recover from this defeat, the whole situation took a turn for the worse, and the subsequent events made it impossible to revive the naval plan.

Ferdinand II, flushed with victory, meant to make the most of it. A fortnight before the conclusion of the treaty of Lübeck he issued the Edict of Restitution. It restored to the Roman Church all property that had been secularized since the treaty of Passau (1552), and expressly excluded the Calvinists from the benefits of the religious peace of Augsburg (1555). Had the edict been carried out to the letter, it would have upset every political and economic arrangement made during the last three generations. However, Ferdinand was taught the limits of autocracy as quickly and thoroughly as Charles V before him. The Electors at once resolved to curb the imperial absolutism; the common danger made them bury their religious differences. They assembled at Ratisbon in July 1630 and unanimously put forward their complaints, ostensibly not against the Emperor, for whom they professed the deepest reverence, but against the alleged outrages of his generalissimo. Ferdinand had to yield to this united front. Wallenstein was discharged from his command and retired deeply embittered against the ungrateful and shortsighted Emperor; and Ferdinand saw himself without an army and therefore without any effective means for pursuing his policy.

The situation of the Emperor was the more embarrassing as the opposition of the Estates was backed, diplomatically and financially, by France. Ever since Richelieu had become the leading minister of the French crown (1622), his aim was to break the encirclement of France by Spain, England and Austria. The peace of Susa (14 April 1629) ended the state of war with England. On 28 June of the same year, the treaty of Alais, which ended the Huguenot wars that had ravaged France for a century, secured the absolute authority of the crown. When, on 5 Nov. 1630, a peace was patched up with Spain, Richelieu had his hands free to deal with Germany. The triumph of the Electors at Ratisbon was his triumph as well. Soon he was able to oppose the Emperor in the field without having to commit France herself, for a man appeared who was to break the Hapsburg hegemony in the interests of France—Gustavus Adolphus, king of Sweden.

In 1587 the Polish diet elected Sigismund, son and heir of King John III of Sweden, their king. When John died in 1592, Sigismund became also king of Sweden; but as he had turned Roman Catholic, the purely Protestant country rose in rebellion against him. His uncle, Charles IX, was appointed lieutenant-governor (1595); after defeating Sigismund and exterminating the pro-Polish party he assumed the title of king (1604), although Sigismund of Poland, who was married to a sister of Ferdinand II, continued to uphold his claims to the Swedish crown. It was therefore natural that Charles's successor, Gustavus II Adolphus (1611–32), should be pledged to a firmly Protestant policy. In fact, his position was much the same as that of Elizabeth of England: the doubtful legitimacy of their kingship compelled each of them to seek the support of that party which opposed their rivals on political as well as religious grounds. Not that Gustavus had not been a devout believer in the righteousness of the Lutheran creed; but his religious tenets and his political advantage both indicated the same course. He soon proved his worth in successful campaigns against Russia and Poland. The former had to cede Karelia and Ingermanland (1617), the land-bridge between the Swedish dependencies of Finland and Estonia. Poland gave up Livonia and the Prussian ports of Memel, Pillau and Elbing (1629). These acquisitions made Sweden the supreme power in the

Baltic and the heir of the German Hanse as well as the Danish aspirations. At the same time, these campaigns established the reputation of Gustavus Adolphus as the first soldier at the head of the finest army of his age, and as the champion of the Protestant cause in the teeth of Russian heterodoxy and Polish counter-reformation. To him it was that the Protestant German Estates and the Catholic French premier looked for deliverance from the Catholic German Emperor.

The truce of Altmark (25 Sept. 1629), which ended the Swedish-Polish war, was brought about by the good offices of Richelieu. Subsequent negotiations led to the Franco-Swedish alliance of Bärwalde (23 Jan. 1631), by which France pledged herself to subsidize the king of Sweden in his struggle with the Emperor. Gustavus was at this juncture already on German soil. He disembarked his force in Pomerania while the Electors were on their way to Ratisbon; and the disgrace of Wallenstein coincided with the Swedish advance into Central Germany.

The Electors, however, were not minded to exchange the whips of Ferdinand for the scorpions of Gustavus Adolphus. Maximilian of Bavaria immediately returned to the side of the Emperor, and the Electors of Brandenburg and Saxony put so many obstacles in the way of their inevitable submission to the Swedes that Tilly scored a great success by taking and sacking Magdeburg, the chief town of the region of the middle Elbe (20 May 1631). When Magdeburg was accidentally destroyed by fire, from which only the cathedral escaped, Swedish propaganda was presented with a godsend: Tilly was stigmatized as a savage incendiary, and public opinion supported by Swedish guns made Brandenburg and Saxony hastily comply with Gustavus's demands. On 17 Sept. Tilly's army was routed at Breitenfeld, and Germany lay open to the conqueror. While the Saxons occupied Bohemia, Gustavus advanced through Saxony, Thuringia and Franconia into the heart of South Germany. A second defeat of Tilly, in which the worthy old general was fatally wounded, allowed Gustavus to enter Munich (17 May 1632). He now contemplated a march on Vienna, to which the Austrian Protestants invited him, but his resources were not adequate to this task. His lines of communication were stretched to the utmost. His high-handed manner had not endeared him to his German allies or to his French associates. His ultimate goal, they suspected, was the imperial throne, and they saw no reason why they should prefer him to the Hapsburg. Apart from his brilliant Swedish troops he could rely only on the smaller German princes and imperial towns who had irrevocably thrown in their lot with the Swedes; and they, too, were reluctant to obey the king's every command.

Gustavus's position was therefore not quite as untroubled as it looked. The less so, as the Emperor had reinstated the only man who was considered a match for Gustavus, namely Wallenstein. Ferdinand, with the concurrence of Maximilian of Bavaria, humiliated himself before his proud subject. Wallenstein was given the supreme command of all imperial forces, and full control of the whole conduct of the war, which, in Wallenstein's interpretation, included the political issues. The charm of his name, his ability for mass organization, and the lavish expenditure of money combined to raise almost out of nothing an imposing and well-equipped army. The Saxons were driven out of Bohemia in as many days as it had taken them weeks to conquer it; and Wallenstein took up a fortified position near Nuremberg which cut off Gustavus Adolphus from his base in the North and gave Wallenstein a central point from which he might turn in any direction. Gustavus hurried back. A fierce contest near Nuremberg remained indecisive, and the king retreated farther northward to collect reinforcements. Wallenstein followed him, and Gustavus Adolphus inflicted a heavy defeat on him at Lützen near Leipzig (16 Nov. 1632). But the Swedish victory was bought too dearly, for amongst the killed was the king himself, and Wallenstein might well consider himself the victor of the day.

The able diplomacy of the Swedish chancellor, Oxenstierna, aided by French pensions and subsidies, kept the smaller German Estates faithful to the Swedish allegiance. The League of Heilbronn (23 April 1633) confirmed this tripartite alliance. On the other hand, the great Estates, above all the Electors, were genuinely seeking for a peaceful settlement. They considered the forces of the Emperor and the foreigners matched so evenly that neither party would upset the balance of power to the detriment of the Empire. They found Wallenstein very much inclined to share their views. As duke of Mecklenburg, and so one of their order, he was himself opposed to the interference of Swedes and Frenchmen in the affairs of the Empire. He wished to employ the imperial forces against these foreigners—and later against the Turks—rather than in the present internecine strife. He therefore opened secret negotiations with Saxony and other Protestant princes and aimed at a general pacification. He miscalculated, however, the influence of his adversaries with the courts of Vienna, Madrid and Munich.

Wallenstein, who had not forgotten the mortification he had suffered at Maximilian's instigation, did not stir when Ratisbon, the key of Bavaria, was seized by the Swedes (14 Nov. 1633); this betrayal, together with other personal and political reasons, drove Maximilian into the ranks of his enemies. Even greater was the hostility of the Spanish court; for a peace which would free the French forces to resume the war with Spain was clearly against the primary interests of Madrid. The ties of blood-relationship between the Austrian and the Spanish Hapsburgs, their common devotion to the cause of their Church, and their common antagonism to France, were strong enough to secure for the Spanish ambassador in Vienna the full confidence of the Emperor. Wallenstein's ruin was decided. The leading generals were won over by promises, bribes, and appeals to their fealty. Driven to extremes, Wallenstein now planned to desert openly to the enemy. 'He did not fall because he rebelled, but he rebelled because he fell', to quote the famous words with which Schiller has summed up the inner reasons of his catastrophe. He was outlawed, the army put under the command of Piccolomini, whom Wallenstein had trusted more than any other of his lieutenants; and at Eger, on 25 Feb. 1634, the generalissimo was foully murdered by some of his officers.[1]

After the murder of Wallenstein the imperial army was placed under the nominal leadership of the eldest son of the Emperor, while the generals Gallas and Piccolomini acted as his advisers. They inflicted a heavy defeat on the Swedes and German Protestants at Nördlingen (5–6 Sept. 1634). It was the last battle in which the massed forces of both sides faced each other. Henceforth, smaller detachments fought in various theatres almost independently. Their unco-ordinated victories and defeats had little influence on the outcome of the war. On the other hand, the disappearance of Gustavus Adolphus and Wallenstein cleared the way for an appeasement between the Emperor and the Protestant Estates, of which the younger Ferdinand was a sincere advocate. As neither party could any longer hope for total victory, the spirit of compromise prevailed.

[1] The murderers and their accomplices were Irish, Scots and English mercenaries to whom loyalty meant nothing, and personal gain everything. Every army that fought on the continent at the time was teeming with foreign adventurers of that kind. Gustavus Adolphus of Sweden trained a number of men who later on played a more or less conspicuous part in the English Civil War: amongst them were Alexander Leslie, first earl of Leven, Sir John Hepburn, Donald Mackay, first Lord Reay, and James, third marquis and first duke of Hamilton.

Saxony, the protagonist of the Protestant Estates, concluded her peace with the Emperor at Prague (30 May 1635). She forsook the Swedish alliance and received in return the margraviate of Lusatia, which had fallen to the Bohemian crown in 1329. This peace gave a new turn to the war. Its initial advantages to the Emperor were soon superseded by its serious repercussions abroad. The Swedes, abandoned by their principal allies, were in danger of losing all the fruits of Gustavus's victories; so Richelieu decided upon a more active part in the struggle. He concluded an open alliance with Oxenstierna, renewed the war with Spain, and took Bernard of Saxe-Weimar, the most gifted of the generals reared in the camp of the late king, into the pay of France (1635). The French frontier districts became the chief theatre of war in the following years. An invasion of France by Piccolomini was repulsed, and the French armies advanced into the Spanish Netherlands; by 1640 they had conquered Artois. At the same time Bernard of Weimar expelled the imperial troops from Alsace and took the important bridge-head of Breisach, which gave the French a secure access into South Germany (1638). As he showed a measure of independence and pursued ambitious schemes of his own, his death from the plague (1639) was not unwelcome to the French. The revolt of Portugal in 1640 which led to the re-establishment of her independence of Spain was a further gain for France. The Swedes confined themselves to North Germany with occasional raids farther afield; they gained two major successes over the imperial troops at Breitenfeld (1642) and Jankau (1645).

Ferdinand III, who succeeded his father in 1637, lacked the latter's religious fanaticism and was his superior in warfare and diplomacy. He therefore soon realized that neither he nor the Empire would gain by prolonging the war; the latest successes of the foreigners made a speedy peace more desirable than ever. Thus it came about that in November 1644 preliminary peace talks were begun at Münster and Osnabrück. While they dragged on without any visible progress, the position of the imperial party grew worse. In 1646, the Swedes and French combined in an attack on Bavaria. Maximilian promptly left the imperial side and concluded a separate treaty with France and Sweden at Ulm (14 March 1647). Having obtained the electoral dignity at the expense of his Palatine cousin, he had lost all interest in the prosecution of the war. Its result could only be the strengthening of the imperial power, or the prevalence of foreign influence in the affairs of the Empire. Neither alternative appealed to him. In 1629, he opposed the Emperor when he threatened to tread the liberties of the Estates underfoot; in 1631, he rallied again to the Emperor, when the king of Sweden seemed likely to become supreme. Now, in 1647, he wanted to secure the gains of his policy. The Emperor, he was sure, would not exert himself in order that the Wittelsbachs might keep the Palatinate and the Rhenish and Westphalian bishoprics, which countries were now in the gift of the French and Swedes. In fact, Maximilian's defection proved very profitable for Bavaria. The greater part of the Palatinate, it is true, had to be restored to the heir of the 'Winter King'; the Protestant powers were pledged to that. Charles Louis of the Palatinate found another strong advocate of his cause in the victorious English Parliament with which he had sided from the beginning as faithfully as his younger brothers, Rupert and Maurice, had espoused the cause of their uncle Charles I. In addition to the Upper Palatinate, however, Maximilian secured for his family the possession of a number of North and West German bishoprics, and, most valuable of all, the lasting friendship of France, which was to outlive the régime of the Bourbons and which made Bavaria the second largest German state when Napoleon handed out the spoils of his victories.

Maximilian was too much a past-master of cunning not to double-cross his new allies. Yet, although he made his peace with the Emperor only a few months after the treaty of Ulm, this treaty proved a decisive step forward towards the general pacification. Another step in the same direction was taken shortly afterwards. On 1 Nov. 1647, the Lutherans acknowledged the Calvinists as their co-religionists. That meant that the Emperor would no longer be able to play off the Lutheran appeasers against the Calvinist firebrands. It further indicated a great slackening of the exacerbating religious issues. A hundred years of internecine strife had at last taught the Protestants that the defence of their common secular interests required tolerance of their doctrinal differences. On the other hand, the Emperor was at last convinced that he must cut his losses, though, if great sacrifices had to be made, he resolved that they should be made at the expense of the Empire, and not of the house of Hapsburg. A last advance of the Swedes into his hereditary possessions, which ended with the capture of Prague by the enemy (July 1648), made Ferdinand willing to accede to the general peace. On 24 Oct. 1648, the treaty was signed in the Westphalian towns of Münster and Osnabrück—from which it derived the name of 'Peace of Westphalia'.

This treaty settled once and for all the constitutional issues between the Emperor and the Empire. The Estates, from the largest Electorate down to the smallest principality, were each accorded the full status of sovereignty and independence in home and foreign affairs. It was a pious hope rather than an obligation that a clause of the treaty stated that this independence should not be used to the detriment of the Empire. The Emperor retained only the honorary presidency of a loose association of which he was a member. The imperial diet, it is true, soon became a permanent institution with its seat at Ratisbon (1663); its functions, however, were no longer those of the controlling organ of a united body politic, but the bargainings of a congress of diplomatists representing sovereign states. Thus the constitution of the Empire was framed in direct contrast to what the Emperors and the Estates had striven after for the last centuries. The Emperor had not obtained a position comparable to that of the rulers of France, England, Spain, or even the small Scandinavian kingdoms. The Estates had failed to transform the Empire into a federal commonwealth guided by its principal member states in harmonious co-operation. For the practical purposes of international policy, the Empire ceased to count as a unit. The smaller territories lost their political significance altogether; and the six or seven larger ones became, or at least considered themselves, great powers. The Holy Roman Empire meant to them nothing but a traditional institution which might from time to time be used as a convenient screen when something was to be gained by it, and could otherwise be disregarded altogether.

The liquidation of the Empire was accelerated by placing the treaty of Westphalia under the joint guarantee of its foreign signatories. Of these, the Netherlands, Denmark and Sweden could only with difficulty keep up their status as European powers, and, in fact, lost their artificial and precarious greatness before the close of the century. It was therefore obvious that this guarantee meant little else than a French protectorate over all those German principalities which could, in future, appeal to the court of Versailles for protection or assistance. Thus France had become the arbiter in the last resort of German affairs.

The religious differences which had played a conspicuous part in the Bohemian, Danish and Swedish wars, or, at least, in the propaganda of the protagonists, receded completely into the background. The equality of rights of Roman Catholics, Lutherans and Calvinists was officially recognized. The maxim of *Cuius regio, eius religio* settled the denominational character of each country; the heterodox were granted no tolerance save the right of emigration. As regards the secularization of ecclesiastical territory, the position of 1624 was regarded as 'normal'. Compared with the former 'normal year' of 1552, this was prejudicial to the Protestants, since the counter-reformation had enjoyed its major triumphs after that date. Although one or two princes subsequently changed their religion, the denominational boundaries henceforth have remained stable; and religious arguments hardly any longer influenced political decisions. The brutal expulsion of 30,000 Protestants by the archbishop of Salzburg in 1731 was a last explosion of the heat and hatred of a bygone period, and was considered an outrage even by the prince's co-religionists. The Lutheran and Calvinistic Estates soon (1653) formed a united *Corpus Evangelicorum* under the presidency of Saxony, which was to safeguard their common interests in the affairs of the Empire.

The territorial changes brought about by the peace of Westphalia further increased the hegemony of France over Germany. The independence of Switzerland and the Republic of the United Netherlands, it is true, was guaranteed by the foreign signatories and recognized by the Empire; but this was the confirmation of a state of affairs that had long since become irrevocable, rather than any fresh loss of territory. As to the rest, France and her allies alone made substantial gains. Austria had to cede to France the whole of the south, and a number of towns and fortresses in the centre and north, of Alsace. Eleven years later, in the peace of the Pyrenees which ended hostilities between France and Spain (1659), France gained Artois and other portions of the Spanish Netherlands. Henceforth, South Germany, the Palatinate, the Rhineland and the Netherlands lay open to the French armies, and the duchy of Lorraine was completely encircled by French territory.

Sweden, to whom France mainly owed the defeat of the Hapsburgs, got the lion's share. She obtained Hither Pomerania and the island of Rügen; the Mecklenburg port of Wismar; the archbishopric of Bremen excluding the imperial town of Bremen itself; and the bishopric of Verden—the latter two countries comprising the whole region between the lower Elbe and lower Weser. Thus it came about that the mouths of every river flowing into the Baltic and North Seas were under foreign control, and Germany was shut off from the open sea. The Memel and Vistula with the ports of Danzig and Elbing were in Polish hands; the Swedes dominated the mouths of the Oder and Weser; the Danes, that of the Elbe; while the Ems, Rhine and Meuse ended in Dutch territory.

There was only one German state that benefited greatly from the Westphalian peace. In 1640, Frederick William of Brandenburg, upon whom his contemporaries and posterity have bestowed the title of the Great Elector, had succeeded his utterly incapable father. Realizing at once that Sweden, backed by France, would be the ultimate victor, he abandoned the policy of appeasement, revoked the peace of Prague, and resumed good relations with the Swedes (1641). He remained their faithful partisan until he had got out of this alliance all it could procure him. Grudgingly he had to leave Hither Pomerania with the important sea places of Stettin, Stralsund and Greifswald to the Swedes. But the peace of Westphalia brought him not only Farther Pomerania and the bishopric of Cammin, but also the bishoprics of Halberstadt and Minden, two small counties in the Hartz mountains, and the reversion of the rich archbishopric of Magdeburg, which occurred in 1680. In addition to these gains, Brandenburg retained her share of the Jülich-Cleves inheritance which she obtained in 1614. Moreover, in 1618, the dukedom of Prussia, a Polish fief since 1466, devolved on Brandenburg when the last duke of this collateral line of the Hohenzollerns died without issue. Thus it was that Brandenburg, in 1609 confined to the barren regions between the middle Oder and middle Elbe, emerged from the forty years of warfare on German soil a great German power equalling Saxony and Bavaria, and inferior only to Austria. Her possessions now stretched from the Baltic through the whole length of North Germany to the left bank of the Rhine. She had ceased to be the poorest and least important of the Electorates, and had become a power that might at any moment make its weight felt by the crowns of Poland and Sweden and the Dutch States-General; a power which even the cabinets of Vienna and Versailles had to take into account.

Austria was crippled in the West. The majority of the German states had gained little or nothing and were suffering from the after-effects of the war. Brandenburg alone came out of the war aggrandized in territory, men and wealth. Now that the links which bound together the German states were loosening, the future history of Germany would be greatly influenced by the policy which the present and later rulers of Brandenburg pursued. Theirs was now the power to consolidate and develop, or to upset and destroy, the Germany that emerged from the council chambers of Münster and Osnabrück.

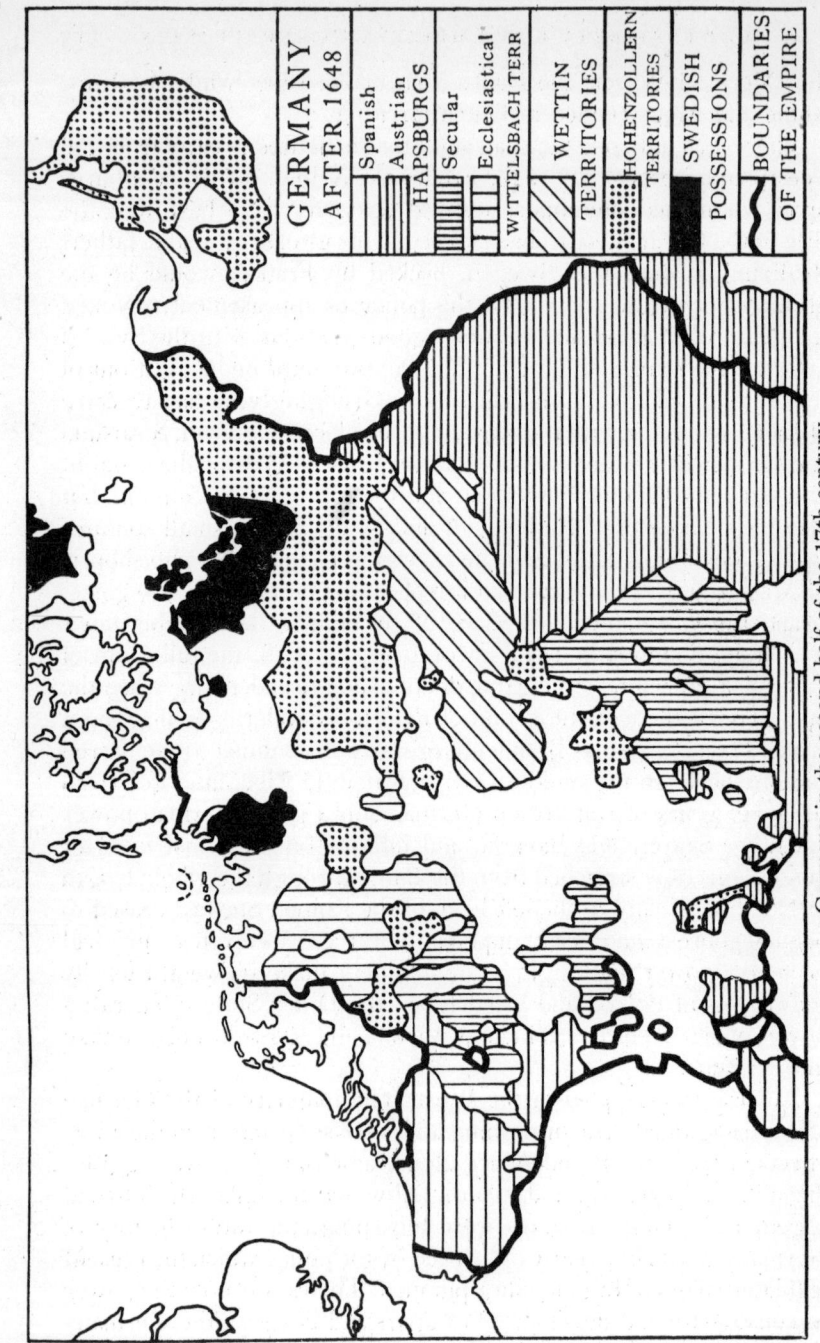

Germany in the second half of the 17th century

CHAPTER V

THE EMPIRE IN DECAY (1648-1786)

From the middle of the seventeenth century onward the term 'Empire' was commonly used to describe exclusively the vast and disorganized mass of petty principalities, imperial cities and villages, and lands of imperial knights in the South-West and West of Germany. These pseudo-sovereignties were in fact the only members of the Empire for whom the old institutions still held some meaning: as the Empire was the only basis of their existence, and their only protection. The larger states went their own ways; they sought and found the means of maintaining themselves within their own boundaries and in alliances with foreign powers. Some of them were, others became, half-foreign powers themselves. Austria, despite the losses she had suffered at Münster, continued to keep guard in the East and West and to expand in both directions. By 1699, she recovered the greater part of Hungary from the Turks; in 1718, she gained the rest, and also parts of Rumania and Serbia. Although the latter territories were abandoned again to the Porte in 1739, the greater part of the Hapsburg possessions lay henceforth outside the boundaries of the Empire. Turkey, Poland and Russia were the powers which influenced Austrian politics in these parts. In the West, the war of the Spanish succession led to the permanent acquisition by Austria of the Spanish (henceforth Austrian) Netherlands and the duchy of Milan in 1714, and to the temporary occupation of Sardinia (till 1720), Sicily and Naples; in 1738 these were exchanged for Tuscany, Parma and Piacenza. The possession of the ports of Ostend and Leghorn made Austria susceptible to the friendly or hostile attitude of the Maritime Powers, above all England, in addition to the traditional tension with France. What, in the face of these international commitments, did the petty quarrels of the German Estates mean to the cabinet of Vienna!

Brandenburg, too, became involved in international politics. The reversion of the duchy of Prussia (1618) demanded a settlement with Poland, of whose crown Prussia was a fief. Pomerania, which Brandenburg thought hers by right of inheritance, had been partitioned between her and Sweden; and designs upon the Swedish portion henceforth dictated the Nordic policy of Brandenburg. By hoodwinking allies and enemies alike, Brandenburg gained her ends: Prussia was released from the Polish suzerainty, and in 1701 the Elector Frederick III had himself crowned king. The eastern provinces of Prussia, however, were never incorporated with the Empire, and the king of Prussia was a prince of the Empire only in his capacity as Margrave and Elector of Brandenburg. Prussia's participation in the war of the Spanish succession brought gains in the West, namely the Rhenish counties of Guelders and Mörs, and the Swiss principality of Neuchâtel. A further portion of Swedish Pomerania, including the capital and seaport of Stettin, went to Prussia as a result of her intervention in the Nordic war (1720). The rape of Silesia from Austria (1742) and the reversion of the principality of Eastern Frisia (1744) added further patches to the variegated map of Prussia. By the middle of the eighteenth century she was the neighbour of Sweden, Poland and Russia, Austria and Saxony, France, the Netherlands and England—and the enemy of nearly all of them.

The coronation as king of the Elector of Brandenburg in 1701 was the reaction to the increase of the international status of another Elector of the Empire, that of Saxony. In 1697, Frederick Augustus I was elected king of Poland, and he and his son after him ruled the two countries together for sixty-six years. In this period, Dresden and Warsaw became the most splendid capitals of Northern Europe, and Leipzig was considered the fashionable German university. The real power of the combined countries, however, lagged far behind their outward grandeur; and it was during this time that Saxony and Poland lost their places in international politics to Prussia and Russia respectively.

The price Frederick Augustus had to pay for the Polish crown was his conversion to the Roman Church. At the same time, adherence to the Protestant religion secured a dazzling reward to the Guelph dynasty of Hanover. More than any other dynasty, except the house of Wettin, the Guelphs suffered for centuries from the inveterate evil of continued partitions and repartitions of their patrimony. It was with great difficulty that Duke Ernest Augustus introduced the right of primogeniture and indivisibility in the younger branch of the house in 1682. He was married to the Princess Sophia, youngest daughter of Frederick V of the Palatinate. When, therefore, the Palatinate fell to a Roman Catholic prince in 1685, he immediately set about procuring for himself a ninth electoral dignity. In order to draw him away from France, Leopold I complied with his wish, and on 19 Dec. 1692 Ernest Augustus was invested with the regalia of the Electorate of Lüneburg, though, as a result of the opposition of other princes, the formal introduction into the College of Electors was delayed until 1708. Meanwhile Ernest August was succeeded by George Lewis (1698). He inherited in 1705 the dukedom of Celle in virtue of the wise provision of his father, and thus united for the first time the Guelph possessions, save the dukedom of Wolfenbüttel, which has remained apart ever since 1267. George Lewis then succeeded to the throne of his maternal ancestor, James VI and I, when Queen Anne died in 1714, the last Protestant Stewart.

While these princes and their successors continued to keep in touch with the affairs of the Empire, other German princes who acceded to foreign thrones became speedily de-Germanized and retained little sympathy for the country of their origin. In 1720, the hereditary prince of Hesse-Cassel became king of Sweden as the husband of the sister and heiress of Charles XII. Being childless, he was succeeded in 1751 by a count of Holstein-Gottorp, whose descendants were afterwards superseded by the Napoleonic dynasty of the Bernadottes. Another prince of the house of Gottorp was adopted by the Empress Elizabeth of Russia. He became Tsar Peter III in 1762, and was in the same year murdered and succeeded by his wife, Catherine II, a princess of Anhalt. The dynasty of Holstein continued to rule the Russian Empire until its last scion met his doom in 1917. Thus in the middle of the eighteenth century all the thrones of Europe save those of France, the Iberian peninsula and part of Italy were occupied by German princes.

When all continental countries and nearly all the member states of the Empire entered the age of absolutism, the traditional oligarchic constitution of the Empire proved a real weakness. Its clumsy apparatus was no match for the efficient administration of the absolute states. Whereas these strove to abolish corporate and regional privileges, those same privileges were the very basis of the Empire. The uniform dynastic, if not yet national, feeling which the bureaucracy of the absolute states was everywhere busy creating weakened even more the common ideals of the Estates of the Empire. In order to counterbalance these centrifugal tendencies, the voluntary associations on regional principles were revived again. Maintenance of order and justice, safeguard of their privileges from imperial interference, and protection of their frontiers against foreign invaders, were the chief aims of these associations. John Philip of Schönborn, archbishop of Mayence (1647–73) and bishop of Würzburg and Worms, tried to emulate his great predecessor Bertold of Henneberg in organizing the Estates of the Empire so that they might play an independent and effective part in German and European affairs. In 1654, the archbishops of Cologne and Treves, the bishop of Münster, and the Count Palatine of Neuburg formed a league which was designed to uphold the Wittelsbach party in the Empire. When John Philip of Mayence joined it in 1655, he at once widened its narrow outlook and insisted on the admission of Protestant princes. Soon Sweden (for her German possessions), the Guelphs, Hesse-Cassel, Württemberg, Brandenburg, and a number of lesser princes, became members of the Rhenish Alliance as it was called. In 1658, the confederates concluded an alliance with France, which they regarded as the natural protector of 'German liberty'. John Philip was, however, not willing to sacrifice vital German interests. He was instrumental in frustrating the aspirations to the imperial crown of Louis XIV and his satellite, Ferdinand Maria of Bavaria, in 1658. He secured the election of Leopold, younger son of Ferdinand III, as the elder, Ferdinand IV, who had been elected Roman king in 1653, had died before his father (1654).

When eventually the aggressive tendencies of Louis XIV became obvious and he attacked the Spanish Netherlands without provocation in 1667, the alliance with France was abandoned and the Confederation came to an end. John Philip, however, remained untiring in his attempts to reform the Empire. At his instigation the great philosopher Leibniz wrote a memorandum on the means and ways of maintaining the *Securitas publica interna et externa* of the Empire (1670). Leibniz suggested that a standing army and its financial upkeep were indispensable for securing the safety and independence of the Empire and its every member. In 1672, the Elector sent Leibniz on a political mission to Paris. He wanted to divert Louis XIV from his schemes against the Low Countries, and Leibniz submitted to the French king the great plan of an expedition to Egypt. Louis and his ministers rejected the idea, and thus missed a great opportunity of expanding the French empire overseas.

How correctly the Mayence cabinet had estimated the European situation and the unpreparedness of the Empire became clear when Louis, in alliance with Charles II and the Bavarian princes of Cologne and Münster, attacked Holland in 1673. The Emperor, Spain, and Lorraine assisted the victim of wanton aggression; and the Empire, too, declared war on France (1674). However, the official participation of the Empire had no influence on the military and political events. The other belligerents waged war and concluded peace with utter disregard for its interests. In the end, the peace of Nijmegen (1679) actually made the Empire the principal loser. It had to cede Freiburg to France; the Wittelsbach princes had to be restored in their countries from which they had been expelled; and Sweden, the faithful ally of France, was given back the territories she had lost during the war. The Empire was not even represented at the peace conference, and the Emperor acted and signed on its behalf.

John Philip of Mayence had also taken the leading part in setting up the capitulation upon which Leopold I had to take his coronation oath in 1658. It became the model for all the following capitulations and shows most clearly the prevailing tendencies of the age, though its influence upon the affairs of the Empire was small. All its clauses were designed to strengthen the absolutism of the princes and, at the same time, to reduce the power of the Emperor. It was the duty of the Emperor, so the capitulation stipulated, to assist the princes of the Empire in keeping down their subjects. The Emperor had, for instance, to prevent the Estates of the countries from assembling without a summons of their sovereign, and from disposing of taxes without the assent of their sovereign. The right of alliance was reserved to the Estates of the Empire, and allowed even against the Estates of the individual states, whereas the latter were expressly forbidden to ally with one another against their sovereign. The imperial Aulic Council (*Reichshofrat*) must never accept complaints of the subjects against their sovereign: thus this important office could no longer be used against the princes, although they had failed to bring it under their control. The *Reichshofrat* had been created by Maximilian I in opposition to the federalistic tendencies of the reform party, in 1498. Ferdinand I made it a permanent office in 1559, and laid down that all the Aulic councillors should be appointed exclusively by the Emperor. In 1654, Ferdinand III issued its final regulations, without asking the opinion of the Estates. The Aulic Council was the supreme court of justice concerning feudal rights and privileges, criminal cases in which immediate Estates were involved, and the reserved rights of the Emperor.

Despite these restrictions, the Emperor through the agency of the Aulic Council intervened several times in favour of the provincial Estates when princes abused their absolute power too flagrantly even for the long-suffering loyalty of eighteenth-century Germans. When Duke Charles Leopold of Mecklenburg (1713–28) tried to abolish his diet with the help of Russia, the Emperor outlawed and deposed him. Here in Mecklenburg, the Estates achieved their greatest success: their final agreement with the ducal house (1755) secured the permanence of the privileges of the Knights, and all attempts at introducing an absolute régime in the eighteenth century, or constitutional forms of government in the nineteenth and twentieth centuries, failed. Mecklenburg remained a curious relic of medieval feudalism until in 1918 feudalism and monarchy collapsed simultaneously.

The only other countries in which the Estates maintained their power were Hanover and Württemberg. After the succession to the English throne of the Elector George Lewis in 1714, the Estates of Hanover were left unmolested in the exercise of their power, and they used it with consideration and benevolence on the model of the English Whigs. The University of Göttingen (founded in 1737) bore witness to the enlightened and liberal régime of the Hanoverian oligarchy: here the natural and political sciences flourished unfettered by a servile censorship, and scholars such as the political economist Schlözer, the philologist Heyne, the orientalist Michaelis, and the anthropologist Blumenbach attracted students from all over Europe. In Württemberg, the Estates gained fresh power when in 1733 the Roman Catholic convert, Charles Alexander, acceded to the throne of the purely Lutheran dukedom. They acted as an independent power, deliberated with Hanover, Prussia, Denmark and other Protestant powers, and eventually appealed to the imperial Aulic Council to have their privileges confirmed. The Aulic Council decided in their favour and Duke Charles Eugene (1737–93), notorious for his oppression of Friedrich Schiller, had to put up with the stiff-necked Estates.

Less consideration was shown to some petty princes who made themselves guilty of the most abominable crimes. The Emperor Joseph II (1765–90) distinguished himself by severely punishing a number of these tyrants whose life was a public scandal. The last Wildgrave and Count Palatine, Charles Magnus, was condemned to ten years' imprisonment; others were deposed or heavily fined. On the whole, however, the princes of the Empire looked with disfavour on this exercise of imperial justice, and they would shield the unworthiest member of their order rather than give the Emperor a handle for interfering with the privileges of the imperial Estates.

These privileges, as laid down in the Westphalian peace, were further strengthened when the Last Recess of the imperial diet

(17 March 1654) completely ignored the constitutional problems, leaving their development to the natural course of events. The recess of 1654 was called the 'last', because the following diet which was summoned at Ratisbon in 1663 was never formally dissolved. It became the 'permanent diet' and disappeared only with the Holy Empire itself in 1806. The diet of 1653–54 took some steps to improve the administration of justice. The permanent diet, however, did little or nothing by way of legislation. The regulation of guilds, issued in 1731, was almost the only practical outcome of its endless deliberations. The diet was an assembly of the envoys of independent states, and these were more anxious to prevent than to promote legislative measures on the part of the Empire, which might interfere with their sovereignty. Therefore voluntary associations of the kind of the Rhenish Alliance, and agreements concluded for limited purposes by individual member states, were more effective than the half-hearted resolutions passed by the imperial diet at Ratisbon.

After the death of John Philip of Schönborn (1673) his projects for the mutual protection of the lesser Estates against the Emperor as well as external enemies were resumed, as far as the military aspect was concerned, by George Frederick, count of Waldeck. He was one of the numerous petty princes whom the administration of their few square miles of territory did not satisfy and who therefore entered the services of some foreign power. George Frederick served in turn the Dutch States-General, Brandenburg and Sweden; he ended his career as Captain-General of William III when the latter left Holland for England in 1689. In 1664, Waldeck was appointed Field-Marshal of the Empire. He brought about a defensive organization of the small Estates of the West and South-West (1679). These concluded the alliance of Laxenburg with the Emperor (10 June 1683), and their troops played a not inglorious part in the liberation of Vienna from the Turks and the subsequent advance into Hungary. Two years earlier, Waldeck accomplished the last great reform to be carried out by the Holy Roman Empire, namely the Military Constitution of 1681 (*Reichskriegsverfassung*). It was laid down that the army of the Empire should consist of a 'Simplum' of 40,000 men; this could be raised to a 'Duplum', 'Triplum', or whatever strength was required in an emergency. The levying and maintaining of the army was left to the Circles, which in their turn apportioned the contingents among their members. This army proved quite effective under the spirited leadership of Waldeck and Margrave Louis William of Baden, his successor as

Field-Marshal of the Empire (1693–1707). They fought successfully in Hungary, defended the Rhine frontier against the renewed attacks of the French (1689–97), and had a glorious share in the victories of Marlborough and Prince Eugene in the war of the Spanish succession. Yet even at this time of its greatest achievements the army of the Empire consisted chiefly of the contingents of the 'Empire' in its narrow meaning, i.e. the Western and South-Western parts of Germany. It was backed by the last large 'association' of Estates which was concluded at Frankfort by the Rhenish, Franconian, Bavarian, Swabian and Westphalian Circles in 1697. When peace was restored in 1714, the association crumbled away, and the military organization deteriorated rapidly. From the beginning, the so-called 'Armed Estates', i.e. those who had a standing army of their own, were unwilling to merge their troops in an imperial army under an independent command. Brandenburg, whose territories lay in four or five different Circles, refused to give up her own uniform organization. Austria, whose possessions were organized in two separate Circles, the Austrian and Burgundian, saw no reason for adapting these to the wishes of other Circles. The 'Not-armed Estates', on the other hand, who had no peace-time armies of their own, were too small and inefficient to raise a homogeneous body of men. Thus the army of the Empire soon became notorious for its inefficiency. There were independent contingents of $1\frac{1}{3}$ infantryman; the companies, battalions, and regiments did not wear the same uniform; they were never inspected, nor did they combine in peace-time manœuvres. In brief, the Military Constitution of the Empire only emphasized, in its own sphere, the fact that the Empire had abdicated in favour of its principal member states. Declarations of war and conclusions of peace on the part of the Empire became little more than formalities; the Emperor, in carrying them out, always put the interests of Austria first. War and peace were decided by the exertions of the individual 'Armed Estates' rather than by those of the Empire as such. Thus, the Empire was a nominal partner of the great alliance which fought Louis XIV from 1689 to 1697. It also joined the anti-French group in the wars of the Spanish succession (1702–14) and of the Polish succession (1734–36). In all these wars, however, important members of the Empire pursued their independent policies: Brandenburg changed sides whenever a change promised her the slightest temporary gain; and the Wittelsbach party, i.e. Bavaria, Palatinate, Cologne, Münster and their vassals, always kept faith with their French protector and ally. It was two Wittelsbach brothers, the Electors of Bavaria and Cologne, against whom the solemn ban of the Empire was proclaimed for the last time, in 1706, when they sided with Louis XIV against the Emperor and Empire. In 1180, the ban of the Empire had been the undoing of the greatest prince of the Empire, Duke Henry the Lion; in 1546, it had broken the power of the Protestant opposition; in 1621, it had sufficed to make Frederick V of the Palatinate a landless exile for the rest of his life. Now, the ban had lost its terror, and had no influence on the final settlement of the dispute: even before the complete restitution of the felonious brothers was made an intrinsic clause of the general peace, the Emperor himself entered into secret negotiations with them. The last serious attempt, on the part of the Empire, at coercing one of its member states ended in complete failure. When Frederick of Prussia wantonly attacked Austria in 1756, the army of the Empire was mobilized, and the 'Elector of Brandenburg' was charged with a breach of the public peace. Frederick simply ignored the legal procedure; and the first battle in which the army of the Empire took part as a corporate unit ended in its complete rout (at Rossbach, 5 Nov. 1757). The very name of the *Reichsarmee* became a word of derision and contempt.

A curious attempt at reviving a concerted Empire policy was made in the religious sphere. In 1785 the Pope established a permanent nunciature at Munich. The nuncio was to supersede the diocesan bishops and to regulate ecclesiastical matters immediately between the Roman Curia and the Bavarian court. The four German archbishops of Mayence, Treves, Cologne and Salzburg took alarm. As a protection of their rights against papal interference they issued the Ems Punctation (25 Aug. 1786), which blended the ideas of the Councils of Constance and Basle with those of the rational philosophers of the age. Radicals even demanded a national synod, the setting up of an autonomous church, and the overthrow of the papal hierarchy. The movement, however, collapsed quickly. The bishops sided with the far-off Pope rather than with their own archbishops. Prussia and Bavaria were opposed to any strengthening of the imperial party. Joseph II himself was quite uninterested in the religious issues. No popular movement backed the archiepiscopal pretensions. A secession from Rome, based on political expediency rather than religious arguments, proved impracticable. In the end, the archbishops had to submit, and the imperial capitulation of Leopold II (1790) restored the old relations between the Roman Church and Empire.

The medieval Empire, despite all its shortcomings, had offered space and opportunity for great exploits. The petty sovereignties which had taken its place were too small even to utilize to the full the capacities of their own subjects. Austria and, from the middle of the eighteenth century, Prussia were the only German states which attracted bold and capable men from abroad. The Savoyard Prince Eugene, the Irishman Maximilian Browne, the Scotsman Gideon Loudon became notable Austrian generals. The Earl Marischal George and his brother James Keith and others who 'had been out' in 1715, 1719 and 1745 served in the army of Frederick II of Prussia. The subjects of the petty German princes went abroad, where they found the scope for their activities which was denied them at home. Dynastic connections with foreign sovereigns of German origin assisted many an adventurous man. German officers lent their arms, German scholars their brains, German writers their pens to foreign potentates. The Rhenish Count Frederick of Schomberg gained a French ducal coronet and field-marshal's baton in the service of Louis XIV and fell by the side of William III in the battle of the Boyne. German officers commanded the Venetian armies in the Levant, and a Lüneburg lieutenant gained notoriety by blowing up the Parthenon of Athens in 1687. The Thuringian physician Struensee became the virtual dictator of Denmark and paramour of the Danish queen (1770-72). German officials reorganized the Russian Empire on Western lines. After the Baltic states were incorporated with Russia (1721), the influence of the Baltic barons was paramount at the court of St Petersburg for more than a hundred years.

Only a few of the lesser German princes devoted their energy to the advancement and improvement of their countries. Noteworthy amongst them is the margrave Charles Frederick of Baden (1738-1811), who made Baden the best governed and most progressive of the German principalities. The majority of the German princes, however, regarded their absolute power merely as a means of enjoying themselves. Louis XIV and his court became the standards of conduct and fashion throughout Germany with the exception of the court of Vienna, which kept to the Spanish ceremonial. Huge palaces on the model of Versailles and the Trianon sprang up in and near every capital. The disparity between the insignificance of the petty principalities and the vast and luxurious pretensions of their sovereigns was grotesque and ludicrous. It was a serious matter, however, to the subjects of these imitators of the *Roi Soleil*. The mania for building and the exorbitant expenses of the court ruined the finances of more than one principality and reduced its subjects to beggars. It was thus that the doctrines of the French Revolution met with an enthusiastic reception in these petty states which had suffered so long under their pygmy tyrants.

Political oppression, economic distress, religious persecution and spirit of adventure drove hundreds of thousands of citizens and peasants from their homesteads and made them seek a new country overseas. North America and especially Pennsylvania became the favourite goal of these emigrants. For a time it was doubtful whether German or English would be the official language of the Thirteen States, and 'Pennsylvania Dutch' has survived as an independent German dialect to the present.

Political and economic understanding of the value of colonies and the desire to equal the greatness of the Maritime Powers combined to tempt some German princes to far-reaching enterprises overseas. The first German colony was established by the Augsburg banking and trading firm of the Welsers. As a reward for their loans to the Emperor Charles V, the Welsers were invested with Venezuela in 1528. On the search for the fabulous gold of El Dorado, their agents advanced as far as Bogotá; but nothing was done for a proper settlement of Venezuela itself, and in 1546 the Spanish government decreed the reversion of the colony. A hundred years later, the Palatine publicist, Johann Joachim Becher (1635–82), revived the schemes of German colonies overseas and substantiated them with mercantilist arguments. Why, he asked his 'brave Germans', should not New Germany be added to New England, New France and New Spain on the maps of the world? The Germans, he argued, had no less intelligence and resolution than other nations; they were hardy soldiers and peasants, as fit as the Dutch or any other nation for enterprises of this kind. Becher was the court-physician of the Archbishop John Philip of Mayence who took up his suggestions. Colbert, the great colonial and economic minister of Louis XIV, favoured a joint Franco-German colonization of Guiana. When this project came to nothing, Becher went to Munich and won over the Elector of Bavaria to similar plans with Dutch and English support; but these projects, too, failed to materialize. The Duke James of Courland (1642–82), however, acquired Gambia and Tobago with the support of Cromwell; and Frederick William of Brandenburg (1640–88) occupied some places on the coast of Guinea and leased a naval base on the Danish island of St Thomas. In the end, however, all these colonies had to be abandoned to the Maritime Powers. In 1721, the last Brandenburg possession in Africa was sold to the Dutch.

These colonial enterprises were prepared and undertaken by trading companies, chiefly on the model of the English East India and the Dutch East and West India Companies. Charles VI of Austria had, during his short reign as Charles III of Spain (1705-11), come into closer contact with oversea affairs than any inland sovereign before him. When he obtained the Spanish Netherlands by the peace of Rastatt (1714), he established an Austrian East India Company at Ostend (1720). The Company acquired some bases on the Coromandel Coast and in Bengal, and also carried on a prosperous trade with Africa and the West Indies. Charles himself, however, wrecked these promising beginnings: eager to reconcile the Maritime Powers with the Pragmatic Sanction, he liquidated the Ostend Company, and the imperial ensign disappeared from the seven seas for the next one hundred and fifty years. An Oriental Company was at the same time established at Vienna (1719). It was meant to oust the Venetians from the trade in the Levant; Trieste and Fiume were made free-ports. The fickleness of the shareholders and the ill-considered expansion of the Company eventually caused its bankruptcy (1734).

All these attempts to gain a share in oversea colonization and world commerce failed for the same reasons. The German states were too undeveloped economically to levy the necessary capital which would have piloted the enterprises through their difficult beginnings. Some of them, such as Bavaria and Mayence, had no access to the sea. Others, such as Brandenburg, Courland and Austria, had naval bases only in the Baltic and Adriatic, which were too remote from the great sea lanes to allow them to compete with the experienced seamanship of the Dutch and English. In the face of these economic and technical difficulties, the ambition of individual princes and the acumen of a few isolated economists were no substitute for the general lack of interest in world affairs. Frederick William I of Prussia spoke for the majority of his contemporaries when he justified the liquidation of the Brandenburg colonies with the words that 'he had always regarded world commerce as a chimera'.

It is an amazing spectacle to watch the poor and insignificant Electorate of Brandenburg gain the hegemony over North Germany, oust the house of Hapsburg from the leadership of Germany and Central Europe, and eventually reach the status of a world power. Brandenburg-Prussia owed its rise to power less than other countries to the favour of its geographical situation, wealth of natural resources, or industrial activities of its population. The original march of Brandenburg was merely created to protect the bishoprics of Magdeburg, Brandenburg and Havelberg. It was remote from the centres of international affairs and the great trade-routes; it lacked metal mines, salt-pits and timber; its sandy soil was unsuited for intensive agriculture and for horticulture. The twin-town of Cölln-Berlin, its capital, was amongst the least important Hanse towns; the University of Frankfurt-on-the-Oder, founded in 1506, contributed little to science and learning. The population was a mixture of autochthonic Slavs and German colonists; only the townspeople, not very numerous, were of pure German stock. The Slav nobility and peasantry accepted the Christian religion and German hegemony in the twelfth century. The nobles thus kept their privileged position and soon fused with the German knights, as did the Slav and German nobles in neighbouring Mecklenburg: the East Elbian Junkers are their direct descendants. The German peasants came into the country as freeholders; the Junkers reduced them to a state of, first virtual, from 1653 legal, serfdom such as existed in Poland and Russia. The almost unlimited power of the lord of the manor is one of the most characteristic features of Brandenburg. All the political and administrative reforms of the nineteenth and twentieth centuries could not stamp it out completely. This relation of lord and serf was carried over to the army and administration. The despotic authority which the officer held over the rank and file, and the state official over the humble subject, was modelled on the godlike superiority which the Junker maintained over the servile fieldhands on his paternal manor farm.

The secularization of the Brandenburg bishoprics (1540) strengthened the position of the Hohenzollerns on the middle Elbe, and the acquisition of Pomerania (1648) that on the lower Oder. Neither expansion was in itself a deviation from the established course of Brandenburg policy. The turn was brought about when the Electors acquired Cleves and Mark in the extreme west, and Prussia beyond the eastern frontiers of the Empire. Brandenburg thus extended her sphere of interest from Memel to Wesel, and became involved in international problems which had been unknown to her former rulers. Prussian historians have always been anxious to vindicate the mystic 'mission' of their country, and to justify it on national, geographic and moral grounds. In actual fact, the Brandenburg-Prussian state, such as it developed from the middle of the seventeenth century, is entirely artificial. It is the deliberate creation of three of her rulers and the servant-master of three others, namely the Great Elector Frederick William, the kings Frederick William I and Frederick II, and the chancellor Otto von Bismarck. These four men, and they alone, have made Prussia and Prusso-Germany idolized by its friends and henchmen, detested by its critics and opponents: an eternal stranger in the European comity of nations. The natural resources of the country proved insufficient for the ambitious role that these men assigned to it once they themselves disappeared from the stage. Under the successor of the Great Elector Brandenburg relapsed into the modest state of an ambitious, but powerless, Estate of the Empire. The Prussia of Frederick the Great met its catastrophe at Jena (1806), and the prussianized Germany of Bismarck ended at Versailles (1919). In each case the bold schemes of the Prussian leaders had outstripped the actual ability and, one may add, the historic destiny of the country. Prussia's great men were at the same time her evil geniuses. For Germany the increase of Prussian power was disastrous. The Great Elector deserted the Empire in its struggle with Louis XIV and assisted France in strengthening her position on the upper Rhine. Frederick the Great made the loss of Alsace and Lorraine irrevocable. By robbing Austria of her most prosperous German province, Silesia, he initiated the final break-up of the Hapsburg Empire, the homeland of twenty-one German Emperors. The partition of Poland which Frederick suggested burdened his country with a moral stain which it was never to live down. Bismarck finally expelled Austria from Germany, made the latter an appendage of Greater Prussia, and thus terminated the peculiar German contribution to European civilization.

The peace of Westphalia brought the Elector Frederick William more territorial gains than any other German prince, thanks to his well-timed desertion to the Swedes. He was disappointed, however, at having failed to obtain the whole of Jülich-Cleves and Pomerania. Henceforth his policy was primarily dictated by the wish to acquire the portions which had fallen to Neuburg and Sweden respectively. While the committee for the execution of the peace of Westphalia was still sitting at Nuremberg, Frederick William suddenly invaded

Jülich (June 1651). This treacherous act, however, miscarried. The Estates of the dukedom, including those of the Brandenburg portion, resisted his blandishments and threats; and the Emperor, Spain and Poland intervened at once against the disturber of the peace that had been brought about with so many difficulties. This resolute action of the Emperor rather appealed to the Elector, the more so as Sweden, his ally, had, most justifiably, not supported his enterprise. He therefore went over to the Emperor, gave his vote to the election of Ferdinand IV and received in return the imperial support in the final delimitation of the frontiers of Pomerania (1653). During the following years, George Frederick of Waldeck directed the policy of Brandenburg. He advocated a close collaboration with the Rhenish Alliance, France and Sweden; and aimed at raising Brandenburg to the leadership of the anti-Hapsburg forces of the Empire; his ideas materialized a century later in the Princes' League which Frederick II brought about in 1785. Waldeck and Frederick William realized that their policy might result in the break-up of the Empire; but they thought of the gains which Brandenburg would make in that eventuality and were ready to accept the risk. Before these schemes matured, Waldeck fell into disgrace (1658), and henceforth the anti-Swedish policy prevailed. Nevertheless, Waldeck made for himself a name in Brandenburg history, for the reorganization of the central administration which he carried out in 1651 remained the basis of the Prussian state until its collapse in 1806.

It was the Nordic war of 1655–60 that deflected Frederick William from the plans outlined by Waldeck, if indeed he ever intended to carry them out. When Charles X Gustavus of Zweibrücken succeeded the daughter of Gustavus Adolphus on the Swedish throne (1654), John II of Poland renewed his claims to the inheritance of the Vasa dynasty of which he was the last male descendant. As the liegeman of the Polish fief of Prussia, the Elector of Brandenburg was deeply interested in the outcome of this struggle. Waldeck urged him to throw in his lot with Sweden and take his part in the destruction of Poland. Before Frederick William made up his mind, Charles X routed the Polish army, and then compelled the Elector to accept his own terms: Frederick William had to change his suzerain and receive Prussia as a Swedish fief. Threatened by a fresh Polish army, the Swedish king shortly afterwards conceded better conditions to the Elector: he was to receive four Polish provinces after their common victory. In the three-day battle of Warsaw (28–30 July 1656) the allied forces gained a brilliant victory over the more numerous Poles; a battle which was afterwards regarded as the Prussian army's baptism of fire. At this juncture the Emperor, Russia and Denmark intervened on behalf of Poland. In his predicament, Charles X now released Frederick William from his feudal obligations (20 Nov. 1656). Having thus been recognized by the Swedes as the sovereign of Prussia, the Elector turned to the anti-Swedish coalition in order to make his gain secure. He made an alliance with Poland, and the Polish king in his turn renounced his suzerainty over Prussia and ceded a few districts bordering on Eastern Pomerania (6 Nov. 1657). Thereupon Frederick William voted for the Archduke Leopold at the election of 1658, and took an active part in the war against his former ally. At the head of an allied army he expelled the Swedes from Denmark and took the strongly fortified island of Alsen (Dec. 1658)—a feat of arms which the Prussian troops were to repeat two hundred years later (1864). In 1659, the Elector conquered almost the whole of Swedish Pomerania and hoped for its final acquisition. At this moment, however, France terminated her long strife with Spain (7 Nov. 1659) and at once cast her weight in favour of her old ally Sweden. In the peace treaty of Oliva (3 May 1660), Sweden was given back all her losses, and Frederick William had to be content with the general recognition of his sovereignty in Prussia, and the small gains of 1657.

Frederick William spent the next years in strengthening his personal rule and unifying his possessions as far as possible. A mail-service between Memel and Cleves was established in 1660. The privileges of the Brandenburg Estates fell into abeyance; and the diet of 1653, which confirmed the villainage of the peasants, was the last ever to be held in the Electorate. The Elector was less successful in establishing his absolutism in the Rhenish-Westphalian provinces of Cleves, Mark and Ravensberg. Here, the Estates maintained some of their privileges and were never reduced to the complete submission of the East Elbian parts of the monarchy. The victory of the sovereign was most complete in Prussia. The Prussian Estates disputed the validity of the declaration of full sovereignty and maintained political contact with Poland—once their right, now regarded as high treason. Frederick William proceeded with brutal energy. The leaders of the opposition were imprisoned for life or beheaded; taxes were levied by military raids, and dragonnades broke the spirit of resistance. By 1674 Prussia was completely subdued. The standing army—*miles perpetuus* as it was called—and the fresh taxes which were required for its maintenance were put under the central administration. The Junkers, moreover, were exempted from the common tax of the excise, which therefore fell exclusively on the towns. The reason for this unjust system of taxation, which lasted well into the nineteenth century, was that the sovereign needed the Junkers as officers for his expanding army. They thus gained indirectly in their social and economic status what they lost in direct political influence.

For ten years, 1657–67, Frederick William kept his alliance with Austria. When he renewed it in 1666, he was, however, already at work to reconcile France. On 15 Dec. 1667, he concluded the first of a long series of treaties and alliances with Louis XIV. Their provisions were in every case much the same: Frederick William was to prevent the Empire from taking active steps against France; he had to allow French troops the benefit of his benevolent neutrality, or even to take an active part on the French side if so required. Furthermore, he promised to vote for the election of Louis XIV or the Dauphin at the next vacancy of the imperial throne. In return, Louis undertook to pay for the Brandenburg army in peace and war, and to grant a handsome yearly pension to the Elector himself.

At the beginning of this close co-operation, Frederick William tried twice to evade his obligations, and sold himself to the States-General and the Hapsburgs for a higher sum. The first of these escapades was speedily settled: in the peace of Vossem (6 June 1673), Louis treated Frederick William's defection as a misunderstanding and simply outbid the Dutch. When Brandenburg nevertheless concluded an alliance with the Emperor (1 July 1674), Louis caused his Swedish allies to invade the march of Brandenburg. Frederick William hurried back from the Rhenish theatre of war and routed the Swedes at Fehrbellin (28 June 1675); from this day it became the habit to call him the Great Elector. In the course of the next years, the whole of Pomerania was conquered, and a Swedish invasion into Prussia repelled. When, however, the Dutch, Spaniards, Emperor and Empire each made their separate peace with France, Frederick William had eventually to follow suit. The peace of St Germain (29 June 1679) restored Pomerania to Sweden, France repaid Brandenburg's war expenses, and the 'close alliance' of 25 Oct. bound Frederick William more closely than ever to the triumphal chariot of Louis XIV.

On the whole, Louis XIV proved the sole gainer in this partnership. Thanks to the support of Brandenburg he acquired the southern fringe of the Spanish Netherlands, Franche-Comté (1678) and Freiburg (1679); and he was also allowed to pursue his policy of 'Réunions' (1679-86), in the course of which he took the greater part of Alsace, including Strasbourg (1681), the Saar district (1680) and Luxemburg (1684). All these districts were part of the Empire and at the time inhabited by a German population, so that the German Empire and nation were the victims of the policy of the Great Elector. This fact must be stressed, as Prussian historiographers have always been anxious to represent Frederick William as a champion of German nationality. The Elector himself liked to parade in this disguise when it suited his purpose. His war propaganda against Sweden was entirely tuned to the phrase: 'Remember you're a German!' One of his pamphleteers 'summarized' the political situation of Germany by the broad hint that 'everything was lost' when Brandenburg failed to obtain 'glorious Pomerania'; thus revealing somewhat imprudently the chief aim for which the Great Elector wanted the 'honest German' to fight. Frederick William absented himself from the greatest enterprise that united the Empire in modern times, namely the defence of Vienna against the Turks in 1683. His professed German patriotism failed him in this hour of supreme need.

Nor can he be given more credit for his alleged Protestant fervour. It is true, he answered the revocation of the Edict of Nantes (18 Oct. 1685) by the Edict of Potsdam (8 Nov.), which granted the Huguenot refugees an asylum in Brandenburg. Shortly afterwards he even concluded an alliance with Sweden in which he renounced his claims to Pomerania (20 Feb. 1686) and a secret alliance with the Emperor against France (22 March). There can, however, be little doubt that Frederick William would have abandoned the French alliance in any case. Louis XIV had achieved all his aims, when the Emperor and Empire recognized the Réunions (15 Aug. 1684); the Brandenburg ally therefore lost his former value and Louis showed less sympathy towards his financial exactions. The revocation of the Edict of Nantes therefore gave Frederick William a welcome pretext for changing sides, and he made the most of its religious propaganda value. In reality he was the first Protestant ruler to unleash in his territories a Church conflict of unprecedented bitterness. Wishing to make the Lutheran and Reformed Churches conform to his state absolutism, he proceeded against the recalcitrant clergy of both denominations by prohibiting their sermons, suppressing their publications, and meting out disciplinary punishment. His noblest victim was Paul Gerhardt, the greatest poet of Protestant hymns next to Luther.

Frederick William's alliance with the Catholic Emperor suffices to throw doubt on the strength of his Protestant feeling in renouncing the French alliance. On this occasion Brandenburg regiments joined the imperial army in Hungary and shared in the storming of Budapest on 2 Sept. 1686. The Great Elector showed himself as eager to combat Louis XIV as he had been to support him. With his nephew, William III of Orange, he discussed the plan of the latter's expedition to England. The watchwords he passed to the Potsdam palace-guard on the last two days of his life were 'London' and 'Amsterdam'. He died on 9 May 1688.

His significance for the growth of Prussia cannot be rated too highly. In the enormous standing army he laid the foundation on which the power of Prussia was built by Frederick the Great. It surpassed the needs and nearly exceeded the economic capacity and man-power of his country. With this army he left behind him the propensity for expansion at anybody else's cost and the tradition of a statecraft to which solemn treaties and alliances were so many scraps of paper, to be discarded whenever the true or imaginary interests of Prussia so required.

The rise of the house of Hohenzollern in North Germany coincided with the foundation of the Austro-Hungarian monarchy in the South-East. Until the middle of the seventeenth century, the component parts of the Hapsburg monarchy were knitted together very loosely; the common dynasty was the strongest, almost the only, bond. Bohemia, Silesia and Moravia were the first countries in which, after the Battle of the White Hill (1620), absolutism was established. In the Austrian crown-lands the Church and nobility retained some of their privileges. Hungary remained an elective kingdom, and the Magyar nobles jealously guarded their excessive privileges. But the Hungary of the Hapsburgs was confined to a narrow strip of land on the eastern borders of Austria and Moravia, while the greater part was still in the hands of the Turks. Next to the dynasty, the Roman Church and the new aristocracy worked for unity. The Hapsburg countries were expressly exempted from the clause in the peace of Westphalia concerning religious freedom, and therefore remained uniformly Roman Catholic. The Protestants had to wait till 1781 before obtaining toleration, and till 1861 for equality of rights. During the Thirty Years War, many noblemen from all over Europe sought service with the Emperor. They now formed a new Hapsburg nobility, whose fortune was bound up with the dynasty, and who were entirely free from the regionalistic sentiment of the native landed gentry. The kinship with the royal house of Spain and frequent inter-marriage with Italian dynasties increased the Romanizing tendencies of the court of Vienna. While the rest of Germany fell under the spell of the Versailles of Louis XIV, Spanish and Italian influences prevailed in art and music, poetry and society in Austria. These foreign suggestions and models blended with the strong artistic and musical talents of the Austrian people. The outcome was the peculiar Austrian baroque of which the architecture of Fischer von Erlach and Lukas Hildebrandt, and the music of Gluck, Haydn and Mozart, are the perfect expression.

Ever since Francis I of France had entered into an alliance with the Sultan against Charles V, Franco-Turkish co-operation was the paramount danger threatening the Hapsburg monarchy simultaneously in the East and West. The rebellion of the Magyar magnates in 1670, the guerilla warfare in Upper Hungary from 1678 to 1682, and finally the great advance of the Turks against Vienna in 1683, were planned in concert with Louis XIV and coincided with French attacks on the Rhine. The threat to the bulwark of Western civilization and Christianity, however, led to a last revival of the spirit of the medieval crusades, to which even Louis XIV had to give way. He refrained from an active support of the Turks, and thus made possible the glorious victory of a truly European army over the infidels at the Kahlenberg (12 Sept. 1683). Under the nominal leadership of King John III Sobieski of Poland and the actual command of Duke Charles V of Lorraine, Austrians and Hungarians, Poles, Saxons, Bavarians, and the contingents of the Empire, Catholics and Protestants, fought shoulder to shoulder. Individual volunteers from all over Europe swelled the ranks of this last genuine crusade which Pope Innocent XI had worked so hard to set on foot.

Military and religious enthusiasm did not abate until, with the conquest of Belgrade by Max Emanuel of Bavaria (6 Sept. 1688), the whole of Hungary and Transylvania had been freed. On 9 Dec. 1687, Joseph, the eldest son of the Emperor, was crowned hereditary king of Hungary. The independent status of Hungary was confirmed, but the Magyars renounced their right of resistance and recognized the right of succession of the male line of the Austrian and Spanish Hapsburgs.

The court of Vienna cherished excessive hopes. The Venetians took Athens (1687), and in 1689 Margrave Louis of Baden, the imperial generalissimo, advanced as far as Nish and Bucharest. The revival of the Eastern Empire and the reunion of the Roman and Greek Churches seemed within reach. However, the Orthodox Christians did not want to be liberated, only to be at once subdued, by the Roman Emperor and Pope. They directed their supplications to the orthodox Tsar, Peter I (1689–1725), who was about to regenerate Holy Russia. The antagonism between Austria-Hungary and Russia, which was to dominate the history of Eastern Europe and the Balkans in the nineteenth and beginning of the twentieth centuries, was ushered in. Russia was, however, as yet too weak to set herself against powerful Austria. Further advance of the Austrian army was rendered impossible by a fresh attack of the French upon the Empire. In September 1687 French troops suddenly invaded Cologne and the Palatinate. Louvois's order *Brûlez le Palatinat!* made the garden of Germany a desolate heap of ruins; the debris of Heidelberg castle is the most conspicuous reminder of a vandalism unparalleled between the times of Nebuchadrezzar and Hitler. For the first time, a genuine national hatred of the French swept Germany. It was an easy matter for William III of England to bring together the Grand Alliance of practically all European states against the peace-breaker of Versailles. Nevertheless, Louis XIV's military power and diplomatic skill were still great enough to secure for himself quite favourable conditions at the peace of Rijswijk (1697). To the Emperor and Empire he ceded little, Freiburg and Breisach to the former, Philippsburg and Kehl to the latter, whereas Strasbourg and Alsace remained French for good.

The war in the West brought the operations against the Turks to a standstill after the battle of Szlankamen (1691), in which Louis of Baden beat the Turkish army led by a staff of French officers. They were taken up again with great vigour in 1697 when Prince Eugene of Savoy was appointed imperial commander-in-chief. Eugene was the son of a niece of Cardinal Mazarin, Louis XIV's prime minister; snubbed by Louis, he entered the service of the Emperor in 1683, and became the greatest general in the history of the Austrian army. Eugene's victory at Zenta (11 Sept. 1697) led to the peace of Carlowitz (26 Jan. 1699). Turkey ceded Hungary, Transylvania, Croatia and Slavonia to Austria; Podolia to Poland; and the Peloponnese to Venice. Confined to the Balkan peninsula, Turkey ceased to be the terror of the Christian world. Austria's position in South-Eastern Europe was firmly established.

There was, however, no time left to pursue the Eastern policy with full vigour, as the problem of the Spanish succession required the undivided attention of the court of Vienna. Charles II, the last male descendant of the Spanish line of the Hapsburgs (1665–1700), had been an invalid from childhood and had no offspring, so that his two sisters and their issue were the legitimate successors. The eldest sister was married to Louis XIV, but had renounced her claim to the throne on her marriage, and this renunciation was confirmed in the peace of the Pyrenees (1659). The younger sister was the wife of Leopold I, and her father had confirmed her right of succession in his testament. She died in 1673, and the only child of the imperial pair had married the Elector Max Emanuel of Bavaria in 1685. The Electoral Prince of Bavaria was therefore the exclusive heir of the Spanish possessions, and Charles II recognized him as such in his testament of 1698. In spite of the legitimate claims of the Wittelsbachs and the less valid but powerfully supported aspirations of the Bourbons, Leopold was eager to secure the rich inheritance for his dynasty. He relied on the numerous family compacts according to which the Hapsburg possessions were never to be alienated from the dynasty. He made his daughter assign her rights to himself and the sons of his second marriage, and promised to compensate the Wittelsbachs with the Spanish Netherlands. However, the Spanish Cortes refused to recognize the validity of this agreement. Leopold further weakened his legal position by offering Louis XIV a partition of the Spanish monarchy, and thus abandoning the maxim of the exclusive rights of the Hapsburg dynasty. Maximilian I of Bavaria and afterwards John Philip of Mayence had been the first to propose partition: from 1689, William III was its principal champion. Partition was considered the best means of adjusting the claims of the various parties; furthermore, it would prevent the Hapsburgs as well as the Bourbons from gaining an exclusive ascendancy over the rest of Europe. The first partition treaty which William III induced all the claimants to accept (Oct. 1698) made the Electoral Prince of Bavaria the heir of Spain, her colonies, and the Spanish Netherlands, while Charles, Leopold's second son, was to obtain Milan, and the French Dauphin Naples and Sicily. The untimely death of the little Electoral Prince upset this scheme (Feb. 1699). William III then drew up a second partition treaty (March 1700). It provided that the Archduke Charles should become the principal heir, while the Dauphin was to have Milan in addition to Naples and Sicily, with the proviso that Milan should be exchanged for Lorraine. Leopold, flushed by his successes in the Balkans, now rejected the idea of partition and refused to ratify the treaty. The Spaniards themselves were deeply hurt by the casual way in which their proud and ancient monarchy was made the object of international bargaining. The united efforts of the Pope and the French diplomatists prevailed in the end: Charles II appointed Duke Philip of Anjou, younger son of the Dauphin, his residuary legatee and died shortly afterwards (1 Nov. 1700). The Spaniards immediately recognized Philip V as their lawful king. The Emperor took up arms at once, and Prince Eugene advanced in Upper Italy. However, the Anglo-Austrian alliance of the Hague (7 Sept. 1701) implicitly recognized Philip V as king of Spain, as it asserted that the French and Spanish crowns should never be united in one hand; on the other hand, Austria was to obtain Italy and Belgium, and the East and West Indies were to go to the Maritime Powers. The war was made inevitable through the folly of Louis XIV. At the death-bed of James II (16 Sept.) he recognized James III as king of Great Britain and thus openly challenged the Act of Settlement just passed in Parliament. Louis thereby roused the English nation to a supreme effort for the defence of their constitution and the defiance of the French hegemony. On 4 May 1702, two months after the death of William III, England declared war upon France and Spain.

The Emperor gained the support of Brandenburg, the most powerful Estate of the Empire from the military point of view, by conceding royal dignity to the Elector Frederick III. On 18 Jan. 1701, the *Roi mercenaire*, as Frederick the Great called him, crowned himself at Königsberg as Frederick I king in Prussia. The Empire declared war on Philip of Anjou (28 Sept. 1702). Only Max Emanuel of Bavaria and his brother, the Archbishop-Elector of Cologne, sided with Louis, from whom they hoped for a greater reward than was to be expected from the Hapsburgs. The armies of the allies were victorious in every theatre of war as soon as Prince Eugene was appointed commander-in-chief of the imperial forces (1703). In conjunction with the duke of Marlborough, the greatest military and political genius England has produced, he inflicted upon the French and Bavarian armies the defeats of Blenheim (13 Aug. 1704), Oudenaarde (11 July 1708) and Malplaquet (11 Sept. 1709). Hanoverian troops took the seemingly impregnable rock of Gibraltar (1704). From October 1705 Charles III resided at Barcelona, protected by the English navy, and for a while (June–Oct. 1706) even in Madrid. Eugene secured Italy by the victory of Turin (7 Sept. 1706). At this juncture, the Emperor Joseph I (1705–11) made a curious attempt to vindicate the imperial rights in Italy. As Pope Clement XI was a partisan of France, Joseph annexed the papal dependencies of Parma and Piacenza as forfeited fiefs of the Empire (1706). He was excommunicated, but his troops invaded the pontifical state. The Maritime Powers, which did not want a further extension of the theatre of war, intervened (1709), and this anachronistic feud between the nominal heads of the Christian commonwealth had no further consequences.

Despite the military successes of the allies Prince Eugene realized that it was beyond their power completely to reduce France and Spain. Louis XIV, too, would have welcomed an acceptable compromise in view of the heavy losses in the field and the financial exhaustion of France. Negotiations were begun, but the presumption of the reigning Whig coterie in London frustrated every attempt to come to an agreement. The sudden death of Joseph I (17 April 1711) changed the situation fundamentally. As he died without male issue, Charles III of Spain, his younger brother, succeeded him. A revival of the monarchy of Charles V, however, was the last thing the Maritime Powers could wish for. Robert Harley, created earl of Oxford, replaced the Whig administration and at once entered into secret negotiations with France. The duke of Marlborough was dismissed from the supreme command (31 Dec. 1711). Prince Eugene went to London on a diplomatic mission, but was unsuccessful, although he was feted by the populace as no foreigner before, and only Garibaldi after him. England, Holland, Savoy and Prussia came to a very advantageous agreement with France. The peace of Utrecht (1713) gave Nova Scotia, New Brunswick, Newfoundland, Gibraltar and Minorca to England, a barrier of Belgian fortresses to Holland, Sicily to Savoy (exchanged for Sardinia in 1720), and Upper Gelderland and Neuchâtel to Prussia. Charles VI refused to accede to the treaty, and continued the war despite the warnings of Prince Eugene. He yielded only after the loss of Freiburg and Landau to the victorious French. The peace of Rastatt (7 March 1714) brought him the Spanish Netherlands and the Italian possessions of the Spanish crown, i.e. Naples, Sardinia, Tuscany and Milan. For a hundred and fifty years to come Austria was to exercise the predominant role in Italy; but in the end Italy proved a liability which contributed much to the final disruption of the Hapsburg monarchy. The imperial diet which was requested to cede Landau to France, objected strongly, but had eventually to yield, being abandoned by everybody else (peace of Baden, 7 Sept. 1714).

The Turks, with whom the peace of Carlovitz was still rankling, missed the opportunity of the Spanish war to act in concert with France. In 1714, however, they hurled themselves on the weak outposts of Venice and recovered the Peloponnese. The Republic of St Mark and the Pope appealed to Austria for help. Prince Eugene led the imperial army in his most brilliant campaign. The victory of Peterwardein (5 Aug. 1716) and the capture of Belgrade (18 Aug. 1717), leading to the peace of Passarovitz (21 July 1718), represent the high-water marks of his career. Austria now obtained the Banat of Timisoara, the last missing corner of Hungary, North Serbia including Belgrade, and Little Walachia, the western part of Rumania; while the Peloponnese remained Turkish for one more century.

At the time when the French hegemony over Western Europe was seriously impaired, Sweden, France's old ally, lost her status as a European great power. Frederick IV of Denmark, Frederick Augustus of Saxony and Poland, and Peter I of Russia expected an easy walk-over when they simultaneously attacked South Sweden and the Swedish possessions in Livonia and Estonia (1700). The military genius of the eighteen-year old King Charles XII, however, frustrated their plans. Denmark was speedily compelled to make peace (18 Aug.), the Saxons were expelled from the Baltic, and the Russians were defeated at Narva (30 Nov. 1700). Charles invaded Poland, had Stanislaus Lesczynski, a willing tool of Swedish and French diplomacy, elected king, and after further defeats of Russians and Saxons conquered the whole of Saxony. In the peace of Altranstädt near Leipzig (24 Sept. 1706) Frederick Augustus had to renounce the Polish crown in favour of Charles's protégé. Charles XII, however, not satisfied with these successes, wanted to bring Russia to her knees and suffered the fate of all invaders of Russia. While he was a virtual prisoner of the Turks after his defeat at Poltava, the anti-Swedish coalition revived (1709). Frederick Augustus of Saxony recovered Poland, the Danes invaded Sweden, and Peter I established himself in the Baltic, where he had previously founded his new capital, St Petersburg (1703). After the close of the war of the Spanish succession Prussia and Hanover joined the allies. Charles XII was killed in the vain attempt to expel the Danes from Norway (11 Dec. 1718); and his successor had to conclude the humiliating treaties of Stockholm (1720) and Nystadt (1721). Sweden lost her Baltic provinces to Russia, Pomerania between the rivers Oder and Peene to Prussia, her possessions in Slesvig to

Denmark, and Bremen and Verden to Hanover. However, Sweden was not annihilated as Russia and Prussia had intended. France intervened on behalf of her old ally, and England wanted to curb the ascent of Russia, in whom the cabinet of St James correctly recognized an antagonist who was to grow more formidable than Sweden. Russia and Prussia had therefore to restore Finland, Western Pomerania, the island of Rügen, and the port of Wismar. Sweden kept these territories until the beginning of the nineteenth century; the suzerainty over Wismar was redeemed as late as 1903. The end of the Spanish and Nordic wars also decided the fate of Bavaria and Saxony. The restoration of Max Emanuel in the former and of Frederick Augustus in the latter was a meagre compensation for the losses in man-power and the ruin of the public finances which the two countries had suffered during twenty years of warfare. The dream of playing a decisive part in European politics was at an end at Munich as well as Dresden.

At the same time, the foundations were laid upon which Prussia rose from the status of an Estate of the Empire to that of a European power. Frederick William I, son of the first Prussian king, created the military and bureaucratic machinery which has ever since embodied the spirit of Prussia. Frederick I had been as unscrupulous as the Great Elector in selling himself and his army to the highest bidder. This was, in his case, the Grand Alliance of the Emperor, Holland and England. Unlike his father, however, he was interested in the arts of peace and the pleasures of life rather than in military glory and territorial expansion. At the instigation of his Hanoverian queen, a sister of George I, the Berlin academies of art and sciences were founded; Leibniz became the first president of the latter. Andreas Schlüter, one of the greatest architects and sculptors of the baroque period, built and decorated the Berlin Arsenal and cast the equestrian statue of the Great Elector, one of the noblest monuments of its kind. All these beginnings of a higher civilization were cut off the moment Frederick William I succeeded his father (1713).

A rigid absolutism was strictly put into force. The royal 'sovereignty was established like a *rocher de bronze*', as Frederick William proclaimed. Prussian absolutism, however, was widely different from the absolutism of Versailles, Vienna, or the small German courts. There was no outward splendour, no patronage of art and literature, no court festivities. Parsimony and stinginess became permanent features of Prussian administration. The civil service was characterized by an iron discipline and absolute incorruptibility, but also by blind obedience and dread of assuming responsibility. Empty titles and decorations, and the feeling of their self-importance, were the chief reward of the underpaid bureaucrats. The proverbial saying *travailler pour le roi de Prusse* was an equivalent of 'working for nothing'. The sole interest of the king and his advisers was concentrated upon the army. It was a microcosm of its own, rigidly separated from the civil population. The most rigorous discipline was enforced, with the goose-step as its outward and visible sign; and the soldier was expected to fear his officer more than the enemy. The army alone of all state departments was grudged no claims to the public revenue. It had consisted of 40,000 men on a war footing under Frederick I; the soldier-king raised the peace footing to 80,000 men, i.e. 10 per cent of the entire population. All the other state departments were rigidly subordinated to the requirements of the army. Its maintenance was made the principal task of the treasury. Compulsory school-attendance was ordered (though not effected) in 1717, because the army wanted a host of non-commissioned officers who had mastered the three R's. After a heavy outbreak of the plague, peasants were settled in the deserted districts of East Prussia, and large-scale ameliorations of bogs and sandy plains were subsidized, because the village supplied the army with the fittest recruits. The manufacture of cloth was encouraged, because the army had to be properly clothed. Industrial life as a whole, with protectionist tariffs here and freedom of trade there, was regulated according to the diverse needs of the commissariat. It is significant that the central administration which Frederick William reorganized in 1722 was called the Directory of War and Domains. The king spared neither himself nor anybody else when the supreme interest of the state as he saw it was concerned. He felt deeply his own responsibility toward God and was sincere in his endeavour to spread His kingdom on earth. But he conceived the Kingdom of God as a vast parade-ground, surrounded by barracks and offices. He himself was God's vicar more absolutely than any Pope has ever claimed to be: 'Salvation belongs to God, everything else must be mine', is a characteristic saying of his. Once the religious and monarchical coverings had worn off, the undisguised deification of brute force was the inevitable outcome of this conception of the state and its head. When Frederick William I died (31 May 1740), he left to his successor the most perfectly adapted instruments of autocracy: the Prussian army and administration.

The thorough militarization of Prussia could have no other purpose but war, yet it is amazing how little the cabinets of Europe realized it. Apart from occasional flirtations with England which never lasted long, Frederick William kept up friendly relations with the Emperor and Russia. In the short war of the Polish succession (1733–35), Prussia, Russia, the Emperor and the Empire fought for the interests of Frederick Augustus III of Saxony, whereas France, Spain and the Wittelsbach Electors of Bavaria, Cologne and the Palatinate supported Stanislaus Lesczynski, father-in-law of Louis XV. In the end, the Elector of Saxony gained the Polish crown. Austria ceded Lorraine to Stanislaus, after whose death (1766) it went definitely to France; and she lost the two Sicilies, which were made a kingdom under a prince of the Spanish line of the Bourbons. Francis Stephen, duke of Lorraine, was to be compensated for the loss of his patrimony with Tuscany, where the last Medici died in 1737. A greater prospect opened up before him when he married Maria Theresa, the heiress of the Austro-Hapsburg possessions, in 1736.

The Austro-Russian co-operation proved equally futile, as far as Austria was concerned, in the war with the Turks which Russia began in 1735 and the Emperor joined in 1737. The victorious Turks recovered Serbia, including Belgrade and Walachia (peace of Belgrade, 18 Sept. 1739).

These severe losses in the Balkans, Italy and the West were overshadowed by a greater threat to the house of Austria and, implicitly, to the Empire. Charles VI, who in 1711 was recalled from Spain to succeed his brother, Joseph I, was the last male descendant of the house of Hapsburg. As the Salic Law excluded women from the succession, Charles was from the first to the last day of his long reign (1711–40) concerned above everything else with securing the right of succession for his eldest daughter, Maria Theresa, and with having this alteration guaranteed by international treaties. In 1713 he issued the family statute of the Pragmatic Sanction which provided for the succession of Maria Theresa and her children after her to the Austrian possessions. The daughters of Joseph I were expressly excluded. Charles's only son, who might have made all these regulations superfluous, died shortly after he was born (1716). In vain Prince Eugene suggested that Charles should set Austria in a state of military preparedness against any disputants of his will. Charles, who like his ancestor Frederick III was at once stubborn and irresolute, put his trust in diplomatic agreements which, as it turned out afterwards, were not worth the paper they were written on. Moreover, he bought the guarantee of the Pragmatic Sanction at a high cost. The status of Hungary as an elective kingdom had to be confirmed, and constitutional disputes with the Magyars never ceased to trouble the chancery of Vienna until 1918. Spain was to be won over by the cession of Naples and Sicily, France by that of Lorraine. The Maritime Powers were placated by the sacrifice of the East India Company which Prince Eugene had established at Ostend.

The extinction of the Hapsburg dynasty involved also a serious problem as regards the succession to the imperial crown, which had been *de facto* hereditary in the house of Hapsburg since 1438. Prior to that the change from one dynasty to another had been fatal again and again to a consistent imperial policy. For the last three hundred years, the patrimonial possessions of the Hapsburgs had been a solid mainstay, though often the only one, of the imperial dignity; the more so since every other means of maintaining the supreme authority had dwindled away. Charles VI sought to uphold dynastic continuity by obtaining the imperial crown for his son-in-law, Francis Stephen of Lorraine. But, although Prussia and the imperial diet ratified the Pragmatic Sanction, the Electors of Bavaria and Saxony refused to abandon their claims to the Hapsburg possessions. They were married to the two daughters of Joseph I and therefore considered their rights better founded than those of Maria Theresa.

When Charles VI died on 20 October 1740, unlamented by his family and his subjects, the guarantors of the Pragmatic Sanction at once went back on their solemn signatures. Only the Austrian crown-lands and Hungary kept faith with the queen of Bohemia and Hungary, as Maria Theresa was styled. She had to assert her rights in the eight years' War of the Austrian Succession (1740–48).

Russia was kept inactive, as the Empress Anne died eight days after Charles VI; and her successor, Ivan VI, was a minor. Prussia struck the first blow: Frederick II overran Silesia in a few weeks, and his field-marshal Schwerin warded off an Austrian army at Mollwitz (10 April 1741). This success paved the way for a number of treaties between Prussia, France, Spain, Bavaria, Saxony, Hanover and Sweden. Bavaria was to receive the Austrian Alpine countries and Bohemia; Upper Silesia and Moravia were allotted to Saxony; Prussia was to obtain Lower Silesia and the Bohemian county of Glatz. The Prussian lawyers hastened to prove the legal claims of the Hohenzollerns to Silesia; but Frederick did not delude himself about his rights. He boldly stated his maxim: 'If there is anything to be gained by being honest, we will be honest; and if it be necessary to dupe, we will be rogues.' He and George II of England exerted themselves to have Charles Albert of Bavaria elected emperor. On 15 Sept. 1741, he received homage as archduke of Austria at Linz; on 19 Dec., he was crowned king of Bohemia at Prague, undeterred by the fate of the previous 'Winter King' of his family; and on 24 Jan. 1742, he was unanimously elected emperor. Although the Pope hastened to recognize him, the bid for the imperial crown brought nothing but misfortune upon the third Wittelsbach Emperor. On the day of his coronation by his brother, the archbishop of Cologne, the Austrians occupied his capital, Munich (12 Feb.). Three years later Charles VII died in misery and despair, and his successor hastened to make his peace with Maria Theresa. Her husband was elected emperor under the name of Francis I, Brandenburg and the Palatinate being the only dissenting Electors (13 Sept. 1745). George II now exerted himself as strongly for him as he had done against him in 1742, for the rapid advance of Prince Charles Edward made a speedy liquidation of the continental war most desirable. Thus, the short interlude of the Wittelsbach emperor resulted only in a further weakening of the imperial position and the permanent antagonism of Prussia and Austria. It was clear by now that the future of Germany would be decided between these two powers.

Meanwhile Frederick II had scored a great triumph. Without regard to his French, Bavarian and Saxon allies, he concluded the preliminary peace of Breslau, followed by the definite peace of Berlin (28 July 1742). Alarmed by French expansion in Central Europe, Britain had drawn nearer to Austria, and the British diplomatist, Lord Hyndford, took an active part in these negotiations. Prussia obtained Silesia and the strategically important county of Glatz. Austria retained some districts of Upper Silesia: they were just those upon which Frederick had based his alleged title for his invasion.

The Maritime Powers, Hanover, Hesse and Austria now combined against France. George II took the command of their so-called Pragmatic Army, and defeated the French at Dettingen near Frankfurt (27 June 1743). It was the last battle in which an English king took command. When Sardinia and Saxony joined the Pragmatic Alliance, Frederick thought it best to save the French from a final defeat. In August 1744, he marched into Bohemia. The pretext for this unprovoked attack was twofold. He maintained that the Allies had made a secret treaty which provided for the recovery of Silesia, and he posed as the champion of the Emperor, Charles VII, and the integrity of the Empire. This was untrue, for it was not until 8 Jan. 1745 that the Quadruple Alliance of Warsaw—Britain, Holland,

Austria and Saxony—was concluded with the purpose of controlling the Prussian peace-breaker. The fortune of war, however, decided in favour of Prussia and France. The French beat the British, Dutch, Hanoverian and Austrian troops under the incapable duke of Cumberland at Fontenoy (11 May 1745); Frederick defeated the Austrians at Hohenfriedberg (4 June); the prince of Anhalt-Dessau inflicted another defeat on the Austrians and Saxons at Kesselsdorf (15 Dec.); and Scotland was in the hands of Charles Edward. Once more, Frederick did not hesitate to abandon his allies. He concluded the peace of Dresden (25 Dec.) by which Austria confirmed him in the possession of Silesia, and Saxony paid an indemnity of a million thalers; in return, Frederick recognized Francis I as Emperor. When Frederick returned to Berlin, his subjects hailed him as 'the Great': Prussia had proved herself a match for a European coalition.

The French, left alone, were unable to set James III on the throne of Great Britain. On the continent, however, they maintained their superiority. The peace of Aix-la-Chapelle, which brought the war of the Austrian succession to an end (18 Oct. 1748), deprived Maria Theresa of the Italian dukedoms of Parma, Piacenza and Guastalla, and Frederick II was given an international guarantee for Silesia and Glatz. The Pragmatic Sanction was confirmed, and was thereafter observed until the end of the Austro-Hungarian monarchy in 1918.

Neither of the two German rivals intended to abide by this decision. Maria Theresa never abandoned the hope of recovering Silesia, 'the most precious jewel of her crown'; Frederick looked about him for further gains. Saxony and Poland, or at least parts of them, would have suited him best. At the same time he was fully aware of the suspicion with which his neighbours looked on his every move. 'The terms of neighbour and enemy are synonymous', he said, and continued to enlarge and train his army: four-fifths of the annual revenue were spent on it.

It was the world-wide struggle between Britain and France which rekindled the latent hostility of Austria and Prussia. When hostilities flamed up in the Ohio Valley and Bengal (1753–54), Prussia was still the ally of France. As Hanover was England's only vulnerable spot on the continent, Frederick suggested that France should invade and annex the Electorate (1755). To protect Hanover against this contingency, England concluded an alliance with Russia which was to defend Hanover in return for English subsidies (30 Sept. 1755). Frederick took alarm, the more so as the French declined his suggestion and would rather have shifted the conquest of Hanover on to himself. Russia, he knew, had been closely allied with Austria since 1746, so that he might have to face Russian and Austrian forces at every point of the compass. So he made a surprising *volte-face*, offered his sword to England, underbid Russia; and on 16 Jan. 1756 signed the convention of Westminster. For an annual subsidy of four million thalers, Frederick put the Prussian army at the disposal of the English government.

An even greater surprise was to follow. On 1 May, Austria and France entered into an alliance by the treaty of Versailles. Kaunitz, the able foreign secretary of Maria Theresa, had suggested it since 1749; but mutual distrust protracted the negotiations for some years. It needed the veiled threat of the Westminster convention to make the courts of Vienna and Versailles forget their secular enmity. Ever since Maximilian I and Louis XI contested the inheritance of Charles the Bold of Burgundy, the antagonism between Austria and France had been the most constant factor in European politics. It was left to Prussia to bridge this century-old gulf, despite herself, and thus to bring about one of the greatest revolutions in the European balance of power. The reconciliation of Austria and France that took place in 1756 had consequences to be compared with the entente and alliance between republican France and autocratic Russia in 1891, and between Britain and Russia in 1907 and 1941: each of them an amazing surrender of age-old prejudices on both sides, and each of them effected by the recurring threat of Prusso-German militarism. A fortnight later (15 May) Britain declared war on France. Without a declaration of war Frederick II crossed the frontier of Saxony on 29 Aug. He demanded the full collaboration of the Saxon army and administration, and when this was refused, compelled the Saxon army to capitulate (15–16 Oct.). In the Dresden archives he very conveniently found the documents which were to justify his act of aggression. They revealed, so Prussian propaganda asserted, the 'dangerous designs' conceived by the Dresden and Vienna courts against Frederick. Saxony was treated as a conquered province; there can be little doubt that her annexation was one of Frederick's principal war aims.

Russia and Sweden acceded to the Austro-French alliance which was renewed on its first anniversary (1 May 1757). After the gory Prussian victory of Prague (6 May), in which Schwerin and Browne, the Prussian and Austrian commanders, were killed, things went badly for Frederick. He had to evacuate Bohemia (battle of Kolin,

18 June), East Prussia, which remained in Russian hands for the duration of the war (battle of Gross-Jägersdorf, 30 Aug.), and Lusatia (battle of Moys, 7 Sept.). The French were victorious in West and North Germany; the duke of Cumberland, of Fontenoy and Culloden memory, was defeated at Hastenbeck (26 July) and concluded the ignominious capitulation of Zeven monastery (8 Sept.). On 16 Oct., Austrian hussars made a daring raid on Berlin. The victories over the French and imperial troops at Rossbach (5 Nov.) and over the Austrians at Leuthen (5 Dec.) restored the balance and showed the military genius of Frederick at its best; Napoleon, the most competent judge, considered them amongst the most brilliant feats of arms in history. But the victories of Duke Ferdinand of Brunswick, Cumberland's successor, over the French at Krefeld (23 June 1758), and of Frederick himself over the Russians at Zorndorf (25 Aug.) were partly offset by Frederick's heavy defeat at Hochkirch, where Marshal James Keith was killed (14 Oct.). From the beginning of 1759 it became clear that a decisive superiority in the field was not to be obtained by either belligerent. Victory and defeat alternated, and the eventual decision was made in the political sphere. In October 1761, Pitt, the leader of the British war party, was succeeded by the marquess of Bute, who undertook to liquidate the war. There was no longer need to spend much money on the defence of Hanover as Ferdinand of Brunswick had been very successful in warding off repeated French incursions; the last French army on the right bank of the Rhine capitulated to him at Cassel on 1 Nov. 1762. So Bute stopped the subsidies to Frederick in April 1762. But now a fresh hope for Frederick flared up in the East. The Empress Elizabeth of Russia, his implacable enemy, died on 5 Jan. 1762. Her successor, Peter III, was a great admirer of Frederick; in quick succession he concluded an armistice (16 March), peace (5 May), and even an alliance (19 June) with Prussia. Sweden, following Russia's lead, made peace (22 May) on the basis of the *status quo*. Peter III, however, was assassinated on 9 July; and Catherine II, his successor, at once terminated the alliance, although she kept to the peace treaty. The preliminary peace of Fontainebleau (3 Nov.) ended the war between England, France and Spain. The withdrawal from the war of the world powers and the complete exhaustion of their own resources in man-power and money made the German belligerents, too, ready for a compromise. On 24 Nov. 1762, Austria, Prussia and Saxony signed an armistice, and on 15 Feb. 1763, the peace of Hubertusburg was concluded. Prussia

restored Saxony but retained Silesia, and on 27 March the Archduke Joseph was unanimously elected King of the Romans. The lasting results of the Seven Years War were twofold: Canada was conquered in Germany, as Lord Chatham put it; and the antagonism between Austria and Prussia was made irreconcilable. There was no room in Germany for both.

In the years following the peace of Hubertusburg, Austria and Prussia consolidated their respective positions. In Austria Maria Theresa remained the leading personality until her death (1780). Francis I (d. 1765) was a nonentity, but Joseph II, their eldest son, who succeeded his father as Emperor, gained an increasing influence. His political ideas differed widely from his mother's. Maria Theresa strove successfully to heal the wounds which the Seven Years War had inflicted upon her country. She was averse to all revolutionary ideas, and looked with deep apprehension upon the passion for innovation that animated Joseph. Her motherly and suave way of handling men and affairs did much to transform the inherited agglomeration of chequered principalities into one body politic, that *totum* which Prince Eugene had demanded as the goal of Hapsburg statesmanship. Joseph II was less patient and far-sighted. He wanted, in the shortest possible time, to recast the polymorphous Hapsburg possessions into a uniform and centralized monarchy, organized on the most modern principles of rationalistic political science. He made German the only official language, abolished serfdom, introduced religious toleration and freedom of the press, placed the church under state supervision, reformed the educational system, and turned his zeal to a hundred other objects. The transformation was as trenchant as short-lived, and caused the inevitable reaction. Soon after Joseph's death (1790), Austria became the most reactionary German state. His rash methods undid much of Maria Theresa's patient statesmanship. He acted with an eye to outdoing Prussia, and his ultimate failure weakened rather than strengthened Austria.

Frederick the Great, too, used the years of peace for a thorough overhauling of the whole state machinery. His chief concern remained the army, which he raised to a peace-footing of 200,000 men. The fiscal system was tightened up to meet the fresh requirements. Protectionist tariffs and monopolies were increased, the tobacco and coffee monopolies creating much bad feeling. The administration of justice was simplified. Under the guidance of Suarez, the greatest Prussian lawyer, a systematic law code was prepared (from 1781) which was to supersede the particular legislation of the various provinces. Next to the army the General Law Code became a pillar of Prussian unity. It took effect in 1794 and remained in force until 1900. Educational reform was carried out by the minister von Zedlitz, an enlightened and liberal disciple of the philosopher Kant, to whom Frederick left a free hand. The king's far-famed religious toleration and lenient censorship of the press were due to his indifference to literary and religious problems. When he left the Jesuits unmolested after the suppression of their Society in all Catholic countries (1773), he did so because he did not want to lose teachers and parsons who cost him nothing. Whenever political or military interests were at stake, Prussian censorship was as ruthless as that of any other less 'enlightened' administration. The obscurantism of Frederick's successor made Frederick's specious liberalism shine brighter than it had been in reality.

There was certainly nothing liberal or enlightened about his foreign policy. In this respect Frederick continued to follow the maxims of his ancestors and to grab any temporary advantage at anybody else's cost. Immediately after the close of the Seven Years War, he approached Russia with a view to controlling jointly the royal republic of Poland. Stanislas Poniatowski, their candidate, was duly elected king in defiance of the legitimate claims of the Saxon dynasty (1764). The weak Polish king was no obstacle to the far-reaching projects of his mighty protectors. In 1769 Frederick submitted to the court of St Petersburg a plan which was to revolutionize the European comity of nations. He coolly suggested a partition of Poland among Russia, Austria and Prussia. No pretext was offered for this unheard-of violation of the most primitive and self-evident rights of nations. Poland was weak, Prussia and her accomplices were strong: two reasons which, in Frederick's view, made further argument superfluous. Frederick's project upset every existing conception of international law. When Russia hesitated, apprehensive of the consequences, Frederick approached Austria. Twice he met Joseph II and Kaunitz (1769–70). Joseph characterized Frederick as 'a genius, but a knave'; Kaunitz would have preferred an Austro-Russian diversion against Turkey. Maria Theresa was in agony; she openly described the partition of Poland as a crime for which the partners would have to pay dearly in God's good time. Her ambitious son, however, overruled her; Russia did not want to leave the spoils to Austria and Prussia; and Frederick achieved his ends. On 5 Aug. 1772, the first partition of Poland was signed. Russia took the lion's share; Austria obtained the most valuable portion, namely the 'Kingdom of Galicia and Lodomeria'. Prussia gained West Prussia, except Danzig, and the bishopric of Ermland, thus bridging the gulf between Brandenburg and Pomerania in the west and Prussia in the east. From this time, Frederick changed his title from 'King in Prussia' to 'King of Prussia'; and the name of Prussia was henceforth used to describe the whole of the Hohenzollern possessions. At the same time, the motto of the highest Prussian order of the Black Eagle, *Suum cuique*, was mockingly quoted outside Prussia as *Suum cuique rapit*.

The struggle between Britain and the rebellious colonies in North America affected the German states only indirectly. The majority of the smaller princes were won over by large British subsidies to let their troops fight against the colonists; and the name of the Hessians has remained odious to Americans to this day as a synonym for mercenaries of despotism. Joseph II exploited the temporary weakness of England and resumed the oversea projects of his grandfather. In 1775 he acquired Delagoa Bay, but sold it to Portugal six years later. Frederick formed a correct estimate of the American chances of success. He lent the rebels one of his staff officers, General von Steuben, who organized Washington's untrained levies on the Prussian model. He was also the first to conclude a commercial treaty with the young republic (1785).

The temporary co-operation between Prussia and Austria did not last long. Frederick frustrated all Joseph's attempts to consolidate Austria's position in Germany. Joseph wanted to round off his possessions and, incidentally, strengthen the German element in them. In 1777 the dynasty of Lewis IV the Bavarian died out, and Bavaria fell to the Palatine branch of the Wittelsbachs. Joseph claimed some districts as reverted fiefs of the Empire and Bohemia. He and the new Elector agreed upon a partition of Bavaria (3 Jan. 1778), and Austrian troops occupied the southern part of the country. Frederick posed as the champion of 'German liberty' and declared war against Austria (3 July). After a listless campaign, Russia and France negotiated the peace of Teschen (13 May 1779). Joseph received the Inn Quarter from Bavaria, and Frederick obtained the reversionary right to Ansbach and Baireuth, two Franconian principalities ruled by a branch of the Hohenzollern family. The reversion took effect in 1791. Joseph, however, did not abandon his Bavarian scheme. This time he took care to secure the benevolence of France and Russia. His sister, Marie Antoinette, married to the Dauphin in

1770, had become queen of France in 1774. A meeting between Joseph and Catherine II in 1780 led to a close collaboration over the problems of the Near East and thus brought to an end the Russo-Prussian entente. Charles Theodore of the Palatinate, whom Frederick had compelled to succeed in Bavaria (1778-99), took no interest in his new acquisition. He lent a willing ear to Joseph's suggestion that he should exchange Bavaria for the Austrian Netherlands, a project Maria Theresa had broached as early as 1742.

At the same time Joseph entertained far-reaching plans for a thorough reorganization of the Empire. Earlier, in 1767, he had set up a commission to examine the High Court of Justice at Wetzlar. It was the first visitation since 1588, and the imperial commissioners found some 20,000 lawsuits in arrears. This reform was foiled by Prussia and Hanover, and the commission was dissolved in 1776. After this, Joseph aimed at a large-scale secularization of ecclesiastical estates, by which Austria and other Catholic princes would, of course, have benefited most. Again, Frederick thwarted this plan. He evoked the memory of the League of Schmalkalden and called up the Estates of the Empire to defend their liberties against the Emperor. Thus the Electors of Brandenburg, Hanover and Saxony concluded the 'Princes' League' on the lines of the associations of the past. Soon afterwards it was joined by the duke of Zweibrücken, heir presumptive of Bavaria, the archbishop of Mayence, arch-chancellor of the Empire, the Duke Charles Augustus of Weimar, and some lesser princes in North and Central Germany. The Electors of Bavaria, Cologne and Treves, the rulers of Württemberg, Hesse-Darmstadt and Oldenburg, and the South German bishops kept aloof. On the other hand, they refused to combine in a counter-league which Joseph suggested. The Princes' League, ostensibly designed to uphold the constitution of the Empire, was in reality a tool of Prussia. Certainly the transference of the Wittelsbachs from Munich to Brussels, the secularization of bishoprics, abbeys and monasteries, the redistribution of petty states, and the modernization of legal and administrative procedure would have benefited the imperial crown and the house of Hapsburg; but the Empire as a whole would also have profited immensely. In fact, the events of the following decade proved the sanity of most of Joseph's suggestions. Belgium was lost to the Empire because Austria could not defend properly this outlying post; and the secularization was carried out ruthlessly at the command of the French conquerors, without regard to traditional ties and interests. Frederick the Great frustrated a reform of the Empire when it was still just possible, for he did not care at all for the German Empire, certainly not for its rejuvenation. What he strove after was the transformation of the Empire into Greater Prussia. The Princes' League of 1785 was the first step towards this goal.

Frederick died on 17 Aug. 1786. He was the last monarch upon whom the appellative 'the Great' was not only bestowed by his contemporaries—as was later on the case with Napoleon I—but to whom this rare distinction has stuck ever since. It is justified in so far as Frederick personified the spirit of Enlightened Absolutism to the same degree as Alexander, Gregory, Charles and Peter embody the essence of Hellenism, Catholicism, Universalism and Despotism. Contemporaries of the most diverse upbringing and outlook, such as Voltaire, Mirabeau, Lessing and Goethe, were fascinated by his personality and paid him unstinted though critical homage, as did Carlyle, Macaulay and Thomas Mann in after times. Frederick was the historian of his own exploits like Julius Caesar before him, an elegant and often witty poet, a composer of taste, and a connoisseur of art. In this respect he has few equals amongst the crowned heads of any age, and he stands out favourably against the pedestrian race of martinets, clod-hoppers and red-tapists with whom the dynasty of Hohenzollern abounded. His literary and artistic taste was exclusively French. In his old age he wrote a bitter pamphlet 'on German literature' in which he disposed of Goethe as an imitator of 'that savage, Shakespeare'. His political outlook was Prussian in the narrowest sense. Yet by the irony of fate this Frenchified Prussian was to become a German national hero; and the heralds of a German national state in the nineteenth century were to draw inspiration from his personality and achievements. Few and far between were the voices of those who doubted that his achievements were an unmitigated blessing for Germany. The more remarkable is the testimony of Ernst Moritz Arndt, the patriot publicist and poet of the war of liberation of 1813 and the revolution of 1848. For him Frederick was a 'noxious creature' and his influence on Germany—as distinct from Prussia—was wholly bad. Certainly, Germany meant nothing to him; it hardly could. All his ideas centred round Prussia, whose best and worst features Frederick the Great personified more completely than any man before or after him.

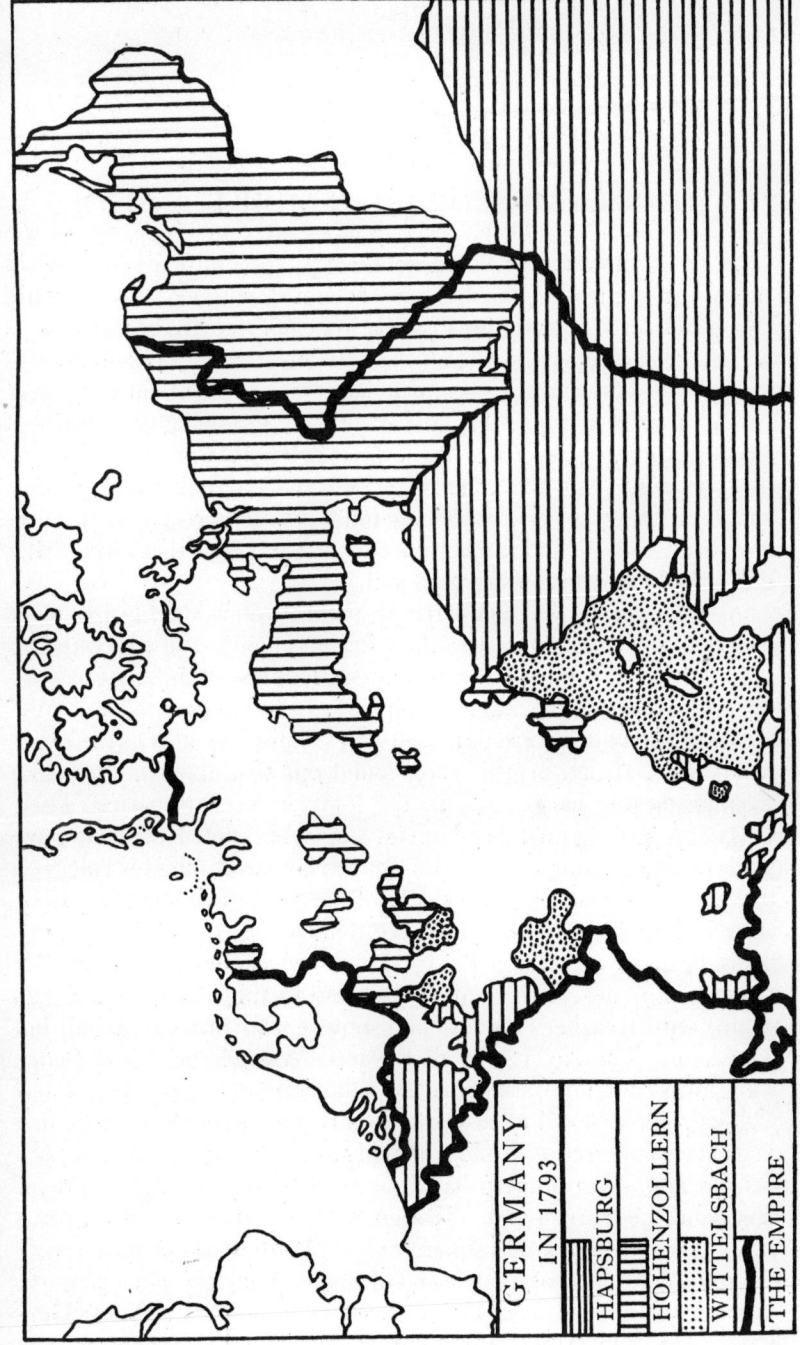

Germany in 1793

CHAPTER VI

THE COLLAPSE OF THE EMPIRE (1786-1815)

GOETHE, who respected the Daemonic (in the Platonic sense) when he saw it, confessed that he was 'Frederick-minded' in his youth though he cared nothing for Prussia. When of riper years, he became no less 'Napoleon-minded', much as he detested the French Revolution whose offspring the great Corsican was. Goethe's attitude may be taken as a symbol. The three decades following the death of Frederick may be described as the age of Napoleon even in a history of Germany. For the radical changes which took place in that country during this period emanated from the French Revolution and its aftermath; and furthermore for fifteen years that Great Man held absolute sway on German soil.

At the beginning, the doctrines of the French Revolution were hailed by the vast majority of the German peoples and execrated by their rulers. When the intoxicating youthfulness of these ideas wore off, many adherents became disillusioned and vaguely felt that 'the bonds of the world were unloosed', as Goethe put it. On the other hand, the German princes soon found out that they might strike most profitable bargains with the loathed revolutionaries. Their crusading zeal against Jacobinism very soon cooled off, and gave place to a disgusting competition for the favour of the new rulers on the Seine. Prussia here got the start of her rivals. Jealousy of Austria, envy of Britain, and the expansive tendency of the Hohenzollerns made Frederick William II (1786-97) and Frederick William III (1797-1840) desert their allies and betray the Empire again and again, until treachery met its punishment, and Prussia was all but wiped out. The sovereigns of Bavaria, Württemberg and Baden were not slow in imitating Prussia and soon outstripped her. Their well-calculated servility towards the French rulers brought them a rich harvest of territorial and personal gains. At the end of this epoch Bavaria and Württemberg had doubled their size and risen to royal rank, and the margraviate of Baden, of 70 square miles, had grown into a grand duchy of 270 square miles. All these acquisitions were made at the expense of Austria and the lesser members of the Empire. Austria was ejected from her possessions in South and West Germany. Her simultaneous gains in Poland and Italy enhanced her multinational and proportionally diminished her German character. The formal dissolution of the Holy Roman Empire was almost accidental in this general upheaval of Central Europe: 'it perished', as an English historian says, 'unwept, unhonoured, and unsung'. Theocracy and feudalism, relics of the Middle Ages, disappeared for good. Their place was taken by nationalism and liberalism, two conceptions introduced into Germany by the French Revolution and Napoleon.

Austria was the first German state to feel the repercussions of the French Revolution. The Austrian Netherlands, provoked by the reformatory officiousness of Joseph II and roused by the events across their borders, broke into rebellion and constituted an independent republic under the name of Belgium (Oct.–Dec. 1789). At the same time Hungary was on the verge of revolution. Joseph abolished the exemption from land-taxes and other privileges of the Magyar magnates, and these conspired with Berlin to overthrow the Hapsburg régime. Joseph was compelled to revoke his rash edicts, and died a broken man (20 Feb. 1790). His brother and successor, Leopold II (1790–92), had a firm and realistic grasp on the situation. Hungary and Belgium were pacified. The victorious campaign against the Turks upon which Joseph had entered together with Catherine of Russia was broken off. The peace of Sistova (30 Aug. 1791) restored Belgrade, which the Austrians had stormed for the second time (9 Oct. 1789), to Turkey. However, the necessity of fighting simultaneously on the Rhine and Danube once more prevented Austria from following up an advantage on either front.

All the while Frederick William II, the profligate successor of Frederick the Great, was hand in glove with the enemies of the house of Hapsburg. The Belgians and Magyars were encouraged and supported from Berlin: alliances with Turkey and Poland guaranteed the integrity of these states against Austrian aspirations. At the same time Frederick William suggested that Poland should cede him Danzig and Thorn and take back Galicia, which Prussian emissaries were busy stirring up to revolt. Poland, backed by Britain, refused. Leopold II, discreet and peaceable, did his best to avoid a war between the two German protagonists, in view of the increasing danger from Paris. He scored a full diplomatic success. In the convention of Reichenbach (27 July 1790) Frederick William abandoned the Princes' League and with it his anti-Austrian policy. For the time being the solidarity which united the two sovereigns against France gave the Austro-Prussian collaboration a semblance of sincerity. The two monarchs pledged themselves to uphold the rights of Louis XVI, if necessary by force (Declaration of Pillnitz, 27 Aug. 1791) and signed a formal alliance for this purpose (7 Feb. 1792). Leopold, however, was not blinded by legitimist prejudices and still hoped to come to an amicable arrangement with France. But the Girondists were bent on a warlike policy so as to maintain themselves in power. After the sudden death of Leopold (1 March), war was declared upon his successor, Francis II. Prussia, in fulfilment of her obligations, thereupon declared war on France. The war opened with the notorious Coblentz manifesto of the duke of Brunswick, the Prussian commander-in-chief, in which he threatened to raze Paris to the ground (25 July). After initial successes the allies were brought to a halt near Verdun and were soon compelled to retreat behind the Rhine. Goethe, who accompanied the army, saw in this turning of the tide 'the commencement of a new epoch of world history'. At the approach of the French, the secular and ecclesiastical authorities collapsed everywhere like houses of cards. 'Golden Mayence' transformed itself into a Jacobin republic of which George Forster, formerly scientific companion of Captain Cook, was a shining light. Soon the left bank of the Rhine and the Netherlands were in French hands, and the conquerors made no secret of their intention to keep them.

The First Coalition, which Pitt brought about in February 1793, seemed to put fresh vigour into the allies. The Empire, too, joined them in March. By the end of the summer Germany and Belgium were recovered and Hood had taken Toulon from the French. While Austria bore the brunt of the continental war, Frederick William of Prussia pursued a selfish policy directly opposed to the common interest and his own pledges. Part of the agreements of Reichenbach and Pillnitz was the guarantee of Polish integrity, as Leopold II wished sincerely to keep the republic as a bulwark against the Russian advance to the West. The fresh vigour which the constitution of 3 May 1791 instilled into Poland gave Russia the pretext to invade the unhappy country and restore anarchy (May 1792). Frederick William went back on his solemn word and signed a secret agreement with Catherine II behind the back of Austria. On 7 May 1793, the second partition of Poland took place between the two. Again, Russia obtained the lion's share; but Prussia was well satisfied with hers: Danzig, Thorn, Posen, Gnesen and Kalisz. A new province, called South Prussia, was established, but the country was far from being pacified. The Poles rose heroically under the spirited leadership of Kosciuszko. A Prussian advance on Warsaw was halted, and the retreating Prussians suffered one reverse after another. When, in the end, the Russians put down the rising with great brutality, Prussia received her new acquisitions as a free gift from Catherine (Nov. 1793). South Prussia was placed under martial law; but terror and corruption kept the spirit of Polish resistance alive.

Meanwhile the successes of the allies in the West were obliterated by a fresh advance of the French. By the end of 1793 Belgium, the Rhineland, and Toulon had changed hands once more. Frederick William threatened to withdraw his troops altogether, but allowed himself to be bought by England and Holland (19 April 1794). This treaty and the subsidies of £50,000 monthly did not, however, prevent him from entering into secret negotiations with the detested French regicides. In October Frederick William ordered his troops back, and only afterwards renounced the treaty with the Maritime Powers. He gave himself the air of universal peace-maker and posed as the defender of the rights of the Empire. But he readily agreed to the cession to France of the German states on the left bank of the Rhine, and was only anxious to secure for himself appropriate compensations for incidental Prussian losses. On this basis the peace of Basle was signed on 5 April 1795: Prussia granted France the Rhine frontier, whereas the French promised to respect the neutrality of Northern and Central Germany for the duration of the war. Hanover and Hesse-Cassel acceded to this agreement, but the imperial diet refused to be browbeaten by the Prussian 'Judas' and authorized the Emperor to represent the Empire at the expected peace conference.

The chief reason why Frederick William liquidated the war in the West was his fear of missing another opportunity in the East. On 3 Jan. 1795, Russia and Austria concluded a secret treaty for the final partition of Poland. Frederick William hastened to join in, and on 24 Oct. the third partition was agreed upon between the three. Austria took Cracow and Western Galicia; Prussia received Warsaw and the territory between the rivers Bug and Niemen; while Russia obtained the rest. The unfortunate king, Stanislas II, abdicated (25 Nov.), and on 26 Jan. 1797 Poland ceased to be an independent state. She was eclipsed for one hundred and twenty years.

While England drove the French flag from the Seven Seas and occupied one colony after another of the French and their Dutch and Spanish vassals, the archduke Charles, the adroit brother of the slow-witted Francis II, successfully withstood the French in Southern Germany. But the brilliant campaign which the twenty-eight-year-old general, Bonaparte, waged in Northern Italy offset Charles's victories. In vain, England and Russia tried to bring the Prussian arms back into the field. But while the French were advancing across the Black Forest into Swabia, the Prussians thought the time come for a further expansion of their frontiers inside Germany. They made a surprise attack on the unsuspecting imperial city of Nuremberg and annexed it to the margraviate of Ansbach-Baireuth (July 1796). The victories of the archduke Charles compelled them to evacuate Nuremberg (1 Oct.), but not before they had secured even greater gains by a secret treaty with the French Republic (5 Aug.). In it Prussia formally renounced the integrity of the Empire, guaranteed the left bank of the Rhine to France, and devised a wholesale redistribution of the territories on its right bank for her own benefit and that of her accomplices behind the Basle line of demarcation. In these circumstances there was nothing left for Austria but to accept the peace which Bonaparte dictated at Leoben (18 April 1797) and Campo Formio (17 Oct.). After Prussia had virtually destroyed the structure of the Empire, Austria vied with her rival in selfish greed. Belgium and Lombardy were ceded to France; the venerable Republic of St Mark with its dependencies on the Italian mainland, in Istria, and Dalmatia was handed over to Austria; and the 'perpetual enlarger of the Empire' gave his secret consent to the cession of the Rhineland and the parcelling out of the rest of Germany.

At the peace conference of Rastatt, which opened on 16 Dec. 1797, the clearing sale of the Empire began. The magic word 'secularization' fascinated the members of the congress. Regardless of tradition, common interests, decency and honour, everyone was bent on carving out for himself the biggest possible slice from the body of the Empire. France took formal possession of the left bank of the Rhine (9 March 1798), and the Peace Deputation of the Empire confirmed the principle of compensating the impaired secular princes for their losses through secularization (11 March). While the bartering continued at Rastatt, Pitt and the Emperor Paul of Russia brought about the Second Coalition and the war flared up again. Prussia, where Frederick William III had succeeded his father on 16 Nov. 1797, remained neutral and regarded France as her natural ally. The new Elector of Bavaria and the Palatinate, Maximilian Joseph (1799–1825), called himself a Frenchman by birth and inclination, and was willing to become the head of a Rhenish Confederation in the service of the French Republic. The coalition soon disintegrated. The Tsar not only withdrew his troops from Italy and Switzerland, but turned against his British ally. He admired the genius of Bonaparte, who at the time made himself First Consul and virtual autocrat of France (9 Nov. 1799). Russia, the Scandinavian states, and Prussia concluded the Northern Confederacy (16 Dec. 1800) and shut the Baltic Sea to British commerce. By this time, Austria had succumbed to the generalship of Bonaparte. The defeats of Marengo (14 June) and Hohenlinden (3 Dec.) led to the peace of Lunéville (9 Feb. 1801), by which the left bank of the Rhine and Italy beyond the rivers Adda and Po were definitively handed over to France.

On 2 Oct. 1801 the Diet of Ratisbon set up an Imperial Deputation with unlimited powers to carry into effect the peace of Lunéville. The undignified bartering of Rastatt was repeated on an even larger scale. The French plenipotentiaries and agents, especially Bonaparte and Talleyrand, were courted and bribed; for it was they who made the final decisions which the Imperial Deputation had only to ratify and register. In England, Pitt was replaced by Addington (14 March 1801), who signed the peace treaty of Amiens (27 March 1802). In Russia, Paul I was murdered (23 March 1801) and succeeded by Alexander I, who came to an agreement with England (17 June) and France (11 Oct.). Prussia, in pursuance of her anti-British policy, occupied Hanover (April 1801), which, however, had to be restored after the peace of Amiens. In May and June 1802, Bonaparte concluded a number of secret treaties with Prussia, Bavaria, Württemberg, Baden and Hesse, which accelerated the disruption of the Empire. Neither the Emperor nor the Imperial Deputation were consulted. Despite the urgent entreaties of the ecclesiastical Estates, Francis II acceded to these negotiations, having obtained certain revisions in favour of Austria.

On 25 Feb. 1803, the Final Recess of the Imperial Deputation (*Reichsdeputationshauptschluss*) was promulgated. The Holy Roman Empire was brought virtually to an end. In fact, the Roman Curia spoke henceforth only of an *Imperium Germanicum*, and Talleyrand called it bluntly the *Fédération Germanique*. The original idea of compensating princes for the losses they had suffered by the cession to France of the left bank of the Rhine served only as a pretext for extensive pillage. Prussia, for instance, lost 48 square miles and received 230 in return. Brunswick, which had had no possessions on the left bank of the Rhine and had therefore lost none, was nevertheless 'compensated' by two rich abbeys. Even the foreign dynasties of Tuscany, Modena and Orange were paid for their losses in Italy and France out of the bankruptcy of the Empire. On the other hand, a large number of lesser princes who lost all their lands, but had neither the money for bribing the French agents, nor the intercession on their behalf of Russia or Prussia, went away empty-handed. One hundred and twelve sovereign states disappeared altogether from the map. Amongst them were those of all the ecclesiastical princes, except the Arch-chancellor who was transferred from Mayence to Ratisbon, the Grand Master of the Teutonic Order, and the Grand Prior of the Order of St John. Only six of the imperial cities were left over, namely Hamburg, Bremen, Lübeck, Frankfort, Augsburg and Nuremberg. The College of Electors was completely changed: Cologne and Treves no longer existed: in their stead, Salzburg (which was given to the grand duke of Tuscany), Württemberg, Baden and Hesse-Cassel were raised to the electoral dignity. Only four of the ten Electors were Roman Catholics; the Bench of Princes was composed of fifty-three Protestants and twenty-nine Catholics; five of the imperial cities were Protestant, one (Augsburg) of religious equality. The bottom was knocked out of the theocratic foundation of the Holy Roman Empire, and it was only a question of time when it would disappear altogether.

The Emperor Francis II naturally wanted to keep the imperial dignity with himself and his house. This seemed to him all the more desirable as Napoleon, too, assumed the title of emperor on 18 May 1804. Francis therefore established formally an hereditary Empire of Austria, of which he called himself the Emperor Francis I (11 Aug.).

The formal end of the Roman Empire was not long in coming. On 9 Aug. 1805, Francis joined the Anglo-Russian alliance of St Petersburg, and took up arms against Napoleon. The German princes sided with Napoleon, from whom they expected further territorial gains. Prussia remained neutral, although Napoleon offered her the British dependency of Hanover which the French had occupied upon the declaration of war by Britain (18 May 1803). She did not change her attitude when the French infringed her neutrality and led an army across Prussia's possessions in South Germany and thereby succeeded in forcing an Austrian army to capitulate at Ulm (19 Oct. 1805). Two months later the combined Russo-Austrian forces were destroyed at Austerlitz in Moravia (2 Dec.). Prussia wished to act as peace-maker, but instead Napoleon enticed the Prussian envoy into concluding the treaty of Schönbrunn (15 Dec.). Prussia received Hanover from France and ceded

Ansbach-Baireuth, Cleves and Neuchâtel. She signed an offensive and defensive alliance with Napoleon, and recognized and guaranteed beforehand the conditions to be imposed on Austria. Thus completely isolated, Austria had to sign the humiliating peace of Pressburg (26 Dec.). The Emperor lost all his Italian and German possessions to Napoleon and Napoleon's satellites, Bavaria, Württemberg and Baden. Tyrol, the most important link between South Germany and Italy, went to Bavaria. Francis had to recognize the international sovereignty of these three princes, two of whom, the Electors of Bavaria and Württemberg, assumed the title of kings.

The final stage of disintegration was reached in the following year. In January 1806, Gustavus IV Adolphus of Sweden was the first to leave the Empire, declaring that the 'decisions of the imperial diet are influenced only by greed and egoism, and he who speaks the language of honour is not listened to'. A North German Empire with the king of Prussia as Emperor was very much in the minds of the Prussian statesmen. The anti-Austrian tendency of this scheme made Prussia completely dependent on Napoleon. The treaty of Paris (15 Feb.) closed the Prussian ports to Britain, and Prussia pledged herself to unconditional support of Napoleon's foreign policy. The Electoral Arch-chancellor of the Empire addressed Napoleon as the new Charlemagne, the saviour of Germany, and the restorer of the Western Empire. On 12 July, sixteen German princes combined in the Rhenish Confederation. Napoleon himself had drawn up the document; Talleyrand gave the princes twenty-four hours to ratify it. Napoleon was made the protector of the Confederation, whose military and economic resources were put at his unconditional disposal. More than seventy princes and counts had not been asked to join; they lost their independence, and their possessions were shared out amongst the Confederates. The rulers of Baden, Hesse-Darmstadt and Cleves—the latter was given to Joachim Murat—assumed the title of grand dukes. The entry into the Confederation of other German states was provided for by a special clause. On 1 Aug., the princes of the Rhenish Alliance declared their formal secession from the Holy Empire. Six days later, a cool note from the Viennese chancellery gave the *coup de grâce* to the creation of Charlemagne and Otto the Great: Francis II abdicated as Roman Emperor and released the members of the Empire from their allegiance. The abdication was illegal, as any political action of the Emperor required the concurrence of the imperial diet to become valid. But nobody cared for the niceties of constitutional law. Unlamented save by the imperial knights the thousand-year-old Empire ceased to exist.

Prussia, so long deaf to the calls of decency and honour, showed herself blind to reality as well. Frederick William III, timid and irresolute by nature, let himself be carried away by the boisterous war-party at Berlin and the blandishments of the Tsar. He chose the moment when Napoleon was the undisputed master of Western Europe to challenge him. A Prussian ultimatum, dispatched on 26 Sept., demanded the withdrawal of the French from Germany, certain territorial restitutions to Prussia, and Napoleon's compliance with a North German Federation under Prussian leadership. Before the Prussian statesmen had time to grasp the impact of Napoleon's refusal, the 'army of Frederick the Great' ceased to exist. In the battles of Jena and Auerstädt (14 Oct.) the Prussian army and its Saxon allies were utterly routed. Three days later Saxony signed an armistice with Napoleon, and Frederick Augustus soon became the most faithful of his German vassals. On 27 Oct., Napoleon made his state entry into Berlin: the Victory monument on the Brandenburg gate was sent to Paris.

The collapse of Prussia was without precedent. The Prussian state was a mechanical automaton without a living spirit; when one particle of the machinery broke, the whole works came to a standstill and became a useless heap of scrap. The recently annexed inhabitants of Hanover and Westphalia rejoiced openly at the downfall of their conquerors. The Brandenburgers, Pomeranians and East Prussians accepted it equably, not a few even with satisfaction. Civil servants and army officers were trained to blind obedience: when they no longer heard the familiar words of command, they were stunned and only too glad that Napoleon at once relieved them from the unwonted necessity of thinking for themselves. Seven ministers swore the oath of allegiance to the victor. One fortress after another capitulated, some of them at the first summons by a handful of hussars. The king and the royal family and scattered fragments of the army fled to East Prussia. A preliminary peace convention was repudiated by the king, who put his trust in the advancing Russians. Peace was restored with Great Britain (28 Jan. 1807); Prussia abandoned her claims to Hanover and promised to continue the war with British subsidies. The undecisive battle of Eylau (7–8 Feb.) showed for the first time that Napoleon was not invincible. He restored, however, his reputation at Friedland on the anniversary of Marengo (14 June). Thereupon the Tsar abandoned Prussia, made a separate peace with

Napoleon (7 July), and persuaded the Prussian diplomatists to sign the peace of Tilsit (9 July). 'In deference to the Tsar Alexander' Napoleon desisted from wiping Prussia altogether off the map. Frederick William was allowed to keep his possessions on the right bank of the Elbe, with the exception of South Prussia and the loot of the third partition of Poland. These districts were made into a grand duchy of Warsaw. It was placed under Frederick Augustus of Saxony, who had made his peace with Napoleon, become a member of the Rhenish Confederation, and assumed the title of king (11 Dec. 1806). Russia and Prussia recognized Napoleon's brothers as kings of Holland and Naples, and Napoleon himself as protector of the Rhenish Confederation. They also consented to the creation of a 'kingdom of Westphalia' under Napoleon's youngest brother, Jerome. This was to consist of the Prussian losses west of the Elbe, including Hanover, and the countries of Prussia's erstwhile allies, the duke of Brunswick and the Elector of Hesse. Jerome, of course, joined the Rhenish Confederation. In a secret treaty, Alexander made an offensive and defensive alliance with Napoleon.

One of the essential points of the treaties of Tilsit was the adherence to the Continental System on the part of Russia and Prussia. From Napoleon's point of view, all the campaigns which France had waged since 1793 were only part of the war against England; his victories in Italy, Germany and elsewhere were important to him only in so far as they served his ultimate purpose. As an invasion of England and Ireland proved impracticable, he resorted to the indirect method of a counter-blockade. While Britain ruled the waves, he could at least exclude British ships and commerce from the continent; and the ruin of her financial and economic system might bring proud Albion to her knees when the direct assault failed. With this end in view, Napoleon issued the Berlin decree of 21 Nov. 1806. It closed the continental ports to British ships and importation, and condemned all goods of British origin or shipment to confiscation and destruction. As the system proved ineffective in the hands of the Dutch, Westphalian and Hanseatic customs administrations, Napoleon annexed Holland and the German coast line as far as Lübeck (July 1810–Jan. 1811). Austria (Oct. 1809) and Sweden (Jan. 1810) had to join the system, but the fishermen of Heligoland became expert blockade-runners and smugglers, fraudulent practices undermined the system, and the secret understanding between Russia and Britain (Dec. 1811) broke its power. The effects of the Continental System were different east and west of the Elbe. Hamburg and Prussia, which lived on the importation of oversea goods and the exportation of grain, were severely hit and impoverished; West and South Germany benefited in proportion. The textile and iron industries of the Rhineland profited doubly by the exclusion of English competition and their own inclusion in the French customs frontiers, thus enjoying every advantage of a highly developed protectionist system.

After the upheaval of the long-established order of things the administrations of the new German states set themselves to a radical reconstruction. The easy-going methods of a traditional semi-feudalism would work no longer. Bavaria, for instance, was no longer the self-contained agricultural duchy between the Alps and Danube inhabited by an exclusively Roman Catholic population of Bavarian stock. The new kingdom comprised also the greater part of Franconia and the eastern fringe of Swabia. Rotten abbeys, sleepy bishoprics, industrious imperial cities, former territories of Austria and Prussia, some of them inhabited by Lutherans and Calvinists—in brief, a multifarious host of alien extraction and tradition had to be amalgamated. Maximilian Count Montgelas, a nobleman of Savoyard origin, carried out this imposing task. Unhampered by Bavarian and Catholic sentiments, Montgelas created a new state on rational and enlightened lines. The administration of justice and police was taken away from the local authorities. State supervision of the churches was extended. Manorial jurisdiction was abolished. The power of the central administration overruled every particular privilege of provinces, corporations, or former sovereignties. Reforms on similar lines were carried out in Württemberg, Baden, Hesse and Westphalia. King Frederick of Württemberg acted with unnecessary harshness. He made the unification of his new kingdom a pretext for abolishing the Estates of the old duchy, which had for centuries been the pride of the Württembergers and more than once their safeguard against the tyranny of their rulers. In Westphalia the administration of the king, Jerome, committed a great many blunders. The king was a profligate, his entourage included numerous adventurers and adventuresses of doubtful qualifications, and the incessant interference with Westphalian affairs on the part of Napoleon gave the country no respite to settle down. Hanover, now divided between France and Westphalia, had for a century past enjoyed a liberal administration on the Whig model, so that the achievements of the French Revolution meant less here than elsewhere in Germany, where they were something like a revelation.

On the whole, however, the subjects of the princes of the Rhenish Confederation were quite satisfied with their conditions. The serfdom of the peasants was abolished, the nepotism of the local corporations had gone, the administration and army of the enlarged states opened fresh prospects, and trade and commerce were everywhere on the rise. The alliance with Napoleon was not considered humiliating; on the contrary, people were rather proud of sharing the glory of the French arms, and taking an active part in the pacification of Europe.

Considering the backward state of Prussia, the reforms attempted in that country from 1807 to 1811 were more ambitious than in any other state. The Prussia that entered upon the war of liberation in 1813 was very different indeed from the Prussia that met her doom at Jena in 1806. The serfdom of the peasants was abolished, following the precedent set by the grand duchy of Warsaw. The administration of the municipalities was modernized, and self-government was introduced on the model of the English boroughs. Freedom of trade was established in conformity with the doctrines of Adam Smith. The unwieldy General Directory of War and Domains was replaced by a collegiate ministry of state consisting of five departments. The provinces were correlated to the central administration. The army was recruited on the principle of universal service; corporal punishment was abolished; and, in theory, commoners were admitted to commissions. This short list shows in itself how much ground Prussia had still to make up. It also shows that the Prussian reformers adopted the principles of English Whiggism rather than those of the Napoleonic system taken over by the rest of Germany. The self-administration of the city corporations, in which English influence is most conspicuous, remained the most lasting achievement. It was introduced gradually in other parts of Germany and became the training school of political liberalism.

Local self-government in the cities was the one section of these reforms which did not immediately interest the Junkers, and therefore escaped the furious onslaught which these gentry made on the reform movement as a whole. They did everything in their power to reduce the efforts of the modernizers to a shadow. Thus they prevented the emancipation of the peasants from being followed by corresponding measures for their protection once they had gained their freedom. It had therefore the same evil effect on the rural population as the break-up of the Scottish clans after the 'Forty-five'. The lords of the manor demanded and received huge compensations in land for their alleged losses; and the emancipated fled the new form of servitude and, in after years, filled the slums of the industrial areas by tens of thousands.

It is noteworthy that nearly all the leaders of the reform party were non-Prussian by birth. The heart and soul of the movement was Karl Baron vom Stein (1757–1831), who was born an independent imperial knight. Hardenberg (1750–1822), who succeeded Stein at the head of the state, was an Hanoverian. So was Scharnhorst, the reformer of the Prussian army; Gneisenau, his closest collaborator, was a Saxon; Blücher, a native of Mecklenburg. Of the spiritual leaders, Arndt was a Swede, Niebuhr a Dane, Fichte a Saxon, and Hegel a Württemberger by extraction. This mixture of nationalities further increased the suspicion with which the true-blue Prussian reactionaries looked upon the remodelling of the state of which they had been the sole stewards for centuries.

For many years past Stein had urged the necessity of a progressive reorganization of the whole administrative machinery; but his pleadings had always fallen upon deaf ears. Untaught by the collapse of Jena, Frederick William dismissed him on 3 Jan. 1807 as 'an intractable, obstinate, and disobedient official, of disrespectful and ill-mannered behaviour'. Ten months later, the 'eccentric man' had to be called back and was made the head of the administration. The king never trusted him; to the court and the nobles he was obnoxious as a 'Jacobin': 'Three battles of Auerstädt rather than one reform edict', as one of them put it. Before any of Stein's major projects had taken shape, he was dismissed again (24 Nov. 1808). He recognized the militaristic, bureaucratic and mechanic system of Prussia as the main obstacle to any thorough-going reform. He hated it passionately, but was crushed by its soulless weight.

The power of the lords of the manor was not destroyed, as the king protected them in the maintenance of jurisdiction and police. The social and political privileges of the officers' caste and nobility were hardly touched. Stein's favourite idea of setting up representative assemblies of districts and provinces, culminating in a national parliament, was rejected out of hand. It served well for a bait in 1815 when, after Napoleon's return from Elba, Frederick William called up his Prussians for a second war. When victory was won, the promise of representative government was forgotten. Hardenberg carried out several of Stein's schemes, but he soon grew weary in the face of the stubborn opposition of the Junkers. Thus it was that in almost every department of national life the reforms fell far short of what their promoters had hoped, and what was carried out in most German states. The latent hostility against Prussia which prevailed in the Rhineland after its annexation in 1815 originated to a large extent in the fact that the Rhinelanders had enjoyed a greater measure of freedom and progress under French domination.

The Erfurt Congress of October 1808 was the zenith of Napoleon's career. The alliance with Alexander of Russia was renewed. Germany was pacified. The two Emperors settled the Prussian war-contribution and the subsequent evacuation of the French army of occupation. Prussia evaded the military clauses of the treaty of Tilsit and secretly built up a considerable army. But Frederick William pinned his hopes exclusively on Russia, and Alexander was not yet prepared to abandon his understanding with Napoleon, although Talleyrand was already conspiring with him against his master.

The imperial tradition of the Roman Empire was still strong enough in Austria for a determined effort to be made to break the French hegemony and restore the ancient leadership of the house of Hapsburg. Philip Count Stadion (1763–1824), who was appointed prime minister after the catastrophe of 1805, held progressive ideas very similar to those of Stein. The archdukes Charles and John supported him. Friedrich Gentz, the greatest German publicist of the time, preached the liberation of Europe under Austrian leadership. Although the Emperor Francis was narrow-minded, reactionary, distrustful of his brothers and ministers, and prevented successfully any internal progress, the population and army were fired by a national enthusiasm when Stadion declared war on France (8 Feb. 1809). But the apprehensions of the archduke Charles, commander-in-chief, were only too justified. Prussia kept aloof; Russia and the princes of the Rhenish Confederation fulfilled their obligations to Napoleon. One or two risings 'from Prussia's timid region' and in Hesse were put down very easily, and Austria herself was unprepared and unable to defy Napoleon single-handed. Nevertheless, the archduke Charles succeeded in inflicting all but a major defeat on Napoleon at Aspern (21–22 May); and the Tyrolese, instructed by the archduke John and led by the popular hero, Andreas Hofer, on the model of the Spanish guerillas, drove the French and confederate troops out of their country. Napoleon's military genius and the superior forces at his command turned the scales. The Austrians were defeated at Wagram (5–6 July) and had to submit to the peace of Vienna (14 Oct.). Austria lost Trieste and Illyria to the French vice-royalty of Italy, Galicia was divided between Poland and Russia, and Salzburg and the Inn Quarter went to Bavaria, which also kept the Tyrol. When the Tyrolese refused to lay down their arms, they were subdued by brute force, and Hofer was court-martialled and shot at Mantua (10 Feb. 1810). Stadion was replaced by the former ambassador to Paris, the Rhenish count Clemens Metternich (1773–1859), who was to dominate German and European history for forty fateful years. The financial bankruptcy of the Austrian state could not be averted (20 Feb. 1811). The Emperor, with whom Metternich concurred completely, was tired of all innovations and, most of all, of popular movements. Austria fell into the slumber of autocratic reaction.

For the time being, Francis and Metternich were convinced of the stability of the Napoleonic system and thought it best to accommodate themselves to it. Francis even stooped to marrying his daughter, Maria Louise, to the Corsican upstart (11 March 1810). He played the role of Napoleon's faithful father-in-law with good will and ill grace, without, however, formally joining the Rhenish Confederation. Prussia, too, entered upon a close alliance with Napoleon, in fact became his submissive vassal when Frederick William pledged himself to supply an auxiliary force for Napoleon's campaign against Russia (4 March 1812). For the erstwhile allies had fallen foul of each other, and Napoleon was about to subdue the last continental adversary before settling his final account with Britain. For the last time he gathered the whole of continental royalty around him at Dresden (May); even Francis and Frederick William were present. Hardenberg and Metternich, however, were already entering into secret negotiations with the court of St James's, and Stein was on his way to Alexander, who had invited him to act as his adviser in the liberation of Europe.

On 22 June, Napoleon crossed the Russian frontier without a declaration of war. The contingents of the Rhenish Confederation marched with the Grand Army; the Austrians under Prince Schwarzenberg and the Prussians under Yorck operated independently and listlessly in Galicia and the Baltic provinces. On 14 Dec. the last remnants of the annihilated imperial army recrossed the Prussian frontier in headlong flight. The Prussian patriots saw the judgment of God in this unprecedented catastrophe; but the sovereigns of Russia, Austria and Prussia showed little faith in their own power to throw off the yoke of servitude. Alexander was persuaded by Stein to carry the war beyond the frontiers of Russia, although

Russian nationalists objected strongly. Frederick William was pushed forward against his conviction and inclination. Yorck signed the convention of Tauroggen on his own responsibility (30 Dec. 1812), according to which the Prussian troops were neutralized. The king never forgave this insubordination. The Austrian government, warned by the former fickleness of Russia and Prussia, concluded an armistice with Russia (30 Jan. 1813) without making further commitments. While Stein and the Estates of East and West Prussia organized the arming of the people, Hardenberg and Scharnhorst forced upon the king the Russian alliance of Kalisz (28 Feb.). The Russians entered Berlin on 11 March, and Frederick William, pressed by Gneisenau and the Tsar, declared war on Napoleon on the 16th. The proclamation 'To my peoples', issued 17 March, was a significant deviation from the old Prussian policy. Its author, Hippel, a disciple of Kant, made the king appeal directly to his subjects, render them account of the reasons for the war, and speak of king and country as a unit. This popular appeal did not fail to rouse an enthusiasm which Prussians had never felt before. Russia and England supplied man-power, money, and equipment.

Contrary to the expectations of Stein and the Prussian patriots, the German princes remained faithful to Napoleon, and their subjects showed no inclination to be liberated by Cossacks and Junkers. Only the petty princes of Mecklenburg and Anhalt left the Rhenish Confederation under Russian military pressure, and the marshal Bernadotte, crown-prince elect of Sweden, was bought by English money and Russian promises to desert his former master. Metternich tried to mediate between the belligerents, but the peace congress of Prague (11 July–11 Aug.) proved a failure. On the one hand, Napoleon, inflated by his victory over the Russians and Prussians at Bautzen (20–21 May), was not prepared to accept the very modest demands of the allies. On the other hand, Great Britain aimed at the complete overthrow of the Napoleonic system, and, bearing the purse, did not allow the allies to make peace save on her terms. Austria therefore declared war on France (11 Aug.). An Austrian officer, Radetzky, devised the plan for a concerted action of the allied armies; and Prince Schwarzenberg was appointed allied commander-in-chief. Metternich was charged with the task of estranging the German princes from Napoleon. Bavaria was the first to be won over (8 Oct.). It was guaranteed its integrity, and joined the alliance as a partner of equal rights. Ten days later Napoleon's power was broken at the battle of Leipzig (16–18 Oct.). Frederick Augustus of Saxony was taken prisoner, his country was placed under Russian tutelage. Jerome of Westphalia fled his kingdom. The Rhenish Confederation ceased to exist; its princes hastened to come to terms with Metternich. Stein and Hardenberg raged at the missing of a great opportunity. They would have preferred to suspend all the petty sovereigns and reshape Germany without regard to the Napoleonic creatures and creations. Frederick William, however, was seriously alarmed by this outbreak of national feeling, which he found incompatible with the Prussian ideas of authority. Francis and Metternich, too, were averse to the resuscitation of the German Empire. They wished to keep Prussia at bay by a confederation of German states over which Austria should preside. Every consideration therefore was shown to the members of the late Rhenish Confederation, except the grand dukes of Berg and Frankfort and two petty princes whose territories were at once declared forfeited.

While the allied forces advanced into France, a peace congress met at Châtillon (15 Feb.–19 March). Napoleon was again offered favourable conditions: France should retain the frontiers of 1792 while renouncing the protectorate over Germany, Italy and Switzerland. Again Napoleon set his claims too high; he would not abandon the Rhine frontier, Belgium and Lombardy. That finished the peace negotiations. The allies entered Paris on 31 March. Louis XVIII was restored, and the allies granted him the most favourable terms in the first peace of Paris (30 May). France kept not only the frontiers of 1792, but received Landau and Saarlouis from Germany and improved her other frontiers at the expense of Belgium, Switzerland and Savoy. A few days later Austria and Bavaria settled their mutual claims. Bavaria was to restore the Tyrol, Salzburg and the Inn Quarter, and to receive the grand duchy of Würzburg and the principality of Aschaffenburg instead (3 June). Thus the decisions of the general peace congress were prejudiced in favour of the largest South German state.

The congress opened at Vienna on 1 Nov. 1814. It was the most brilliant meeting that ever brought together the sovereigns and statesmen of Europe. The splendid façade, however, could not conceal the deep rifts that separated the partners. Thus Talleyrand quickly succeeded in making defeated France almost the arbiter of her quarrelling conquerors. The Tsar wished to incorporate the whole of Poland with Russia, and therefore supported the Prussian claims to the whole of Saxony. Castlereagh, Metternich and Talleyrand were united in their endeavour to curb the expansion of Russia and Prussia. The outbreak of a war between Russia and Prussia on the one side, and the rest of Europe on the other, was imminent. It was averted only by the return from Elba of Napoleon, of which the congress heard on 7 March. The common hatred and fear of Napoleon and of the popular movements which he might stir up overcame the dissensions of the sovereigns and diplomatists. The alliance was renewed; France, Denmark, Spain, the Italian and German states joined it. The reshaping of Europe and the reorganization of Germany, the two main tasks of the congress, were dispatched with utmost speed. The Final Act of Vienna was signed on 9 June. It was preceded by a day by the constitution of the German Confederation. On the 18th, Wellington and Blücher defeated Napoleon at Waterloo. Louis XVIII re-entered Paris on 8 July, followed by the allied monarchs on the next day. The second peace of Paris (20 Nov.) deprived France of some frontier districts, of which the Saar territory went to Prussia and Landau to Bavaria. On 26 Sept., Alexander of Russia, Francis of Austria and Frederick William of Prussia signed the Holy Alliance; the Prince Regent of Britain joined it on 20 Nov. Napoleon, who had put himself under British protection, disembarked on St Helena on 17 Oct. The age which has been called after him had come to its close.

The foundations of the new European order laid at Vienna were more solid than those of any former or later date. For forty years to come no war disturbed the peace of Europe; and for forty-five years the map of the continent was not altered by force. It was unfortunate for the posthumous fame of the congress that the diplomatists did not confine themselves to stabilizing the outward relations of the European powers, but tried at the same time to regularize their internal affairs. Shaken with the fear of the ideas of 1789, they regarded liberalism, democracy and nationalism as the common enemies. It was only the dynastic interests which were taken into consideration at Vienna; the needs and aspirations of the peoples found no champion. Poland remained divided amongst her neighbours; Russia acquired the greater part of the portion formerly allotted to Prussia. Italy lost the unity she had enjoyed under Napoleon; Venetia and Lombardy fell to Austria; and Austrian influence was supreme throughout the peninsula except in Savoy.

Germany was redistributed on the principles of 1803, that is to say, for the greed and convenience of the great, without regard to racial, economic, or historical considerations. Prussia regained the greater part of her old possessions on the left bank of the Elbe; these and the former territories of Cologne, Treves, Jülich, Berg, and a dozen more petty principalities and abbeys, were combined in the two new provinces of Rhineland and Westphalia. Swedish Pomerania and the isle of Rügen, coveted ever since 1640, became Prussian, while Sweden took Norway from Denmark, which also ceded Heligoland to Britain, receiving the duchy of Lauenburg in compensation. Saxony got the worst treatment as a punishment for Frederick Augustus's unshakable belief in Napoleon's star: two-thirds of the country came under Prussian rule. Charles Augustus of Weimar also received some spoils; he had hoped to become the Protestant king of undivided Saxony, which he thought would suitably atone for the betrayal of the Protestant cause by the Duke Maurice and the Elector Augustus the Strong. Charles Augustus and the dukes of Mecklenburg and Oldenburg assumed the title of grand dukes. Hanover was made a kingdom and enlarged by East Frisia, the bishopric of Hildesheim, and the imperial city of Goslar.

Austria retired completely from the West and South-West of Germany. Its century-old championship of Germany against France passed over to Prussia. This gave fresh directions to the political outlook of Prussian as well as non-Prussian politicians. The eastern and western parts of Prussia still lacked a geographical connection. It was only to be expected that Prussia would, at the first opportunity, annex the parts of Hanover and Hesse-Cassel lying between. The task of keeping the watch on the rivers Rhine and Memel would always serve as a pretext for strengthening Prussia's position inside Germany. Metternich undoubtedly underrated the Prussian lust for expansion when he agreed to a Prussia extending from Memel to Aix-la-Chapelle.

Stein and other patriots hoped in vain for an organic reconstruction of Germany. Metternich carried the day, and his scheme materialized in the German Confederation. It consisted of the princes and free cities which were left over from the Holy Roman Empire and was set up as an international association of sovereign states under the presidency of Austria. The 'Federal Diet' which met for the first time at Frankfort on 5 Nov. 1816 was in reality a congress of diplomatists. The German peoples were excluded from participating in their own affairs. The confederate governments had only yielded to the popular movement in so far as one clause of the draft of the Federal Act of 8 June 1815 provided that 'representative constitutions shall take place (*sic*) in all member states'. Even this vague concession was eventually robbed of compulsory power, and 'shall' was replaced by the non-committal 'will'. Furthermore, the Federal Act was made an integral part of the Final Act of Vienna, so that the future constitution of Germany was made the joint concern of Europe. Neither the constitutional nor the national problems of Germany were solved. The placing of the Federal Act under the guarantee of foreign powers made it almost inevitable that even legitimate national aspirations would have to be pursued in defiance of Europe, much as the constitutional wishes had to be attained in defiance of the German monarchs.

MAP VIII

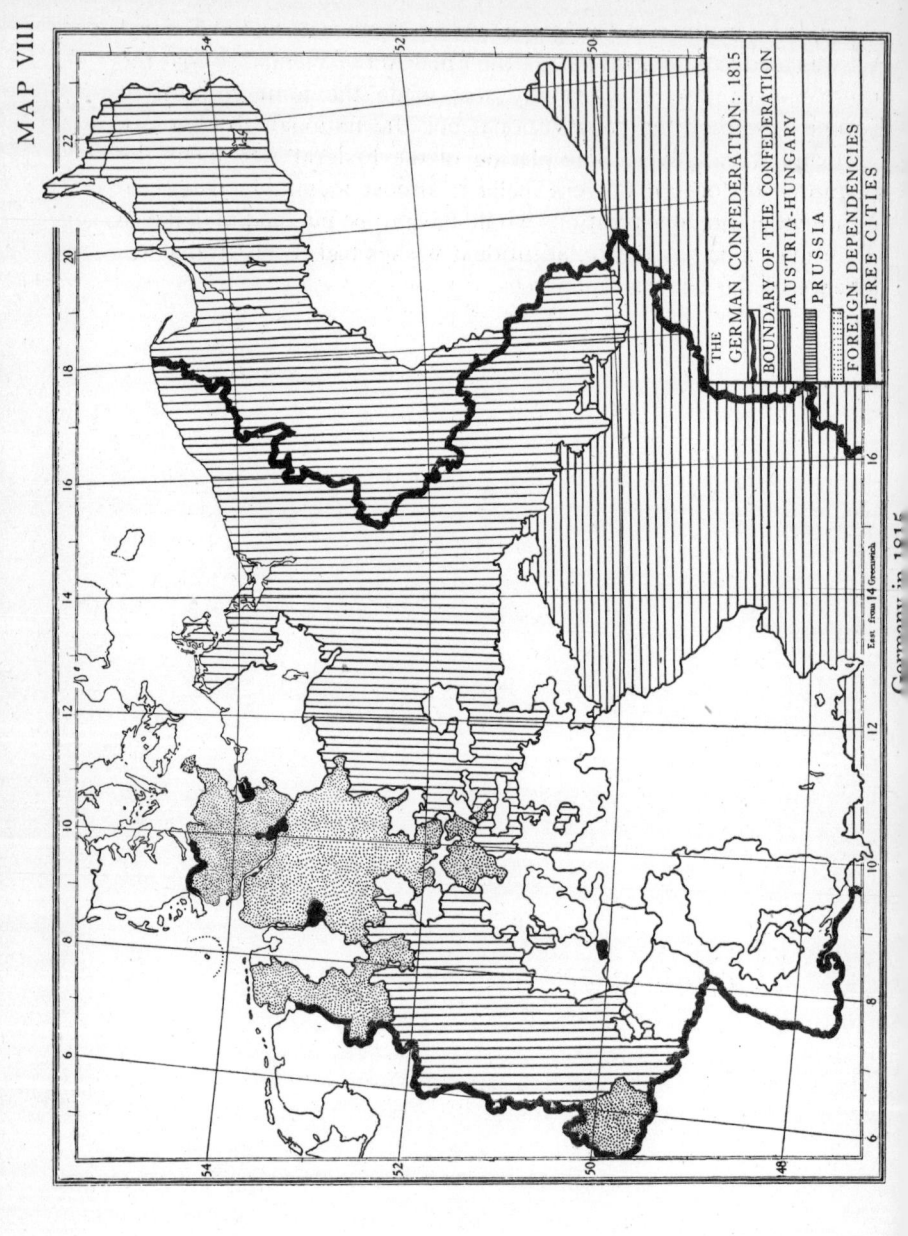

Germany in 1815

CHAPTER VII

THE GERMAN CONFEDERATION (1815-1866)

Two men dominated the German political scene in the nineteenth century. The period stretching from the Congress of Vienna to the revolution of 1848 may be described as the age of Metternich, and the second half of the century as that of Bismarck. The names of Metternich and Bismarck stand not only for the opposing powers of Austria and Prussia; they also represent contradictory political methods. Both were confronted by the prevalent forces of liberalism and nationalism; neither of them was a liberal or a German nationalist himself. Metternich sought openly to crush the liberal and national movements, and was vanquished. Bismarck used them for his own purposes and conquered them. Having attained his ends, he promptly stifled and all but killed the liberal spirit of Germany, and diverted the national movement into the channels of Prussian power politics. 'Bismarck'—as Theodor Mommsen, the great historian and liberal politician, put it—'enlarged Germany and reduced the Germans.'

When the monarchs and their advisers returned from Vienna and Paris in 1815 they were united in one resolve: that a recurrence of the revolutionary upheaval of the last generation must be prevented by every means at their disposal. All of them wanted external and internal peace; some, like Austria and Prussia, because of the sacrifices, others, like Bavaria, Württemberg and Baden, because of the gains which had just accrued to them. Nearly every German state had undergone great territorial changes for the better or the worse; and the constitutional change from the Holy Roman Empire to the German Confederation concerned them all. Talleyrand quickly convinced the victorious allies that the France of the restored Bourbons was no longer the aggressor of the Convention and Napoleonic days. The Holy Alliance set the seal upon the pacific tendencies which were only too natural after the carnage of the past twenty years. Thus the work of reconstruction and maintaining peace at home could be entered upon without disturbances from abroad. The German governments, however, were by no means agreed upon the course by which to secure this end.

In Austria, the time-honoured idea of a supra-national organization was still alive. The Holy Roman Empire was based on it: in theory, it comprised the entire *Res publica Christiana* regardless of national and racial distinctions. Both the German Confederation and the Austrian Empire retained these supra-national features. The king of Great Britain and Ireland was a member of the German Confederation in his capacity as king of Hanover; the king of the United Netherlands, as grand duke of Luxemburg; and the king of Denmark, as duke of Holstein. On the other hand, the Emperor of Austria and the king of Prussia had possessions outside the German Confederation, namely those portions of their monarchies which had not been parts of the Holy Roman Empire. As far as Austria was concerned, this was the greater part of the Empire. Moreover, even half of the section which did belong to the German Confederation was inhabited by non-German races. Thus the still operative tradition of the Holy Empire and the naked will of self-preservation pointed in the same direction: that the statesmen of Vienna should pursue a policy of supra-national co-operation, and therefore oppose the spirit of isolationist nationalism.

The German Confederation was certainly not an ideal creation; but it was something more than a temporary makeshift, and might have developed into the nucleus of a larger European federation. In the light of the accelerating armaments race which harassed Europe after the dissolution of the German Confederation, it is worth remembering that the Confederation was not once involved in a foreign war, whether as aggressor or as victim of aggression. Its military exploits were entirely confined to police actions against recalcitrant members of its own organization. The break-up of the union of the Netherlands and Belgium (1830) did not directly affect the Confederation, as the Dutch portion of Limburg was eventually admitted into it in place of the western half of Luxemburg, which was allotted to Belgium (1839). The structure of the German Confederation received its first blow when the union of Hanover and Great Britain was terminated by the death of William IV (1837). Hanover, no longer part of an international great power, was not now in a position to stem the advancing tide of Prussian aggressiveness, and eventually fell a victim to it (1866). Had Hanover still been connected with Great Britain, Prussia would not have been allowed to eject Denmark from the German Confederation (1864). In this case Austria was shortsighted enough to abandon her principles and follow docilely the Prussian lead—with the result that two years later the tables were turned against herself. The disruption of the German Confederation in 1866 finally severed the supra-national ties which up to that time bound up Germany with Europe. The thoroughly Prussianized Empire of the Hohenzollerns stands at the end of a period which began with the hope of a federated Central Europe.

Half-way between these two attempts to reconcile the traditional variety of German politics with the comparative simplicity of the rest of Europe stands the third solution which was aimed at in 1848. In that year the attempt was made to create a truly national state out of the German peoples. Those parts of the Germanies which contained foreign populations were to be discarded. Prussia was to give up the Polish-speaking districts of her Eastern provinces; Austria was to be dismembered, and Poles, Magyars, Czechs, Yugoslavs and Italians to be left to seek their own salvation. The failure of the Frankfort parliament to reshape Central Europe on these lines was due to various causes. On the one hand the Austrian and Prussian governments were violently opposed to abandoning voluntarily any part of their historic inheritance. Neither of them cared for a national German state. On the other hand, the advocates of this national state were divided against themselves, and that for very natural reasons, although only a few of them were aware of them. They were fogged by romantic ideas of nationhood and accepted blindly the theories of the French Revolution. They did not realize that this German nation which they wanted to unite in a single indivisible state consisted in reality of half a dozen different nationalities. A federal union was quite compatible with their centrifugal interests; and there were economic, constitutional and cultural issues which might profit by a tightening of the loose bonds of the German Confederation. But a centralized state built on a 'national' foundation would never satisfy the natural needs of the Germanies: it could only be brought about if a single state assumed the hegemony by overriding all the other members. None of the parliamentary leaders of the 1848 movement dared to assume this responsibility and crush the vital interests of others for the aggrandisement of his own tribe. Bismarck was not moved by such scruples; on the other hand, he lacked any enthusiasm for the cause of Germany. In fact, his 'German Empire' of 1871 was not the consummation of the longing for national unity. While Bismarck deliberately excluded the Germans of Austria, he did not hesitate to incorporate with his Empire several millions of Poles, Frenchmen and Danes—not on a federal basis, with which these foreign nationals might have agreed, but as subject races under a foreign yoke. Not German nationalism, but Prussian militarism was the foundation stone of the Bismarck Empire.

The 'Empire of Austria', as the Hapsburg possessions were officially called from 1804 to 1867, comprised a greater variety of races than ever before. It was in fact a microcosm of Central and Eastern Europe. The majority of its population was of non-German stock. Poles, Ruthenes and Italians had been added to its former German, Czech, Slovak, Croat, Magyar and Rumanian subjects. Their amalgamation would have tested the wisdom of any statesman at any time. The problem that confronted the chancellor Metternich was even more formidable. For a new element was added to the dynastic and administrative issues, which required a tactful handling. The Romantic movement that swept European life and letters in the first three decades of the nineteenth century made the nations fully conscious of their racial, intellectual and political traditions, and stirred them to maintaining and increasing this inheritance of their own. The modern French idea of the 'Nation State' transformed the memory of a glorious past into aspirations for an even more glorious future. Goethe was among the first to appreciate the national poetry of Czechs and Yugoslavs, and Ranke wrote the first Serbian history in a Western tongue. Could the legitimate claims to national independence be reconciled with the supra-national structure of the Hapsburg Empire?

Three different attempts were made to solve this problem. Metternich flatly denied and defied the legitimacy of any national aspirations and insisted strictly on imperial unity and uniformity. The revolution of 1848 proved this system untenable: the patriotic fervour of the Germans, Czechs, Magyars, Italians, dammed up too long and unharnessed too suddenly, tore down all barriers. Before the ensuing chaos could clarify itself, the revolution was put down with brutal force. However, it needed the loss of the Italian provinces, the defeat of Königgrätz at the hands of the Prussians, and the threat of another national upheaval of the Czechs and Magyars—fomented by Bismarck—to convince the Emperor Francis Joseph of the advisability of a fresh approach. The result was the reconstruction of the Empire on a dualistic basis in 1867: Hungary and the 'kingdoms and countries represented in the imperial Diet'—this was the clumsy official title of what is commonly called the Austrian half of the Dual Monarchy—were separated administratively. Their common ties were the monarch and the ministries of foreign, military and financial affairs. In either half of the Empire, the racial minorities were sacrificed to the respective 'master race', the Magyars and Germans. The Magyars suppressed Germans, Slavs and Rumanians with ruthless force and subtle stratagems. The Germans, on the other hand, gradually lost their dominating position in 'Cisleithania' in favour of Poles and Czechs, without, however, yielding an inch of their claim to absolute mastery, and still looked down upon Slavs as their inferiors. The internal conditions of the Dual Monarchy went from bad to worse. As early as 1900 shrewd foreign observers regarded it as doomed to destruction. The Archduke Francis Ferdinand, whose assassination at Sarajevo unleashed the furies of the Four Years War, outlined a scheme of reconstruction which, if put into force, might have saved the Hapsburg monarchy. His 'trialistic scheme' provided for a federation of three sections, in each of which Magyars, Slavs and Germans would have been supreme respectively, while racial minorities would have enjoyed a legal protection, and foreign, military and economic affairs would have been their common concern. As the Emperor Francis Joseph and the Magyar nationalists opposed this plan, it came to nothing, and in 1918 the unreformed monarchy split up into its component parts without safeguards for the protection of either racial minorities or common economic interests.

One of the difficulties besetting the Hapsburg monarchy at the beginning of the nineteenth century was the peculiar position of the Poles and Italians. Under the rule of Napoleon and his satraps they had enjoyed a measure of liberty and unity which had been denied to the Italians for centuries, and to the Poles for a generation. Both Italy and Poland were now shared out again amongst foreign rulers. The Poles in Austria were the more fortunate when compared with their co-nationals under Russian and Prussian domination. Their influence in Galicia soon became paramount, and they abused it badly by suppressing the Orthodox Ruthenians in Eastern Galicia. In course of time they also gained a fair share in the central administration of Austria. In 1870, the Austro-Hungarian premiership fell for the first time to a Pole; and Poles continued to play a leading part in Austrian politics until 1918.

Conditions in the Lombardo-Venetian kingdom were different. Its population saw across the Austrian frontier two independent Italian states, the kingdom of Piedmont and the pontifical state, each of which might lay claims to the political or religious allegiance of all Italy. While liberals hoped for the unification of Italy under the crown of Piedmont, conservatives expected a federation of the peninsula under papal presidency. Both groups alike detested the Austrian tyranny. They did not wish for its humanization, but its complete abolition, as Daniel Manin said. Confronted by these racial and political aspirations the Emperor Francis I and his chancellor, Metternich, found it easiest to ignore them in theory and suppress them by force whenever they tried to assert themselves. Francis was of an utterly ignoble nature: selfish, pedantic, heartless, incapable of lofty actions himself, and incapable of conceding lofty motives to others. He personally supervised every detail of the daily life of the Italian patriots, who after the failure of the conspiracy of 1821 were incarcerated in the notorious Spielberg fortress in Moravia. While some, such as Antonio Panizzi and Gabriele Rossetti, succeeded in escaping to free Britain, other men of the highest integrity, such as the poet Silvio Pellico and the Marquis Pallavicino, spent up to fifteen years in Austrian dungeons; and Francis made it his special concern to think of fresh vexations with which to torment his victims. Only Francis's death, in 1835, freed most of those who had not succumbed to the mental and physical tortures of their imperial jailer.

Whereas the reactionary and uncompromising attitude of the Emperor sprang from the aridity of his heart and the sterility of his mind, Metternich's policy, though it coincided with that of his master, originated in a very different personality. Born and bred at Coblentz, the archiepiscopal court of Treves, he always retained something of the easy grace of the most lascivious court of that most lascivious period. The intrigues of the boudoir and ball-room influenced, in the fashion of the eighteenth century, his political decisions more often than was compatible with the problems of the new age. A perfect man-about-town and a witty conversationalist, he had a fatuous weakness for regarding a question as solved when he had enshrined it in a brilliant epigram. His philosophy was eighteenth-century rationalism, with the inevitable preponderance of mechanics and medicine. Metternich liked to compare himself to a 'physician in the great hospital of the world'. His mechanistic view of men and affairs led him to underrate the spiritual forces in liberalism and nationalism. With all his political knowledge and psychological perspicacity he meddled with the symptoms of the diseases of his age, rather than applied a thorough treatment. A cosmopolitan by nature and inclination, he considered European politics his proper sphere of action. Austria and Germany came into his range of vision only in so far as they were component parts of the wider unit. He envisaged a European system, well balanced and regulated like a clock, in which Austria, supported by the Germanies, would play the part of a central weight and thus counterbalance the powers of Russia and France. His ignorance of sea-power, customary with continental statesmen, caused him largely to neglect Britain. In any case, Britain played a minor part in his political conceptions; he was to realize his miscalculation when he met with Canning's and Palmerston's support of the liberal and national movements all over Europe.

Considering the age-old rivalry between Austria and Prussia, it is amazing to see the faithfulness, even the subservience, with which the Berlin statesmen accepted Metternich's leadership for more than thirty years. As a matter of fact, they found no fault with his policy of *quieta non movere*, and whole-heartedly supported his measures to extinguish the liberal and national ideas; for these threatened the traditional structure of the Prussian state hardly less than that of Austria. The Polish population in West Prussia and Posen, the liberal intelligentsia in East Prussia and the Rhineland, and the disciples of Stein and Kant entertained ideas which were utterly alien to the autocratic and militaristic foundations of Prussia. The royal promise of a charter given in the hour of supreme need was forgotten as soon as victory was achieved. It was, however, not forgotten by the youth who had enthusiastically waged war for the new Prussia which Stein, Scharnhorst and Humboldt had conjured up; nor by the Rhenish and Westphalian industrialists who fought the battle of the industrial revolution against bureaucratic reaction. One lesson, however, long neglected by Junkers and bureaucrats, had been learned by the rulers of Prussia from the bitter experience of the past decade, namely the importance of spiritual and economic factors in public life. Wilhelm von Humboldt had inaugurated a new era in education when he became Minister of Public Instruction in 1809. He carried into effect the ideal of compulsory and free school attendance for the whole population, reformed secondary education on classical as well as modern lines, and made the universities sanctuaries of unfettered research. This educational system, admirable in itself, was now put under strict state control, and subjected to the peculiar exigencies of Prussianism. Altenstein, Minister of Education from 1817 to 1838, was an enlightened and moderately liberal man. But the man who stamped his mark upon Prussian education was Hegel, the philosopher (1770–1831). For twenty years none but his disciples occupied the chairs of philosophy, education and political economy at all Prussian universities; and many generations of schoolmasters were grounded in the doctrines of

Hegelianism, which they in turn imparted to untold hosts of schoolchildren. In fact, Hegel became the very *praeceptor Borussiae*. His philosophy is the epitome of Prussianism. In a deliberately obscure language, he and his disciples taught those conceptions which, reduced to popular and vulgar slogans, were eventually embodied in the Nazi system: the doctrine of the omnipotent state beside which the fate and happiness of the individual count for nothing; the doctrine of the revelation of the Almighty in and through successive nations culminating in His present embodiment as the 'German God'; the equation of the Divine will to the interests of the state—always with the tacit or openly proclaimed understanding that 'the state' is the Prussian monarchy.

Next to the School, the Church was to be co-ordinated. The multiplicity and variety of denominations were an eyesore to an administration accustomed to the dressed ranks of uniform battalions. Frederick William III, a martinet on the parade ground and a Philistine in intellectual matters, set himself to redress this irregularity. As the supreme head (*summus episcopus*) of the non-Roman churches, he enjoined the amalgamation of all these denominations in a centralized ecclesiastical body, the Prussian Union (1817). A great many pastors and congregations, chiefly Lutheran, resisted this compulsory fusion, and a ruthless persecution of the recalcitrants broke out. Those who survived the years of an embittered struggle were eventually granted a meagre toleration, but the spirit of the Protestant Church as a whole was broken. It was transformed into a willing tool of the Hohenzollerns. The complete submission of the 'altar' to the 'throne' had the most disastrous consequences for the Church. All the liberal, democratic and socialist elements which opposed existing political conditions were incidentally pushed into hostility to a Church which identified itself completely with the secular powers of the day. From that first Church struggle onward, political opposition was accompanied by indifference if not antagonism to the Church and Christianity, on the part of the nominal members of the Protestant Churches in Prussia.

The Roman Catholic Church was the next victim of the ever expanding *étatisme*; but the Catholic clergy and laity held their ground more firmly than the Protestants. The trouble arose simultaneously in the Rhenish and Polish provinces; in both cases, the religious issue was exacerbated by liberal sentiments on the part of the Rhenish and by national susceptibilities on that of the Polish populations. The Prussian government tried to reduce the Catholic clergy to state officials such as the Protestant pastors had become; this determined their attitude to the intricate questions of mixed marriages and the language to be used in divinity lessons and in the pulpit. When the Catholic clergy persisted in their resistance to state interference in canonical matters, the administration resorted to force (1837). The archbishops of Cologne and Posen were imprisoned; public gatherings throughout the Catholic provinces of Rhineland and Westphalia were broken up by cavalry attacks. The Catholic population was subjected to every form of chicanery and oppression, but they remained firm. Frederick William IV, who succeeded his father in 1840, broke off the hopeless struggle. Irreparable mischief, however, was done: the Rhinelanders and Poles, who had come not too willingly under Prussian rule in 1815, were irretrievably alienated from the Prussian state. The second Church struggle, Bismarck's Kulturkampf, 1871–78, intensified their animosity, and they never felt at home in the Hohenzollern monarchy, nor did the Prussian government ever regard them as loyal citizens.

While Prussia failed conspicuously to gain the hearts of her recently acquired subjects, her endeavours to exploit the sphere of economics for her exterior aggrandisement were altogether successful. Here, Prussian statesmen had not to contend with popular movements of an emotional and irrational character with which they had not learned—and were never to learn—to cope. The opponents who were to be goaded into economic 'collaboration' with Prussia were the governments of the lesser and petty German states; they could be cajoled, threatened or forced into compliance by economic pressure or show of military strength.

These German states, hemmed in between the great powers of Austria and Prussia, had to tread very warily. However much the rigid police system of Metternich and his Prussian followers contributed to the smooth running of the government machine at home, the very fact that it was the system of Austria and Prussia made the lesser German states restive. Proud of their international status of sovereignty, recently won and more recently confirmed, they were anxious to stress their independence and not to seem mere appendants to one of the great powers. As the latter had chosen the path of undiluted coercion and reaction, the rest of the Germanies saw their opportunity in following a liberal course. Hesse-Cassel made a noteworthy exception. The old Elector had spent his exile from 1806 to 1814 in amassing a vast fortune by dubious transactions with the Rothschilds. Back at Cassel, he hit on the ingenious idea of simply putting the clock back to 1806. The interlude of the kingdom of Westphalia was to be wiped out: the colonel was reduced to the rank of lieutenant, the burgomaster moved back to the clerk's desk, and the Elector himself retained his electoral title although there was no longer an emperor to elect. This utter disregard for the signs of the time was, however, not imitated anywhere else.

The South and Central German states—Bavaria, Württemberg, Baden, Hesse-Darmstadt, and a number of lesser principalities—had by no means fared badly when they had adapted themselves to the political tenets of Napoleonic France. They saw therefore no reason why they should renounce the means by which they had gained so much. Little Saxe-Weimar, ruled by the benevolent and progressive Charles Augustus, took-the lead: as early as 1816 a constitutional charter was granted. The larger South German states soon followed suit, and from 1820 onward a vigorous political life grew up. All these charters were modelled more or less on the famous French *Charte* of 1814. As was the case in France, the government retained the final decision; and in some departments, such as foreign and military affairs, the representatives of the people had no say whatever. The deputies were also barred from the government bench; and the franchise was strictly limited to the upper classes. Yet parliamentary life, rudimentary as it was, brought the middle classes into closer contact with public affairs than ever before. Political parties made a tentative appearance and helped to educate inarticulate subjects into responsible citizens. Parliaments and parties combined to bring forth the first-fruits of political oratory, experience and leadership. A great number of adroit tacticians, well-informed politicians, and unselfish statesmen stepped forth from the Diets of Munich, Stuttgart, Karlsruhe and Darmstadt, when the German people were called to take their destiny into their own hands, in 1848.

It was no longer exclusively kings and courts, diplomatists and secretaries of state who decided the fate of nations. Public opinion made itself felt throughout the Germanies. Neither the doctrinaire reaction which kept down Metternich's Austria, nor the militaristic bureaucracy which constrained the Hohenzollern monarchy, could bar their own middle classes from taking an increasing interest in state affairs which they gradually learned to regard as their own. The greater political activities in the constitutional states could not fail to be watched carefully across the frontiers. In return, the parliamentary debates and political agitation in these countries received an additional stimulus. The politicians of Baden and Württemberg were conscious of their joint responsibility for the peoples of Prussia, Austria and other states who could not yet voice their grievances and aspirations themselves.

The two main topics with which the contemporary newspapers, periodicals, pamphlets and public debates resounded were the rights of the individual citizen and the reorganization of Germany. The advocates of progress demanded the introduction of constitutional charters where there existed none, and the development towards fully parliamentary forms of government where the existing charters had paved the way. However, liberal tenets which aimed at the greatest possible freedom from state interference in the affairs of the individual, and democratic ideas which demanded the fullest participation in state affairs on the part of the individual, were not clearly defined; they overlapped even in the pronouncements of the same publicist or politician. The conservative democracy of Arndt and Uhland, the liberal doctrines of Rotteck and Dahlmann, and the socialist radicalism of Georg Büchner, were for a long time considered mere nuances of the one idea of civic progress.

The same confusion persisted in the various ideas put forward for the future of Germany. Some radicals championed a centralized republic with a president, elected for two years, at its head. As this was clearly utopian, the majority favoured a development of the existing Confederation towards greater efficiency and unity. Opinions, however, were divided as to how this goal should be attained. Should the Holy Roman Empire be revived in a form better suited to the exigencies of modern times? Those who advocated this solution were to be found chiefly among the South-West German politicians, with whom the memory of the 'Empire' was strongest. This group was to become known as the 'hereditary imperial' (*Erbkaiserliche*) or 'Greater Germany' (*Grossdeutsche*) party, as the emperorship of the Hapsburgs and the inclusion of the German-speaking provinces of the Austrian monarchy were two main items of their programme.

The other extreme was represented by those who advocated the unification of Germany under Prussian leadership. As Austria could not be expected to bow to a Hohenzollern Emperor, the entire Hapsburg monarchy would have to be excluded from the German Empire, although the two should become close allies. This group was later on nicknamed the 'Little Germany' (*Kleindeutsche*) party. It recruited its adherents chiefly from Prussia. But just as a great many Catholics of the Rhenish and Westphalian provinces of Prussia preferred a Hapsburg Emperor to a Hohenzollern, many South German Protestants looked for a Hohenzollern Empire rather than a resuscitated Holy Roman Empire.

Various other schemes were mooted, among which that of a diarchy found a not inconsiderable following. According to this scheme, Austria and Prussia should alternate in the rule of Germany; or else the Emperor of Austria should be installed as the actual German Emperor while the dignity of a perpetual Imperial Generalissimo, including the supreme command over all forces, should be vested in the king of Prussia.

None of these plans for a reform of the political superstructure of Germany coincided wholly with any of the programmes which aimed at promoting constitutional liberty. Groups which were agreed upon, say, the principle of ministerial responsibility in Baden or the abolition of feudal tithes in Hesse, might easily find their members in opposite camps when the problem of fitting Austria into the framework of a united Germany was under discussion.

An intrinsic weakness of all these political groups was their almost religious belief in the magic power of the written word. This was a consequence, perhaps an inevitable one, of the fact that two-thirds of the nation were entirely excluded from active participation in public affairs and that even the third part was not allowed full responsibility. All classes thus lacked that political experience which exercises such a sobering influence on high-flown theories. With a consistent party programme and a legally flawless charter, they thought that every political problem could be solved, indeed was solved already. This passion for the correct formula, and the unending theoretical struggles which needs must arise from it, remained a characteristic feature of public life in Germany. Heresy hunting and the casting of suspicion on the intellectual integrity of political opponents were the inseparable consequence.

Having anticipated the growth of political thought up to the revolution of 1848, let us return to the situation of 1815. There was a unanimous desire to give the German Confederation a fair trial. The Federal Diet (*Bundestag*) at Frankfort was opened by an address for which Metternich was responsible (5 Nov. 1816): an unfettered public opinion and the national interest, so it said, should be the guiding stars of their deliberations. The Hessians were granted protection against the wild schemes of their Elector, who wished to annul all business agreements contracted during his exile; the constitution of Saxe-Weimar was taken under the guarantee of the Confederation, as the Grand Duke Charles Augustus had asked; and clause 13 of the Confederate Act, according to which parliamentary representations should be set up, was recalled to the various governments. Even in Prussia, whose militaristic structure was least compatible with popular institutions, Hardenberg was allowed to convene a royal commission for the preparation of a charter, and Wilhelm von Humboldt was nominated its chairman (1819).

By this time, however, reaction was in full ascendancy. Rioting by university students gave timid administrations ample reason, and determined reactionaries welcome pretexts for curbing the rising tide of radicalism. Inflated by their real and imaginary heroism in the War of Liberation, filled with romantic ideas of German nationhood (*Volkstum*), this generation of students felt called to great deeds. Their revolutionary nationalism was fomented by a number of professors, who supplied the theoretical justification for intolerance, Frankophobia and anti-Semitism. The moderates, who stood for an organic development of popular rights and national consolidation, were swept aside. On the three-hundredth anniversary of the day that Luther promulgated the ninety-five theses (31 Oct. 1817), hundreds of students, chiefly of Jena University, flocked to Wartburg castle. The meeting ended in a rude commotion. A number of books of an 'anti-student' tendency and some insignia of Prussian militarism, Austrian despotism and Hessian reactionism were publicly burnt. This *auto-da-fé* gave the signal to the governments of Austria, Prussia and Russia to make serious representations to the other German governments: revolution, they argued, was imminent, and the universities were its hotbed. This fear grew when the playwright and publicist, Kotzebue, who was paid by the Tsar to attack the Teutomaniacs, was murdered by a Jena student of divinity (23 March 1819). When shortly afterwards another attempt was made on a harmless official of Nassau, Metternich convened a conference of the principal German states at Karlsbad. The Karlsbad decrees, issued on 1 Sept. 1819, aimed at exterminating the dreaded 'German revolution' root and branch. A strict censorship was set up for all printed matter of less than 320 pages; the universities were placed under close supervision; professors were to be dismissed at the discretion of the university curators; students were forbidden to associate. A Central Investigation Committee was instituted at Mayence, and a Provisional Executive Ordinance prescribed military execution against member states which might be unwilling to carry out these draconian measures.

Sweeping regulations such as the Karlsbad decrees cannot fail to produce blunders and injustice. The examining magistrates vented their spite against anybody who for any reason had incurred their displeasure. Amongst the victims of this so-called 'persecution of demagogues' were noble and lofty characters such as Arndt and Schleiermacher, and harmless boys such as Fritz Reuter, who in after years was to become one of the foremost poets in Low German dialect. The Prussian judges showed themselves the most ruthless, whereas Charles Augustus of Weimar displayed his wonted benevolence and did not interfere with his little parliament or the privileges of Jena University, much as he was pressed to do so. Although his lenient views were shared by a number of other potentates, the Karlsbad decrees set the seal on the final victory of reaction in Prussia. Frederick William III was more than ever convinced of the propriety of Metternich's policy, and the scheme of a representative constitution was buried once and for all.

Metternich was not slow in following up his advantage. A conference of all the member states of the German Confederation accepted the Final Act of Vienna (15 May 1820), which was embodied in the constitution of the Confederation. It interpreted the sovereignty of the confederate monarchs in such a way that it could not be restricted by constitutional institutions; and it obliged the monarchs to succour each other against recalcitrant subjects even if a ruler should be prevented by those subjects from calling upon the aid of the Confederation—which meant the wholesale release from the oath upon the constitution which the princes had taken.

The Final Act of Vienna put an end to the independent activities of the Federal Diet at Frankfort. The representatives of Württemberg and two Hessian principalities, who tried to uphold the original purposes of the assembly, were forced by Metternich to leave Frankfort. The publication of the minutes of the diet was discontinued. The diet itself was nothing more than the recipient and forwarder of the orders of its president, the Austrian representative. Throughout the decade from 1820 to 1830 the central organ of the Confederation was paralysed, Austria and Prussia remained impervious to any political innovation, and the lesser states had to tread very warily so as not to imperil their precarious status.

The one great change Germany underwent during this period took place outside the official machinery of the Confederation, almost outside the political sphere altogether. It was the preparation of the German Customs Union, and it was originated by Prussia.

The last triumph of Hardenberg's statesmanship had been the amalgamation of the old Prussian provinces with those recovered from the late Rhenish Confederates and the fresh acquisitions made at the expense of Saxony and the secularized and mediatized West German princes. In 1818 the whole monarchy was divided into ten provinces, each of which was placed under a Lieutenant-Governor (*Oberpräsident*) and subdivided into Administrative Districts (*Regierungsbezirke*). Each *Regierungsbezirk*, in its turn, was comprised of a number of Circles (*Kreise*) headed by a Sheriff (*Landrat*). This organization worked most satisfactorily, was extended to the provinces acquired in 1864 and 1866, and survived the republican and National-Socialist revolutions of 1918 and 1933.

At the same time the economic amalgamation of the Prussian provinces was carried out by the Director-General of Taxation, Karl Georg Maassen (1769–1834). His customs law of 26 May 1818 superseded sixty-seven local tariffs and became the cornerstone of Prussian and German trade policy until Bismarck initiated the era of protectionist tariffs in 1879. Maassen's decree was based on free-trade principles; he was a disciple of Adam Smith, and resolutely abandoned the prohibitive system of Frederick William I and Frederick the Great. Moderate duties on the importation and transit of foreign products encouraged foreign and home trade, and raised the standard of living of the population without making the industry unfit for competition abroad. This policy, if carried out in an even larger territory, would obviously appeal to neighbouring states. Friedrich Adolf von Motz (1775–1830), the Prussian Minister of Finance, envisaged a Central European customs union under Prussian leadership and worked patiently towards this goal. The petty states of North and Central Germany were more or less compelled to choose between joining the Prussian system and being starved. Schwarzburg-Sondershausen, a Thuringian principality, was the first country to conclude a tariff treaty with Prussia (1819). She handed over her customs administration to the big neighbour for a proportionate share of the revenue, and renounced an economic policy of her own. Other small states followed suit during the next years and the economic power of Prussia increased correspondingly.

The South German states wished to reap the fruits of an enlarged customs district without giving up their economic independence to Prussia; and Bavaria, Württemberg and Hohenzollern therefore set up a customs union of their own (1828). Contrary to the treaties concluded by Prussia, this association did not infringe upon the sovereignty of the partners, so that Prussia had to grant similar rights to Hesse-Darmstadt when she joined the Prussian customs union in the same year. A third group of states, in which Saxony, Hesse-Cassel and Hanover took the lead, concluded the Commercial Association (Sept. 1828). The members of this association pledged each other not to join either of the rival customs unions. However, the economic power of the Prussian system and the political pressure behind it were too powerful. In 1829 a working arrangement was achieved between the Prussian and South German groups. The Commercial Association was ground down and several of its members joined the union individually. Finally, on 22 March 1833, the German Customs Union (*Deutscher Zollverein*) was established. It came into force on 1 Jan. 1834, and comprised about four-fifths of the future Germany of Bismarck. Only Baden, Nassau, Brunswick, Mecklenburg, the Hanse towns and the Danish, English and Dutch dependencies kept aloof. They, too, gradually came round: Baden and Nassau in 1836, Brunswick and Luxemburg in 1842, Hanover in 1851. The Elbe duchies, Mecklenburg and Lübeck were included in 1867, Alsace-Lorraine in 1872. Hamburg and Bremen held out longest; it was only in 1888 that they abandoned the many advantages accruing from their singular position as free ports.

Prussia had been careful from the beginning to make no overtures to Austria. This in itself shows sufficiently that Prussia wanted to use the customs union for her political ends. Metternich did not underrate the political significance of the Customs Union, but he shunned energetic steps which might have endangered his general policy. When Karl Ludwig von Bruck (1798–1860) took over the Austrian Ministries of Commerce (1848) and Finances (1855) it was too late to unsettle Prussia from her leading position in German economics. Bruck was a native of Elberfeld, one of the industrial centres of the Prussian Rhineland; and he applied most successfully the lessons he had learned at home to the conditions of his adopted fatherland. It was he who transformed the Hapsburg monarchy into a unified customs district, created the Austrian chambers of commerce, founded the Austrian Lloyd at Trieste, and by a skilful handling of all problems of taxation and tariffs re-established Austria as a political and economic great power after the downfall of 1848. He aimed at creating a vast Central European customs union which would have stretched from the North and Baltic Seas to the Mediterranean and the Black Sea: in fact, he anticipated by two generations the Central European idea of Friedrich Naumann. When he broached

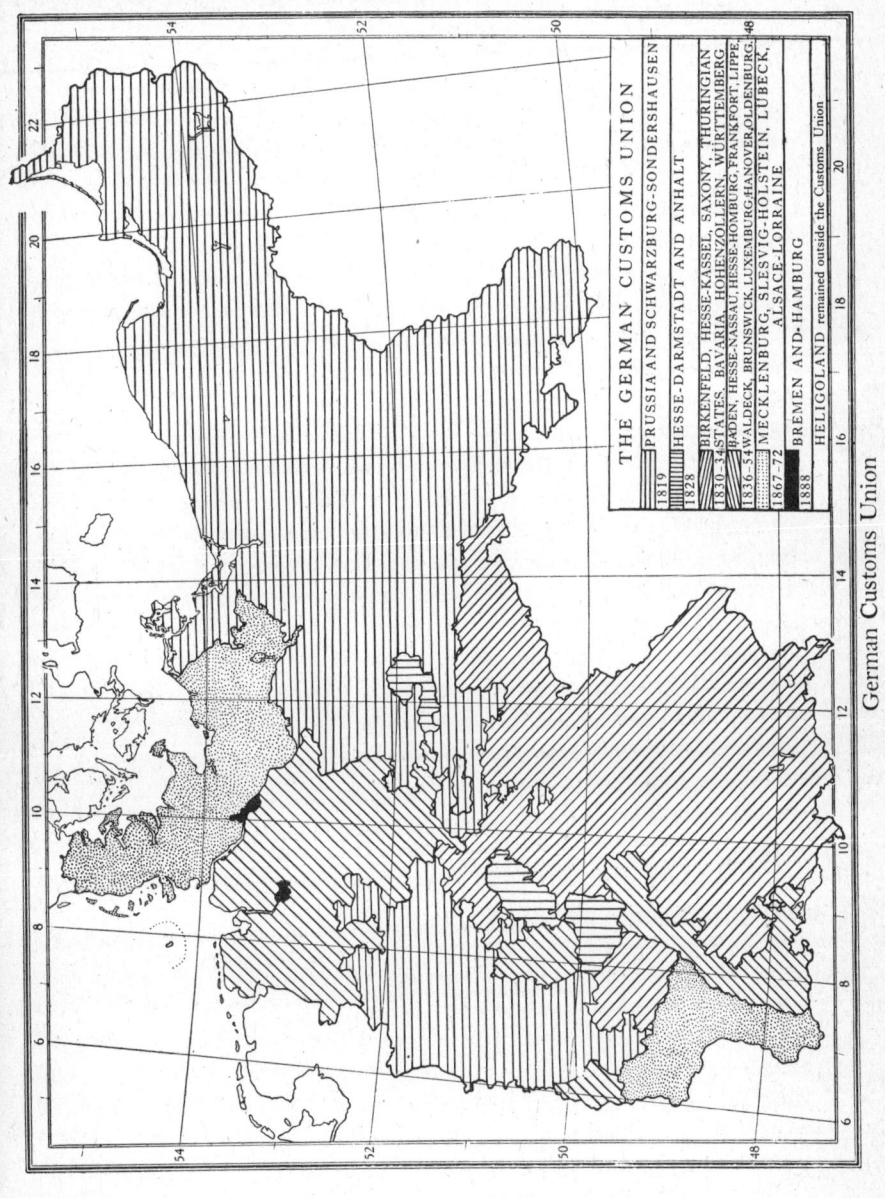

German Customs Union

the fusion of the German Customs Union with Austria, he met with the ready support of the lesser German states. They welcomed the plan which would have expanded their commercial sphere and at the same time relieved the one-sided pressure from Prussia. Political, not economic reasons caused Prussia to veto this extension of the Customs Union. When the treaties were renewed in 1853, Hanover and Oldenburg were admitted to full partnership. Austria, however, had to be content with a commercial treaty which came into force on 1 Jan. 1854 and expired on 31 Dec. 1865. On this very day Prussia concluded a commercial treaty with Italy, at that time the chief enemy of Austria; and less than six months later Prussia and Italy were to declare war on Austria.

It was not without reason that the German Customs Union was concluded shortly after the year 1830. For the revolutions which in this year overthrew the Bourbon monarchy in France and the house of Orange in Belgium had violent repercussions in Germany. The political stagnation which characterized the 'twenties came to an abrupt end. Austria and Prussia, it is true, were hardly touched by the revolutionary agitation. Their police system worked too well for that. Those governments of the lesser states, which had refused any concession to the demand for parliamentary representation, had to bear the brunt of popular indignation. Brunswick, Hesse-Cassel, Saxony and Hanover became the scenes of the first genuine revolutions in Germany. The duke of Brunswick, the perfect copy of an Asiatic despot, had to flee his country, and was replaced by his younger brother. The rulers of Saxony and Hesse-Cassel had to accept their respective heirs as co-regents, and thus virtually abdicated. Count Münster, the actual regent of Hanover under the popular viceroy, the duke of Cambridge (1816–37), had to resign. All these countries were given charters (1831–33). The Hessian constitution even stipulated the right of refusing to pay taxes and demanded the oath on the constitution from the army officers.

The liberals and democrats in South Germany felt encouraged by these happenings. They convened a great meeting at Hambach in the Palatinate (27 May 1832), and the speeches made on this occasion reflected the general trend of thought common to the progressive politicians up and down the Germanies. A German union based on the sovereignty of the people, and co-operating harmoniously within a European league of nations, was the chief tenet. The liberation of the Poles and the emancipation of women were amongst the main items of foreign and home politics. The black, red and gold colours, originally those of the Jena *Burschenschaft* (students' association), were now generally adopted as the colours of German liberty and unity.

The Hambach festival gave Metternich and his Prussian henchmen the long-desired pretext for intensifying the persecution of liberals and democrats. The Federal Diet prohibited all political associations, popular meetings, and the showing of black, red and gold cockades, and suppressed a large number of newspapers (5 July 1832). These repressive measures were increased even more when, on 3 April 1833, a small number of revolutionaries made a foolhardy attack on the main guard station at Frankfort. They hoped to raise the whole of Germany once they had got control of the Federal Diet, but nobody stirred on their behalf, and they were overpowered in a few hours. The Vienna conferences (Jan.–June 1834), under Metternich's chairmanship, decided upon the strictest coercion of university students and professors. Peace—the peace of the police-sabre —was restored once more. But it was an uneasy peace and the popular movement had gained too much power and self-confidence to suffer such treatment indefinitely.

The critical attitude of public opinion became apparent on the flagrant breach of the constitution of Hanover by its sovereign. With the death of William IV in 1837, the union of Great Britain and Hanover came to an end, for the young Queen Victoria was debarred by the Salic law from the succession to the German patrimony of her dynasty. The heir to this throne was the duke of Cumberland, the wickedest of the 'wicked uncles', who, according to *The Times*, had committed every crime save suicide. Scarcely had he settled in Hanover when he abolished by a stroke of the pen the charter of 1833. Seven professors of the University of Göttingen solemnly protested against this act of despotism, amongst them the brothers Grimm, Gervinus and Dahlmann, the historians, and Wilhelm Weber, the inventor of telegraphy. The king dismissed the seven on the spot. But public indignation seized the whole of Germany irrespective of party opinions. A strong minority of the Federal Diet urged an intervention of the Confederation against the perjured king. Austria and Prussia had to throw in their full weight to save him from the fate that had overcome his cousin of Brunswick seven years earlier. Even so, Prussia admitted the Grimms and other professors to her universities, and four of them were to reappear on the tribune of the Frankfort National Assembly in 1848.

While the succession of the half-witted Ferdinand to the Austrian throne (1835) was of no importance in German politics, as Metternich retained his preponderant influence, the accession of Frederick William IV in Prussia had a rousing effect even beyond the frontiers of Prussia. The 'romantic on the throne of the Caesars' as he was called was the most un-Prussian Hohenzollern monarch. He was interested in art, literature and music, averse to militarism, easily swayed by enthusiastic impulses, but lacked steadiness of purpose and staying-power. The mental disorder which overtook him in 1858 cast its shadow upon him long before.

His first acts roused general applause. He gave an amnesty to the victims of the 'persecution of demagogues', reinstalled dismissed professors and officials, composed the quarrel with the Roman Catholics in the Rhineland and Posen, and moderated the rigid censorship. As a romantic admirer of the splendour of the medieval empire he willingly accepted the Austrian hegemony in German affairs. He was ready to 'merge Prussia in Germany', as he himself put it later on, trusting that Prussia as well as Germany would be the mutual gainers by this combination. He was also anxious to set going constitutional life in Prussia, to show that his monarchy no longer meant to lag behind the rest of Germany. At this point, however, the gulf soon became visible which divided Frederick William's romantic autocracy from the spirit of the age. He was a convinced adherent of the political philosophy of C. L. von Haller, the romantic publicist. Haller proclaimed that 'princes were not set up or made by the people; on the contrary, they gradually assembled their subjects round themselves and took them into their service. The people do not take priority over the prince, but on the contrary, the prince is prior to the people, just as the father exists prior to his children.' Haller also denounced the idea that the prince is the administrator, servant, or trustee of the commonwealth as 'emanating from the spirit of revolution': the exercise of government, he contends, is his right, not his duty.

With these ideas of kingship Frederick William IV combined a sincere admiration of English constitutional life. England, he said, enjoyed a constitution which had grown naturally and had not been 'ready made' as were the continental constitutions on the French model. The difficulty of transplanting institutions from the Thames to the Spree, however, was not made less formidable by the warnings which Metternich, the Tsar Nicholas I (Frederick William's brother-in-law), and Prince William, the king's brother and heir presumptive, poured into his ears. Valuable years were thus wasted.

When at last Frederick William moved, the popular enthusiasm which had greeted his accession had long given way to disappointment. On 3 Feb. 1847, Frederick William summoned the United Diet which was composed of the diets of all the Prussian provinces. Its composition and the limitation of its rights completed the general disillusionment over the king's ideas of popular representation. The high aristocracy and the nobility comprised nearly half of the assembly; periodicity of sessions, the chief demand of the progressionists, was expressly rejected by the king. The atmosphere of the diet which met at Berlin on 11 April resembled very much that of the States-General at Versailles in 1789. The majority threw out every bill proposed by the government. On 26 June, the United Diet was dissolved. The king and deputies parted in ill-humour.

Despite this meagre result, the political development of Prussia in the 'forties deeply impressed Germany. At last one of the great powers which had so long blocked the way of progress seemed to wheel round into the path of German liberalism and nationalism. National feelings had been roused to a high pitch by the French threat of war in 1840. In that year France was excluded from the London treaty which Britain, Russia, Austria and Prussia signed for the protection of Turkey against Mehemed Ali of Egypt, the French protégé. Thiers, the then French premier, spoke of another Waterloo and was prepared to rehabilitate the honour of the French arms by crossing the Rhine and the Alps. Prussia, especially Prince William, was eager to take up the challenge and chastise France; the recovery of Alsace was mentioned as a desirable prize. This Prussian bellicosity put Metternich and Palmerston in a pacific mood, as neither of them wished to see Prussia gain fresh laurels in a popular war. After Louis Philippe had dropped Thiers, France was admitted to signing the Convention of the Straits (13 July 1841).

The firm attitude of Prussia enhanced Frederick William's reputation throughout Germany, and especially in the South-West, which would have borne the brunt of French aggression. Prussia came to be considered the natural champion of Germany against the hereditary enemy—a role that had been Austria's for three centuries.

This national *élan* found fresh inspiration when Holstein was in danger of being torn from Germany. The legal position of the Elbe duchies, Slesvig and Holstein, was a curious relic of feudalism which baffled the most perspicacious historians and lawyers. The duchy of Slesvig had been considered part of the Danish monarchy ever since 1025, when Conrad II formally ceded it to King Canute. The duchy of Holstein had been an integral part of the Empire ever since it was Christianized and Germanized in the early twelfth century. When in 1460 the king of Denmark and duke of Slesvig also succeeded to Holstein, the two duchies were declared 'inseparable for ever', although Slesvig continued to remain a part of the Danish monarchy and Holstein a member of the Holy Roman Empire and, later on, the German Confederation. Apart from the northern fringe of Slesvig, the population was German. The national movement of the early nineteenth century opened the eyes of the Danes as well as Slesvig-Holsteiners to their racial differences, and the peaceable companionship slowly gave way to friction. The influence of Slesvig-Holsteiners at the court and in the administration of the Danish monarchy, which had been supreme in the seventeenth and eighteenth centuries, waned. The complicated and delicate situation became even more precarious when the royal house of Denmark was about to die out. In Denmark and Slesvig the distaff line of the house of Holstein-Glücksburg was qualified for the succession. In Holstein, however, the Salic law was in force, so that the dukes of Augustenburg, the next male agnates, were to succeed. The result would thus have been similar to the separation of Hanover from England in 1837, had not the clause 'inseparable for ever' barred this solution. The Danes naturally wanted to keep Holstein; the Holsteiners and Slesvigers wanted Slesvig severed from Denmark. In 1846, King Christian VIII issued an 'Open Letter' in which he implicitly announced that the Danish order of succession was valid for Holstein as well. The Slesvig-Holsteiners protested vigorously. The Federal Diet asserted, in terms cautious but unmistakable, the rights of the German Confederation, the house of Augustenburg and the Slesvig-Holstein Estates. When the childless Frederick VII succeeded to the throne (20 Jan. 1848) he made things worse by reducing the duchy of Slesvig to the status of a Danish province and severing its ties with Holstein (23 March). The very day after, a German government of Slesvig-Holstein was set up to defend the right of the duke of Augustenburg, and this rebellion was speedily followed by open war in which Prussia took the lead.

These events, however, must be seen in connection with the greater upheaval which, in the meantime, had seized the whole of Germany.

From 1839 onwards at fairly regular intervals the deputies of the South German diets held informal meetings at which they discussed problems of common interest. Reform of the German Confederation was the main topic of these conferences. The convocation and failure of the Prussian United Diet induced the meeting at Heppenheim, on 10 Oct. 1847, to accept the suggestion that in every parliament a motion should be put that a German National Assembly should be convened. When the preparatory committee took up its task at Frankfort, on 31 March 1848, the whole of Germany was aflame. Hopes and expectations outstripped everything the promoters of the assembly expected six months earlier. All Germany was in the turmoil of revolution.

The revolutions of 1848 started in Sicily, but the movement was seen to be of European-wide dimensions when the Orleans monarchy in France was overthrown. Its repercussions in Germany were spontaneous and far-reaching. Everywhere administrations were overthrown, leaders of the opposition called into office, and the principal demands of the liberals granted: freedom of the press, freedom of associations and political meetings, trial by jury, and extension of self-government. It was a revolution of the bourgeoisie; progressive noblemen supported it, the peasantry followed, as did the working class. The industrialization of Germany was still in its infancy, and the organization of labour was rudimentary. Although Marx and Engels had just published the *Communist Manifesto* in London, the German workmen threw in their lot with the professional classes, industrialists, and students, the three chief representatives of the new order.

Along with these 'achievements of March', the German question, i.e. the reorganization of the German Confederation, was taken in hand. The Heidelberg congress of the South-West German parliamentarians (5 March) prepared the convocation of a National Assembly. Even the Federal Diet realized that some measures had to be taken. They suggested 'a revision of the federal constitution on a truly modern and national basis', and hoisted the black, red and gold flag on their council-chamber.

Most remarkable was the speedy success of the revolution in Austria and Prussia, the very pillars of stability and legitimacy. A short encounter between the population of Vienna and the military (13 March) sufficed to make the government yield. Metternich resigned and fled to England, where he and Louis Philippe were soon joined by Prince William of Prussia. The Hapsburg monarchy broke asunder. The Italian provinces rose on 22 March, and three days later the Sardinian troops marched into Lombardy. Hungary had to be granted an independent government and parliament. The Czechs gained the longed-for administrative separation from the German portion of Bohemia. Only the Croat and the Polish peasantry remained faithful. An insurrection of the Polish nobility was therefore easily crushed, and the Croat regiments had subsequently the greatest share in suppressing the revolution in Vienna, Hungary and Italy.

For the revolution was not over when Metternich relinquished his office. The concessions were granted hesitatingly and late, and lagged behind the increasing demands. The court fled to Innsbruck, and Vienna became the seat of a radical committee of public safety (May). This, however, was the turning point of the revolution in Austria. The army, though composed of a dozen nationalities and languages, showed a surprising coherence. The military genius of Radetzky routed the Piedmontese and Tuscans at Curtatone (29 May), Vicenza (10 June) and Custozza (25 July) and compelled them to sue for an armistice (9 Aug.). At the same time Prince Windischgrätz crushed the Czech attempt to establish a Bohemian state (17 June). The radical governments at Vienna and Budapest were already isolated when, on 22 July, the Constituent Assembly for the Hapsburg monarchy opened.

Events took a similar course in Prussia. Royal proclamations promising the recall of the United Diet and a reform of the German Confederation lagged behind events. Street fighting broke out in Berlin (18 March), and although the military got the upper hand, the terrified king ordered them to evacuate the capital. Ministerial changes took place, and on the 21st Frederick William, preceded by black, red and gold flags, made a theatrical round on horseback. On this day, he spoke the famous words: 'Prussia shall henceforth be merged in Germany.' However, steeped in legitimist prejudices he let slip the moment when Germany might have been reorganized under Prussian leadership with the voluntary concurrence of the nation. Only the constitutional reform of Prussia was carried out without delay. Ludolf Camphausen, the leader of the Rhenish liberals, was appointed prime minister (29 March). A Prussian National Assembly, elected by universal suffrage, met on 22 May and carried a number of progressive bills which considerably reduced the power of the Junker caste.

Despite the stirring events in Vienna and Berlin, public attention was focused rather on Frankfort, where the National Assembly met on 18 May. The radical democrats of South-Western Germany had hoped to forestall the decision of the Assembly by proclaiming a

German republic; but their rising was crushed by Baden and Hessian troops (20 April). The natural reaction to this ill-advised coup was an overwhelming victory of the monarchical and moderate candidates on polling day. The draft of a constitution which was submitted to the Frankfort parliament was drawn up by Dahlmann, the historian. It provided for a centralized monarchy with an hereditary emperor at its head, and a two-chamber legislature, the lower house of which was to be elected by universal suffrage. Austria, Prussia and the majority of the other states opposed this draft from the outset: Austria, because the charter tacitly implied the leadership of Prussia; Prussia, because of its democratic basis; and the rest, because of its centralizing tendencies.

Before the committee reported to the National Assembly, the latter created a 'provisional central administration'. Archduke John of Austria, the popular youngest brother of Francis I, was elected Vice-regent (*Reichsverweser*) and appointed a liberal cabinet. The Federal Diet and the individual governments recognized him at once; but they were slow to comply with the political and financial demands of the provisional government, whose power was theoretical rather than real. The test came soon. Frederick William IV had championed the cause of the provisional government of Slesvig-Holstein, and Prussian troops under General Wrangel advanced far into Denmark (April–May). The hostile attitude of Britain, Russia and France, however, cooled off his enthusiasm. He halted his troops and in the end abandoned the Elbe duchies to Denmark (truce of London, 26 Aug.). The Frankfort Assembly, whose nominal agent the king was, foamed at this betrayal of the national cause, but they lacked the means for continuing the war and eventually had to ratify the truce (16 Sept.). After its termination the Slesvig-Holstein troops made headway into Jutland, but eventually succumbed to the superior Danish forces. Prussia left them to their fate by signing first an armistice (10 June 1849) and then a peace (2 July 1850) with Denmark; and the Danes had little difficulty in stamping out the rising. The London Protocol of 2 Aug. 1850 reaffirmed the indissoluble integrity of the Danish monarchy. The general indignation over the handling of the Slesvig-Holstein affair caused the radicals to attempt a rising at the very seat of the Assembly (18 Sept. 1848). Two leaders of the right were assassinated. Hessian and Austrian troops suppressed the revolutionaries, with much bloodshed. The authority of the Assembly suffered a severe blow, and the right and left groups became more and more embittered against each other.

The debate about the constitution began under ill omens on 19 Oct.

By this time the revolutionary tide in Austria and Prussia was in full retreat. The Constituent Assembly of Vienna was, to a large extent, frustrated by the rivalries of the national groups which were to impede the activities of every subsequent Austrian parliament. The jurisdiction of the lord of the manor, statute-labour, and other burdens of the peasantry, were indeed abolished; but this legislation was the only real achievement. The Austrian peasants, their urgent demands thus satisfied, lost their revolutionary zeal and relapsed into apathy and loyalty. The government felt strong enough to take vigorous steps against the Magyars. An attempt to enlist the Viennese troops for the campaign against Hungary failed, however. The Viennese democrats refused to be accomplices in the crushing of their fellow-democrats. A mutiny broke out, several ministers and deputies were foully murdered, the court had to flee again, and Vienna was in the hands of the most radical section of the revolutionaries (6–7 Oct.). Prince Windischgrätz advanced in force against the rebellious capital, bombarded it, and took it by assault. A régime of terror followed. Amongst the many victims was Robert Blum, a member of the Frankfort Assembly, whom his immunity as a deputy, if not his innocence, should have saved from being courtmartialled. But the imperial government was past caring for parliamentary privileges. The Constituent Assembly was moved to the little town of Kremsier in Moravia and subjected to as strict a control as ever Cromwell exercised over the Rump. The imbecile Emperor, Ferdinand, abdicated and his nephew, Francis Joseph, acceded to the throne (2 Dec.). The Diet of Kremsier was forcibly dissolved (7 March 1849). The government of Prince Schwarzenberg promulgated a charter for the Austro-Hungarian monarchy, which was antedated on 4 March. It was strictly centralistic, flouted all national aspirations, and did away with the greater part of the achievements of the revolution. It needed more than a revolution to exorcise the ghost of Metternich from the Austrian body politic.

Even so, Schwarzenberg was not powerful enough to cope with Hungary, which found in Kossuth a national leader of the highest moral and political qualities. The Austrian government solicited and received Russian military aid. The Austrian general, Haynau, and Paskievitch, the Russian commander who had smothered the Polish rising of 1830–31, made a concentric advance. The main body of the Magyars surrendered to the Russians at Vilagos (13 Aug. 1849).

Haynau restored the Hapsburg power by martial law, the firing squad and the hangman.

In Prussia, it was the Junkers who took up the challenge when they saw their privileges and vested interests threatened by the legislators at Berlin. To counteract the spirited agitation of the progressive parties, the *Neue Preussische (Kreuz-) Zeitung* was founded. It acted according to the time-honoured principles of the Junkers, which were aptly described by their opponents in a popular rhyme:

> Let the King be absolute,
> If our will he execute.

One of the paper's earliest contributors and, incidentally, one of the most spirited leaders of the parliamentary conservative group was one Otto von Bismarck. The increasing radicalism of the Assembly greatly embarrassed the liberal cabinets of Camphausen and his successor, Auerswald. The weak king was pushed on by the reactionary camarilla. On 21 Sept., he appointed a ministry of moderately conservative bureaucrats; but the actual power was concentrated in the hands of General Wrangel. The discussion of the charter further infuriated the king, especially when the house deleted 'by the grace of God' after his title. The suppression of the October rising in Vienna hastened the victory of the Prussian diehards. A purely conservative ministry was formed under the nominal leadership of Count Brandenburg, the strong man being Manteuffel, the Home Secretary and an intimate friend of Bismarck's. When, with signal lack of grace, Frederick William received the last deputation of parliamentarians, a democratic member uttered the memorable words: 'It is the misfortune of kings that they will not listen to truth.' Count Brandenburg moved the Assembly to Brandenburg, and Wrangel occupied Berlin and kept down any attempt at disorder. On 5 Dec. the Assembly was dissolved and the king granted a charter of his own making. It was meant to assuage popular indignation and therefore not altogether reactionary: but Frederick William never even thought of abiding by it.

The eclipse of the revolution in Austria and Prussia had its inevitable effect upon the Frankfort Assembly. The debate on the constitution showed that the men of St Paul's Church, Frankfort, were indeed the élite of the German nation. Their lofty idealism, brilliant oratory, profound knowledge of history and constitutional law, and keen perception of the spirit of the age, were unequalled by any German parliament, perhaps by any other assembly except the first Congress of the United States of America. All those problems which have again and again beset German statesmen and historians were discussed and examined from every point of view. Centralism and federalism, historical frontiers and rational readjustment, royal prerogative and parliamentary rights, the thorny problem of racial minorities within and without the German-speaking countries, class privileges and rights of man—in brief, there was no basic problem of German history that did not come before that august assembly.

Their deliberations, however, were doomed to failure, since neither Austria nor Prussia was willing to sacrifice a tittle of sovereignty. Schwarzenberg bluntly declared that the unimpaired continuance of the Hapsburg monarchy must on no account be questioned. This was a heavy blow to the majority of the Assembly, who wanted neither to sever the bonds with the Austro-Germans nor to include in a reconstituted Germany the non-German nationalities of the Danube monarchy. In June, an amendment conferring the provisional executive power upon the king of Prussia had been rejected amidst shouts of laughter and was not even read for the first time. After Schwarzenberg's statement, the Little Germany party gained the upper hand. The preliminary question whether the imperial dignity should be hereditary or elective was decided in favour of heredity by a majority of four; and on 28 March, Frederick William IV, king of Prussia, was elected hereditary Emperor of the Germans by 290 votes, 248 members abstaining. Although twenty-eight lesser states dispatched a collective note to Berlin in which they declared their full agreement with the election, Frederick William was firmly resolved to refuse this unsolicited honour. He wanted a Hapsburg at the head of the Empire. Nothing appealed to him less than the crown of a democratic empire which he described in a private letter to Bunsen, his envoy in London, as 'an imaginary diadem baked of mud and clay'. After some shilly-shallying the Frankfort Assembly was notified of his final refusal (28 April).

This inevitably meant the breakdown of the work of the Assembly. The attitude of the various governments became more and more hostile when they realized the impotence of the parliament to which, a short while ago, they had tremulously paid lip service. The majority of the representatives returned home, disillusioned and despairing of the ideals of their youth. Most of them resigned themselves to a fatal compromise: if German unity and German liberty could not be attained together—might it not be preferable to have unity without liberty? This was the mood which afterwards converted not a few of the old men of 'Forty-eight' to Bismarck's policy.

The Rump parliament, naturally enough, turned radical. Agitation for a general rising in defence of the constitution was rife. In South-West Germany, the Rhineland, Silesia and Saxony popular risings broke out (May); Richard Wagner, the composer, fought on the Dresden barricades. Prussian troops led by Prince William drowned the revolution not only in the Prussian provinces, but also in the Bavarian Palatinate, in Saxony and in Baden in rivers of blood. While these risings still seemed to have a chance of success, the Rump moved from Frankfort, which was threatened by Prussian troops, to Stuttgart, the capital of Württemberg. Here 105 members held their last meetings from 6 to 18 June. On the latter date the Württemberg military scattered them. Amongst the last to stay was Ludwig Uhland, the Swabian poet, who decried Prussian hegemony and the exclusion of Austria and advocated a democratic confederation with a periodically elected emperor at its head. Friedrich Theodor Vischer, the philosopher and novelist, in his last speech compared the Stuttgart Assembly with King Lear 'who wanders about in the stormy night, homeless and bareheaded, cast out by his daughters upon whom he has conferred crowns'.

Thus ended the one attempt to create a democratic Germany.

While the revolution lay in its agonies, the Prussian cabinet made an attempt to garner its wheat without the tares of democracy. Radowitz, a close friend of Frederick William IV, outlined the constitution of a Little Germany federation under Prussian leadership. The 'Three Kings' Alliance' with Saxony and Hanover, concluded on 26 May, was the first step. The Hereditary Empire party promised its support at a meeting at Gotha (24–28 June). On 20 March 1850, the first parliament of the 'Union', as the federation was called, met at Erfurt under the presidency of Radowitz. By this time, however, the Hungarian revolution was quelled, and Schwarzenberg was in a position to defy the Prussian scheme. The South German kingdoms looked askance at the Union; Saxony and Hanover thought of deserting it at the first opportunity. Schwarzenberg reconstituted the Confederation by an 'Interim' regulation (30 Sept. 1849); it met with no resistance, even with approval. On 10 May 1850, he summoned the Federal Diet back to Frankfort, and Hanover and Saxony now publicly resigned from the Union.

The Elector of Cassel, nominally a member of the Union, fled to Frankfort and asked for the assistance of the Confederation against his subjects, who were resolved to maintain their hard-won liberties. Schwarzenberg concluded a military alliance with Bavaria and Württemberg (12 Oct.), and made the Federal Diet decide upon Federal action to be executed by Bavarian troops against the recalcitrant Hessians (16 Oct.). He was assured of the help of the Tsar Nicholas, whom he had obliged by the adherence of Austria to the London Protocol of 2 Aug.

Radowitz, appointed foreign secretary on 26 Sept., and Prince William were all for taking up the Austrian challenge. But the Tsar convened a conference of the Emperor Francis Joseph, Schwarzenberg and the Prussian premier, Count Brandenburg, at Warsaw, and forced the latter to abandon the Union and rejoin the Confederation. The king, Prince William, and Radowitz opposed this course. On the day when Count Brandenburg died (6 Nov.), the Prussian army was mobilized. But Radowitz, worn out by the secret and powerful opposition of the reactionary camarilla, resigned office, and the new premier, Manteuffel, at once set out to come to terms with Austria. An ultimatum from Schwarzenberg led to the complete submission of Prussia. Schwarzenberg and Manteuffel met at Olmütz (29 Nov.), and the latter agreed to the full restitution of the German Confederation, the restoration of the Elector of Cassel, the submission to Denmark of the provisional government of Holstein, and the immediate reduction to a peace footing of the Prussian army. Austria gained a complete diplomatic victory, and the 'shame of Olmütz' rankled deeply with the Prussian militarists.

The revolution of 1848 failed to establish a united Germany based on the principles of liberty. Throughout the first half of the nineteenth century the national and liberal movements had marched side by side and mutually inspired each other. They continued to do so in Italy. In Germany, however, the advocates of unity now parted company with the champions of popular freedom. The former made their peace with Prussia, the great power that alone seemed to be able to accomplish the unification of the Germanies; and they sacrificed their youthful enthusiasm for the popular cause on the altar of Disciplina and Bellona, Prussia's supreme goddesses. Their sacrifice was made the easier when they fell under the spell of the great Prussian statesman who slowly began to dominate the scene—Bismarck. The liberals and democrats of sterling character, on the other hand, continued the fight against the soulless efficiency of Prussian bureaucracy and militarism. Hundreds of thousands of them, it is true, sought a new country across the Atlantic, and Germany's loss was America's gain. Carl Schurz, Lincoln's home secretary, was amongst them. Those who remained persevered gallantly, and for a time even with success. The opposition in the Prussian diet rose from 136 deputies in 1852 to 305 in 1863, whereas the ministerial parties fell from 213 to 38 in the same time. Never before or after were the masses of the German nation, and especially the people of Prussia, so strongly permeated by the spirit of independence and democracy as in the decade following the breakdown of the revolution of 1848. But all the burning zeal and political talent of the opposition was wasted in a barren negation, as they had no hope or prospect of ever being called into office. In his first speech before the Prussian diet, Bismarck stated bluntly the principle which ever guided Prussian policy, namely that 'the great problems of the age are not decided by speeches or majority decisions, but by blood and iron'. The triumph of this principle, as manifested in the Civil War of 1866 and the war against France four years later, extinguished the flame of civic freedom, and won over Germany to the Prussian doctrine of blood and iron.

As the immediate result of the agreement of Olmütz, the German Confederation was restored in its old form. The Federal Diet set up a committee which naïvely called itself the Committee of Reaction and gleefully revised the constitutions of the member states in a retrograde sense. The order of the day, as Frederick William IV put it, was 'to sweep out of the German constitutions the democratic dirt of the year of shame'. The lesser states entirely lost their influence upon the shaping of Germany's status, and had no alternative left but to follow obediently in the wake of either Austria or Prussia. For ten years, all attempts to reform the constitution of the Confederation were nipped in the bud. Outwardly, Austria exercised the presidential rights at Frankfort with greater vigour than before; but behind the curtains, the Prussian plenipotentiary successfully counteracted any measure that would have strengthened either the hegemony of Austria or the power of the Confederation as such. The man who thus gained an intimate knowledge of German affairs, and an ever increasing influence upon their destiny, was Bismarck.

Prince Schwarzenberg abolished his own constitution of 4 March 1849 on 31 Dec. 1851, and he and his successors ruled for ten years without a constitution, supported by the police and the Jesuits. The concordat of 1855 handed over to the Roman Catholic Church the whole educational system, jurisdiction in matrimonial cases, and the censorship. On the other hand, the Austrian statesmen were fully aware of the impossibility of letting things alone, which had been Metternich's policy. They wanted to raise the internal efficiency of the monarchy so as to enable it to regain and maintain a decisive part in European affairs. A centralized bureaucracy was imposed upon the whole Empire; the medieval organization of Hungary was abolished. Special attention was paid to economic problems; the role which Bruck played in this respect has already been mentioned. This modern absolutism, however, failed to gain the affection of the population; the Italians, Czechs and Magyars continued to regard it as a foreign yoke, and all of them, including the Germans, as a tyranny.

Frederick William IV had conscientious scruples about annulling the Prussian constitution. It was, however, re-issued on 30 Jan. 1850; and this new version considerably strengthened the royal prerogative. Moreover, the franchise for the diet was indirect, divided the electorate into three classes, and thus gave the landed and moneyed classes a preponderance out of all proportion to their numbers. An arbitrary demarcation of the constituencies and a shameless corruption of the voters were designed to return an obsequious majority. In 1854 a House of Lords was installed which consisted almost exclusively of members of the landed nobility. The Political Police gained a sinister ascendancy: the independence of the civil servants, the freedom of the press, and the livelihood of every citizen were entirely at their tender mercies. The influence of the prime minister Manteuffel was eclipsed by that of Hinckeldey, the all-powerful chief of police, who even set his informers on the tracks of Prince William and Bismarck.

The preoccupation with problems of domestic policy, administrative and economic, prevented the two great powers and the Confederation from making their weight felt in the trial of strength between Western and Eastern Europe which came to a head in the Crimean War of 1853–56. The Tsar as well as the French Emperor were anxious to secure the support of either or both of the central powers. There were champions of a pro-Russian and anti-Russian course at the courts of Berlin and Vienna. Radetzky and Windischgrätz advocated an alliance with Russia; with the connivance of Russia, they argued, Austria would gain a firm foothold in the Western Balkans and strengthen her position in Italy. The Tsar himself invited Austria to occupy Bosnia and Serbia and to secure the port of Salonika, while Russia was to acquire the Rumanian and Bulgarian principalities.

In Prussia, Prince William and Manteuffel favoured the Western course, whereas Bismarck gave his wholehearted support to the Russophil camarilla. The lack of real statesmanship in Vienna and Berlin eventually cast the balance in favour of a weak compromise. An Austro-Prussian defensive alliance (20 April 1854) was followed by an Austrian *sommation* delivered at St Petersburg. It was, in reality, an ultimatum which forced the Russians to evacuate the Danubian principalities. On 2 Dec. 1854, an alliance with the Western powers was concluded in Paris, but, it remained a dead letter. Austria, unlike Piedmont, did nothing by way of military support, and peace parleys in Vienna (March–June 1855) led to nothing. Austria remained neutral.

The death of Schwarzenberg in 1852, it is true, had robbed Austria of a first-rate statesman; but the true reason for her vacillation was her fear of Prussia. If Austria undertook military commitments, would not Prussia see an opportunity to make herself paramount in Germany, or even to stab Austria in the back? It was known in Vienna that Bismarck had suggested to the king the concentration of an army in Upper Silesia which might be thrown into Russia or Austria at a moment's notice. Frederick William, however, recoiled from any decisive step, with the result that Prussia was completely neglected at the peace conference of Paris (Feb.–April 1856). Manteuffel was only admitted when the important points had been settled. All the same, the position of Prussia was not quite unfavourable although she was cold-shouldered for the moment. The good relations with Russia had been dimmed for a time but not fatally injured. Shortly afterwards they were restored to intimacy by Bismarck, who represented Prussia at the Tsarist court from 1859 to 1862. Napoleon, too, made overtures to Prussia when he made up his slow-working mind to eject Austria from Italy.

Cavour, the Piedmontese premier, had boldly put the Italian question before the Congress of Paris and never ceased to challenge Austria. Diplomatic relations between the two countries were broken off in 1857; and in 1858 he obtained from Napoleon the definite promise of French assistance. The Austrian war party played into his hands. Against the warnings which Metternich uttered on his death-bed, the mediation offered by Russia and England was refused, and an ultimatum was dispatched to Turin (23 April 1859). Napoleon at once threw his army into Italy; for the first time, transport by railroad played an important part in military history. The Austrians failed to use the start they had gained by their precipitation.

'They would not wait, when they ought to have done so, and now they do nothing', the shrewd Queen Victoria observed. Within a few weeks, the Austrian dependencies and protectorates in Northern and Central Italy were liberated and the Austrian army cleared out of Lombardy. The gory battle of Solferino (24 June) was inconclusive, but the military situation of the Austrians looked very serious, when an unexpected event occurred. Ten days before Solferino, Prussia mobilized her army and proposed the mobilization of the South German contingents of the German Confederation in support of Austria. Prince William, who on 7 Oct. 1858 had been appointed regent for his insane brother, and Moltke, the Chief of the General Staff, urged an immediate crossing of the French frontier. Bismarck advocated the opposite course. He wanted to keep France quiet and benevolent until Prussia had settled the German question, i.e. ousted Austria from Germany. The imminent intervention of Prussia drove Napoleon as well as Francis Joseph to conclude the preliminary peace of Villafranca (11 July). The latter preferred to renounce all his Italian possessions, with the exception of Venetia, rather than to owe his salvation to the Prince of Prussia, who had already demanded the supreme command of all Federal troops as the price of his support.

The change of ruler in Prussia was indeed of the greatest importance. Prince William, although sixty years of age, gave the lie to those who expected him to live up to the evil reputation he had gained as the arch-reactionary of 1848. Unlike his brother, he accepted the changed situation with all sincerity. Under the influence of his intellectual queen, who had been brought up under the eyes of Goethe at the court of Weimar, he adopted views which, by Prussian standards, might be called liberal; and these tendencies were strengthened when his eldest son married the Princess Royal of Great Britain, in 1856. Nevertheless, he was certainly more Prussian than Frederick William IV: a soldier above everything, soberminded and tenacious, 'a humdrum fellow' as he described himself. His greatest asset, perhaps, was his clear recognition of his own limits; he always subordinated, if reluctantly, his opinions to those of his political and military advisers. The 'New Era', as his regency was called, began with the appointment of a number of liberal and moderately conservative ministers of whom Auerswald, the erstwhile premier of 1848, was the most conspicuous. It seemed indeed that Prussia was to make the 'moral conquests in Germany' which Prince William announced in his first address as regent. In September 1859 a German National Association was founded under the presidency of the Hanoverian, Rudolf von Bennigsen, and the protectorship of Duke Ernest of Coburg, the elder brother of the prince consort of England. It rallied the liberal, Protestant and national bourgeoisie to its standard, and propagated the idea of a united Little Germany under Prussian leadership.

The defeat in the Italian war and the success of Prussian propaganda combined to make a revision of the Austrian administration unavoidable. A period of constitutional experiments began. The 'October diploma' of 20 Oct. 1860 terminated the era of absolutism and centralization. The centre of gravity was shifted to the diets of the crown-lands. Only affairs concerning the whole monarchy were reserved to the imperial diet, which was to be composed of delegates of the provincial diets and members appointed by the government. Nobody was satisfied. The German liberals resented the federal principle and wanted the imperial diet to become the chief body. The nationalities, on the other hand, especially the Magyars, considered the federalization not extensive enough to meet their demands. The government shrank back. The 'February patent', of 26 Feb. 1861, reversed the distribution of power in favour of centralism. The imperial diet (*Reichsrat*) was to become the centre of constitutional life. It consisted of two chambers and dealt with all matters not expressly reserved for the diets of the crown-lands. A complicated electoral system was designed to secure a German majority. This and the centralizing tendency of the 'February patent' wrecked its operation: the Magyars refused to have any dealings with the imperial diet, and the Czechs kept out of it from 1863. The government therefore suspended the constitution altogether in 1865. The war of 1866 altered the whole situation, and made imperative a fundamental re-orientation.

Unsatisfactory though these constitutional changes turned out in the end, they did not fail favourably to impress public opinion in Germany. Austria seemed to be sincerely bent on a liberal course. She recovered much ground lost in the previous decade of reaction. Even the protector of the National Association, Duke Ernest of Coburg, went to Vienna and explored the possibility of a closer collaboration with Austria. For Prussia, recently the hope of the national liberals, had most cruelly disappointed the expectations aroused by the beginnings of the New Era. The crown and parliament headed for an open conflict. The Prince Regent had set his heart on carrying out a thorough reform of the Prussian army. He wanted a considerable increase of its actual strength, an extension of the years of service, and a drastic curtailment of the territorial army. The reform of the regular army was defensible for military reasons, as the organization had not been altered since 1814 and was certainly out of date. The remodelling of the territorials, however, was prompted by political considerations. The militia was created as a democratic body; it was a corps of citizens in arms and its officers lacked the unquestioning royalism of the professional army men.

The diet was willing to vote the increase of the contingents, but objected to the extension of the time of service, and flatly refused to have the militia made part and parcel of the regular army. Prince William appointed General von Roon (1803–79) Minister of War (5 Dec. 1859), the very model of the reactionary Junker and arrogant officer. The attitude of the sovereign became more inflexible after he succeeded to the throne (2 Jan. 1861). He considered himself the Lord's Anointed and, though no mystic by nature, adopted just enough of the theory of the Divine Right of Kings to override parliamentary decisions without feeling uneasy in his conscience. The liberal ministers of the New Era were replaced by reactionary diehards and the recalcitrant diet was twice dissolved (Dec. 1861, March 1862). Despite all kinds of direct and indirect pressure on the part of the administration, the electors remained firm. The Progressive Party, which was founded in June 1861 as the rallying point of the opposition, obtained 82 seats in Dec. 1861 and increased to 141 members in May 1862, whereas the conservatives were all but wiped out. Although the united opposition parties had a comfortable two-thirds majority, they were still ready for a compromise. But the king remained obdurate. He even threatened to abdicate, an unheard-of event in the annals of Prussia. In the end, Roon found the man who was prepared to defy the representatives of the people, to uphold the royal prerogative in Prussia, and to establish Prussian hegemony over Germany. On the day when the diet rejected the army budget, 23 Sept. 1862, Bismarck was appointed Minister of State and President of the Council.

On New Year's eve, 1870, the Prussian crown prince, reviewing the events of the past eight years, wrote in his diary: 'Bismarck has made us great and mighty, but deprived us of our friends, the sympathy of the world, and—our clear conscience. I am still of the firm opinion that Germany could have made moral conquests without blood and iron, solely with her good right; and thus might have become united, free, and powerful: but the reckless and brutal Junker has willed it differently.'

'Bismarck: to be used only when the bayonet rules unrestrictedly'; with these words Frederick William IV once refused to appoint him as a minister. When he took office in 1862, everyone expected that the unrestricted rule of the bayonet would be the order of the day. Bismarck, however, was more flexible and subtle than either his friends or his opponents thought him. He never for a moment lost sight of his ultimate goal, namely, to make Prussia supreme in Germany and to gain for her the role of arbiter in the affairs of Europe: but the resources of which he disposed for furthering this end were legion, and the appeal to brute force was the least among them. He would even have preferred a compromise to an open conflict with the diet, in order to get his hands free for a vigorous foreign policy. But the house did not trust his promises, and stated formally that any expenditure out of the rejected budget would be unconstitutional and that the ministers were personally liable for the money thus spent. Therefore Bismarck made the king say in his speech from the throne (13 Oct. 1862) that the government was compelled to find the necessary funds without the constitutional provisoes.

The majority of the diet felt sure of their final victory. The king was uneasy and spoke of Strafford and Charles I. The crown prince became all but the leader of a fronde. Bismarck remained unperturbed. He knew that the battle was for the principle of Prussianism as laid down by the Great Elector, Frederick William I, and Frederick the Great. He knew also that the two traditional pillars of Prussianism were on his side. The loyalty of the army could not be questioned. The bureaucracy, which to a large extent was permeated by liberal ideas, was speedily brought into line: municipal and state officials who were suspected of progressive leanings were reprimanded and dealt with by the hundred. Bismarck also sought contact with Lassalle and Marx, the leaders of the rising working class. He hoped to win their support by the promise of universal suffrage, following the precedent of the Second Empire. Thus he calculated the intractable bourgeoisie might be crushed between the two millstones of royalism and socialism. Lassalle, however, was killed in a duel, before any definite agreement had been reached (1864), and Marx was less amenable than Bismarck had hoped.

On the whole all this did not worry him very much. He was rather inclined to look down upon the constitutional conflict as an unnecessary embarrassment of his foreign policy, to which he gave his undivided interest at the first possible moment. In the past years, the reform of the German Confederation had been taken in hand by the lesser states. Dissatisfied with merely following the Austrian or Prussian lead, they met several times at Würzburg to discuss current affairs. On 15 Oct. 1861, they published the draft of a German constitution, drawn up by Beust, the prime minister of Saxony. It provided for a directory of three and a national assembly composed of 128 members of the various diets, and made Hamburg and Ratisbon the alternating seats of the Federal Diet. The plan was at once rejected by Austria and Prussia, but it showed the chancelleries of Vienna and Berlin the necessity for bestirring themselves. Prussia resumed the scheme of Radowitz and suggested that a closer union should be created within the framework of the Confederation (20 Dec. 1861). Austria, Bavaria, Hanover, Württemberg, Saxony, Hesse-Darmstadt and Nassau sternly protested in identical notes. Austria then came forward with motions aiming at an extension of the Customs Union and the creation of a common law code as preliminary steps for a national unification. Bismarck bluntly threatened Prussia's withdrawal from the Confederation should any of these motions be carried; with the result that the Federal Diet rejected them by a narrow majority (22 Jan. 1863).

Nevertheless, the favourable reception with which these suggestions met throughout non-Prussian Germany encouraged the Austrian government to put forth a far-reaching reform programme, and the Emperor Francis Joseph invited all German princes to a meeting at Frankfort. It took place from 16 Aug. to 1 Sept. 1863. At the same time, 318 parliamentarians from all over Germany assembled at Frankfort; the Federal Diet even hoisted the black, red and gold flag. It seemed as if the aspirations of 1848 were about to be fulfilled under the leadership of Austria and with the concurrence of the German princes and peoples. This would have meant the shipwreck of Bismarck's plans, and he did not hesitate to bring up his heaviest guns. For the first time, he threatened the king with his resignation: for the first time, the king yielded to this threat: it was to remain one of the strongest weapons of Bismarck's armoury as long as William I lived. The king refused to attend the Princes' Meeting at Frankfort. This meant the end of the Austrian attempt to reform the German Confederation, as the majority of the German states were of the opinion expressed by the Bavarian representative at Frankfort: 'We do not want the

Confederation without Austria, neither, however, do we want it without Prussia.'

Bismarck could dare to defy Austria because he had meanwhile scored a success in the field of foreign policy. In January 1863, a great rising broke out in the Russian parts of Poland, and public opinion throughout Europe showed the greatest sympathy for the heroic Poles. Napoleon III had a mind to exploit the acute embarrassment of the Tsarist government for one of his cherished diplomatic triumphs; and England and Austria supported his repeated *démarches* at St Petersburg. But Bismarck took a firm stand by the side of Russia. He concluded a military convention with the Russian government, which was thus able to suppress the Polish rising and to reject the suggestions and threats of the Western powers. Thus Bismarck secured for Prussia the benevolence of Russia should future contingencies make such a backing desirable. In fact, Bismarck's calculation proved correct. For thirty years to come, the Russo-Prussian entente was the backbone of Bismarck's policy. All his great achievements were made possible by having his eastern flank secure; whereas Austria had alienated Russia once more without achieving the active support of Napoleon.

The first-fruits of Russia's benevolent neutrality was the opportunity it gave Prussia to settle the Slesvig-Holstein question. On 30 March 1863, King Frederick VII of Denmark issued a letter patent by which the administrations of Slesvig and Holstein were separated. The Danish diet passed a new constitution which reduced Slesvig to the status of a Danish province (13 Nov.). Two days later the king died and was succeeded by Prince Christian of Slesvig-Holstein-Sonderburg-Glücksburg, in accordance with the London Protocol of 1852.

The Federal Diet answered the letter patent of 30 March by decreeing a federal execution against Denmark, which was entrusted to Hanover and Saxony (1 Oct.). When Christian took the oath on the new Danish constitution, public opinion throughout Germany burst into flames. Prince Frederick of Augustenburg, the son of the pretender of 1848, proclaimed himself the lawful duke of Slesvig-Holstein, and his cause was taken up with enthusiasm by the Greater Germany and Little Germany parties alike. The kings of Bavaria and Saxony, the grand duke of Baden, and the crown prince of Prussia were foremost amongst his champions. Bismarck alone opposed the popular current with all his might. The stablishment of one more German prince would have strengthened the non-Prussian element of the German Confederation. It might, moreover, provoke the intervention of the guarantors of the London Protocol, which expressly excluded the Augustenburg succession. Lastly, there can be no doubt that, from the very beginning of the dispute, Bismarck meant to acquire the Elbe duchies for Prussia. For this end, however, he needed the provisional support of Austria. It was his first great triumph in the field of foreign policy that he succeeded in aligning Berlin and Vienna against Denmark. On 16 Jan. 1864, the two powers dispatched an ultimatum to Copenhagen in which they demanded the repeal of the Danish constitution of 13 Nov. It was a clever stroke of diplomacy, as this constitution was not covered by the London Protocol. The Danes therefore looked round for help in vain. On 1 Feb., Prussian and Austrian troops crossed the frontier of Holstein where Saxons and Hanoverians had been operating since 23 Dec. Thanks to the strategical plans of the Chief of the Prussian General Staff, Moltke, the allies forced the Danes out of Holstein and Slesvig within six days, occupied Jutland in March, and paved their way to the isles and Copenhagen by the capture of the heavily fortified redoubts of Düppel (18 April).

Meanwhile Palmerston tried to bring together the signatories of the London Protocol. After the success of Düppel Bismarck abandoned his obstruction, and the conference met in London. An armistice was signed, but nothing further was achieved. The Danes, by their obstinacy, wrecked Palmerston's endeavours to arrange an acceptable compromise, so that hostilities were resumed on 27 June. A fortnight later the Prussian and Austrian banners were hoisted on Cape Skagen, the northernmost point of Jutland, and the invasion of the Danish isles had begun. Panic broke out at Copenhagen. The king dismissed the war cabinet, and the new premier sued at once for an armistice. The preliminary peace was signed at Vienna on 1 Aug., and was followed by the definite treaty on 30 Oct. Denmark ceded unconditionally the three duchies of Slesvig, Holstein and Lauenburg. Austria and Prussia took them in condominium.

This provisional state of affairs could not last long. The Austrians soon realized that nothing but the wholesale annexation of the duchies would satisfy Prussia. Bismarck, according to his own words, had put the duke of Augustenburg as an ox to the plough, and unyoked him as soon as the plough was on the move. The internal difficulties of Austria, however, made her give in for the time being. The treaty of Gastein (14 Aug. 1865) provided for an administrative division of the duchies, while the condominium was nominally maintained. Holstein was taken over by Austria, Slesvig by Prussia; Lauenburg was sold to Prussia. Moreover, Prussia was given the right to establish a naval base at Kiel and to build a canal, two military roads and a telegraph line through Holstein; and both duchies joined the German Customs Union. They were, for all practical purposes, already under Prussian control and the grateful King William made Bismarck a count (15 Sept.).

Bismarck now set to work to gain the moral and military support of France and Italy for his next move. At a meeting with Napoleon at Biarritz (Oct.) no definite agreement was reached with France, but it was sufficient for Bismarck that Napoleon encouraged the Italians to seek a closer understanding with Prussia. On 8 April 1866, a defensive and offensive alliance was signed at Berlin. It pledged Italy to declare war on Austria if within three months Prussia should be obliged to attack her in pursuance of the necessary reform of the German Confederation.

To gain this end, the conservative Prussian premier did not refrain from a revolutionary step. He put to the Federal Diet the motion that a National Assembly should be elected by universal and direct suffrage, and that this Assembly should deliberate on a reform bill to be worked out by the confederate governments. It was a bombshell, as Bismarck had to face the unanimous opposition of Prussia, Germany and Europe. The king and the Prussian conservatives were horrified by the appeal to the masses; the liberals and catholics abhorred the prospect of a fratricidal war between Germans. A radical youth attempted Bismarck's life (7 May), and the overwhelming majority of the nation mourned his failure. Queen Victoria, the Tsar, and Napoleon counselled peace, the last hinting at compensations in the Rhineland.

In the end, it was the Austrians themselves who played Bismarck's game. For months they could not make up their minds as to what course to take: whether they should cede Slesvig-Holstein and thus placate Prussia, or give up Venetia to Italy and thus get their hands free in the North. It was the old story of Austria's irresoluteness over again, which Grillparzer aptly formulated in the verses:

> It is the curse of our proud dynasty
> To move half-heartedly, stop half-way, and
> Adopt half-measures hesitatingly.

After the mobilization of the whole army at the end of April, four precious weeks were squandered in futile negotiations. An agent of Bismarck suggested in Vienna that Austria and Prussia should partition Germany between themselves and, with both their armies mobilized, 'dictate the law to Europe'. Simultaneously Napoleon broached the plan of a great European congress at Paris which should settle the Italian and German problems. Contrary to the wishes of the Austrian Foreign Office the military party in Vienna saw to it that both these suggestions were refuted. On the same 1st of June when Napoleon was thus mortified, the Austrian government challenged Prussia by submitting the Slesvig-Holstein question to the Federal Diet at Frankfort. On 12 June, the Austrian and Prussian envoys at Berlin and Vienna asked for their passports.

Two days later the Federal Diet passed an Austrian motion to mobilize the non-Prussian army-corps. The Prussian representative thereupon declared the constitution of the German Confederation null and void, and invited the German governments to join a modified union under Prussian leadership. The German Confederation thus ceased to exist. A twelve-hour ultimatum was dispatched to Hanover, Dresden and Cassel: at the same time the Prussian troops received orders to cross the frontiers of Hanover, Saxony and Hesse, as Bismarck neither expected nor wanted the ultimatum to be accepted. Within a fortnight these countries were occupied, and the brave Hanoverian army, after having defeated a Prussian detachment at Langensalza (27 June), was compelled to capitulate.

The Italians, too, declared war on Austria (20 June), but were speedily defeated at Custozza by the Archduke Albert, the son of the victor of Aspern (24 June). The Austrians were, however, unable to follow up this victory, as meanwhile the Prussian armies had begun a concentric advance into Bohemia. Benedek, the Austrian commander-in-chief, wanted to extricate his troops from the threatened encirclement, but the Emperor Francis Joseph forced him to accept battle. On 3 July, Moltke all but annihilated the Austrian and Saxon forces between Königgrätz and Sadowa. The Prussians advanced to the gates of Vienna and Pressburg, and Bismarck drafted proclamations to stir up the 'glorious Czech nation' and the Magyars—when suddenly an armistice was concluded (22 July).

The Austrians, at last convinced that they could not cope simultaneously with Prussia and Italy, requested Napoleon's good offices to bring about peace with Italy. On the day of Sadowa they ceded Venetia to him, and twenty-four hours later Napoleon announced that he intended to intervene. Bismarck at once realized the danger. It is true that the Prussian armies operating against Hesse, Bavaria, Württemberg and Baden had so far gained easy victories; and

Moltke and Roon had the plans ready for a war against France. On the other hand, the Austrians gained a brilliant naval victory over the Italians at Lissa (20 July), the Prussian troops in Bohemia suffered appalling losses from cholera, and England, Russia and Denmark might enforce a peace which would wreck Bismarck's ambitious schemes.

Bismarck therefore abandoned the far-reaching plans which the king and generals cherished. He yielded to the French pressure in so far as he confined the immediate extension of the Prussian sphere of influence to North Germany, consented to a plebiscite in Slesvig and guaranteed the integrity of Austria. It may be mentioned in parenthesis that the plebiscite in Slesvig was first delayed indefinitely, and afterwards formally annulled by Bismarck (1878); it was carried out under the provisions of the treaty of Versailles in 1920, and in the northern zone about 74 per cent of the votes were cast for Denmark. In order to eliminate further French interference, Bismarck hastened to conclude the preliminary peace of Nikolsburg (26 June), which was confirmed by the definite peace of Prague on 23 Aug.

The peace of Nikolsburg was Bismarck's diplomatic masterpiece. The generals would have liked to establish Prussian military rule throughout Germany and finish Austria once and for all; and King William wanted to take something from everybody. Bismarck calculated very differently. The intervention of Napoleon clearly ruled out the unlimited aspirations of the Prussian generals, more especially the destruction of Austria. Until he was able 'to requite the Gaul', as he put it, he had to treat Austria, the South German states, and Saxony with leniency, the integrity of the latter being made a point of honour on the part of Austria. Moreover, he saw rightly that it would not pay to tear away bits and pieces from Austria, Saxony, Bavaria, Hesse and Hanover as the king suggested. Petty spoliations would only infuriate these countries and antagonize them against Prussia for good, without crippling them beyond recovery and revenge. Bismarck therefore decided to annex some of the enemy countries lock stock and barrel, and to deal with the rest in such a way that further collaboration would be facilitated rather than blocked.

Consequently the kingdom of Hanover, the electorate of Hesse-Cassel, the duchy of Nassau, the free city of Frankfort-on-Main, and the duchies of Slesvig and Holstein were incorporated with Prussia. Austria had to recognize the dissolution of the German Confederation, give Prussia a free hand to reorganize Germany, and to pay a nominal war-indemnity of 20 million thalers (£3 million). Italy received Venetia from the hands of Napoleon; while her claims to South Tyrol and Trieste were passed over with scorn. When the Italians complained about the Prusso-Austrian armistice, Bismarck told them contemptuously that the Prussians, when taking their ease for a few days, did nothing but what the Italians had done throughout the campaign.

The armistice with the South German states was concluded on 2 Aug., the peace treaties following a fortnight later. They had to pay war-indemnities of 50 million florins (£5 million); Bavaria and Hesse-Darmstadt ceded a few frontier districts; Upper Hesse, the northern part of the grand duchy, was to join the North German Confederation. Most important of all, Bavaria, Württemberg and Baden signed military conventions by which their armies were placed under the command of the king of Prussia in case of war. This hypothetical contingency was to become a reality four years later. Many years later Moltke summed up the reasons for which Prussia had fought the war of 1866. It did, he coolly stated, 'not spring from self-defence against a threat to our own existence, nor was it called forth by public opinion and the voice of the nation; it was a fight for hegemony, which the cabinet had recognized as necessary, for long contemplated, and calmly prepared'.

The Hohenzollern monarchy now stretched in an unbroken chain from Memel to Aix-la-Chapelle and from Hadersleben to Frankfort. It included sections of every German tribe, except the Bavarians. Even Swabia was represented by the tiny principality of Hohenzollern, the patrimony of the dynasty, which the collateral line reigning there from 1192 had ceded to the king of Prussia in 1849.

It is an indisputable fact, too often overlooked by outsiders and intentionally obscured by Prussian historiographers, that the forcible dissolution by Prussia of the German Confederation meant the virtual end of Germany as this word had been understood for a thousand years. The term Germany had always described the federal association of, first, the German tribes, and, later, the German principalities. Henceforth it was used for the centralistic power-state of Greater Prussia padded out with those remainders of the old system which were allowed to vegetate on Prussian sufferance. Nor could the disappearance of Germany proper and its replacement by Greater Prussia fail to make itself deeply felt in the sphere of European affairs at large. The repercussions abroad were aptly summarized by Constantin Frantz, the greatest and most neglected publicist of the Bismarck era. Frantz wrote in 1879: 'Impotent and imperfect as the Confederation may have been, one thing cannot be denied, namely, that it was of paramount importance for the whole European system, if only passively. It operated moderatingly, it was in fact an instrument of peace. Its dissolution in 1866 made the whole European system lose its former stability so that from that moment onward the relations of all European states became based upon bayonets, and the whole continent groans under the burden of militarism.' Frantz's idea of a remodelled Europe is worth conjuring up again. He envisaged a truly federal organization of the continent, with a federated Germany that would be dominated by neither Prussia nor Austria. The hitherto oppressed nations in the East and South-East should enjoy equality of rights with their older and consolidated sister nations; the reconstitution of a strong Polish state was amongst Frantz's primary demands. This European union, he further suggested, should form a branch of a world union which was to be established on similar lines of regional federalization.

The actual course of events after 1866 took a very different shape.

MAP X

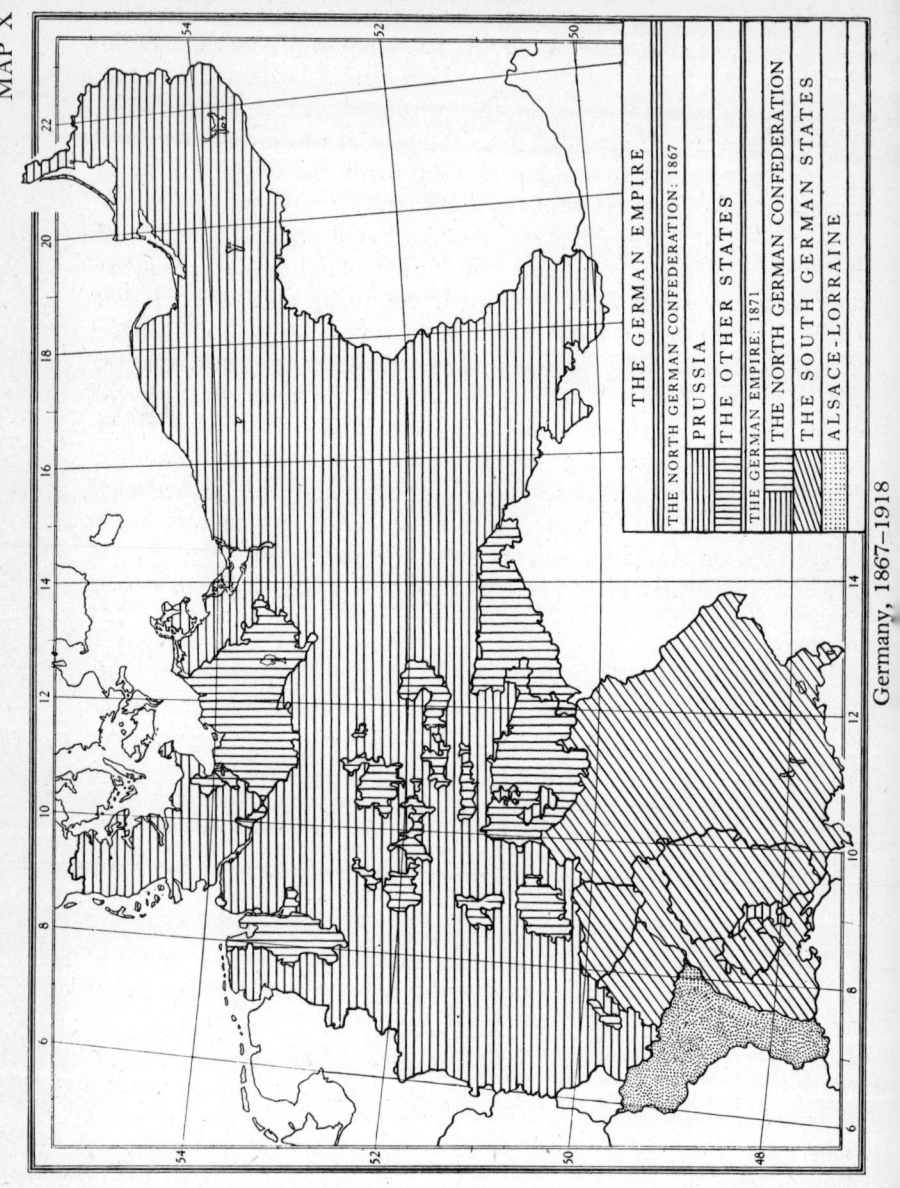

Germany, 1867–1918

CHAPTER VIII

THE BISMARCK EMPIRE (1867–1890)

THE German Empire which came into existence on 18 Jan. 1871 was not the United Germany for which the men of 'Forty-eight' had fought and died. It was not Germany in which Prussia and the lesser states were merged; it was Prussia which absorbed the rest of Germany. It followed that the principles on which Prussia had thriven pervaded the new creation as well. The absolutism of the crown, the loyalty of the army, and the efficiency of the civil service were the three mainstays of Prussia. The rights which the South and Central German rulers reserved for themselves and the concessions which had to be made to the liberal spirit of the age, however, made it inopportune to apply the Prussian system wholesale to the German Empire. Moreover, Bismarck himself was not a soldier, and the difficulties arising from the peace negotiations in 1866 and 1871 brought him into sharp opposition to Moltke, Roon and the rest of the generals; their aversion was mutual. He also despised the civil servants; having reduced them to mute and sullen obsequiousness, he somewhat unreasonably complained of their lack of initiative and vision. So he concentrated the supreme power in the 'presidency' of the North German Federation and, later on, the German Reich. Nominally, it was vested in the king of Prussia as the President of the North German Federation and Emperor of the Empire. In reality, it was wielded by the imperial chancellor, who at the same time held the office of Prussian premier. For there were neither imperial ministers nor an independent imperial administration. The 'offices'—the term 'ministries' was studiously avoided—of foreign affairs, the interior, the finances, and so on were sub-departments of the imperial chancellery; and their chiefs were mere subordinates of the imperial chancellor, in whose hands all the reins of government were united.

The figment of a voluntary association of the German princes was kept up in so far as the policy of the North German Federation and the German Empire was not simply determined by Prussia, but nominally controlled by the Federal Council (*Bundesrat*). Its members were delegated by the federate governments. Prussia had 17 out of 58 votes in her own right. However, the votes of ten or twelve petty principalities such as Brunswick, Schaumburg-Lippe and Reuss-Gera were always at her disposal, that of Waldeck even by permanent delegacy; and as the imperial chancellor was the ex-officio chairman of the Federal Council, Prussia virtually ruled this body and through it the Empire.

For the *Reichstag* was little more than a popular façade to hide the autocratic fabric of the new Empire. By granting it the universal, direct and secret suffrage, Bismarck seemed to have met the demands of the liberals and democrats. But the Reichstag had no influence upon the composition and policy of the imperial government, from which the deputies were expressly excluded. Therefore, neither the chancellor nor the heads of departments were responsible to the house. Its influence was confined to making suggestions which the government was at liberty to accept or refuse, to checking the proceeds and expenditure of the budget, and to passing such bills as did not affect the imperial prerogative of foreign and military affairs. The gulf which separated the government bench from the seats of the deputies was not bridged until October 1918 when, after the constitution had been amended, deputies were appointed secretaries of state for the first time.

Bismarck found it easy to manage the Reichstag. Moderate sections left the conservative as well as the progressive parties; and the new groups of 'free conservatives' and 'national liberals' formed a solid block upon which he could rely for carrying out his home policy during the decade 1867–78. These moderate parties represented accurately the new bourgeoisie whose growth coincided with the foundation of the Empire. A hundred years after it originated in England, the Industrial Revolution seized Germany. If industrialization was less complete in Germany than in England, it was carried out more methodically, and its effect was hardly less farreaching. The windfall of the French war-indemnity of 1871, the peculiar German talent for careful and thorough organization, and the co-operation of industrialists and scientists combined to make Germany very quickly a powerful competitor for international markets. Nor did the growth of industrialism fail to make itself felt in the political sphere. Moltke and the Prussian General Staff realized very early the military importance of railways; first in Prussia, later on in the other federal states, they were bought up and developed by the *fiscus*; and strategical considerations often played as large a part as economic needs. The heavy industries of iron and steel, too, enjoyed the care and indirect subsidies of the state. The armaments factory of Krupp at Essen soon developed into one of the biggest and most renowned firms of its kind, and the Moroccan interests of the Mannesmann steel works even led Germany to the verge of a war with France in 1911.

What the ambitious industrialists, and the middle classes at large, wanted was stability and security at home, and the diffusion of German goods and *Kultur* in the world. These aims were quite compatible with the Prussian ideas of an authoritarian régime at home and expansion abroad. The bourgeoisie and the Bismarck Empire joined hands, and the ascending and energetic middle class became the surest supporter of imperialism. However, they failed to gain the respect and influence in society and politics which the English middle class obtained in the Victorian age. They paid the piper, but Junkers and officers continued to call the tune.

The establishment of the preliminary North German Federation took many months. As late as 17 April 1867 the federal constitution was promulgated. The relations of Prussia with South Germany remained cool despite the military alliances. Bismarck had to threaten the termination of the Customs Union before Bavaria consented to the reorganization of this body. It was brought into line with the institutions of the North German Federation, and a German *Zollparlament* (Customs parliament) was set up. But 49 out of the 85 deputies who were conceded to South Germany were anti-Prussian, and the debates of the *Zollparlament* made it very doubtful whether it could easily be turned into a pliable *Vollparlament* (parliament proper) such as Bismarck wanted. Even within the North German Federation dissatisfaction was rife. The Prussian conservatives lamented the alleged abandonment of Prussian tradition in favour of German nationalism; whereas the liberals found it hard to accommodate themselves to this same Prussian tradition. The recently annexed provinces of Hanover, Hesse-Nassau and Slesvig-Holstein did not easily accept their new status. The German Hanoverian party openly drilled their adherents for the war of liberation against the Prussian usurper. Bismarck thereupon sequestrated the property of the deposed king, George V (1868), and used the 'Guelph fund' for large-scale briberies and the other corrupt practices of his secret service. However, the success of the Prussian arms in 1866 settled, at least, the constitutional conflict concerning the military budget. The Prussian diet which was elected on the day of Sadowa comprised a majority of moderate deputies. Bismarck asked them formally for an indemnity for the violation of the constitution, and he was given it.

On the whole, however, Bismarck was anything but satisfied with the course of events. In 1869 he thought it would take thirty more years to accomplish the unification of Germany. Only an international crisis could precipitate things, and he did not scruple to create one and to exploit it to the full. The restless ambition of Napoleon, as Bismarck calculated correctly, might furnish him with a suitable pretext for overcoming the reluctance and distrust of the non-Prussian Germanies. A quarrel about the right to garrison Luxemburg was composed by the intervention of England, Austria and Russia. The Prussian troops evacuated the fortress, which was dismantled; the grand duchy was declared neutral under the joint guarantee of the great powers, but remained a member of the German Customs Union (London Conference, May 1867). It looked like a diplomatic victory for Napoleon; but it fell short of the big increase of power which he had led the French nation to expect. The Empress Eugénie put the problem in a nutshell when she said (8 May 1869) that only a war could avert the overthrow of the dynasty. In September 1869, an exchange of letters between Napoleon, Francis Joseph and Victor Emmanuel brought about a kind of entente between France, Austria and Italy, although the thorny problem of the secular régime of the Pope stood in the way of a formal alliance.

The blow, however, was to fall from an unexpected quarter. In September 1868 the Spaniards expelled their queen Isabella, whose conduct had kept the *chronique scandaleuse* of Europe going for twenty years. After the king of Portugal and two junior members of the house of Savoy had refused the Spanish crown, it was offered to Prince Leopold of Hohenzollern. He was a scion of the Swabian, Roman Catholic branch of the Hohenzollerns, and was considered acceptable to the neighbours of Spain as the son-in-law of the king of Portugal, and a second cousin of Napoleon through his Beauharnais mother. His elder brother Charles had, in 1866, ascended the throne of Rumania and proved himself a capable ruler. Leopold's candidature was inspired and financially backed by Bismarck: he wished to 'apply the Spanish fly to Napoleon's neck', that is, to gain a foothold on the other side of the Pyrenees. On the other hand, it is hardly credible that he should have deliberately chosen the Spanish candidature as a *casus belli*. For the affair might well have ended in a major diplomatic triumph for Napoleon had he not overshot his mark by tactical blunders which Bismarck could not have foreseen.

On 2 July 1870 the provisional Spanish government promulgated the candidature of Prince Leopold. On the 6th, the French foreign secretary, the Duc de Gramont, told the Legislative Assembly that France would never allow a foreign power to install one of her princes on the throne of Charles V. France was apparently resolved upon war, but Napoleon's ambiguous diplomacy not only ruined the slender prospects of a peaceful settlement, but at the same time manœuvred France into political and military isolation. Pressure was brought to bear upon Leopold's father to make his son waive his candidature, and upon King William of Prussia to renounce it in the name of the house of Hohenzollern. This aim was fully achieved. The king let his cousin know that he would approve the renunciation, and on the 12th, the candidature of Prince Leopold was officially withdrawn. All would have been well for Napoleon if he had stopped here. However, egged on by the Empress and public opinion, he and Gramont wanted to add humiliation to defeat. The French ambassador, Benedetti, was instructed to demand of King William that he should give a solemn promise never to allow the prince to accept a candidature in the future; moreover, the king was to write a letter of apology to Napoleon embodying this declaration. Benedetti delivered this message at Ems, where the king was taking the waters, on 13 July. The king was annoyed, described the demand as 'impertinent' and at once informed Bismarck of Benedetti's *démarche*.

The peace negotiations of the past week had deeply depressed Bismarck, and he thought of resigning office. The 'Ems Dispatch', which he received in the company of Moltke and Roon, restored his spirits. Napoleon had done the spade-work for him, like the Danes and Austrians in 1864 and 1866. Napoleon had tried to block Prussia's retreat. Bismarck turned the tables, and, in his turn, made war inevitable. He revised the 'Ems Dispatch', which was composed in the worst red-tape diction, from a 'chamade' into a 'fanfare', to use Moltke's words. The mild rebuff which the king had given Benedetti sounded in Bismarck's version like a blunt, offensive, and final dismissal. The publication had the provocative effect Bismarck intended it to have, that of a 'red rag to the Gallic bull'. On the following day, the French Chambers voted for war 'with a light heart'; and on the 19th, the declaration of war was delivered at Berlin.

The impolitic and tactless procedure of the French government achieved within a couple of days what Bismarck had estimated would be the work of a generation, namely the unification of Germany. The North German diet voted the war budget unanimously save for the two Social Democratic members. The South German states acknowledged the *casus belli* and placed their troops under Prussian command. The 'Patriotic fraction' in Bavaria, i.e. the Roman Catholic group, was outvoted, and the Bavarian prime minister aptly summed up the situation in the sentence: 'The Spanish candidature is finished, the German question has begun.'

An earlier blunder of Napoleon's enabled Bismarck to secure the benevolent neutrality of Britain. The chancellor published in *The Times* the text of an offensive and defensive alliance which the Emperor had offered him in August 1866. It stipulated amongst other things the annexation by France of Belgium and Luxemburg. This exposure of Napoleon's ambitions sufficed to stifle any sympathy with France on the part of the British government and public opinion.

The excellent relations which Bismarck had studiously kept up with Russia ever since 1859 also bore fruit. They had ripened into an informal alliance (1868), and now the Tsar intimated at Vienna and Copenhagen that he would come to the succour of Prussia should Austria or Denmark try to reverse the issues of 1864 and 1866. Italy was more fortunate than wise. Victor Emmanuel was ready to attack Prussia in the middle of August. By this time, however, the Prussians had gained a series of successes which made him abandon his intention. Instead, he marched on Rome, which the French had evacuated, and overthrew the secular régime of the Papacy (21 Sept.).

Before that, the rule of Napoleon was brought to an end. The German victories of Weissenburg (4 Aug.) and Wörth (6 Aug.) shook its foundations. The largest French army under Marshal Bazaine was put out of action and hemmed in at Metz; this fortress with 175,000 men surrendered on 27 Oct. The main field army under the command of Marshal MacMahon was pushed northward towards the Belgian frontier. Around the little fortress of Sedan it was overpowered by the superior German artillery, and capitulated on the morning after the battle (2 Sept.). Amongst the prisoners was the Emperor himself, who had in vain sought death on the battle-field. Two days later the republic was proclaimed in Paris, and the Government of National Defence pursued the war with the greatest vigour. A *pourparler* between Bismarck and Jules Favre only showed the incompatibility of their respective claims. While Favre protested that he would not cede 'an inch of our territory, a stone of our fortresses', Bismarck, backed by military experts as well as public opinion, demanded the cession of Alsace and the German-speaking part of Lorraine, the fortresses of Metz, Strasbourg and Belfort included.

This open avowal of the annexation of Alsace and Lorraine stirred up the depth of Gladstone's liberal convictions, and he was prepared for an intervention in favour of France. However, the majority of the cabinet opposed his policy; and Thomas Carlyle's famous letter to *The Times* strengthened the pro-German tendency of public opinion. The firm attitude of the Tsar eventually prevented the other neutral powers from effectively assisting France, much as many of them, especially Austria, desired it.

In order to widen the breach between Russia and England, Bismarck suggested to Alexander II that he should seize the opportunity to free himself from the restrictions which the treaty of Paris (1856) had imposed upon Russian sovereignty in the Black Sea. England became alarmed, and attention was drawn away from the French theatre of war. In the end, the London Conference (17 Jan.–13 March 1871) complied with Russian wishes, and Bismarck had obliged Russia once more at somebody else's cost.

All that Britain and the United States did to strengthen the weak French Republic was to allow a large-scale traffic in arms for the benefit of the republican armies. The Germans, in fact, suffered some reverses, but the final issue was never in doubt. The republican levies were dealt with one after another: the Eastern Army was forced to cross the Swiss frontier, and on 1 Feb. Belfort was the only place over which the tricolour was still flying, for Paris, too, had fallen after a siege of four months (19 Sept.–28 Jan.). Contrary to the military advice of Moltke and the humane remonstrances of the queen and crown princess, Bismarck insisted on a ruthless bombardment of the capital, which began on 27 Dec. He was impatient to bring the war to an end. Its main purpose—the unification of Germany—was achieved. Its prolongation might lead to the intervention of neutral powers; it certainly raised the prestige of the generals higher than he cared for. The preliminary peace negotiations at Versailles were therefore concluded with great speed. Thiers and Favre were no match for Bismarck. They thought they had scored a triumph when Bismarck abandoned his claim to Belfort and reduced the demand for a war-indemnity from 6000 to 5000 million francs. As a matter of fact, they might also have saved Metz for France, as Bismarck put forth the demand for it only at the instigation of the General Staff. The signing of the final peace was, however, delayed by the internal difficulties of the French government. Bismarck even got into touch with the leaders of the Paris Commune and Napoleon, who now lived at Chislehurst, and thus eventually frightened the republican government into the peace of Frankfort which confirmed the preliminary arrangement with insignificant modifications (10 May 1871). France ceded unconditionally the three eastern departments of Moselle, Haut Rhin and Bas Rhin, and had to pay the 5 milliards within three years, during which a third of the metropolitan area was to remain under German occupation. The deputies from Alsace and Lorraine solemnly protested against their country being bartered away without their consent; but their voices died away in the national mourning of France and the national rejoicing of Germany.

While the siege of Paris was approaching its final stage, the unification of Germany under Prussian leadership was celebrated by an impressive ceremony. On 18 Jan. 1871, one hundred and seventy years after the coronation of the first Prussian king, William I was proclaimed German Emperor in the Gallery of Mirrors at Versailles. The popular enthusiasm that accompanied the outbreak of the war throughout Germany provided Bismarck with the lever with which to overcome resistance. King Lewis II of Bavaria, the insane patron of Richard Wagner, was prevailed upon to copy a letter of Bismarck's in which he was made to suggest that the king of Prussia should assume the imperial title (1 Dec.). King William was alternately furious and downhearted. He did not wish, he said, to exchange the 'glorious crown of Prussia' for 'this crown of mud', and contemptuously compared the title of emperor with that of a 'brevet major'. In the end, Bismarck coaxed him into submission, and, after a last crisis on the eve of the proclamation, King William even accepted the somewhat anaemic title of 'German Emperor' instead of 'Emperor of Germany', the latter having been rejected by the South German rulers as implying territorial sovereignty.

Not without some justification, the new Emperor described his Empire as an 'artificially manufactured chaos'. There was, first of all, a glaring disparity in the size and population of the twenty-six federal states which were in theory equal partners. They ranged from Prussia, comprising 134,616 English square miles and 24.7

million inhabitants, down to the tiny principality of Schaumburg-Lippe, with 131 English square miles and 32,000 inhabitants (1871). There were four kingdoms, six grand duchies, five duchies, seven principalities, and three republics, each with its own constitution and representative system. Nine of them had two chambers, the majority only one house, while the two Mecklenburgs were still ruled by their medieval Estates. The franchise varied from state to state: universal suffrage, suffrage limited by property and other qualifications, chambers partly nominated by privileged corporations, direct and indirect voting, single and plurality votes—there was hardly a system that was not tried out somewhere. Popular representation was most genuine in the South, whereas Prussia and Hamburg vied with one another in falsifying the will even of their carefully sifted electors by reactionary methods of polling. The member states furthermore retained practically the whole internal administration, including direct taxation, railways, police, education, the administration of justice, and the control of local government. Saxony and the South German states also had their own armies, whereas those of the North German states were amalgamated with the Prussian army; only the navy was an imperial institution.

Moreover, the South German states had wrested from Bismarck a number of 'reserved rights' (*Reservatrechte*), which included their own postal services and some titular rights in foreign policy. Prussia, it is true, had ceased to exist as an international power in her own right—and loud were the complaints of the Junkers that the despised democrats and Catholics of the South should have a say in determining the affairs of the Empire. However, this same Empire was, for all practical purposes, a coercive extension of Prussia rather than a voluntary 'permanent league for the protection of the federal territory and the welfare of the German nation', as the imperial constitution proclaimed. For the traditional Prussian spirit and the traditional Prussian methods of government soon permeated the whole Empire. Friedrich Theodor Vischer, the Württemberg democrat, scorned as early as 1873 the spreading of Prussian militarism in the half-humorous verse:

> Soldiers exist for the sake of the state,
> Not for the soldiers' sake has the state been made.

Alsace and Lorraine, although they were described as Imperial Territory, were subjected to a ruthless régime of Prussian generals and officials who succeeded in keeping the flame of French nationalism burning in the country. Subsequent alterations of the constitution of the provinces, although they introduced a certain measure of self-government, did not remove the feeling of the Alsace-Lorrainers that they were looked upon and treated as 'second-class Germans'. After forty years of German rule, the Zabern affair of 1913 revealed that the provinces were as far as ever from being reconciled to the Hohenzollern Empire.

Nor was the internal policy of Bismarck likely to enlist the support of many Germans except those who were prepared from the outset to follow his lead without any mental reservation. Bismarck was the last man to admit the necessity or even the desirability of an opposition for the smooth working of constitutional machinery. Opposition had no place in the Prussian conception of the state; if there was any, it had to be crushed forthwith. Nor were supporters welcome who reserved to themselves the right of criticism. Unconditional surrender to the state of mind, body and soul was required.

No sooner was the Empire established than Bismarck embarked upon a large-scale attack on what he described as the 'enemies of the Empire'. They were the Roman Catholics, Socialists and Liberals. The attack on the Catholic Church was launched with the help of the Liberals, the Liberals were overcome with the help of the Catholics, and the whole bourgeoisie was called out to beat the Socialists. From these battles the Catholics emerged unbroken and the Socialists greatly strengthened, but the liberal bourgeoisie was all but wiped out between the right and the left.

The fight against the Catholic Church began in 1871 and lasted until 1878. It was styled a 'fight for civilization' (*Kulturkampf*) by the Liberals, who honestly regarded the Roman Church as the embodiment of the powers of retrogression and darkness. Bismarck, however, was only concerned with the political aspect. The Roman Catholics had organized themselves in a political party which for want of something better was called the Centre Party (June 1870). Hanoverians, Poles and Alsace-Lorrainers affiliated themselves to it. The Centre stood for the independence of the Church, the political federalization and administrative decentralization of the Empire, the reduction of the military budget, and the extension of the social services. Every point of this programme was a challenge to Bismarck's and the Liberals' conception of a centralized, warlike, secular and capitalistic empire. The Centre Party returned sixty-three deputies to the first imperial diet in 1871 and thereby at once became the second largest party of the house. It rose to the first place after the defeat at the polls of the National Liberals in 1881, and kept it until 1912, when the Social Democrats outstripped it.

The *Kulturkampf* reached its climax with the four 'May laws' of 1873. These aimed at reducing the Church to a state department, and its priests to state officials. The Catholic population, clergy and laity, rose as one man, and not a few devout Protestants, amongst them the Empress Augusta, took their side. Bismarck resorted to draconian measures. The archbishops of Cologne and Posen were imprisoned, four other bishops deposed, and about 1500 priests expelled from their parishes. Fines, imprisonment, and the deprivation of pastoral cures did not break the spirit of resistance. In vain Bismarck boasted that he would never 'go to Canossa', as did Henry IV in 1077, in order to submit to the Pope. In the end, he was forced to beat a retreat. The *Kulturkampf* revived the age-old distrust of Prussia throughout Catholic Germany. The heir presumptive to the Bavarian throne, afterwards King Lewis III, told the duke of Connaught 'how much he hated Prussia'. The worst impression was made upon the strictly religious populations in Alsace-Lorraine and the eastern provinces. Here, Catholic Germans joined hands with their French and Polish co-religionists and thus swelled the ranks of the 'enemies of the Empire'. The Christian trade-unions and journeymen's associations, which were originally founded with a view to counteracting the influence upon the working classes of the irreligious socialist unions, were also driven into opposition. Their sympathy was wholly with their 'red' comrades when Bismarck directed his onslaught against socialism and trade-unionism.

The accession of the diplomatist Pope, Leo XIII (1878), facilitated Bismarck's change of policy. By 1887 nearly all the *Kulturkampf* laws were repealed. Only state supervision of all schools and obligatory marriage before a registrar remained in force, and the Jesuit Order was excluded from German soil until 1904. In 1885 Bismarck even chose the Pope as arbitrator in a quarrel with Spain about the Caroline Islands, and was rewarded for his '*civilis prudentia*' by a high decoration and a flattering letter from Leo XIII. Nevertheless, his relations with the Centre Party remained mutually cool and distrustful; but meanwhile he was on the warpath against two other enemies.

First of all the Socialists had to be exterminated. They were obnoxious to Bismarck as republicans, pacifists, internationalists and enemies of the capitalist system. They were represented only by twelve deputies, but the number of Socialist voters had steadily risen from 124,000 in 1871 to 493,000 in 1877. Two attempts on the life of the Emperor (May and June 1878) gave Bismarck a welcome pretext for striking the long-prepared blow. Although none of the assassins was a member of the Socialist Party, he brought in a bill 'against the socialist machinations dangerous to the common weal', which completely outlawed the party. This measure was aimed not only at the Socialists, but in a subtle way also at the Liberals.

Bismarck's alliance with the Liberals had become inconvenient to him for various reasons. For ten years the Liberals had supported him through thick and thin. It was their parliamentary majority which passed the unifying legislation of the first years of the Empire, which introduced the gold standard and mark currency (1873), established the Reichsbank (1875), and set up a uniform legal system for civil, criminal and bankruptcy proceedings (1876). Now the Liberals presented their bill and intimated that the time had come for enlarging the rights of parliament, and to appoint two or three parliamentarians as ministers responsible to the house. This constitutional issue was aggravated by serious dissensions about economic policy. The Liberals upheld the tenets of free-trade as embodied in the Prusso-French treaty of 1862 which, in its turn, was modelled on the famous Cobden treaty of 1860. Unfettered economic liberalism received a severe blow when the prosperity period following the victorious war and overfed by the milliards of the French war-indemnity collapsed in 1873. Agrarians and industrialists were the first to clamour for protectionist tariffs. They set up powerful organizations—*Deutscher Landwirtschaftsrat* (1872), *Zentralverband der deutschen Industrie* (1876)—and through them gained a firm hold on the political parties of the right. In 1877 Bismarck embraced the protectionist creed, and introduced legislation to that effect in the following year.

Both the law against the Socialists and the protectionist tariff went against the most cherished liberal convictions of political and economic freedom. The Reichstag threw out the former bill, Bismarck at once dissolved it, and the Liberals lost a third of their seats as the bourgeoisie was frightened by the bogey of a red revolution and went over in masses to the Conservative camp. The new Reichstag passed the law against the Socialists (18 Oct. 1878), and it was regularly renewed until 1890. The rigour with which the police administered it caused much suffering, created martyrs, and alienated the working class irretrievably from the Hohenzollern Empire. At the same time, the Socialist Party was welded into a disciplined and militant body, and marshalled 1½ million voters at the election in 1890, when it became the largest party in the country, though not yet in parliament.

As the majority of the working class, especially the trade-unions, cared less for the theoretical aspects of revolutionary Marxism than for improving the workmen's lot forthwith, Bismarck inaugurated a policy of social reforms by which he hoped to take the wind out of the sails of the Social Democrat Party. After he had shed the Liberals (1878), who had shortsightedly opposed any measures which might stain the purity of their theories of economic and individual freedom, Bismarck deliberately used social legislation as a means to humiliate his erstwhile allies and to oblige his present supporters, Conservatives and Centre. The latter had for some decades taken an active interest in factory legislation, health insurance, and old-age pensions; while the Conservatives favoured similar schemes as being in accordance with their idea of the patriarchal and omnipresent state. Thus Bismarck cleverly asked the Reichstag 'to heal social evils by means of legislation based on the moral foundation of Christianity' (1881). Against the stubborn resistance of the Liberals a number of social reforms were passed, which included compulsory insurance against sickness (1883), accidents (1884), and old age (1889). However progressive these measures were, they did not give Bismarck that political gain for which he had chiefly introduced them; for the working classes were not appeased and continued to demand political rights which they would not barter away for a mess of pottage.

Whereas the Centre and Socialist parties successfully withstood Bismarck's onslaught, the Liberals were completely overwhelmed. The socialist scare cost them a third of their power; the tariff legislation halved the rest; the number of National Liberals fell from 155 in 1874 to 99 in 1878 and 47 in 1881. Henceforth they lived on Bismarck's sufferance. In order to carry the protectionist legislation, Bismarck had to approach the Centre. A majority of Conservative and Centre deputies passed it in 1879. The price the chancellor had to pay was the 'Franckenstein clause' named after the principal speaker of the Centre. It stipulated that the surplus revenue of the new customs duties should go to the federal states instead of the imperial exchequer. Thus the unifying tendencies of the liberal era were reversed. Bismarck was not altogether dissatisfied with this development, for it allowed him to strengthen the Prussian hegemony within the Empire. 'The German Empire is just jogging along. You try and make Prussia strong!' he advised the future

Emperor William II. A Prussian Economic Council was set up in 1880, and the Prussian State Council (which had been created by Hardenberg in 1817, but lain dormant for thirty years) was reorganized in 1884 so as to paralyse the Federal Council. After the death of the last Guelph duke of Brunswick (1884) a Prussian prince was installed as regent, with a view to amalgamating the duchy altogether. The Prussian diet with its conservative majority based on the three-class electoral system also backed Bismarck's next onslaught against one more 'enemy of the Empire', the Poles. Polish influence upon education and administration was to be exterminated and the eastern provinces were to be completely Germanized. Anti-Polish legislation culminated in a bill which provided that Polish landowners should be expropriated and replaced by German peasants and workmen (1886).

The reverses Bismarck suffered in home politics were, however, in his view outweighed by his successes in foreign affairs. The complicated system of security, which he began to build up even during the war of 1870–71, can be reduced to the simple formula which he himself once used, namely, that Germany should always be the third in any possible combination of the five great European powers of Austria-Hungary, France, Germany, Great Britain and Russia.

France, of course, was excluded from any scheme of alliances. The loss of her eastern provinces made her an implacable enemy of Germany. Bismarck tried every means to keep her in a state of impotence and isolation. He fomented internal dissension and threw his weight into the balance against any monarchical restoration. The republic behind which loomed the shadow of the Paris Commune would bar France from the society of the respectable monarchies of Europe. A 'preventive war' which the German General Staff suggested in 1875 was averted by British and Russian intervention. Bismarck, who had added fuel to the fire by inspiring provocative press comments, thereupon changed his tactics. He encouraged France to extend her oversea empire in Tunisia, Indo-China, Madagascar and Central Africa (1881–84), in order to turn the attention of the French from the Vosges to distant parts of the globe where friction with England was almost inevitable.

A close understanding with Russia continued to be the cornerstone of Bismarck's foreign policy. At the same time, he succeeded in restoring amicable relations with Austria. On 22 Oct. 1873, the three Emperors of Russia, Austria-Hungary and Germany signed an alliance. Its main purpose in Bismarck's view was 'to prevent

Austria and Russia, firstly, from tearing each other to pieces and, secondly, from combining at Germany's expense'. The Three Emperors' Alliance was wrecked by the Balkan war of 1876–78. Bismarck refused to take sides in the war which threatened between Austria and Russia, and preferred the part of the 'honest broker' at the Congress of Berlin (1878). Although he thought that he now 'drove Europe four-in-hand', the Berlin Congress marked, in reality, an ominous turning-point in German history; Russia lost faith in the value of her alliance with Germany, and Austria could therefore raise the price of her partnership: it was the beginning of the road that led to the Russo-French alliance of 1891 and Germany's submission to Austria's foolhardiness in 1908 and 1914. The Berlin Congress was the first stepping-stone on Germany's way into world politics while her diplomatic, military and economic equipment were inadequate for her role on this stage.

Still, Bismarck's consummate skill succeeded in laying the ghosts which he himself had conjured up. A close alliance with Austria (7 Oct. 1879) was concluded and met with an enthusiastic welcome in Germany, as it seemed to redress the effects of the fratricidal war of 1866. William I was almost the only one to regard it with misgivings; he considered it perfidious towards Russia, and looked upon the Danube monarchy as a broken reed. The Dual Alliance was converted into a Triple Alliance when Italy joined it with the approval of England (20 May 1882). Alliances concluded by Austria with Serbia (28 June 1881) and Rumania (30 Oct. 1883) further extended the sphere of influence of this weighty Central European bloc.

At the same time, Bismarck succeeded in restoring friendship with Russia. On 18 June 1881, a fresh Three Emperors' Alliance was signed. It was duly renewed in 1884, but the Bulgarian crisis of 1885–87 undermined Austro-Russian relations beyond repair. As Russia firmly refused to renew the Three Emperors' Alliance, but was willing to continue on friendly terms with Germany, Bismarck found a solution in the Russo-German Re-insurance Treaty of 18 June 1887. It pledged the two powers to mutual neutrality in any conflict, except a Russian attack on Austria or a German attack on France; thus Germany obtained security against becoming the victim of a joint Russo-French attack, while Russia was reassured against the danger of a hostile Austro-German combination.

The part which Britain played in Bismarck's complicated system of European alliances is not easy to define. He was anxious to reach some kind of *entente* with the power that was best fitted to counter-

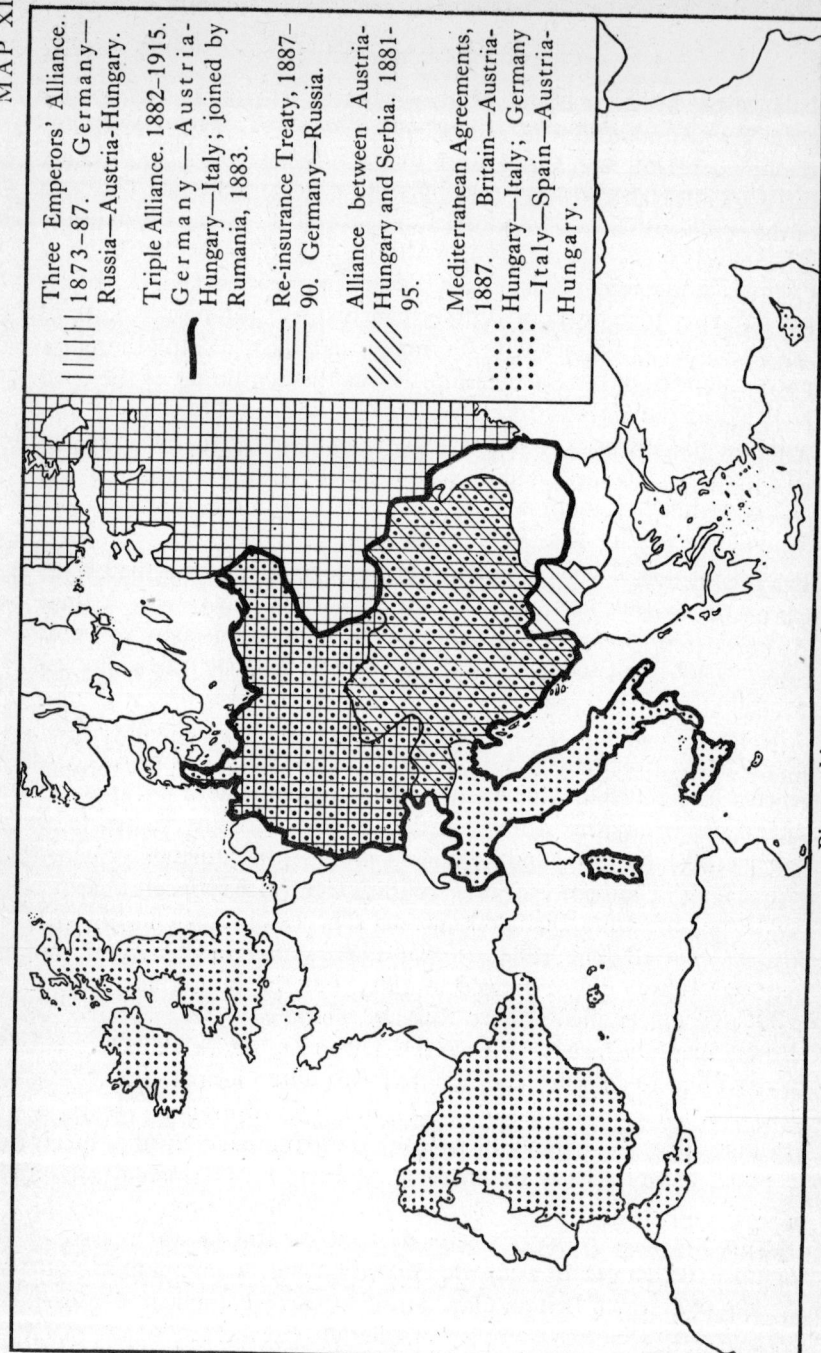

Bismarck's system of alliances

balance the heavy pressure exercised by the Russian colossus. He certainly had no design to rival British sea-power. This was one of the few points in which he saw eye to eye with Moltke, who stated categorically that Germany 'could never make claim to the command of the sea', and was therefore the natural continental ally of Britain. Various overtures to come to terms were, however, turned down by Gladstone, who described Bismarck as 'the devil incarnate'; and Beaconsfield and Salisbury, who were inclined to an Anglo-German *entente*, were out-voted by their cabinets. Bismarck would have liked England to become a kind of sleeping partner of the Triple Alliance. Italy was expressly exempted from her obligations if the Triple Alliance should become involved in a war with England—a clause which can only be interpreted as proof that Bismarck considered this contingency impossible. Moreover, he encouraged his junior partners to conclude the London Alliance of 12 Dec. 1887, by which Britain, Austria and Italy pledged themselves to maintain the *status quo* in the Near East. In the same year, an agreement was signed by Austria-Hungary, Italy, Spain and Germany to safeguard their interests in the Western Mediterranean. Both these informal anti-French alliances lapsed in 1895.

Neither Gladstone nor Salisbury raised any objections to Germany's acquisition of colonies. In December 1882, a German Colonial Association was formed with Bismarck's approval. German trading and shipping companies bought territories in Central, South and East Africa and in the Pacific; and in 1884–85 Togoland, the Cameroons, South-West Africa, Tanganyika, Zanzibar, North-East New Guinea and the Bismarck Archipelago were proclaimed German 'protectorates'. Bismarck took little interest in these colonies, and only meant to use them for political bargaining with Britain. Even less interest in colonial matters was shown by the Reichstag and the nation in general. An instinctive foreboding of the dangers involved in oversea adventures prevailed until the warning voices raised by Conservatives, Liberals and Socialists alike were drowned by the fanfares of Tirpitz's propaganda.

Despite these seemingly sincere proofs of mutual good-will, Bismarck approached the problem of Anglo-German relations with caution. He was afraid of too close a contact with a nation of anti-militaristic and liberal leanings. He viewed with apprehension the approaching death of the old Emperor, as the heir apparent and his consort, 'that Englishwoman', openly showed their preference for liberal politicians and institutions. A complete change of German policy might indeed have taken place when William I died on 9 March 1888 in his ninety-first year. But the new Emperor who for years had waited for this moment was fast dying from laryngeal cancer. What might have become a turning-point of history dissolved into the pitiful tragedy of the '99 days'. On 15 June, Frederick III followed his father into the grave. With him was buried the hope of a liberal evolution of German home politics; and the whole generation of public men who in correspondence and conversation with the Princess Royal had for years been mapping out the future policy of social and cultural progress, disappeared from the stage. The dismissal of the Prussian Minister of the Interior, Puttkamer, the most reactionary member of the cabinet (6 June), was the only act by which the dying Emperor indicated his intentions.

The young man of twenty-nine who ascended the throne was a stout supporter of Bismarck, an idolator of the Prussian army, and a hater of democracy and socialism. His idiosyncrasies were founded on a mystical belief in the world-mission of the house of Hohenzollern, and an unlimited vain-gloriousness. His instinct often showed him the right way, but he was too unsteady to act upon his own convictions if they required serious study and tenacity of purpose. William II was, as his uncle Edward VII described him, 'the most brilliant failure in history'.

It was inevitable that the young Emperor and the old chancellor should collide. It was, as sycophants insinuated to the eagerly listening monarch, a question whether the Hohenzollern dynasty or the Bismarck dynasty should rule over Germany. The crisis developed early in 1889. The Emperor asserted his autocratic power, demanded legislative measures, interfered with the administrative routine, and made it increasingly clear that he wanted 'to be his own chancellor'. Bismarck retaliated '*à corsaire, corsaire et demi*', treated his sovereign with deliberate contempt—on one occasion 'he all but threw an inkstand at my head', the Emperor afterwards said—and opposed on principle the Emperor's every suggestion. In the end, William II brusquely ordered Bismarck to tender his resignation. Complying with this demand, Bismarck charged the Emperor with the exclusive responsibility; and the latter dared not publish the statesmanlike letter. On the anniversary of the revolution of 1848 (18 March 1890), 'the pilot was dropped'; and the 'sure destroyer of the Empire', as Bismarck described him, announced the new course with the words 'Full steam ahead!'

CHAPTER IX

THE EMPIRE OF WILLIAM II (1890–1918)

THE period from 1890 to 1918 is known as the Wilhelmian era, not because William II was a strong personality who impressed his will and authority upon his generation, but because the absence of any outstanding man made him the prototype of the weaklings who for twenty-five years shaped the destiny of Germany. In no sphere of activities was this more obvious than in that of foreign affairs, which Bismarck had made his exclusive domain. The Reichstag was allowed to discuss them, but had no influence on their course, and the Federal Council, which had the authority, never used it. The Emperor's prerogative of personal intervention in foreign affairs soon therefore gained an importance which Bismarck had never conceded to his sovereign; and Germany's foreign policy from 1890 to 1914 clearly reflects the inconsistency of its imperial originator. William II's impulsive vagaries were by no means counterbalanced by the chancellors who succeeded Bismarck. General von Caprivi (1890–94) was a worthy old soldier; Bethmann Hollweg (1909–17) was an uninspired administrative official; neither of them had any experience of, or settled views on, foreign affairs. Prince Hohenlohe (1894–1900), it is true, was a trained diplomatist; but, being seventy-five years of age when he took office, he was too old and inert to resist the flighty impromptus of his imperial nephew. Lastly, Bülow (1900–9) responded to the Emperor's sudden flashes with an unscrupulous alacrity which increased rather than checked their dangers. Similarly, fawning courtiers adapted themselves to their master's every whim, although not a few of them—such as Count Waldersee, Moltke's successor as Chief of the General Staff, and Prince Eulenburg, a base flatterer though well versed in foreign affairs—expressed in diaries and confidential letters their despair of the Emperor's ruinous policy; they even hinted at his being mentally deranged. The Emperor's unconstitutional *politique à l'opérette*, however, provided a leading role for an actor of demoniacal gifts: it was Fritz von Holstein, councillor at the Foreign Office, who, though bearing no formal responsibility, was for sixteen fateful years the chief agent of German foreign policy. The central motive of Holstein's activities seems to have been a fiendish hatred of Bismarck and an excessive lust for destruction; and though he sought to out-Bismarck his former master's statecraft, he entirely failed to grasp the simple principles underlying Bismarck's seemingly complicated system. Holstein wove William II's inconsistencies into a super-sophisticated pattern, the only recognizable leitmotif of which was that the more waters Germany troubled the more fish she might catch.

It was probably Holstein who decided the first event of importance after Bismarck's dismissal. The Russo-German Re-insurance Treaty was allowed to lapse, although Russia offered very favourable conditions for its renewal. The corner-stone of Bismarck's edifice was thereby broken, and only one year later the Franco-Russian alliance which Bismarck had dreaded more than anything else was initiated (Aug. 1891). The traditional friendship between Russia and Prussia gave way to an increasing hostility on both sides which became fatal when Germany began to interfere in the main sphere of Russian interests, the Balkans and Turkey. William II fondly believed that the personal relations between the houses of Hohenzollern and Romanov would be sufficiently strong to adjust the policies of their respective empires. For twenty years (1894–1914) he kept up a regular correspondence with Tsar Nicholas II in which he displayed all his great charm and greater tactlessness. He regarded it as a masterpiece of diplomatic cunning when he made the weak and ignorant Nicholas sign the treaty of Bjoerkoe (July 1905), which pledged the two countries to an almost unconditional brotherhood in arms. The childish monarchs were speedily shaken out of their autocratic illusions, for their foreign ministers at once derided the treaty of Bjoerkoe as a chimera. The hostile camps of the Triple Alliance and the Dual Alliance—the latter complemented by the Anglo-French Entente of 1904—could no longer be reconciled by the well-meaning efforts of crowned amateurs.

If thus the ties of friendship with Germany's oldest ally were lightheartedly severed, it could not be expected that relations with the 'hereditary enemy' would improve. In fact, Franco-German relations never passed beyond the stage of icy formality. On the other hand, William II had, at the beginning of his reign, a genuine desire for a close friendship with Britain; and up to August 1914, he never ceased to entertain a secret love for the country whence his mother had come. British national character and statesmanship inspired in him a curious blend of intense admiration and passionate hatred. The exchange of the German protectorate of Zanzibar for the British possession of Heligoland, which took place a few months after Bismarck's dismissal, seemed to indicate that the Emperor was anxious to avoid far-flung overseas commitments which might embroil Germany with Britain. But, as was so often the case with his political ambitions at home and abroad, he eventually brought about the very opposite of his original intentions. Heligoland soon became the pivot of German naval strategy; and the navy more than anything else became the Emperor's chief obsession and, more than anything else, made inevitable the final rupture between England and Germany. In 1897, Alfred von Tirpitz was appointed naval secretary; nine months later (March 1898) the first navy bill was passed, followed in quick succession by more and bigger ones (1900, 1906, 1908), which transformed the German navy from an instrument of coastal defence into an offensive high-seas force. Tirpitz proved himself to be a pastmaster in stimulating public interest in naval and oversea matters: titles, decorations, promotions and veiled subsidies were lavished upon university professors, artists, authors, journalists and industrialists; and the Emperor's word that 'Germany's future lies on the water' became the leitmotif of countless public speeches, periodicals, books and press comments.

The navy was originally hardly more than a personal hobby of William's. But this very fact aptly illustrates the desultoriness of his whole policy. Personal likes and dislikes made him again and again take up fresh ideas only to drop them, thereafter remaining indifferent to their fate. William II was often sincerely surprised when he realized what shape his intuitions had taken in the hands of anonymous and irresponsible courtiers, generals and officials. That was, for instance, the case with the notorious telegram in which he congratulated Kruger, the president of the Transvaal Republic, after the Jameson Raid (3 Jan. 1896). That this was an empty gesture was proved a few years later when Kruger, travelling Europe as a suppliant, was not even received by the Emperor. But the sinister wording of the telegram and the simultaneous landing of German marines at Delagoa Bay could not but create the suspicion that Germany, far from respecting the loudly heralded sovereignty of the Boer republics, had designs of her own upon them.

At this time, English public opinion began to realize that their statesmen had committed a blunder when handing over Heligoland to Germany. However, neither the German navy programme nor the Kruger telegram were sufficient in themselves to seal the fate of Anglo-German relations. On the contrary, there followed a series of earnest attempts on the part of Britain to come to a closer understanding with her troublesome neighbour. After careful preparations Joseph Chamberlain, the colonial secretary, openly offered Germany an alliance with Britain (1898). Cecil Rhodes was full of enthusiasm for the plan and discussed it at length in Berlin; William II and Bülow examined further details with the British government in London and at Windsor (1899). Salisbury's cabinet associated themselves wholeheartedly with the project, and Chamberlain continued as its chief sponsor. In 1901, Lansdowne had a draft of the treaty ready; Japan was to be the third partner.

It was certainly not the fault of the German diplomatists on the spot which in the end caused the negotiations to break down. For thirty years, Germany was represented at the court of St James by her best diplomatists who, advocating Anglo-German friendship, had the interests of both countries and of universal peace very much at heart. They were Count Hatzfeldt (1885–1901), who played an important role in the negotiations with Chamberlain; Count Wolff-Metternich (1902–12), who fought a heroic but unavailing struggle against the blindness of the Emperor and the Berlin Foreign Office, and was dismissed when he reported that the failure of the Haldane mission meant war with England, France and Russia, in 1915 at the latest; and Prince Lichnowsky (1912–14), who worked hand in hand with Sir Edward Grey to the last minute and whose gloomy warnings awakened no more response than those of his predecessor, but earned him the implacable hatred of the pan-Germans. The failure of the Anglo-German negotiations was entirely due to the complete absence of the spirit of compromise in Berlin; 'all or nothing' was a characteristic reply to one of Lansdowne's proposals.

Statesmen, generals and admirals alike overestimated the power of Germany, and underestimated that of her potential enemies. Bülow haughtily refused 'to play the part of England's continental mercenary'; the General Staff had worked out to the very day its time-table for the defeat of the French and Russian armies, just as later on the Naval Staff confidently prophesied the date when the U-boat warfare would bring England to her knees. Moreover, Holstein's dictum was generally accepted as gospel truth—that Britain and Russia could under no circumstances come to terms with each other. The Anglo-Russian convention of 1907 shattered these illusions like a bolt from the blue. But, instead of making the responsible men reflect and retrace their steps, it only drove them on to even greater exertions: the navy bill of 1908, the army act of 1911, and the combined army and navy bills of 1912—drafted by Ludendorff—brought the world war nearer step by step.

Just as the beginnings of the German navy were accompanied by the discordant notes of the Kruger telegram, this increased danger to world peace was emphasized by another outburst of the Emperor's. On 28 Oct. 1908, the *Daily Telegraph* published an interview which William II had granted to an English host. It was nothing more startling than the usual imperial blend of offensive threats and more offensive flatteries, and the *Daily Telegraph* even hoped to improve Anglo-German relations by its publication: but this interview was a perfect epitome of all the vagaries with which William II had bluffed and disquieted the world for twenty years—and the world took full notice of it. Even the long-suffering and politically blind and deaf German people at last took alarm; and Bülow had to apologize to the Reichstag for his imperial master. It was, however, a storm in a tea-cup, and Germany relapsed into apathy and fatalism.

It was again the British government which made a last superb stand against the onrushing tide of war. Asquith, Lloyd George, Haldane and Churchill were ready to come to a compromise which was to minimize Anglo-German rivalry in the naval and colonial spheres. A general pacification might follow since Britain and Germany could easily exert their influence on their respective allies to this effect. As the German chancellor, Bethmann Hollweg, sincerely strove for peace, the prospect of Haldane's mission to Berlin (Feb. 1912) seemed indeed good, although the friendly spirit of the Chamberlain era had meanwhile given way to cautious suspicion on the part of the British government. In fact, the negotiations were doomed to failure from the beginning. No concession of Churchill's (the 'adventurer' with whom Tirpitz refused 'to sit at a conference table') could have overcome the firm resolve of Tirpitz to uphold his shipbuilding programme at any cost. Tirpitz, backed by the army leaders, was stronger-willed and knew better what he wanted than either the weak chancellor or the opportunist foreign secretary, Kiderlen-Wächter, neither of whom, moreover, was in the Emperor's confidence.

The Anglo-German negotiations in 1898–1901 had offered an opportunity to reverse the diplomatic setbacks which Germany had sustained since Bismarck's dismissal. For, ten years after this fateful event, Germany had manœuvred herself out of the focus of a carefully planned system of alliances into an isolation that was anything but splendid. The Austro-Hungarian monarchy was the only reliable friend left, and its international authority was dwindling fast in proportion to its increasing internal difficulties. The Triple Alliance, though it was regularly renewed, lost its value with the breakdown of the Anglo-German negotiations, as the maintenance of cordial Anglo-Italian relations had been a primary condition of Italy's adherence to the alliance of 1882. While England and France were drawing more closely together, Italy settled her quarrels with France over North Africa (1 Nov. 1902). Any possible doubt about Italy's position was finally cleared when at the conference of Algeciras (1906) she openly sided with the Western powers against her nominal allies. It was obvious that no active support was to be expected from her in case of war, and it became more and more probable that she might even be found in the hostile camp. Germany and Austria-Hungary facing the rest of Europe and possibly the world—this was the constellation with which Germany had to reckon ten years before it became a bloody reality.

Such was the result of the policy of the Emperor who had promised that he would 'lead Germany into glorious days'. Intoxicated by meretricious slogans of his own invention, such as 'our fist must grasp the trident', he had made a dramatic entry upon the stage of 'world politics'. Henceforward, he thought himself entitled to appear and make himself heard on every political scene throughout the wide world. In 1895 Germany joined Russia and France in stopping Japanese aggression in China: two years later Germany's protégé had to foot the bill and cede Kiaochow to her protector. Both Japan and China were thus given offence, in return for which Germany acquired a possession of no economic value and moreover indefensible in any armed conflict. In the Spanish-American war of 1898, a German squadron was sent to the Philippines, and the United States was all but provoked to war. Two years later, the Emperor demanded and obtained German leadership of the international force in China; on the occasion of a send-off speech to his troops, he admonished them to emulate the Huns in savagery—a word which the world was never to forget.

Undeterred by experience, Germany continued to embark upon one adventure after another. Each of these departures might have precipitated a major conflagration and each ended in a diplomatic defeat which made Germany's position ever more desperate. The Foreign Office, since Bismarck's dismissal always under the pressure of the neurasthenic Emperor, was now subjected also to the expansionist demands of big business. German industry and capital were on the look-out for foreign markets, as their expansion had by far outrun the demands of home consumption. In almost every branch of production Germany had outstripped her rivals; only England and the United States were her superiors, and year by year she was narrowing the margin between herself and them. Capital investments abroad rose from £2500 millions in 1880 to £15,000 millions in 1913 (Great Britain: £15,000 millions to £38,000 millions); the German percentage of the world output of pig-iron increased from 15 to 21 per cent from 1890 to 1913 (U.S.A. 34 to 40 per cent; Great Britain: 30 to 13 per cent); and in 1910 Germany's annual share in world trade was £8000 millions, as compared with £10,000 millions of Great Britain and £7000 millions of U.S.A.

Economic expansion took two principal directions—Turkey and Africa. The Ottoman Empire fell an easy prey to the political, military and financial attractions that Germany had to offer. The Emperor's visit to Palestine and Syria in 1898 paved the way. He declared himself the protector of all the Moslems, and he so successfully curried favour with the notorious Abdul Hamid II, that the construction of a railway from Constantinople to Baghdad was granted to German concessionaires (1899). Economic penetration was followed by military agreements. Most of the leaders of the Young Turkish revolt of 1908 had received their military training in Germany. After they had deposed the wily old Sultan (1909), the Young Turks feverishly imitated Germany in what they correctly considered her strongest point, the organization of the army. Baron von der Goltz, formerly a military adviser of Abdul Hamid, was appointed chief instructor of the Turkish army, which, in 1913, was virtually placed under the command of a German general, Liman von Sanders. The slogan 'Berlin-Baghdad' had become one of the principal tenets of German foreign policy. Might not the economic penetration of Turkey be followed by that of Persia, Afghanistan, and, perhaps, India? These thoughts kindled the imagination of adventurous youngsters and calculating business men alike. In any case, the Berlin-Baghdad route seemed safer and more promising than the jump across the Mediterranean which had for a long time stood in the foreground of political considerations at Berlin. The eyes of the heavy industrialists were fixed on the rich ore deposits of Morocco, and it seemed still possible to challenge the vaguely defined French protectorate. Holstein forced the Emperor, against the latter's unusually firm resistance, to defy the French by a state visit to Tangier (31 March 1905), on which occasion he affirmed

Germany's disinterested friendship for a sovereign and independent Morocco. Delcassé, the French foreign secretary, opposed with great vigour the obvious German threat to the French North African empire, but he had to resign under heavy German pressure. For this short-lived triumph of blackmail, Bülow was rewarded with the title of prince, which Bismarck had received after the victorious end of the Franco-German war. But the Emperor and chancellor rejoiced too early. Instead of following up his success and settling the problem with the intimidated French cabinet, Bülow insisted on a European conference which was to be his counterpart of Bismarck's Congress of Berlin. At the conference of Algeciras (Jan.–April 1906), however, Germany found herself confronted by a solid phalanx of opponents, Austria alone supporting her claims. The threat to Gibraltar and the Spanish south coast sufficed to rally Britain and Spain behind France, even if Britain had not been pledged by the Entente of 1904; Russia stood unhesitatingly by her ally; and Italy for the first time openly deserted the Triple Alliance. The result was a crushing diplomatic defeat of Germany.

Five years later, Morocco became the scene of another mad adventure which ended in another public exposure of Germany's dangerous isolation. In July 1911, a German gunboat, the *Panther*, was sent to Agadir 'for the protection of German interests'—in reality, to secure the profits of an iron-ore concern—and this open challenge brought Germany and France to the brink of war. A tactful but firm speech by Lloyd George saved the situation: his hint that Britain would stand by France in her hour of need made the German diehards recoil. By the treaty of Berlin (4 Nov. 1911), Germany secured, it is true, a large slice of French territory bordering on the Cameroons, but in return she abandoned all her claims in Morocco, and once more she saw herself faced by a united Europe. Moreover, her reputed superiority and determination had suffered a serious shock.

The political events in the Balkans during these years did little to offset the loss of prestige suffered in Africa. In the turmoil of the Turkish revolution, Austria-Hungary annexed the Turkish provinces of Bosnia and Herzegovina (5 Oct. 1908). They had been placed under Austrian administration by the Congress of Berlin, and their formal annexation in no way increased the actual power of the Danube monarchy. It was an open insult to Russia, and the tension became so acute that the Austro-Hungarian army was mobilized. However, Russia, still suffering from the aftermath of the war with

Japan and the revolution, had to accept the *fait accompli* when William II assured the world of Germany's 'Nibelungen loyalty' to Austria—a signally unfortunate metaphor since, in the legend, the loyalty sprang from the guilty conscience that binds together the assassin and his abetter. As at Algeciras, Germany and Austria again stood alone, for Italy again went into opposition. She protested against the violation of the Triple Alliance treaty which stipulated the maintenance of the *status quo*, and claimed compensations for herself.

The Bosnian crisis revealed for the first time that the leadership of the Triple Alliance had passed to Austria: it was the inevitable outcome of William II's political adventures, which had driven Germany into an isolation in which the last remaining ally could extort any prize for his loyalty lest he, too, should desert her. Her reputation for duplicity and faithlessness was further increased when Italy, her nominal ally, attacked Turkey, her professed friend, in 1911, and Berlin was unable and unwilling to restrain the one or support the other. The Balkan wars of 1912 and 1913 again diminished Germany's prestige. Her statesmen were torn by conflicting desires: to counteract British influence at Constantinople, to oblige the Bulgarians whom it became the fashion to describe as the 'Prussians of the Balkans', to keep Rumania faithful to the Triple Alliance pact, and to improve relations with Greece whose king, William II's brother-in-law, was reputed to be Germanophil. These aims were, however, mutually incompatible, so that in the end nothing was left to the German diplomatists but to follow the Austro-Hungarian lead through thick and thin. The Magyars—for it was they who dominated the policy of the Hapsburg monarchy—succeeded in setting up a German princeling as king of Albania, and in cheating Serbia and Montenegro out of the rewards they had expected for their exertions; but this cheap triumph was paid for by driving not only the Serbs, but also the Rumanians and Greeks, their allies, into the camp of the Triple Entente. It was a meagre gain for the Central Powers that Bulgaria and Turkey entered into an informal collaboration with them, for both were terribly weakened by three successive wars and neither of them felt attached to Germany for reasons other than fear and selfishness.

The regrouping of the Balkan powers and the failure of the Anglo-German negotiations over the armaments race caused the British cabinet not only to strengthen their ties with France by exchanging written promises of mutual consultation (Nov. 1912), but also to make a last effort to arrest Germany on her way to Armageddon. Excluding naval questions and thereby the sinister influence of Tirpitz, aided at the same time by the death of the Anglophobe Kiderlen-Wächter (Dec. 1912), Grey and Lichnowsky mapped out a comprehensive agreement on the outstanding problems of common interest in the Middle East and Central Africa. The German and British spheres of influence were defined to their mutual advantage; above all, the Baghdad railway was to be continued by a joint Anglo-German company which was to secure the political safety of India as well as the economic interests of Germany. The agreement was initialled in London on 15 June 1914. It was the first success of German diplomacy for the past twenty-five years, and might easily have become the starting-point for a new departure in Anglo-German relations. *Dis aliter visum.* A fortnight later, the shots were fired at Sarajevo which killed the Archduke Francis Ferdinand and heralded the first world war.

The tremendous growth of German man-power and industrial capacity during the Wilhelmian era was not accompanied by a corresponding extension of democratic institutions, as the Empire remained a semi-autocracy, the middle and lower classes being excluded from any share in the government. There was not even an attempt to lift Bismarck's stigma on democrats, socialists, Catholics, Poles, Danes and Alsatians, although these 'enemies of the Empire' mustered 6·5 out of 12·2 million voters in 1912. The policy of either exterminating or reconciling the foreign nationalities within the Empire was already doomed to failure when the last pre-war chancellor, Bethmann Hollweg, made a last attempt to solve the problem. In 1911 Alsace-Lorraine was at last given a constitution which brought the country, for forty years treated like a backward mandate, nearer to the standard of a self-governing colony; but the notorious Zabern incident of 1913 revealed that neither the arrogance of the Prussian officers nor the hostility of the population had undergone a change. The Zabern incident also confirmed the conviction of all progressive elements that the actual power in Germany was vested in the military caste, which used the civil authorities only as a convenient screen. Similarly sterile was the Prussian policy towards the Poles, who numbered about 10 per cent of the population. The laws of expropriation were made severer, but the Junkers failed to realize that it was no longer the Polish squires, but the Polish artisans and peasants, who formed the backbone of national resistance, so that the anti-Polish laws remained for the most part ineffective.

Bethmann eventually decided not to apply them, but he could not replace them by anything better.

A complete deadlock was also reached in the official attitude towards the 'internal enemy' of German blood, the Social Democrats. After the law against the Socialists expired in October 1890, some of the Emperor's speeches suggested that he was willing to give the working class its proper place in the social and political structure of the Empire. But his reforming zeal quickly subsided when the enthusiasm he had expected was not forthcoming. With his usual inconsistency he changed over to the side of the employers and bade the 'fellows without a fatherland' 'shake the dust of Germany off their feet'. In a natural reaction the Social Democratic Party stiffened and became the intransigent champion of orthodox Marxism, until from 1899 a 'revisionist' wing instilled a more realistic outlook into the party. In consequence, the Socialists of Baden voted for the budget in 1904, for the first time in any German state. In the Reichstag, however, the Socialists rejected the budget, root and branch, and thus forewent the chance of offering the government an alternative majority. For the Reichstag, impotent though it was on the whole, might gradually have obtained a greater share in the government by prudently using its few prerogatives: but it never used its powers to impress its will upon the administration. The so-called bourgeois parties were, by their social structure and political ideology, incapable of taking the reins of government into their own hands.

The Conservative Party remained representative of Prussian tradition; and the prerogative of the Prussian crown and the sovereignty of the Prussian state were the mainstays of its programme. As its safe constituencies were situated in the East Elbian provinces, its outlook was chiefly that of the squirearchy of these parts. Its revised party programme of 1892 stressed its semi-feudal, agrarian, militaristic and anti-semitic character; colonial policy and protectionist tariffs were two important new items. The Free Conservatives who in the seventies and eighties had been on the way to becoming a modern Tory party dwindled from 1890 onwards to a small though influential group of high officials and reactionary industrialists.

It was a calamity for the external and internal policy of the Empire that the worship of power politics was not restricted to the nominally conservative parties. The National Liberals dropped to a great extent their liberal tenets and over-compensated this loss of half their original programme by becoming the typical representatives of a specifically German brand of nationalism. This German nationalism identifies national power with military power, regards international law as binding only when it coincides with German interests, and therefore considers the sword the only judge in international affairs. Such was the doctrine—never, of course, stated in so many words—to which the National Liberal Party rallied industrialists, big business men, shipowners and the educated classes, i.e. university professors, officials, secondary school teachers and fashionable writers.

From the Conservative and National Liberal groups the Pan-German League, founded in 1892 by Hugenberg and Carl Peters, the champion of colonial expansion, enlisted its members. Never strong in numbers, but thanks to the social status of its followers not uninfluential, the League demanded that 'the first military power of Europe' should become 'the paramount power in world affairs', and that 'all people of German blood everywhere in the world' should be 'organized in support of German national aims in every country'. The Progressive Party and other liberal secessionists were hardly considered 'national' by these patriots of the strictest observance. Their followers were the small industrialists of West and South-West Germany, artisans, shopkeepers, the peasants of certain North and Central German districts, and a handful of intellectuals, amongst whom Theodor Mommsen, the historian, and Rudolf Virchow, the pathologist, enjoyed an international reputation. But these radicals, too, failed to keep abreast of the times; they were free-trade doctrinaires, opposed social legislation, and, while defending the indefensible positions of the Manchester school, completely lost sight of the political issues of liberalism; and Eugen Richter, their leader, led them, despite his great gifts, from defeat to defeat by tenaciously clinging to the letter of liberal orthodoxy.

In full contrast to the left-wing Liberals, the Centre Party had few principles which it would not forgo provided the interests of the Roman Church were safeguarded. In all other questions it was as ready to go with the Conservatives as with the Liberals and even the Socialists, especially after the Christian trade-unions, ably led by Matthias Erzberger, the youngest member of the Reichstag in 1903, had won the upper hand within the party. Thus none of the political parties was either willing or able to engage wholeheartedly in developing the slender beginnings of constitutional life into full parliamentary and democratic government. In the legislation of 1890–1914, military and naval bills took pride of place, especially as a number of other acts indirectly served the same purpose. When the protectionist tariffs, introduced by Bismarck in 1879, were qualified by Caprivi, the Prussian Junkers openly rebelled and brought about the downfall of the chancellor in 1894; and from 1902 onward the tariff walls were steadily and steeply raised. The value of German imports rose from 6·3 milliard marks in 1903 to 11·6 in 1913, that of exports from 5·3 to 10·9 milliard marks; and the mercantile marine grew from 2·6 million tons in 1900 to 5·2 million tons in 1913.

Bethmann Hollweg, the most enlightened of William's chancellors, was fully aware of the many weaknesses of the Empire's structure, and he did his best to mend some of its most glaring deficiencies. However, he failed in this respect as he failed in foreign affairs, for he was a sensitive philosopher and no match for the hardheaded Junkers and industrialists who knew their own minds very well and, moreover, knew that the Emperor would never back up this conciliatory civilian against the spokesmen of pan-Germanism. The chancellor suffered his most serious defeat over the reform of the Prussian franchise, which he rightly considered the touchstone of German home affairs. Although the draft which he submitted to the Prussian diet in 1910 contained only very few and meagre improvements of the existing three-class system, not only the Conservatives, but also the National Liberals and Centre, raised so many objections that the bill was eventually withdrawn.

Only twice did the Reichstag make any serious attempt to impose its will on the government in questions of political import; and both times Bülow, a pastmaster of glib tactics, succeeded in stifling the opposition by emotional appeals to patriotism and loyalty.

In January 1904 the warlike tribe of the Herreros in South-West Africa rose against their German masters, and it took more than three years to quell the rising. The war was waged with the greatest ruthlessness and ended in the extermination of the Herreros. When the government asked the Reichstag for further supplies, Catholics and Socialists seized the opportunity to censure very sharply the whole colonial administration in which corruption and abuses of all kinds were rife. The supplementary estimates were refused by 178 to 168 votes, and Bülow at once dissolved the diet (Dec. 1906). Nationalistic slogans did their work, and the Socialists lost 38 of their 81 seats, although the Centre retained its strength. Bülow then 'mated' the Conservatives and Liberals, and with this comfortable majority governed for eighteen months. However, the natural antagonism of the two partners proved too strong even for a consummate juggler like Bülow. The 'bloc' split over the proposed reform of the financial system, as the Conservatives opposed and the Liberals supported direct taxation. Bülow resigned after Centre and Conservatives had rejected the bill (24 June 1909). This new majority, the 'black and blue bloc', then passed a number of bills increasing indirect taxation. It looked as if the principle of parliamentary responsibility had won a decisive victory.

In fact, however, Bülow was not overthrown by the Reichstag, and he might have continued in office despite his defeat, had he not incurred the Emperor's displeasure for personal reasons, by backing the deputies' second attempt to influence foreign affairs. The publication of the Emperor's *Daily Telegraph* interview led to a two-day debate in the Reichstag (10–11 Nov. 1908), in the course of which speakers of every party, including the Conservatives, poured out the resentment which for twenty years past had accumulated against the Emperor's personal rule. Worse, the chancellor himself exposed his imperial master to the censure of the representatives of the people. It was this 'disloyalty' which decided Bülow's fate, and was the reason why William II, who had quickly abandoned his first impulse to abdicate, 'sacked the dirty swine', while the Reichstag, frightened by its own courage, relapsed into its wonted subservience.

If the Reichstag, the representative of the centralistic tendencies, failed to assert even its limited rights, the Federal Council displayed an equal unwillingness to exert its theoretically considerable power in favour of the federalistic interests. The federal states were still the mainstays of the Empire, and their political life still flourished. Much was done in Prussia to improve further the efficiency of its already highly efficient bureaucracy; in Bavaria, the reigning clerical democracy cultivated a vigorous particularism which gave the kingdom a peculiar political character. Saxony, the 'red kingdom', which in 1903 returned only socialist deputies to the Reichstag, clung to its conservative home government, but became a model state in some spheres, such as slum-clearing, garden cities, and elementary and adult education. Württemberg and Baden retained the tradition established in the early nineteenth century of democratic and liberal principles in public life, and here as elsewhere in the small states art, the theatre, music and literature received intelligent appreciation and generous support. But the federal governments had almost ceased to take an active share in the political affairs of the Empire.

The first world war was, in the military sense, lost by Germany on the Marne (9–15 Sept. 1914), when Gallieni, by a bold stroke, smashed the infallible Schlieffen plan on which the General Staff had staked all its expectations. The hope for a draw was lost when the battle of Jutland (31 May–1 June 1916), although claimed by the Germans as a victory, definitely established British naval supremacy; and the convoy system, introduced by the Admiralty on 4 May 1917, proved the deadly counterblow to the last German effort to bring Britain to her knees. It put at the disposal of the allies the untapped resources of the United States, the weight of which eventually crushed Germany and her satellites.

While the German armies seemingly marched from victory to victory—and the German public never realized that these victories were but tactical gains bought at the price of strategical failures—a second war of equal ferocity, though no bloodshed, raged on the home front. Never before in German history, it is true, had there been such an internal unity as in the first days of August 1914. The Emperor's slogan 'No more parties, Germans all!' became a reality when the Socialists wheeled into the national front and the Reichstag unanimously voted the war expenses. Very soon, however, rifts became visible in the imposing structure of national unity, or *Burgfriede*, as it was called. This medieval term implied that all personal quarrels should cease within the pale of a besieged fortress; but it was quickly interpreted by the ruling classes that every patriotic citizen should refrain from criticism not only of the military conduct of the war, but also of political, social and economic conditions at home. It was three questions which split public opinion into two opposing camps, namely those of political war aims, the submarine warfare, and the democratization of the imperial and Prussian governments. In none of these problems did the Emperor or the government guide public opinion towards a definite goal, for they themselves had no definite policy on any of them. With critics muzzled and the government perplexed, the forces of reaction and militarism established a complete ascendancy, while the Emperor, nominally the supreme war-lord, and the imperial government, nominally the sole executive organ, had virtually abdicated in favour of the High Command.

This state of affairs came to a head when in August 1916 Hindenburg, the most popular general, was appointed Chief of Staff. He was a mere figure-head—and was to play a similar role in a later crisis—and the real power was vested in his quartermaster-general,

Ludendorff. The perfect type of the hard-working, efficient, ambitious and narrow-minded Prussian officer, Ludendorff made himself the master of Germany, and nothing was too great or small in military, political, administrative or economic affairs to be brought under his personal control. It was Ludendorff who enabled the Junkers, heavy industrialists and big business men to impose their will upon the civil administration in all the major questions of political warfare.

The first of these problems arose at the end of 1914 when the first enthusiasm had cooled and the question of the peace settlement began seriously to engage public opinion. Two schools of thought faced each other. The one strove for an order which would combine German hegemony over East and South-East Europe with a harmonious co-operation with Great Britain in the rest of the world; and this 'Western orientation' was advocated by the chancellor, Bethmann Hollweg, and the parties of the left, Progressives and Socialists. On the opposite side stood the Conservatives, National Liberals and the Prussian Centre, backed by the army and navy staffs. These, the 'Easterners', wanted to see 'God punish England' and to bring under German control French ore, Belgian coal, English shipping and oversea trade. With each victory the demands of the pan-German annexationists increased until nothing less than absolute world-domination would satisfy their appetite.

The discussion of war aims was soon followed by no less heated arguments on the means for bringing the war to a speedy and victorious end; a discussion which concentrated on the question of submarine warfare. Should this terrible weapon only be used within the limits imposed upon it by international agreements to which Germany had subscribed; or should its full fury be let loose upon belligerents and neutrals? All those who regarded the break-up of the British Empire as the principal war aim favoured the radical course. Bethmann Hollweg and the parties of the left who wanted to maintain a modicum of international law realized that the last hope for an understanding with England would disappear with the beginning of unlimited submarine warfare. They were fortified by the warnings about the danger of America's entry into the war, sent by Count Bernstorff, the German ambassador in Washington.

However, in both these questions—war aims and submarine warfare—the diehards carried the day. Their first victim was Bethmann Hollweg. For more than two years he had withstood the noisy agitation for unrestricted submarine warfare, and Tirpitz, its chief advocate, had relinquished office over this dispute (15 March 1916).

In the end, however, Bethmann was tired out by the unremitting attacks which Tirpitz, Stresemann, Erzberger and their disreputable henchmen were directing against him with an unprecedented indulgence in personal abuse. He gave way, and on 31 Jan. 1917 unrestricted U-boat warfare was proclaimed; three days later the U.S.A. broke off diplomatic relations with Germany, and on 6 April openly joined the Allies. This sacrifice of principles, however, did not satisfy Bethmann's opponents, who put forward the demigods of the High Command for the final onslaught. The crown prince, Hindenburg and Ludendorff peremptorily demanded Bethmann's immediate dismissal, and the Emperor bowed to this ultimatum (11 July 1917).

The alliance of Conservatives, National Liberals and the Centre, which had brought about this change, broke, however, at the moment of their apparent triumph. Erzberger and Stresemann had so far supported a wild policy of annexationism. Yet private information on the true military and economic situation, which Erzberger received from the Austrian court and the Roman Curia, shook his faith in the superior wisdom of the General Staff and made him increasingly critical of the military and political conduct of the war. Stresemann, the leader of the left wing of the National Liberals, also felt more and more uneasy about the internal conditions, although he continued to follow the military leadership in foreign and strategical matters. It was the issue of 'internal re-orientation' which drew together National Liberals, Centre, Democrats and Socialists. They realized that the nation which willingly sacrificed its all in this war could no longer be excluded from its full share in determining its political fate. The government of the Empire, they concluded, had to shed its semi-autocratic character and to be transformed into a democracy; and, at the same time, the Prussian diet must be changed from a stronghold of squirearchy and big business into a body truly representative of two-thirds of Germany. The four parties succeeded in setting up a committee of the Reichstag which was to prepare a reform of the imperial constitution; they failed dismally, however, to make even the slightest progress in Prussia. Here the Junkers did not intend to make the least concession to the spirit of the age. These professed stalwarts of royalism even turned against their feudal overlord when William II, in his capacity as king of Prussia, issued the 'Easter message', supplemented by the 'July message', of 1917, in which Bethmann made him promise universal suffrage. It was a shameful spectacle when the two houses of the

Prussian diet turned down the government bill for which the king had pledged his word; to the last, the Prussian Junkers stuck to their prerogatives and prejudices, cynically impervious to counsels of either reason or equity.

They had good reason to consider that their caste still ruled Germany, for they won a decisive victory over the majority of the Reichstag on the issue of war-aims. A week after Bethmann's downfall Centre, Democrats and Socialists passed a motion which defined Germany's war aims on the very lines which Bethmann had been pursuing; for this reason the National Liberals refused their support, without, however, breaking with the coalition parties. In this resolution the Reichstag declared for 'peace by negotiation and for permanent reconciliation of the nations' and against 'annexations by force, and political, economic, or financial oppression of the vanquished'. However, though the parties which carried this motion spoke for the majority of the nation, they did not speak for the imperial government. The new chancellor, Michaelis, was a mere cipher and an obedient tool in Ludendorff's hands, and at once proved his submissiveness to his master. After the peace resolution had been carried by 212 to 126 votes, he stated that he accepted it 'as I interpret it'—which, in fact, meant that he rejected it. Had there been any hope that the Allies would meet Germany on the basis of the resolution, it was crushed by this scarcely veiled avowal of a *vae victis*.

Germany's foreign policy during the war was almost forced upon her. She found herself in the same position as at Algeciras: Germany and Austria-Hungary facing the whole world. In this situation she had no choice; at all costs Italy, Rumania and the U.S.A. must be kept neutral. She failed with all three. Italy and Rumania went over to the Allies because the political leadership of the Central Powers lay at Vienna, and the Austrians refused concessions satisfactory to Italy, while the Magyars were quite obdurate towards Rumania. As to the U.S.A., it was the military and naval leaders and the Prussian reactionaries who deliberately provoked the great republic, in the sure expectation that 'the Americans can neither swim nor fly across the Atlantic; the Americans won't come', as a Prussian minister put it. Military and economic pressure only succeeded in winning Turkey and Bulgaria as allies, and their doubtful military strength and political reliability were glossed over by rosy schemes of a permanent Central European bloc with the Berlin-Baghdad railway as its lifeline extending to the gates of India. While German diplomacy was thus reduced to complete bankruptcy, no annexationist scheme was too chimerical to be propagated by the 'Fatherland Party', which was founded by Tirpitz and an East Prussian official, Wolfgang Kapp, on the anniversary of Sedan, 1917, and backed by the High Command, to counter the growing influence of the moderate parties as expressed in the Peace Resolution. What the world had to expect from a German victory inspired by Tirpitz and dictated by Ludendorff was revealed in the peace treaties of Brest Litovsk (3 March 1918) and Bucharest (7 May 1918) which Russia and Rumania were respectively forced to sign. Quite apart from huge cessions of territory—Russia lost every district she had acquired since 1605—these treaties were designed to reduce the two victims to impotent objects of unlimited economic exploitation, and to leave them perpetually at Germany's mercy. It was only in keeping with these tendencies when Ludendorff, by now the omnipotent dictator, sacked the foreign secretary, Kühlmann, who faintly doubted the possibility of bringing the war to an end by military power alone, and replaced him by an admiral who held political ideas convenient to himself (9 July 1918). Again the chancellor—the seventy-five-year-old Bavarian Count Hertling had succeeded the inept Michaelis (1 Nov. 1917)—was but a figure-head to screen Ludendorff's responsibility from the nation and the Reichstag.

From 1914 to 1918 centralistic ideas undoubtedly gained considerable ground; as early as 1915 it was, for instance, as good as settled that railways and waterways should be nationalized. On the other hand particularism, too, gained in strength. In August 1914 the Reichstag conferred emergency powers on the Federal Council, which the latter used to subject industry, trade, labour and social services to state control. Above all, Prussia and Bavaria developed agricultural policies and rationing schemes of their own, often in defiance of the measures taken by the imperial government. The rationing of commodities, especially foodstuffs, led to a 'bread-card particularism' which showed the old political divisions as vigorous as ever. They came, however, most clearly to the fore when the problem of sharing out the occupied countries was broached. The Wettiners of Saxony put forward their old claim to the Polish crown, and when in 1916 Poland was to be given to an Austrian archduke, they demanded Lithuania instead. The Hohenzollerns coveted the Baltic duchies; the house of Württemberg alternately wanted Lithuania and Flanders; the Hessian princes desired Finland; smaller dynasties also entered into competition, and Bavaria and

Baden wanted to be compensated by portions of Alsace and Lorraine. This greedy haggling came to a sudden end when in November 1918 old and new crowns alike fell into the dust.

When in September 1918 the Allied armies victoriously advanced on all European and Asiatic fronts and the three allies of Germany simultaneously collapsed, Hindenburg and Ludendorff surprised the unsuspecting German public by their sudden demand for an armistice and peace (29 Sept.). Under the impression of this stunning blow the imperial government fell into a panic. What ought to have been the result of careful deliberation was thrown upon a wholly unprepared nation: Germany awoke to find herself a parliamentary democracy. Contrary to established parliamentary habits, however, the leaders of the parties which supported the Peace Resolution were called upon to form the government; and they shared out the ministerial portfolios amongst themselves on the principle of proportionate representation. The Weimar Republic was to suffer severely from this initial misunderstanding of parliamentary practice. Only after the ministers had been nominated, did William II appoint as chancellor Prince Max of Baden, a cousin of his (3 Oct.). A double task awaited this democratic and anti-militaristic South German prince: to establish modern constitutionalism and to liquidate the war. He succeeded with the former task, and the Republic took over the machinery of government as Prince Max had devised it. And it was not his fault that the 'peace offensive' ended in complete failure and revolution. When President Wilson had proclaimed his Fourteen Points (8 Jan. 1918), they had been rejected by the German government acting on Hindenburg and Ludendorff's instructions. Now, the same generals demanded an immediate offer of armistice and the opening of peace negotiations on the basis of these Fourteen Points. For the High Command were now as despondent as previously they had been overbearing, and would not allow the chancellor twenty-four hours in which to consider the whole situation. Prince Max was forced to dispatch the petition for an armistice in the night following his appointment.

While the negotiations with President Wilson were proceeding, Prince Max strengthened his authority by dismissing Ludendorff, who had recovered from his fit of nerves and resumed his sinister quasi-political activities (26 Oct.). Wilson's ignorance of European and even more of German affairs, however, failed to secure a peace that would have rendered Germany militarily impotent, without plunging Central Europe into chaos. The President mistook the semblance of authority for authority itself, and, instead of giving the government of Prince Max a fair chance to overcome the power of generals and Junkers, concentrated his attack on the dynasty and especially on the Emperor, who had already lost all real authority. The result was that an agitation for William II's abdication interfered with, and eventually overshadowed, the internal reorganization, and that in the end the Emperor lost his crown, but the Prussian spirit, after a short eclipse, reappeared as powerful as ever.

When on 7 Nov. the armistice commission, led by Erzberger, now a secretary of state, crossed the front line on the way to Compiègne, Germany was already in the turmoil of revolution. It had begun at Kiel where the sailors refused to sail for a last desperate enterprise against the Flemish coast. Following Bolshevist precedent, the men of the battle fleet hoisted the red flag (3 Nov.). Within a few days mutiny changed into revolution which overran the whole of Germany. Bavaria was the first state to proclaim herself a republic (8 Nov.). On the following day the movement spread to Berlin. In vain Prince Max tried to stem its tide by announcing that the Emperor and crown prince had abdicated and that a council of regency under the Social Democrat leader, Ebert, had been set up for William II's eldest grandson. The Emperor himself had hurried to General Headquarters on 29 Oct. and was practically out of reach of his political advisers. Now Hindenburg himself informed him that his abdication had become inevitable. But events outstripped the Emperor's indecision and the chancellor's good intentions. Confronted with the imminent proclamation of a Soviet republic, the Social Democrat deputy, Scheidemann, proclaimed the German republic (9 Nov.). On hearing this news the Emperor fled to neutral Holland, and his example of simply yielding to the revolutionary forces was speedily followed by every one of the other twenty sovereigns, none of whom lifted a finger for the defence of his throne.

Within five weeks Germany had been transformed from a semi-autocratic monarchy first into a parliamentary monarchy and then into a semi-socialist republic. The transition was too sudden to be sincere, much less to have any roots from which to grow. For a moment it seemed as if the monarchical idea had been uprooted, as if German imperialism had completely disappeared, as if the belief in the divine nature of the state had collapsed, as if generals, bureaucrats and Junkers had lost their sway over Germany. In fact, nothing of that kind had happened. Monarchism, it is true, lost its attraction for a generation which witnessed the contemptible behaviour of most of the last occupants of the various thrones. All the other traditional forces, however, which had made Prussia and subsequently subjugated Germany to Prussia, went only temporarily into safe hiding. They wanted to burden the democratic republic with the liquidation of the military and political disaster of their making, and only bided their time, ready to establish themselves in their old glory. Before the republic had found its bearings, the sworn enemies of liberty, democracy and justice were already busy sharpening the daggers which were to stab the German nation in the back.

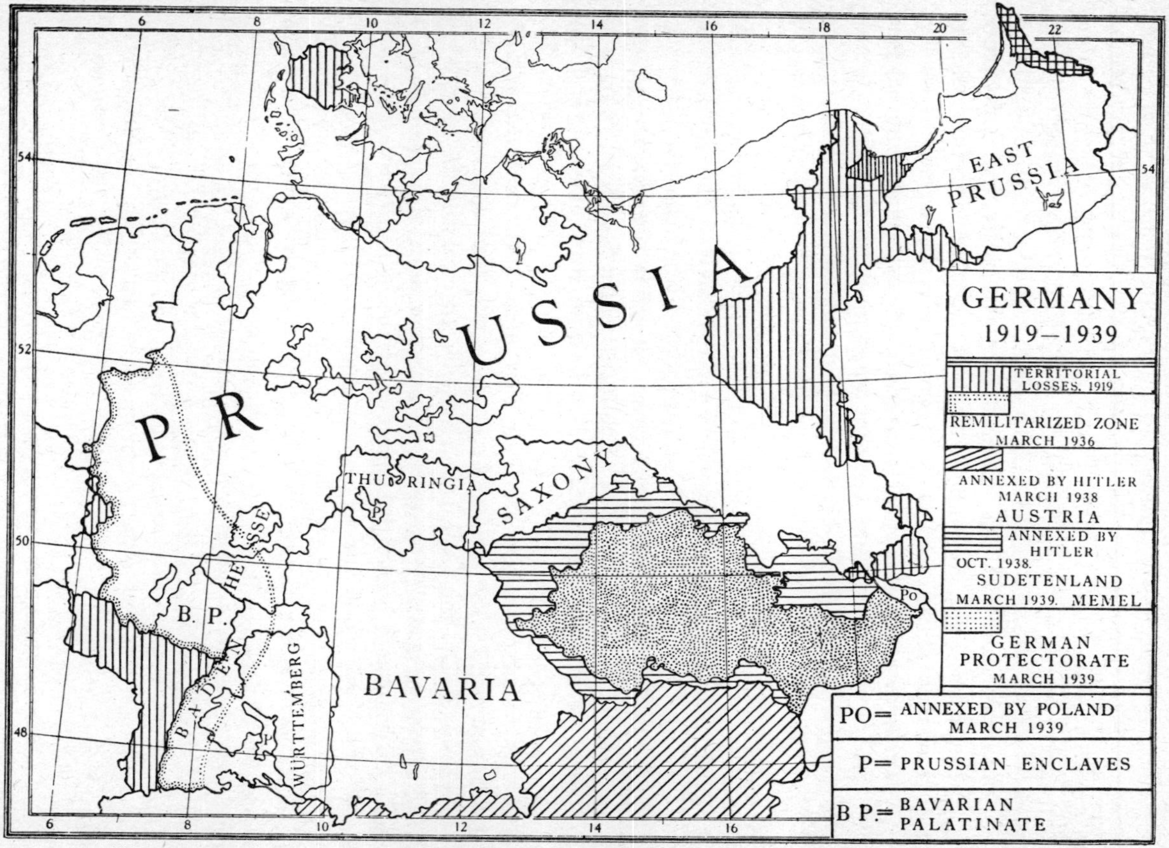

MAP XII

GERMANY 1919–1939

- TERRITORIAL LOSSES, 1919
- REMILITARIZED ZONE MARCH 1936
- ANNEXED BY HITLER MARCH 1938 AUSTRIA
- ANNEXED BY HITLER OCT. 1938 SUDETENLAND MARCH 1939 MEMEL
- GERMAN PROTECTORATE MARCH 1939

PO = ANNEXED BY POLAND MARCH 1939

P = PRUSSIAN ENCLAVES

B P = BAVARIAN PALATINATE

Germany, 1919–38

CHAPTER X

THE WEIMAR REPUBLIC (1918–1933)

ON the unceremonious disappearance of royalty and royalists, a Council of People's Commissars took over the fluttering reins of government; but, as it was composed of evolutionary and revolutionary socialists in equal proportion, it was divided against itself and incapable of taking energetic steps in any one direction. Simultaneously with the Council of People's Commissars, 'Workers' and Soldiers' Councils' modelled on the Russian Soviets sprang up all over Germany; and, at the same time, particularist movements displayed great vigour not only in the federate states proper, but also in the Rhineland and to a lesser degree in Hanover, Slesvig-Holstein, Hesse-Cassel and Silesia. The first problem which the new authorities had to decide was whether Germany should be organized as a Soviet republic or as a democracy. The Independent Socialists, vying with the recently established Spartacus League, forerunner of the Communist party, advocated the dictatorship of the proletariat. The right-wing Socialists stuck to their democratic convictions, and, supported by the Central Congress of the Workers' and Soldiers' Councils and the federal governments, they carried the day. Writs for the election (on the principle of Proportional Representation) of a Constituent National Assembly were issued, and universal, equal, direct and secret suffrage was granted to all men and women over twenty years of age (19 Dec.). Thus thwarted, the champions of the proletarian revolution took up arms; irregular gangs of so-called sailors fought the remnants of the old army which had placed themselves at the disposal of the government. The fighting in Berlin (23 Dec. 1918–13 Jan. 1919), during which the radical members withdrew from the Council of People's Commissars, ended with a complete victory of the government; and on 19 Jan. the elections for the National Assembly took place in good order, the Communists abstaining.

The most serious consequence of the armed revolts was the making of a secret agreement by Ebert, the chairman of the People's Commissars, with the generals of the demobilized army, according to which the latter were empowered to raise corps of volunteers. These 'free-corps', originally meant to uphold the Council of People's Commissars' authority, became not only the recruiting ground of the Reichswehr, but also the rallying centre of all opponents of the new order. Eventually these free-corps became the nucleus of Hitler's storm troops. In the spring of 1919 fresh risings in Berlin, Brunswick, the Ruhr district, and elsewhere, all of which had been fanned by Independent Socialists and Communists, were, with comparative ease but much wanton bloodshed, suppressed by the free-corps; only Bavaria presented a more formidable problem. The Munich government, which was set up on 8 Nov. 1918, represented a queer mixture of federalist, socialist, agrarian and pacifist tendencies. It was almost at once exposed to the attack of both monarcho-nationalistic and anarcho-syndicalist extremists; and Eisner, its first premier, fell, the first victim in a long list of assassinated representatives of the republic (21 Feb. 1919). The chaos which followed Eisner's foul murder ended in the proclamation of a Bavarian Soviet republic (7 April), which, however, was quickly confined to the capital, Munich; it took the free-corps several weeks to overcome the resistance of the fanatical idealists whose rash deeds of violence were soon eclipsed by the systematic reign of terror which the victorious free-corps set up after the capture of the town (2 May). Loyalty to the ancient dynasty of the Wittelsbachs returned almost on the heels of its overthrow; anti-semitism, hitherto unknown in Bavaria, began to thrive on the anti-Christian attitude of Eisner; but it was the experience of the Soviet republic which provided the most penetrating argument for all enemies of the republic. 'Fight against Bolshevism' became the principal catchword with which to stir up the emotions of anybody who felt dissatisfied with any aspect of the new order. The many members of the free-corps who permanently settled in Bavaria took care to keep alive the memory of the red terror, which lost nothing in the repeating. They organized themselves in fellowships which fostered militaristic and nationalistic ideas, and soon spread a network of secret organizations all over the country; one of the most insignificant of them was the National Socialist German Workers' Party, which was joined by one Adolf Hitler, a shady *agent provocateur* of the military intelligence.

It was, however, only a section of the free-corps which took part in the civil war in Germany. Others were marching into the Baltic countries, which had been overrun by the Russians after Lenin had repudiated the treaty of Brest Litovsk (13 Nov. 1918). The free-corps were called in by the German barons to defend their social and economic supremacy against the land reform which the newly established governments of Estonia, Latvia and Lithuania had taken in hand; and they were promised farmsteads to be taken from the Bolshevists. As there was no farmland in the hands of Bolshevists, but only in those of the German barons, the free-corps, after having expelled the Russians by May 1919, stayed in the Baltic burning with racial contempt for the native governments, and with social resentment against the barons. When the Allies compelled the German government to recall the free-corps (Dec. 1919), hosts of mercenaries returned to Germany who gloried in the barbarities of what they looked back upon as a crusade. They were alienated from civilian life, and deeply imbued with militant nationalism, a vague kind of socialism, and a sovereign contempt for law and order. They were the very men to join the secret organizations which, by this time, had fully established themselves all over Germany, with their headquarters in Bavaria. In conjunction with the generals who had lent their sword and experience to the socialist People's Commissars and crushed the left-wing radicals, every foundation was laid to make military influence as paramount in the new republic as it had been under the monarchy.

The Constituent National Assembly met at Weimar on 6 Feb. 1919; the place was chosen for sentimental reasons—it was meant to show that the spirit of Goethe's Weimar had triumphed over that of Frederick the Great's Potsdam. The membership of the Assembly, however, proved that the form rather than the spirit had changed. It was not only for the greater part the same men of the Reichstag of 1912 who were returned, but the system of parties, too, practically remained the same. Conservatives and Free Conservatives had combined in the German National People's Party; they dared not openly advocate a restoration of the monarchy, but opposed democracy and social progress, championed the ideas of revenge, rearmament, pan-Germanism and anti-Semitism, and stoutly defended the landed and vested interests of Junkers and heavy industrialists. Hugenberg, at one time a principal in the Prussian ministry of finance, later on a director of Krupp's, financier and landowner, press-lord and manager of the biggest film-concern and newsagency, personified to perfection this combination of nationalism and capitalism. He had been pulling wires behind the scenes years before he came into the limelight when he took over the leadership of the German National Party (1929) and afterwards made a spectacular alliance with the National Socialist Party (Oct. 1931): it was he who thus paved the way for Hitler's rise to power.

Ideological quibbles and personal friction stood in the way of a strong and united liberal party. At first, the German Democratic Party attracted the vast majority of the progressive bourgeoisie, under the leadership of Friedrich Naumann, who for twenty years past had advocated the reconciliation of 'Empire and Democracy' (the title of one of his books). After his untimely death (Aug. 1919), his successors failed to amalgamate the cultural and economic tenets of their liberal and democratic adherents; dissatisfied by weak compromises, employers and employees in large numbers deserted the party, which by 1924 was reduced to a splinter party of able and often brilliant individuals without a following. Its loss was the gain of the German People's Party. This party, founded by Stresemann and a mere handful of right-wing National Liberals, pursued from the beginning that course of sentimental nationalism, non-committal liberalism, and mealy-mouthed capitalism which irresistibly attracts the German middle class. Learning by hard-won experience Stresemann gradually became a statesman with an international outlook; but when death cut short his career (1929), his party relapsed into smug mediocrity and, to say the least, put no spoke in Hitler's wheel. The Centre and Socialists retained their programmes, recruiting grounds and parliamentary strength almost unchanged from 1919 to 1933. When Socialists and Independents combined in 1922, the Communists subsequently snatched a few seats from the United Socialists without altering the combined figures of the Marxist parties. In the Weimar assembly the Socialists were the strongest party, which they remained until July 1932, although they could not maintain their numbers of 1919, when they comprised two-fifths of the house; it is an interesting coincidence that in 1933 the National Socialists had the same percentage of deputies; in fact, Proportional Representation led to the inevitable result that no party was ever able to obtain a majority by itself. Consequently, Germany was ruled from February 1919 to July 1933 by coalition governments which entailed all the weaknesses of a mostly insincere and always uneasy alliance. At first the parties which had already co-operated during the war—Centre, Democrats and Socialists—combined in the 'Weimar Coalition'; in 1923, Stresemann, by adding the German People's Party to the former combination, formed the 'Great Coalition' which reappeared in 1928; in between, 'Bourgeois Coalitions' of various composition were in power. In 1930 Brüning, the then leader of the Centre Party, being unable to obtain a majority, introduced the first of a series of 'presidential cabinets' which ruled by emergency decrees and relied on the President of the Reich and the Reichswehr rather than on parliament, which was justly suspicious of personal rule.

After the National Assembly had elected Friedrich Ebert President of the Reich (11 Feb.), it began to discuss the constitution which was drafted by Hugo Preuss, a professor of constitutional law and Minister of the Interior. It provided for a centralized and unitary republic, with rationally repartitioned provinces; it was a perfectly logical construction and therefore hardly compatible with reality. The federal governments, although in the hands of Socialists, stood up unanimously for their traditional rights, of which they preserved as many as the unitarian prejudices of the day allowed. Above all, the federalists retained the Federal Council, although with diminished powers, under the new name of *Reichsrat* (Imperial Council), as a counterweight to the Reichstag. The men of Weimar, however, failed to solve the main problem of the Empire: Prussia remained the chief stumbling-block of a satisfactory reorganization of Germany. The personal and, to a large extent, real union between the governments of the Reich and Prussia as established by Bismarck might have been preserved; or, as Preuss suggested, Prussia might be reduced to her original size while her later annexed provinces could be re-established as federal states. The National Assembly chose a third solution, the worst possible: the union between the Reich and Prussian governments was dissolved, but Prussia was not dismembered. It was quite inevitable that the co-existence of two powerful governments in Berlin and the existence of a great power—whose population equalled that of France and surpassed that of Poland—within a great power must lead to all kinds of tensions between Prussia and the Reich, Prussia and the other federal states, and lastly, the Reich and all its members. The National Assembly thought to overcome these difficulties by strengthening the central government. Direct taxation, railways and waterways, and the army, were taken over by the Reich from the federal states which, so as to mark their loss of sovereignty, were henceforth known as 'lands'. But the lands soon proved that they were still vigorous and powerful enough to defy the theory of legislators. Above all, they successfully withstood all attempts on the part of the central administration to interfere with church, school and police. The traditional organization of the churches remained intact, and three different bills aiming at a uniform school-system were successively thrown out by the Reichsrat and Reichstag—facts which proved beyond doubt that the various regions of Germany were still anxious to maintain the independence of their distinct cultural spheres. The creation of the land of Thuringia out of eight principalities (1920) and the incorporation with the Prussian province of Hesse-Nassau of the petty principality of Waldeck (1929)—at the time hailed by the unitarians as important steps towards a centralized Germany— in reality only stressed the prevalence of regional feeling, as they merely undid some of the arbitrary delimitations of dynastic family-pacts, without changing any frontiers of the ancient tribes.

While the debate about the constitution was proceeding and before the constitution was promulgated (11 Aug.), the National Assembly had to cope with the problem of the peace treaty. The alternative of accepting or rejecting its conditions split the nation from top to bottom. Bismarck's distinction between 'national' and 'unnational' parties revived, and the government neglected to counter a raving nationalist propaganda by calling to account the men who in reality had caused Germany's ruin. In the end, a shaky majority passed the peace treaty, which was signed at Versailles on 28 June. The treaty was harsher than was expected in Germany, where a vague recollection of some of Wilson's Fourteen Points had led people to hope for a general pardon. Compared with the treaties of Brest Litovsk and Bucharest the treaty of Versailles was neither harsh nor unjust; its main fault was that it was a patchwork without clarity of purpose, reflecting the mutually inconsistent war aims of the political, military and economic leaders of the Allied and Associated Nations. All clear-cut demands were accepted as inevitable: and the complete loss of the navy, Alsace-Lorraine, and the colonies left none of the rankling resentment which was caused by the perplexing half-measures with which the treaty abounded: such as the cession of fringes all along the frontiers, the creation of the Polish corridor, and the dubious position of the Free City of Danzig (which resulted in Poland at once becoming the furiously hated 'secular enemy'), the nebulous provisions for reparations in cash and kind, and the vague implications of war-guilt and war-criminals.

However, neither the bogey of Bolshevism nor the agitation against the 'dictated peace' seized the whole nation; it was only the middle classes which found in them a convenient outlet for their habitual inferiority complex. Unfortunately it was the same classes which fell a victim to the economic catastrophe of the inflation: people living on their private means or savings, officials, professional men, traders and small industrialists, the very descendants of the nineteenth-century champions of liberty and progress. When they saw themselves expropriated, they blamed democracy and the republic for their misfortune, not realizing what huge profits were made out of the inflation by the financial wire-pullers of the nationalist parties. Amongst them Hugo Stinnes, a Rhenish industrialist, built up the biggest horizontal and vertical combine that ever existed; he, together with Thyssen, even offered to buy cash down the whole German state railway system. The sinister political influence which Stinnes exerted in Berlin and at international conferences was forgotten as quickly as his super-trust crashed in the period of recovery. Meanwhile, however, national and social resentment was skilfully exploited by the capitalist and industrialist diehards of the type of Stinnes and Thyssen to rouse middle-class indignation against social reform, in which sphere the republic was achieving considerable results, such as the eight-hour working day, unemployment insurance, collective labour agreements, the improvement of housing, and educational and recreational facilities for all classes and ages. Salvation was expected by the middle classes from the 'expert' as opposed to the parliamentarian, and it was even suggested that politics should be 'abolished' in favour of a corporative economic order.

The lingering malaise developed into an open crisis when, on 13 March 1920, Ludendorff, Kapp, and the commander-in-chief of the new army, Lüttwitz, tried to overthrow the republican régime with a few discontented regular troops and the Baltic free-corps which, for the first time, on this occasion displayed the Swastika as the symbol of a 'new nationalism'. The Kapp revolt collapsed four days later thanks to the unanimous resistance of the workers and employees and the well-calculated reticence of most officers and officials. But when the defenders of the republic tried to carry out the necessary purge of army and civil service, the government again succumbed to the bogey of Bolshevism, again made common cause with the generals, and let loose against the workers of Saxony, Thuringia and the Ruhr the free-corps which quickly stifled the awkward memory of the Kapp revolt in a fresh wave of terrorism. The most far-reaching consequence of the Kapp revolt took place in Bavaria, whose new premier, Kahr, openly protected the illegal societies and made himself the spokesman of intransigent nationalism.

The foreign policy of the republic was complicated by the unwillingness, or perhaps incapability, of all parties to face facts without blinkers. Hardly anyone was prepared to acknowledge the Western powers as the victors of the Great War, to carry out loyally the peace treaty, to accept Poland and Czechoslovakia as equals in the European comity of nations, and to abandon the principles of power politics. The fate of Walter Rathenau, the leading economic thinker of the Democratic Party, is typical in this respect. As Minister for Reconstruction (1921) and of Foreign Affairs (1922) he inaugurated the 'policy of fulfilment', i.e. he tried to overcome the tension with the Western powers, especially France, by honestly fulfilling the clauses of the treaty of Versailles; and thus obtained for the first time a place of equality for Germany at the conference of Genoa. At the same time he put relations with Russia on a sound basis by the treaty of Rapallo (16 April 1922), without committing Germany either to an Eastern or Western course. Two months later (24 June) he was assassinated by members of one of the secret organizations, who considered him their most dangerous enemy because his policy began to bear fruit and to deprive the nationalists of their strongest arguments against the 'enervated and treasonable Jew republic'.

The murder of its foreign secretary at last stirred a government that had let pass almost unnoticed the assassination of Erzberger by gangsters of the same type (26 Aug. 1921). A 'law for the protection of the republic' was passed which filled the republican masses with fresh hope; but its observance was soon paralysed by the open defiance of the Bavarian government and its covert sabotage by judges and juries. With Rathenau's murder the policy of fulfilment, too, came to an end. It was succeeded by one of deliberate provocation, after the industrial magnates had succeeded in replacing the Weimar Coalition by a cabinet of 'experts'. With malice aforethought they gave the French a convenient pretext, in the non-delivery of reparations, for occupying the Ruhr district (Jan. 1923), and the policy of passive resistance gave the secret societies more than a pretext for poisoning public opinion with the virus of revenge. While the Ruhr industrialists converted their patriotism into ready money, the nation as a whole lost its last savings in the mad whirlpool of inflation, with the result that all order and decency was relaxed and the country for some months resembled a madhouse of gamblers and lunatics. An illegal army, the 'Black Reichswehr', was organized, Bavaria and the Rhineland threatened to make themselves independent, Saxony and Thuringia were in the throes of communism, and the cabinet of experts was at its wits' end. In this extremity, Stresemann formed a cabinet of the Great Coalition (13 Aug. 1923), which broke off passive resistance, stabilized the currency, and persuaded the Allies to set up a committee under the American, Dawes, to investigate the whole problem of reparations. Desultory risings of the Black Reichswehr in Eastern Prussia, the Saxon and Thuringian Communists in Central Germany, and the Rhenish separatists in the West, were easily suppressed by the army. A National Socialist revolt that took place under the joint leadership of Hitler and, again, Ludendorff at Munich on 9 Nov., was quelled by the same Bavarian government, which had all the time winked at every nationalist excess and was now horrified to realize the utter incompatibility of its reactionary particularism with the National Socialists' revolutionary pan-Germanism. But they soon forgot this lesson. Ludendorff was altogether acquitted, while Hitler was sentenced to five years' 'honourable imprisonment', from which he was unconditionally released after he had served only six months in a Bavarian fortress. It was there that he wrote, with the assistance of his fellow-prisoner Rudolf Hess, his autobiography *Mein Kampf* (My Struggle), which was to become the Bible of Nazi Germany. After his release he was able to re-found his party and his private army of Storm Troopers (S.A.), with the tacit consent of the Bavarian government.

Within a twelvemonth from Stresemann's courageous acceptance of responsibility, Germany's whole situation fundamentally changed. When the Dawes agreement was signed in London (16 Aug. 1924), the country was factually and psychologically pacified. Its economic prosperity, made possible by the new regulation of reparations and the subsequent influx of foreign credits and loans, was, however, deceptive, as under the calm surface the political situation remained thoroughly unsound. The unsatisfactory relation between the Reich and the large 'lands' had from the beginning led to one crisis after another, and the disturbances in 1923 had been overcome only by concentrating the executive power in the hands of the chief of the army. But the government did not draw the obvious conclusion that it must go back on the half-way structure of the Weimar Constitution and, as complete centralization was out of the question, revise it on federalistic lines. The reorganization of the economic and financial system in 1924 would have provided a suitable handle, and the Bavarian government came forth with sensible suggestions. These were, characteristically enough, turned down on account of an unfavourable memorandum of the Defence Ministry which, beside the governments of the lands and the organizations of capital and labour, had by this time become the most powerful unconstitutional factor of German politics. In fact, political democracy was the most notable of the countless victims of the inflation period, and its place was largely taken by the economic and professional organizations. This led, paradoxically enough, to a consolidation of the republican idea, since the industrial magnates, despite their sentimental monarchism, had come to realize how well they could make money in and with the republican system.

The cause of monarchism further declined after Ebert's death when the imperial field-marshal Hindenburg was elected President of the Reich (26 April 1925). As he remained a convinced monarchist at heart, his example converted millions of his partisans from open hostility to tacit approval of the new order. It was fatal, though, that Hindenburg lacked any experience and even interest in non-military matters so that, already seventy-seven years of age in 1925, he fell with increasing senility more and more under the spell of irresponsible advisers who were naturally the feudal and military companions of his East Elbian youth. This sinister back-door influence was first felt when Hindenburg in 1928 suggested large-scale subsidies to the East Elbian landowners who, though the inflation had freed them from all their former debts, had contracted huge fresh debts and saw themselves faced by complete ruin. Instead of transforming their *latifundia* into thousands of farms and thereby replacing the Junker caste by a healthy peasantry, Hindenburg's counsel prevailed, and the German taxpayer was obliged, by the *Osthilfe* (help for the East) legislation, to maintain out of his pocket the hereditary enemies of social progress.

All these problems of internal reconstruction were thrown into the shade by the exigencies of foreign politics, which Stresemann continued to direct as foreign secretary. He adopted the course which Rathenau had initiated, but cleverly substituted the term 'national *Realpolitik*' for the ominous 'policy of fulfilment'. But whereas Rathenau had envisaged a new European community, Stresemann's vision reached only as far as a revival of power politics on more modern and less objectionable lines than those of Bismarck, who remained his idol of statecraft. He turned a blind eye to all but the most fantastic attempts to circumvent the disarmament clauses of the treaty of Versailles; and enough leaked out to keep alive a justified distrust in Germany's professed sincerity. Nevertheless, Stresemann not only gained full recognition of equality for Germany, but incidentally eased international tension throughout Europe. The Locarno treaties (Oct. 1925), which cleared the way for a sympathetic collaboration with the Western powers, Germany's admission to the League of Nations (8 Sept. 1926), the evacuation of the first and second zones of occupied Rhineland (31 Jan. 1926 and 30 Nov. 1929), and the further considerable reduction of reparations through the Young plan (Aug. 1929), were the high-water marks of his career. Between the first and second reparation conference at The Hague—the latter settling the final evacuation of the Rhineland by 30 June 1930—Stresemann died (3 Oct. 1929). His death left Germany without a real statesman at a moment when she had to face the economic world crisis ushered in at the New York Stock Exchange on Black Friday (28 Oct. 1929). Germany's sham prosperity collapsed at once, and with it all the hidden maladies of the German body politic broke again to the surface. The new situation pitilessly revealed the fundamental drawback from which public life had been suffering all these years, namely that the Socialists and Centre lacked leadership, Democrats and Liberals lacked followers, and the Nationalists were void of ideas. There remained the National Socialists, who had a leader of unparalleled demagogic power, masses of blind followers, and intoxicating ideas of a German millennium.

For a while it seemed as if the new chancellor Brüning was the man to cope with the situation: he was a moderate Catholic with connections both with moderate conservatives and trade-unionists, an expert in financial and social problems, and he had first-hand knowledge of England; on the other hand he was lacking in determination, was infected with a mystic idea of the Holy Empire, and suffered from the subaltern's inferiority complex in his dealings with the generals of the Reichswehr and with the field-marshal president. Unable to forge a working parliamentary majority, he ruled by means of emergency decrees which article 48 of the Weimar Constitution empowered the president to sign. This resource, originally intended for situations of extreme danger and subject to parliamentary ratification, became in Brüning's hand the normal way of conducting the business of government. Even so all his measures to reorganize the broken-down fiscal and economic system could not keep pace with the world crisis. When therefore the National Socialists, exploiting the social unrest, raised the numbers of their deputies from 12 to 107 (14 Sept. 1930), Brüning made an abortive attempt to outrival them by a 'national' foreign policy.

On 12 March 1931 the world was surprised by the announcement of a customs union with Austria. The move could but be understood as the precursor of a political union, and the confidence in German determination to follow the policy of international collaboration which Stresemann had created was badly shaken. Foreign credits were called in, the reserves of gold and foreign securities melted away, banks and industrial undertakings went bankrupt, and a whole year's labour of reorganization, however imperfect, fell to the ground. In this emergency Brüning showed his mettle. The projected union with Austria was dropped; he cleared, by personal meetings with British, French and Italian statesmen, the international atmosphere, unconditionally accepted the Hoover plan and disarmament conference, and brought about a standstill agreement with Germany's foreign creditors. At home, he secured Hindenburg's re-election as president against Hitler's candidature (10 April 1932), and took up a firm attitude against the National Socialists, whose brown hordes roamed about the country spreading terror and murder. He was preparing for the final reparation conference at Lausanne when Hindenburg suddenly and gruffly dismissed him (30 May 1932). Brüning's downfall was brought about by the chiefs of the Reichswehr bent on setting up an authoritarian dictatorship, in conjunction with the industrialists who wanted to get rid of state interference and trade-unions; and the Junkers who were alarmed by Brüning's tentative suggestions of a land reform. These three groups were in close touch with Hitler, whose demagogic powers they meant to use for their own ends, confident in their ability to throw him over afterwards. Hindenburg, who utterly despised the 'scallywag lance-corporal', was coaxed into compliance by the threatened land reform, and on 1 June 1932 he appointed a presidential cabinet under Herr von Papen, who had given ample proof of his capacity for mischief-making as military attaché in Washington (1915–17), chief of staff in Palestine (1918), and the most unscrupulous intriguer in the Centre Party (from 1921).

The course which Papen would take was sufficiently indicated by the fact that seven of the ten ministers of his cabinet were members of the aristocracy, the most resourceful and powerful of whom was Kurt von Schleicher, the Defence Minister, a pastmaster of political backstair intrigues. The militant National Socialist formations of the S.A. (Storm Troops) and S.S. (Black Guards) were again made legal, and street fights and political murders became everyday events. As the cabinet had no contact with popular feeling and no majority in the Reichstag—which was at once dissolved—and still shunned an open alliance with Hitler, they tried to cement their power by usurping the administrative machinery and police force of the strongest land, Prussia. From 1919, Prussia had been governed almost uninterruptedly by the Weimar Coalition under Social Democrat leadership, which was quietly transforming the bulwark of the Junkers into a progressive democracy, and was therefore the target of the incessant attacks of all anti-democratic forces. Now the reactionaries secured their object. By means of an emergency decree of the President, the Prussian government was removed from office and Papen appointed Reich commissar (20 July). But the Papen cabinet was no more capable of solving the economic problems than Brüning had been. The increasing unemployment was reflected in the elections of 31 July, which raised the National Socialist seats from 107 to 235, the Communists from 77 to 89, and all but wiped out the Liberal and pseudo-Liberal parties, while Socialists and Centre fairly held their own, and Hugenberg's Nationalists sustained further losses. Schleicher, who entertained sincere but vague ideas about social and economic reforms, at once entered into secret negotiations with Hitler with a view to overthrowing Papen, whose feudal, agrarian and capitalistic tendencies were odious to both of them, though for different reasons. But Papen's influence prevailed with Hindenburg, who mortified Hitler at their first meeting by offering him the portfolio of postmaster-general under Papen, instead of the chancellorship.

Open warfare ensued between Papen and Hitler. The Reichstag passed a vote of censure on the cabinet, which was supported only by the thirty-seven Nationalist deputies; and Papen dissolved it after its first meeting. Although the National Socialists lost forty seats at the polls (Nov.), Papen's position was in no way improved, and Schleicher's intrigues, now launched with might and main, finally forced Hindenburg to dismiss Papen and appoint Schleicher chancellor (4 Dec.). There was a great chance of splitting the National Socialist party. Gregor Strasser, Hitler's chief whip, was ready to join Schleicher's cabinet with the immediate support of at least forty deputies, while more were certain to follow later; and at this juncture the industrialists stopped their subsidies to Hitler. But Schleicher let the occasion slip, and Hitler expelled Strasser from the party. At the same time, Schleicher lost the confidence of the industrialists when he publicly declared that he subscribed neither to capitalism nor to socialism; nor did his idea of setting up 'Prussian Socialism', which was to be based on the trade-unions and run by the generals, appeal to organized labour. In vain Schleicher tried to gain popular support by directing public attention to the scandalous corruption connected with the *Osthilfe*. Of his intention to have Hindenburg declared feeble-minded and Papen and Hugenberg arrested, just enough transpired to make these three men overcome their reluctance to co-operate with Hitler. Schleicher, whom Hindenburg had assured that he would be his 'last chancellor', suffered Brüning's fate: on 28 Jan. 1933 he was curtly dismissed. On the basis of a coalition between the German Nationalists and National Socialists, Hitler was appointed chancellor and Papen vice-chancellor on 30 Jan. The torchlight procession with which the National Socialists honoured their Leader on the same night was the funeral procession of the German nation and empire. On the following morning the Nordic master-race set out to make the world its living-space.

EPILOGUE

THE NAZI DICTATORSHIP

How did it come about that almost the whole German nation at once tamely submitted to a régime which meant the complete negation of everything that was best in German life and tradition? Two answers to this question have been put forward. One school of thought maintains that Nazism is nothing but the undisguised expression of the eternal German spirit, whereas the opposite school regards the Nazis as a mad minority which has temporarily imposed its will upon a decent and innocent nation. Neither of these arguments can satisfy the historian. The nation that has produced men such as Gutenberg, Luther, Dürer, Bach, Kant, Goethe, Röntgen, Robert Koch cannot be described as an abomination to the rest of the world, unredeemed and unredeemable. The very fact that the Nazis have maintained themselves in power only by the brutal methods of the concentration camp and the omnipresent Gestapo (secret police) clearly shows that they do not represent the German nation as a whole. On the other hand, it cannot be denied that the vast majority of the people either openly hailed, or at least raised no objections to, the political aims and methods of Hitler and his henchmen, from the abolition of the fundamental rights of man in Germany to the cold-blooded extirpation of millions of men, women and children all over Europe.

There is no doubt that the Nazis have succeeded in appealing to some instincts of some people in every section of the German community. Their nationalist and militaristic outlook made them welcome to the leaders of the right and the generals of the Reichswehr: their professed hatred of Communism and trade-unions secured for them the financial support of the industrialists, bankers and landowners. All these groups were, at the same time, convinced that they would be able to manage the Nazis for their own purposes, and to discard them at will should they outgrow their usefulness. When Hugenberg concluded the alliance of the 'National Opposition' at Harzburg (Oct. 1931), he little foresaw with what ease Hitler would drop him from the government (27 June 1933) and a fortnight later wipe out the German Nationalist Party together with all the despised parties of the centre and left.

The Centre Party did not on principle object to trying out a political partnership with the Nazis, which they were confident of keeping or dissolving as they had at various times done with the Conservatives, Democrats and Socialists; and it was not before the organized attack on Church and Christianity started in September 1933 that the leaders of the Catholic community awoke from their dreams of a deal with Hitler.

Up to 1933, the pseudo-socialistic slogans of the Nazi programme made little or no impression upon the working classes. But there was alive a tradition amongst organized labour which first fatally weakened their power of resistance and later on made them more pliable to Nazi leadership than they themselves realized. Ever since August Bebel (1840-1913) had begun to play a leading role in the labour movement—he was the first socialist deputy to be elected in the North German Diet of 1867 and the German Reichstag of 1871 —this son of a professional Prussian N.C.O. had shaped the party organization on the model of the Prussian army and administration, those twin paragons of efficiency; and sixty years of party drill taught the rank and file of Social Democracy to fall in and turn about at the party leaders' command like any demonstration squad of the Prussian army; and independent thinking and action of individuals and groups was discouraged in the party offices not less than in the royal barracks. The result was that after 1933, when their leaders had been exiled, gagged, imprisoned or assassinated, the masses of the former Socialist and Communist parties were stunned, and not a few of them felt almost relieved when they found themselves again under the marching orders of autocratic party bosses.

The Social Democratic Party, it is true, never had any illusions about the real aims of the Nazis; and it is to their honour that they voted against the enabling bill even in the packed Reichstag of March 1933. However, for many years past their uninspired and uninspiring conduct of home and foreign affairs in general had reduced the masses to a state of listlessness from which they were not easily roused. The Communists, on the other hand, though they posed as the champions of the proletariat against fascist tyranny, did not mind lending their full support to the Nazis in every division that took place in the Reichstag from 1930 onwards; for to the last they were undecided as to whether a Nazi dictatorship with—as they thought—civil war in its wake was not preferable to a democratic republic. As the Communists, however, were the most militant section of all non-Nazi groups, they had to pay most dearly when parliamentary democracy was at last overthrown. After Göring had set fire to the Reichstag building (27 Feb. 1933), the Communist party was outlawed and its followers massacred by the thousand.

Of greater importance, however, than the attitude of the organized parties was that of the unorganized masses of the bourgeoisie. The main reason which drove millions of middle-class voters without fixed party loyalties into the National Socialist camp, and made some more millions tacitly bow to the new régime, can be traced back to the unprecedented upheaval of inflation and mass-unemployment. These created an atmosphere of hopelessness and panic, which made people frantically look round for any 'movement', any programme, and any leader promising to give them economic security, to restore to them social stability, and to relieve them from making their own choice. There were many who had tried out all parties from the left to the right, naïvely hoping that some one of them might have the panacea for all evils, and who in the end supported the National Socialist Party, whose programme offered something for everybody. The small shopkeeper was to be freed from the competition of chain stores, and the landless farmhand was led to expect a share in the *latifundia*; whereas, at the same time, the industrialists were to be rid of the trade-unions, and the landed gentry were assured of the sanctity of private property. Rearmament promised employment to millions of workers and fat dividends to the shareholders of iron, steel and textile companies.

Women were altogether to be taken out of the labour market, and were to be reinstated as guardian angels of hearth and home; and this appeal to the primeval instincts of the German *hausfrau* made the National Socialists the first radical party of either the right or the left to obtain a majority of female votes. Even stronger was the appeal to youth. The old parties had neglected to take the younger generation into their councils and to train them in responsible leadership. Here, as everywhere else, National Socialist propaganda addressed itself to noble and base emotions alike. The spirit of comradeship and adventure, a feeling of frustration, youth's natural longing for hero-worship, a sense of national and racial superiority, the real and alleged iniquities of the treaty of Versailles—all passions were stirred up, to the display of colourful uniforms and the rousing music of brass bands, until huge masses of inflammable boys and girls were filled with a burning desire to give themselves up to the Leader, who, with their help, would one day dictate his law to the world—while at the same time the less idealistically minded looked forward to the sharing-out of the spoils among the members of the master-race. Thus an earthly paradise was painted in glowing colours to a nation which was tired of the lack of action in an ordinary democracy; and the prospect of ruling the whole world, with the remote and hardly dreaded risk of a glorious death on the battle-field, seemed to many an ample compensation for the loss of civic rights.

Civic rights mean very little to a nation which has no Magna Carta, Bill of Rights, Declaration of Independence by which to kindle the imagination and love of freedom of every successive generation. The one occasion when the Germans had taken their fate into their own hands—the revolution of 1848—had ended in complete defeat; and Prussian historians have been assiduous in representing the men of 'Forty-eight' as a motley of well-meaning but rather muddled ideologists who by turns misled, or were carried away by, a disorderly and cowardly rabble. In fact, the Germans had never achieved any political and social progress by their own exertions, but had always been granted it from above. The serfs were liberated, the municipalities were accorded self-government, and representative institutions were set up as free gifts by gracious and benevolent autocrats. Social legislation was introduced by Bismarck as a weapon of political warfare against Socialists and Liberals. Even the change to parliamentary government in October 1918 was, at least in form, brought about by the Emperor in consultation with the Federal Council. No Bastille Day and no Fourth of July reminded the Germans of the fundamental truth that political freedom and social progress must be fought for and are achievements worth fighting for.

Brought up in the idea that the government's function was to give orders which the subject had to obey without questioning, and that the Reichstag's function was only to criticize and restrain a government on whose composition it had no influence whatever, the electors of the Republic failed to grasp the fact that it was no longer sufficient to be 'agin the government', but that they had now to choose between the government in office and the alternative government. Self-determination seemed a burden rather than a privilege to a nation which for so long had been relegated to barren criticism, and they continued to look for guidance to the government, until they were finally relieved of all responsibility by the Leader.

The totalitarian programme of the National Socialists could be accomplished only by eradicating every other political and ideological system at home and abroad. At home, National Socialism meant unlimited despotism; abroad, it meant world-domination. This double aim was clearly expressed in a favourite song of the Hitler Youth, the refrain of which runs:

> To-day we are Germany's masters,
> To-morrow the whole world will be ours!

For some years this ultimate aim was hidden from most foreign observers by the smoke-screen of Goebbels's propaganda. Hitler seemed indeed only to consummate the nation-state idea of the nineteenth century when he abolished the last vestiges of independence still left to the German lands and set up a thoroughly centralized administration on the model of the *république une et indivisible* (31 March 1933); when he united in himself the offices of Chancellor and President of the Republic after Hindenburg's death (19 Aug. 1934); when he annexed Austria, the Eastern march of the medieval empire (12 March 1938); and even when he claimed and received the German-inhabited frontier districts of Czechoslovakia (29 Sept. 1938). Hitler, it was argued, acted within the rights of national sovereignty when he suppressed the trade-unions (2 May 1933) and all political parties save the National Socialist movement (14 July 1933); when he excluded the Jews from every trade and vocation and finally put them outside the pale of the law (15 Sept. 1935); when he set up a complete state control of economic life, which culminated in a comprehensive four-year plan (19 Oct. 1936); and when universities and schools, newspapers and wireless, literature and art were expurgated and made to conform to the principles of National Socialism. The abolition of the fundamental rights of man, the horrors of the concentration camps and the persecutions of the Christian churches were officially regarded as internal affairs of Germany. Even when Germany withdrew from the disarmament conference and the League of Nations (14 Oct. 1933), repudiated the military clauses of the peace treaty and re-introduced universal military service (16 March 1935), denounced the Locarno Pact and occupied the demilitarized Rhineland (7 March 1936)—even after these unmistakable signs of aggressive intentions, few and far between were those who realized that Hitler was bent on war unless the rest of the world would voluntarily accept his rule.

In fact, Hitler began to prepare for war the day after he took office. On 31 Jan. 1933, Göring was appointed Air Minister and ordered to build the strongest air force in the shortest time possible. On the same day, Hitler met the army chiefs and won them over to his policy. The last misgivings that the professional officers entertained against the party rule were dispersed when Hitler yielded to their demands and suppressed the rival army of the S.A. which Captain Röhm, its chief of staff, wished to incorporate with the regular army, with himself as Defence Minister. On 30 June 1934, Hitler butchered Röhm and a number of other S.A. leaders; and he and Göring seized the opportunity to square accounts with other one-time adversaries. Amongst the dead were Kahr, Schleicher, Gregor Strasser, and the private advisers of Brüning and Papen. In return for this purge the generals transferred their allegiance from Hindenburg, who died on 2 Aug., to Hitler and later accepted the former lance-corporal as their supreme war-lord (4 Feb. 1938).

The timely support of the army was the more necessary for Hitler as the elections of 5 March 1933 disappointed him. Although the fire of the Reichstag building, planned and carried out by Göring (27 Feb.), furnished the pretext for outlawing the Communists and appointing the S.A. and S.S. as a special constabulary, the Nazis obtained only 44 per cent of the votes and even together with the Nationalists commanded only 52 per cent of the Reichstag. The two-thirds majority which was necessary for a change of the constitution was provided by the Centre Party, under the pressure of the S.A. men who thronged the lobbies of the house. Thus, on 23 March, the enabling act was passed which freed Hitler from every legal and constitutional restriction on the exercise of his power. By means of this *carte blanche* he subordinated the state to the party which not only occupied every vantage-ground in the administration, but at the same time built up an administrative machinery of its own, parallel with and soon superior to the constitutional authorities. It was this party organization which carried out the racial legislation culminating in the pogroms of November 1938, and propagated the mythical creed of the master-race and its Messiah-Leader. The standard-bearers of this crusade were the S.S. who, after the purge of the S.A., held all key positions in the executive, especially the secret police. Outside Germany the way for Hitler's ascendancy was prepared by what was later described as 'Fifth Column' work. Minorities of German descent and representatives of German business firms, who resided in practically every European and American country, were their spearhead; but its most useful and active agents were indigenous politicians—men thwarted in their ambitions, fanatics, mentally unbalanced zealots, and hired traitors, to whom the Norwegian, Quisling, eventually gave his name as the lowest common denominator. Once the master-race had established their rule over the various dependencies, protectorates, possessions and slave-colonies—graded according to their blood relationship with the Nordic race and their economic and military usefulness—the Fifth Columnists were to obtain their reward as subordinate taskmasters over their compatriots of lesser breed.

The non-aggression pact for ten years which Hitler concluded with Poland on 26 Jan. 1934 was the first step towards the conquest of Eastern Europe, as it lulled Poland into a false security and incidentally poisoned Polish relations with Russia, Czechoslovakia and France. Two years later, the remilitarization of the Rhineland gave Hitler the commanding ground from which to launch his later attack on Holland, Belgium and France; and effectively obstructed military co-operation between France and Czechoslovakia. The ominous inertia with which Britain and France looked at Hitler's sweeping away one international obligation after another was most encouraging to the Leader; and the tension between Britain and Italy which ensued from Italy's predatory raid on Abyssinia allowed him to redress a former blunder of his own. In June 1933, and again in July 1934, his Austrian followers had tried to seize power by a *coup d'état*, and the Austrian chancellor, Dollfuss, was foully murdered at the second attempt. Mussolini had upheld the independence of Austria, threatened Germany with war, and entered into a common front with Britain and France at the conference of Stresa (April 1935). Now, snubbed but not reduced by the application of League sanctions, he lent a willing ear to Hitler's wooings. He withdrew his protection from Austria and on 1 Nov. 1936 proclaimed the Berlin-Rome axis. This, the first blast of the war-trumpet, was quickly followed by official recognition of the Franco régime in Spain (18 Nov.), which accomplished the encirclement of France and incidentally drew North-West Africa into Hitler's orbit: while the pact with Japan (24 Nov.) gave him a foothold in the Far East and the Pacific, which threatened British, Dutch, French, Portuguese and American territories. Fascist revolts in Palestine, Iraq, and various South American republics, from 1936 to 1938, indicated Hitler's growing interest in the Middle East and the Western hemisphere. The naval agreement with Great Britain (17 July 1937) closed the last chink in his armour, as by it the building of a strong German submarine force was explicitly sanctioned by the only power which Hitler regarded with fear. Having thus secured his ground in every direction, Hitler started the offensive. In March 1938 he annexed

Austria; in April he demanded first full autonomy, soon complete cession of the German-speaking parts of Czechoslovakia. The reaction in London and Paris was exactly as Hitler had expected. Mr Chamberlain only intensified the policy of appeasement and helped Hitler to his triumph at the conference of Munich (29 Sept. 1938).

It was Hitler's next step that unmasked him as the 'thrice perjured traitor' that he was. On 15 March 1939, he invaded Czechoslovakia, which he had previously robbed of her natural and military defences, and dismembered the country, assigning Bohemia and Moravia as a 'protectorate' to himself. The incorporation of ten million Slavs terminated the nation-state and racial ideologies which had so far served him as smoke-screens, and established the principle of the New Order in which the master-race staked out its living-space. Faithful to his cunningly naïve procedure, Hitler then prepared the gigantic eastward drive, the earliest and most cherished item of his programme, by signing a non-aggression pact with Russia (21 Aug. 1939). A week later, 1 Sept., he invaded Poland and thereby provoked the second world-war, which may, perhaps, be described as an international civil war in which Christianity, civilization and humanity are arrayed against the spiritual hosts of wickedness everywhere throughout the world. Mr Winston Churchill, the accepted leader of the United Nations, concluded his monumental history of the first world-war with a question which has lost nothing of its pertinence and may appropriately stand also at the end of this chapter of German history:

'Is this the end? Is it to be merely a chapter in a cruel and senseless story? Or will there spring from the very fires of conflict that reconciliation of the giant combatants which would unite their genius and secure to each in safety and freedom a share in rebuilding the glory of Europe?'

INDEX

Aargau, 73
Abdul Hamid II (1842–1918), Sultan of Turkey (1876–1909), 247
Abyssinia, 284
Acre, 49
Adalbert, Abp of Bremen (1043–72), 23, 28, 29, 30
Adalbert I, Abp of Mayence (1111–37), 35, 36
Adaldag, Abp of Hamburg (936–88), 8, 11
Adda, river, 161
Addington, Henry, Lord Sidmouth (1757–1844), 161
Adelaide of Burgundy, Q. of Otto I (d. 999), 10, 14
Adolf, Count of Nassau (1277), King (1292–98), 60
Adolf II, Count of Schauenburg and Holstein (1131–64), 37
Adrianople, truce (1545), 90, 93
Adriatic Sea, 59, 128
Aethelstan, K. of England (924–40), 6
Afghanistan, 247
Africa, 1, 128, 236, 239, 246–8, 250, 284
Agadir, 248
Agnes of Poitou (d. 1077), Q. of Henry III (1043), 22, 28
Aix-la-Chapelle, 7, 14, 147, 174, 220
Alais, treaty (1629), 107
Albania, 249
Albert I, D. of Austria (1282), King (1298–1308), 59, 60
Albert II (1397–1439), D. of Austria (1404), K. of Bohemia and Hungary (1437), German King (1438), 60, 71, 72
Albert IV (1447–1508), D. of Bavaria (1460), 99
Albert V (1528–79), D. of Bavaria (1550), 86, 90, 99
Albert Alcibiades (1522–57), Mg. of Kulmbach (1541), 91
Albert, Austrian Archduke (1817–95), 218
Albert the Bear (d. 1170), Mg. of Nordmark (1134) and Brandenburg (1150), 37, 42, 62
Alexander the Great (356–323 B.C.), 154
Alexander III, Pope (1159–81), 41
Alexander I (1777–1825), Tsar of Russia (1801), 161, 164, 165, 169–73, 189

Alexander II (1818–81), Tsar of Russia (1855), 217, 228, 229
Alfonso X (1226–84), K. of Castile (1252–82), German King (1257), 58
Algeciras, 246, 248, 249, 258
Allenby, Edmund, Viscount (1861–1936), 50
Alps, vii, 9, 20, 32, 40, 47, 66, 99, 145, 166, 197
Alsace, viii, 74, 91, 111, 114, 130, 134, 137, 197, 229, 230
Alsace-Lorraine, 192, 231–3, 250, 260, 269
Alsen, 132
Altenburg, 40
Altenstein, Karl von (1770–1840), 183
Altmark, truce (1629), 108
Altranstädt, peace (1706), 141
America, 81, 83, 95, 127, 283, 284
Amiens, peace (1802), 161
Amsterdam, 96, 135
Anacletus II, Pope (1130–38), 36
Andrew II, K. of Hungary (1205–35), 49
Anglo-Saxons, vii, 1, 3, 5
Anhalt, 62, 119, 171
Anne (1665–1714), Q. of Gt Britain (1702), 119
Anne (1693–1740), Empress of Russia (1730), 145
Anno, Abp of Cologne (1056–75), Saint (1183), 28, 29
Ansbach-Baireuth, 152, 160, 163
Anselm, Abp of Canterbury (1093–1109), 34
Antwerp, 96
Apulia, 11, 48
Aquitaine, 20, 22, 24, 46
Arabs, 4, 10, 14, 18, 21, 81
Aragon, 33
Archipoeta (fl. 1160–65), 38
Ardoin, Mg. of Ivrea, K. of Italy (1002–13; d. 1014), 17
Arles, 20, 40
Arndt, Ernst Moritz (1769–1860), 154, 168, 187, 190
Arras, 74
Artois, 74, 111, 114
Ascalon, 38
Ascanian dynasty, 37, 62
Aschaffenburg, 172
Asia Minor, 38, 44
Aspern, battle (1809), 169, 218
Asquith, Herbert Henry (1852–1928), 245

INDEX

Athens, 126, 136
Auerstädt, battle (1806), 164, 168
Auerswald, Rudolf von (1795-1866), 203, 210
Augsburg, 10, 54, 57, 58, 82, 95, 127, 162
Augsburg, diet (1500), 78, 79; diet (1530), 84; diet (1555), 91, 97, 106
Augusta (1811-90), Q. of William I, 210, 229, 233
Augustenburg, Christian, D. of (1798-1869), 198, 215
Augustine, St, 3, 83
Augustus (1526-86), Elector of Saxony (1553), 94, 99
Augustus the Strong, *see* Frederick Augustus I of Saxony
Auhausen, Union of (1608), 101-4
Austerlitz, battle (1805), 162
Australia, 81
Austria, archdukedom, 64, *et passim*
Austria, empire (1804-48), 162-202 *passim*
Austria, margraviate and duchy, viii, 23, 31, 37, 40, 44, 50, 59, 60, 71
Austria, republic, 60, 275, 282, 284, 285
Austria-Hungary, 23, 137, 146, 202, 211, 236, 237, 239, 245-9, 258
Aversa, 21
Avignon, 20, 52, 64

Babenberg dynasty, 31, 50
Bach, Joh. Sebastian (1685-1750), 278
Baden, margraviate, 54, 126, 156, 161-3
Baden, grand duchy, 156, 163, 166, 177, 186, 188, 192, 201, 205, 215, 218, 220, 251, 254, 260
Baden, peace (1714), 140
Baghdad, 247, 250, 258
Baldwin of Luxemburg (1285-1354), Abp of Treves (1307), 60-2
Balkans, 44, 105, 137, 138, 144, 208, 237, 242, 248, 249
Baltic countries, ix, 7, 126, 141, 170, 259, 265, 266; *see also* Courland, Estonia, Latvia, Lithuania, Livonia
Baltic Sea, 7, 15, 41, 49, 54, 59, 96, 106, 108, 114, 115, 128, 161, 192
Bamberg, bishopric, 18, 22, 23, 25
Barcelona, 33, 139
Baring, bankers, 102
Bärwalde, treaty (1631), 108
Basle, 7, 20, 54, 60
Basle, council (1431), 70, 125; peace (1795), 159, 160
Bautzen, battle (1813), 171
Bavaria, duchy and electorate, vii-ix, 4, 7-10, 13-16, 18, 20, 24, 25, 30, 33, 34, 36-8, 40, 42, 47, 53, 61, 86, 90, 98-104, 110, 111, 112, 115, 124, 125, 127, 128, 136, 138, 139, 142, 144-6, 152, 153, 156, 160, 161, 163
Bavaria, kingdom, x, 163, 166, 170-3, 177, 186, 191, 206, 214, 215, 218-20, 225, 228, 230, 233, 254, 259
Bavaria, republic, 261, 265, 266, 270-2
Bazaine, François Achille (1811-88), 228
Beaconsfield, Benjamin Disraeli, Earl of (1804-81), 239
Beatrice of Burgundy (d. 1184), Q. of Frederick I (1156), 40
Bebel, August (1840-1913), 279
Becher, Johann Joachim (1635-82), 127
Becket, Thomas, English Chancellor (1155), Abp of Canterbury (1162-70), Saint (1173), 39
Beirut, 45
Belfort, 20, 229
Belgium, kingdom, 178, 228, 256, 284; before 1830, *see* Netherlands (Spanish)
Belgrade, 92, 136, 141, 144, 157
Benedek, Ludwig von (1804-81), 218
Benedetti, Vincent, Comte de (1817-1900), 227
Benedict VIII, Pope (1012-24), 17-19
Benedict IX, Pope (1032-48), 19, 22
Bengal, 128, 147
Bennigsen, Rudolf von (1824-1902), 211
Berengar, Mg. of Ivrea, K. of Italy (950-64; d. 966), 8-11, 17
Berg, 102, 172, 174
Berg, Claus (fl. 1501-33), 58
Bergen, 57
Berlin, 25, 54, 55, 129, 142, 146, 147, 149, 164, 165, 171, 192, 200, 202, 217, 227, 244, 245, 247, 258, 261, 264, 265, 268, 284
Berlin, congress (1878), 237, 248; treaty (1911), 248
Bernadotte, Jean Baptiste (1763-1844), K. Charles XIV of Sweden (1818), 119, 171
Bernard, Prince of Saxe-Weimar (1604-39), 111
Bernard of Clairvaux (d. 1155), 36-8
Berne, 73
Bernstorff, Johann, Count (1862-19), 256
Bernward, Bp of Hildesheim (993-1022), 15
Besançon, 20
Bethmann-Hollweg, Theobald von (1856-1921), 241, 245, 250, 251, 253, 256-8
Beust, Friedrich Ferdinand, Count (1809-86), 214
Biarritz, 217

Bismarck, Otto von (1815–98), x, 130, 177, 179, 180, 185, 191, 192, 202, 205–43 *passim*, 248, 268, 269, 273, 281
Bismarck Archipelago, 239
Bjoerkoe, 242
Black Sea, 192, 229
Blenheim, battle (1704), 139
Blücher, Gerhard Leberecht, Prince (1742–1819), 168, 173
Blum, Robert (1804–48), 202
Blumenbach, Johann Friedrich (1752–1840), 122
Bogotá, 127
Bohemia, dukedom, 7, 13–15, 17, 18, 23
Bohemia, kingdom, 32, 37, 40, 52, 58–72, 78, 92, 97, 98, 102–5, 108, 109, 111, 113, 135, 145, 146, 148, 152, 200, 218, 219, 285
Boleslav Chrobry, K. of Poland (992–1025), 15, 17, 21
Boleslav II, D. of Bohemia (967–99), 15
Bologna, 38, 93
Bolshevism, 261, 264–6, 269, 270
Bosnia, 208, 248, 249
Bouvines, battle (1214), 47
Boyne, battle (1690), 126
Brabant, 44, 74
Brandenburg, bishopric, 8, 129
Brandenburg, margraviate and electorate, ix, 37, 40, 52, 55, 62, 64, 68, 71, 82, 95, 100–2, 108, 115, 117, 118, 120, 123–5, 128, *et passim*
Brandenburg, town, 7, 203
Brandenburg, Friedrich Wilhelm, Count of (1792–1850), 203, 206
Breisach, 111, 137
Breisgau, 54, 74
Breitenfeld, battle (1631), 108; battle (1642), 111
Bremen, archbishopric, 17, 23, 28, 114, 142
Bremen, city, 49, 55, 87, 96, 114, 162, 192
Brenner pass, 66
Breslau, 54, 146
Brest Litovsk, 259, 265, 269
Bretislav, D. of Bohemia (1034–55), 23
Britain, 1; *see also* England
Brittany, 80
Brixen, bishopric, 22
Browne, Maximilian, Count of (1705–57), 126, 148
Bruck, Karl Ludwig von (1798–1860), 192, 208
Bruges, 57, 66, 74
Brüning, Heinrich (1885–), 267, 274–7, 283
Bruno, Count of Egisheim, *see* Leo IX

Brunswick, city, 42, 54, 55, 265
Brunswick-Lüneburg, duchy, 48, 87, 95, 118, 126
Brunswick-Wolfenbüttel, duchy, 90, 95, 119, 161, 165, 192, 194, 195, 224, 236
Brussels, 74, 80, 153
Bucharest, 137, 259, 269
Büchner, Georg (1813–37), 187
Budapest, 93, 135, 200
Bug, river, 159
Bulgaria, 13, 14, 49, 208, 237, 249, 258
Bülow, Bernhard von (1849–1929), 241, 244, 245, 248, 253, 254
Bunsen, Josias von (1791–1860), 204
Burgundians, 3
Burgundy, duchy, 73, 74, 80, 81, 91, 93, 124, 148
Burgundy, kingdom, 4, 7, 10, 17, 20, 35, 40, 45
Bute, John Stuart, Marquess of (1713–92), 149
Byzantine empire, 4, 10, 11, 13, 14, 18, 21, 23, 32, 45
Byzantium, *see* Constantinople

Caesar, Caius Julius (100–44 B.C.), 154
Calabria, 11
Calixtus II, Pope (1119–24), 35
Calvinists, 97, 99, 100, 102, 106, 112, 113, 114
Cambrai, league (1508), 80; peace (1529), 85
Cambridge, Adolphus Frederick, D. of (1774–1850), 194
Cameroons, 239, 248
Cammin, bishopric, 115
Camphausen, Ludolf (1803–90), 200, 203
Campo Formio, peace (1797), 160
Can Grande della Scala (1291–1329), Lord of Verona (1308), 61
Canada, 150
Canning, George (1770–1827), 183
Canossa, 31, 233
Canterbury, 17, 23, 34
Canute, K. of England, Denmark and Norway (1014–35), 17, 21, 197
Capetian dynasty, 4, 14, 25
Caprivi, Leo von (1831–99), 241, 253
Carinthia, 13, 20, 24, 59, 62, 75
Carlovitz, peace (1699), 137, 141
Carlyle, Thomas (1795–1881), 154, 229
Carniola, 62
Carolines, 233
Carolingian dynasty and empire, vii, viii, 3–5, 8, 14
Casimir I, D. of Poland (1034–58), 23
Casimir IV (1427–92), K. of Poland (1447), 72

INDEX

Cassel, 149, 185
Castile, 57, 81
Castlereagh, Robert Stewart, Viscount (1769–1822), 172
Catherine II (1729–96), Empress of Russia (1762), 119, 149, 153, 157–9
Catholic Church, *see* Roman Catholic Church
Cavour, Camillo, Count di (1810–61), 209
Celestin III, Pope (1191–98), 44
Celle, dukedom, 119
Centre Party, 232, 233, 235, 252–4, 256–8, 267, 274–6, 279, 283
Ceprano, peace (1230), 48
Chamberlain, Joseph (1836–1914), 244, 245
Chamberlain, Neville (1869–1940), 285
Charlemagne, Frankish King (768), Roman Emperor (800–14), vii, viii, 3, 4, 7, 10, 12, 23, 34, 38, 76, 154, 163
Charles IV (1316–78), King (1346), Emperor (1355), 24, 52, 59, 64–8, 71, 78
Charles V (1500–58), K. of Spain (1516) and Roman Emperor (1519–56), 76, 77, 81–93, 106, 127, 136, 140, 227
Charles VI (1685–1740), Emperor (1711), as C. III, K. of Spain (1700–11), 128, 138–40, 144, 145
Charles, Austrian Archduke (1771–1847), 159, 160, 169
Charles II (1804–73), D. of Brunswick (1815–30), 194
Charles the Bold (1433–77), D. of Burgundy (1467), 74, 80, 148
Charles I (1600–49), K. of England (1625), 105, 112, 213
Charles II (1630–85), K. of England (1660), 120
Charles III the Simple, K. of France (893–929), 5, 6
Charles IV (1294–1328), K. of France (1322), 64
Charles VIII (1470–98), K. of France (1483), 20, 80
Charles V (1643–90), D. of Lorraine (1675), 136
Charles I (1839–1914), K. of Rumania (1866), 226
Charles II (1661–1700), K. of Spain (1665), 138, 139
Charles IX (1550–1611), K. of Sweden (1604), 107
Charles XII (1682–1718), K. of Sweden (1697), 119, 141
Charles of Valois (d. 1325), 60
Charles VII Albert (1697–1745), Elector of Bavaria (1726), Emperor (1742), 76, 145, 146

Charles Alexander (1684–1737), D. of Württemberg (1733), 122
Charles Augustus (1757–1828), D. of Saxe-Weimar (1758), Grand Duke (1815), 153, 174, 186, 189, 190
Charles Edward, Prince (1720–88), 146, 147
Charles Eugene (1728–93), D. of Württemberg (1737), 122
Charles Frederick (1728–1811), Mg. (1738) and Grand Duke (1806) of Baden, 126
Charles X Gustavus (1622–60), Count Palatine of Zweibrücken (1652), K. of Sweden (1654), 131, 132
Charles Leopold (1678–1747), D. of Mecklenburg-Schwerin (1713–28), 121
Charles Louis (1617–80), Elector Palatine (1648), 112
Charles Magnus, Wildgrave, 122
Charles Theodore (1724–99), Elector Palatine (1742) and of Bavaria (1777), 152, 153
Charles William Ferdinand (1735–1806), D. of Brunswick (1780), 158
Chartreuse, 33
Chatham, William Pitt, Earl of (1708–78), 149, 150
Châtillon, congress (1814), 172
Cherusci, 1
China, 246
Chislehurst, 230
Christian IV (1577–1648), K. of Denmark and Norway (1588), 102, 105, 106
Christian VIII (1786–1848), K. of Denmark (1839), 198
Christian IX (1818–1906), K. of Denmark (1863), 215, 216
Christian I, Abp of Mayence (1165–83), 41
Christopher (1515–68), D. of Württemberg (1550), 94
Churchill, Winston (1874–), 245, 285
Cilicia, 44, 45
Cimbri, 1
Citeaux, 33
Cividale, 48
Clement II, Pope (1046–47), 22
Clement III, Pope (1080–1100), 32, 33
Clement V, Pope (1305–14), 61
Clement VI (1291–1352), Pope (1342), 63
Clement XI (1649–1721), Pope (1700), 140
Cleves, duchy, 71, 101, 102, 115, 129, 130, 132, 163
Clovis, Frankish King (481–511), viii

INDEX

Cluny, 17, 19, 22, 33
Cobden, Richard (1804-65), 234
Coblentz, 63, 158, 182
Colbert, Jean Baptiste (1619-83), 127
Cölln, 129
Cologne, archbishopric, 12, 18, 20, 28, 39, 42, 46, 47, 52, 68, 97, 98, 100, 120, 124, 125, 137, 139, 144, 146, 153, 162, 174, 185, 233
Cologne, city, 44, 46, 51, 54, 58, 66, 74
Colonies, 127, 128, 239, 253, 269
Columbus, Christopher (d. 1506), 81
Communist Party, 199, 264, 265, 267, 271, 272, 276, 279, 280, 283
Compiègne, 261
Connaught, Arthur, D. of (1850-1943), 233
Conrad I, D. of Franconia (906), King (911-18), 5, 11
Conrad II, King (1024-39), Emperor (1027), 19-22, 24, 29, 197
Conrad III, anti-King (1127-35), King (1138-52), 36-8
Conrad IV (1228-54), King (1237), 48, 51, 52
Conrad, anti-King (1093-1101), 32, 33
Conrad, D. of Lorraine (944-55), 10, 19
Conrad, D. of Masovia (1200-26), 49
Conradin (1252-68), 52
Conservative Party, 234, 235, 239, 251-4, 256, 257, 266, 279
Constance, 42, 54
Constance, Council (1414), 68, 69, 125
Constance (d. 1198), Q. of Henry VI (1186), 42, 44, 45, 47
Constantine the Great, 7, 16
Constantine I (1868-1923), K. of Greece, 249
Constantinople, 10, 13, 22, 23, 54, 247, 249
Cook, James (1728-79), 158
Copenhagen, 216, 228
Cordoba, 10
Coromandel, 128
Corsica, 40
Courland, 49, 127, 128
Cracow, 66, 159
Crécy, battle (1346), 63
Crimean War, 208, 209
Croatia, 137, 180, 200
Cromwell, Oliver (1599-1658), 104, 127, 202
Cromwell, Thomas (1485-1540), 101
Crusades, 33, 37, 38, 44, 45, 136
Culloden, battle (1746), 149
Cumberland, D. of, *see* Ernest Augustus
Cumberland, William Augustus, D. of (1721-65), 147, 149

Cunigonda, Q. of Henry II (d. 1039), 19
Curtatone, 200
Custozza, 200, 218
Customs Union, 190-4, 217, 225, 226
Cyprus, 45
Czechoslovakia, 271, 282, 284, 285
Czechs, 7, 58, 59, 69, 70, 179-81, 199, 200, 208, 211, 218

Dahlmann, Friedrich Christoph (1785-1860), 187, 195, 201
Daily Telegraph, 245, 254
Dalberg, Karl Theodor von (1744-1817), Abp of Mayence (1802), 162, 163
Dalmatia, 160
Damascus, 38
Damasus II, Pope (1047-48), 22
Danes, *see* Denmark
Dante Alighieri (1265-1321), 61
Danube, 8, 54, 157, 166
Danzig, 54, 114, 152, 157, 158, 269
Darmstadt, 186
Dawes, Charles (1865-), 272
Delagoa Bay, 152, 243
Delcassé, Théophile (1852-1923), 248
Democratic Party, 267, 271, 274, 276
Denmark, vii, 6, 7, 11, 13-15, 17, 21, 23, 24, 34, 37, 50, 57, 73, 81, 95, 102, 105, 106, 108, 113, 115, 122, 126, 127, 132, 141, 142, 168, 173, 174, 178, 179, 192, 197, 198, 201, 206, 215, 216, 219, 227, 228
Dessau, battle (1626), 105
Dettingen, battle (1743), 146
Dijon, 74
Dnieper, river, 9
Dollfuss, Engelbert (1892-1934), 284
Donauwörth, 101
Dorpat, 54
Dortmund, 56
Dresden, 118, 142, 147, 148, 170, 205
Düppel, 216
Dürer, Albert (1471-1528), 58, 77, 279
Dürnkrut, battle (1278), 59
Düsseldorf, 102

East Elbia, 7, 129, 132, 251, 273, 277
East Prussia, *see* Prussia, dukedom
Eberlin von Günzburg, Johann (1465-1530), 87
Ebert, Friedrich (1871-1925), 261, 264, 268, 273
Ebro, river, 3
Eck, Leonhard von (1475-1550), 99
Edith, Q. of Otto I (d. 946), 6
Edward the Elder (899-925), 6
Edward I (1239-1307), K. of England (1272), 60

INDEX

Edward III (1312-77), K. of England (1327), 62, 63
Edward VII (1841-1910), K. of Gt Britain (1901), 240
Eger, 40, 110
Egypt, 120, 197
Eider, river, 21
Eisner, Kurt (1867-1919), 265
Elba, 168, 173
Elbe, river, 6-8, 14, 40, 54, 66, 96, 108, 114, 115, 129, 165, 173
Elbe duchies, *see* Slesvig-Holstein
Elberfeld, 192
Elbing, 107, 114
Elizabeth (1533-1603), Q. of England (1558), 57, 94-6, 103, 107
Elizabeth (1596-1662), Electress of Frederick V (1613), 102-4
Elizabeth (1709-62), Empress of Russia (1741), 119, 149
Elizabeth, Landgravine of Thuringia (1207-31), Saint (1235), 49
Emden, 96
Ems, river, 115; spa, 125, 227
Enea Silvio Piccolomini, *see* Pius II
Engelbert I, Abp of Cologne (1216-25), 47
Engels, Friedrich (1820-95), 199
England (= Britain), 3, 6, 10, 15, 17, 21, 24, 25, 27, 31, 34, 38, 42, 44-8, 50, 51, 57, 58, 60, 62-4, 66, 68, 69, 74, 79, 80, 90, 92, 95, 96, 101, 103, 105, 107, 110, 112, 113, 117, 118, 122, 123, 127, 128, 135, 137, 139, 140, 142, 146-9, 152, 153, 156-7, 170-4, 178, 182, 183, 192, 195-9, 201, 209-11, 215, 219, 224-9, 236, 237, 239, 242-50, 255, 256, 274, 275, 284, 285
Erfurt, 169, 205
Ermland, bishopric, 152
Ernest II (1818-93), D. of Coburg (1844), 211
Ernest, D. of Swabia (1015-30), 19, 20
Ernest Augustus (1629-98), D. of Kalenberg (1679), Elector of Hanover (1692), 118, 119
Ernest Augustus (1771-1851), K. of Hanover (1837), 195
Erzberger, Matthias (1875-1921), 252, 257, 261, 271
Erzgebirge, 94
Essen, 225
Estonia, 57, 107, 141, 266
Eugene, Prince of Savoy (1663-1736), 105, 124, 126, 137, 139-41, 144, 145, 150
Eugénie, Countess of Montijo (1826-1920), French Empress (1853-70), 226, 227

Eulenburg, Philipp, Prince (1847-1921), 241
Eylau, battle (1807), 164

Favre, Jules (1809-80), 229
Fehrbellin, battle (1675), 133
Ferdinand I (1503-64), King (1531), Emperor (1556), 81, 83, 90, 92, 93, 95, 97, 121
Ferdinand II (1578-1637), K. of Bohemia (1617) and Hungary (1618), Emperor (1619), 24, 77, 99, 102-11
Ferdinand III (1608-57), Emperor (1637), 110, 111, 112, 120, 121
Ferdinand IV (d. 1654), King (1653), 120, 131
Ferdinand (1793-1875), Emperor of Austria (1835-48), 195, 202
Ferdinand (1452-1516), K. of Aragon (1479), 81
Ferdinand (1721-92), D. of Brunswick (1735), 149
Ferdinand Maria (1636-79), Elector of Bavaria (1651), 120
Fichte, Johann Gottlieb (1762-1814), 168
Finland, 23, 107, 142, 259
Fischer von Erlach, Johann (1656-1723), 136
Fitznigel, Richard (d. 1198), 38
Fiume, 128
Flanders, 24, 36, 74, 86, 96, 259, 261
Florence, 56, 68, 69
Fontainebleau, peace (1762), 149
Fontenoy, battle (1745), 147, 149
Forster, George (1754-94), 158
France, *passim*
Franche-Comté, 74, 91, 134
Francia, duchy, 4, 8
Francis I Stephen (1708-65), D. of Lorraine (1744), Emperor (1745), 144-6, 147, 150
Francis II (1768-1835), Roman Emperor (1792-1806), as Francis I, Austrian Emperor (1804-35), 158, 159, 161-3, 169, 170, 172, 173, 182, 201
Francis I (1494-1547), K. of France (1515), 82, 83, 90, 136
Francis Ferdinand (1863-1914), Austrian Archduke, 181, 250
Francis Joseph (1830-1916), Austrian Emperor (1848), 180, 181, 202, 206, 210, 214, 218, 226, 236
Franckenstein, Georg von (1825-90), 235
Franco, 284
Franconia, 4, 5, 7, 11, 12, 18, 19, 25, 53, 86, 101, 108, 124, 152, 166
Frankfort, National Assembly (1848), 179, 195, 199-205

Frankfort-on-Main, 25, 40, 58, 66, 79, 82, 124, 146, 162, 172, 174, 188, 190, 195, 205, 207, 214, 218–20, 230
Frankfort-on-Oder, 129
Frankish empire, *see* Carolingian empire
Franks, vii, 1, 3, 7, 10, 11
Frantz, Constantin (1817–91), 221
Frederick I Barbarossa, D. of Swabia (1147), King (1152), Emperor (1155–90), 38–44
Frederick II (1194–1250), King (1211), Emperor (1220), 45, 47–52, 58
Frederick III (1415–93), Roman Emperor (1439), 72–6, 144
Frederick (1286–1330), D. of Austria (1308), King (1314), 56, 61, 62
Frederick, Prince of Augustenburg (1829–80), 215, 216
Frederick I (1372–1440), Mg. of Brandenburg (1415), 71
Frederick III (1657–1713), Elector of Brandenburg (1688), as Frederick I, K. in Prussia (1701), 118, 139, 142, 143
Frederick II (1712–86), K. of Prussia (1740), 66, 125, 126, 130, 131, 135, 139, 145–57, 164, 191, 213, 266
Frederick III (1831–88), Emperor (1888), 212, 213, 215, 239, 240
Frederick IV (1671–1730), K. of Denmark (1699), 141
Frederick VII (1808–63), K. of Denmark (1848), 198, 215
Frederick, Count of Hohenstaufen, D. of Swabia (1079–1105), 31
Frederick V (1596–1632), Elector Palatine (1616–23), K. of Bohemia (1619–21), 102–4, 112, 118, 125, 146
Frederick of Rothenburg (d. 1167), 38, 40
Frederick III the Wise (1463–1525), Elector of Saxony (1486), 82, 84
Frederick II, D. of Swabia (1105–47), 36
Frederick I (1754–1816), Duke (1797), Elector (1803) and K. of Württemberg (1806), 166
Frederick Augustus I (1670–1733), Elector of Saxony (1694), as F. A. II, K. of Poland (1697), 142
Frederick Augustus II (1696–1763), Elector of Saxony (1733), as F. A. III, K. of Poland (1733), 118, 141, 144, 174
Frederick Augustus III (I) (1750–1827), Elector (1763) and King (1806) of Saxony, Grand Duke of Warsaw (1807–13), 164, 165, 171, 174
Frederick William (1620–88), Elector of Brandenburg (1640), 115, 127, 130–5, 142, 213

Frederick William I (1688–1740), K. in Prussia (1713), 128, 130, 142–4, 191, 213
Frederick William II (1744–97), K. of Prussia (1786), 156–60
Frederick William III (1770–1840), K. of Prussia (1797), 156, 160, 164, 165, 168–73, 184, 190
Frederick William IV (1795–1861), K. of Prussia (1840), 185, 196, 197, 200, 201, 203–10, 213
Free Conservative Party, 224, 251, 266
Freiburg (Breisgau), 34, 54, 58, 121, 134, 137, 140
Freising, bishopric, 37, 100
Fribourg (Switzerland), 54
Friedland, battle (1807), 164
Friedland, duchy, 105
Frisia, 51, 74, 118, 174
Friuli, 4
Fuggers, Augsburg bankers, 82
Fulda, 98

Galicia, 152, 157, 159, 170, 181
Gallas, Mathias, Count (1584–1647), 110
Galliéni, Joseph (1849–1916), 255
Gambia, 127
Garibaldi, Giuseppe (1807–82), 140
Gastein, treaty (1865), 216
Gebhard, Bp of Eichstätt, *see* Victor II
Gelasius II, Pope (1118–19), 35
Gelnhausen, 40
Genoa, 18, 50, 56, 271
Gentz, Friedrich von (1764–1832), 169
Geoffrey II, D. of Upper (1044) and Lower (1065) Lorraine (d. 1069), 24, 29
George Lewis (1660–1727), Elector of Hanover (1698), as G. I, K. of Gt Britain (1714), 119, 122, 142
George II (1683–1760), K. of Gt Britain (1727), 145, 146
George IV (1762–1830), K. of Gt Britain (1820), 173
George V (1819–78), K. of Hanover (1851–66), 225
Gerbert of Aurillac, *see* Silvester II
Gerhardt, Paul (1607–76), 135
German People's Party, 267, 274, 276
Gervinus, Georg Gottfried (1805–71), 195
Geza, D. of Hungary (972–97), 15
Ghent, 74
Gibraltar, 139, 140, 248
Gladbach, 101
Gladstone, W. E. (1809–98), 229, 239
Glatz, county, 145–7
Gluck, Christoph Willibald (1714–87), 136

Gneisenau, Neithardt, Count (1760–1831), 168, 171
Gnesen, 70, 158
Goebbels, Joseph (1897–19   ), 282
Goethe, Johann Wolfgang (1749–1832), ix, 58, 154, 156, 158, 180, 210, 266, 278
Goltz, Colmar von der (1843–1916), 247
Göring, Hermann (1893–19   ), 280, 282, 283
Goslar, 25, 41, 56, 105, 174
Gotha, 205
Gotland, 57
Gottfrid of Strasbourg (fl. 1210), 57
Göttingen, 122, 195
Gramont, Antoine, Duc de (1819–80), 227
Granada, 81
Greece, 249
Greenland, 23
Gregory I, Pope (590–604), 154
Gregory VI, Pope (1045–46), 22, 23
Gregory VII, Pope (1073–85), 27, 28, 30–3
Gregory IX, Pope (1227–41), 50
Greifswald, 115
Grey, Edward, Viscount (1862–1933), 244, 250
Grillparzer, Franz (1791–1872), 217
Grimm, Jakob (1785–1863), 195
Grimm, Wilhelm (1786–1859), 195
Gross-Jägersdorf, battle (1757), 149
Guastalla, duchy, 147
Guelders, 74, 118, 140
Guelph dynasty, x, 36, 37, 40, 44–6, 48, 51, 55, 76, 118–20, 225, 236
Guelph IV, D. of Bavaria (1070–1101), 33
Guelph V, D. of Bavaria (d. 1119), 33
Guelph VI (d. 1191), 40, 41
Guiana, 127
Guinea, 127
Guinegate, battle (1479), 74; battle (1513), 80
Gustavus II Adolphus (1594–1632), K. of Sweden (1611), 107–11, 131
Gustavus IV Adolphus (1778–1837), K. of Sweden (1792–1809), 163
Gutenberg, Johann (d. 1467/8), 58, 279

Hadersleben, 220
Hague, The, 139, 274
Hainault, 74
Halberstadt, bishopric, 115
Haldane, Richard, Viscount (1856–1928), 244, 245
Haller, Carl Ludwig von (1768–1854), 196
Hambach, 194, 195

Hamburg, 8, 11, 49, 55, 56, 66, 95, 96, 162, 165, 192, 214, 231
Hamilton, James, D. of (1606–49), 110
Hanover, ix, 71, 97, 118, 122, 139, 141, 142, 145–9, 153, 159, 161, 162, 164–6, 168, 174, 178, 192, 194, 195, 198, 205, 214–16, 218, 219, 225, 232, 264; *see also* Brunswick-Lüneburg
Hanse, 49, 54–7, 67, 95, 96, 108, 129, 165, 192
Hapsburg dynasty, 50, 58–62, 64, 72, *et passim*
Harald Bluetooth, K. of Denmark (950–86), 11, 15
Hardenberg, Karl August, Prince of (1750–1822), 168, 170–2, 189, 191, 236
Hartz mountains, 5, 25, 115
Harzburg, 278
Hastenbeck, battle (1757), 149
Hatzfeldt, Paul, Count (1831–1901), 244
Hauteville dynasty, 18
Havel, river, 7
Havelberg, bishopric, 8, 129
Haydn, Joseph (1732–1809), 136
Haynau, Julius von (1786–1853), 202, 203
Hedwig, Duchess of Silesia (d. 1243), Saint (1267), 50
Hegel, Georg Wilhelm Friedrich (1770–1831), 168, 183, 184
Heidelberg, 97, 100, 104, 137, 199
Heilbronn, League of (1633), 109
Heligoland, 165, 174, 243
Henneberg, Bertold von (1442–1504), Abp of Mayence (1484), 78, 79, 84, 120
Henry I, D. of Saxony (912), King (919–36), 5–8, 11, 16
Henry II, King (1002–24), Emperor (1014), Saint (1146), 13–20, 25
Henry III, King (1026), Emperor (1046–56), 20–5, 28, 36, 40
Henry IV (1050–1106), King (1056), Emperor (1084), 12, 19, 25, 27–34, 62, 233
Henry V, King (1098), Emperor (1111–25), 19, 33–6, 48
Henry VI, King (1169), Emperor (1191–97), 40, 42, 44, 45, 49, 51
Henry (VII), King (1220–35; d. 1242), 47, 48, 50
Henry, King (1147–50), 38
Henry Raspe, Lg. of Thuringia (1227–47), King (1246), 51
Henry VII, Count of Luxemburg (1288), King (1308), Emperor (1312–13), 60, 61, 73
Henry of Almaine (1235–71), 58

294 INDEX

Henry Jasomirgott, Mg. and D. (1156) of Austria (1141–77), D. of Bavaria (1142–54), 37, 40
Henry II, D. of Bavaria (955–95), 8, 10
Henry the Proud, D. of Bavaria (1126–39) and Saxony (1137), 36, 37, 40
Henry the Lion (1129–95), D. of Saxony (1142) and Bavaria (1156), 37–42, 45, 46, 48, 53, 54, 125
Henry (1489–1568), D. of Brunswick (1514), 90
Henry I, K. of England (1100–35), 34
Henry II, K. of England (1154–89), 39, 41, 42
Henry III, K. of England (1216–72), 48, 58
Henry IV (1367–1413), K. of England (1399), 68
Henry VII (1457–1509), K. of England (1485), 80
Henry VIII (1491–1547), K. of England (1509), 80, 82, 90, 101
Henry I, K. of France (1031–60), 20
Henry II, D. of Silesia (1238–41), 50
Hepburn, Sir John (1598–1636), 110
Heppenheim, 199
Herder, Joh. Gottfried (1744–1803), ix
Hermann, Count of Salm, King (1081–88), 32
Hermann of Salza, Grand-master of Teutonic Order (1210–39), 49
Herreros, 253
Hertling, Georg, Count (1843–1919), 259
Herzegovina, 248
Hess, Rudolf, 272
Hesse-Cassel, Landgraviate and Electorate, vii–x, 87, 90, 119, 120, 146, 152, 159, 161, 162, 165, 174, 185, 188, 189, 192, 194, 205, 206, 218, 219, 259, 264
Hesse-Darmstadt, 153, 163, 166, 186, 192, 201, 214, 218, 220
Hesse-Nassau, Prussian province, 225, 269
Heyne, Christian Gottlob (1729–1812), 122
Hildebrand, see Gregory VII
Hildebrandt, Lucas von (1668–1745), 136
Hildesheim, bishopric, 16, 100, 174
Hinckeldey, Karl von (1805–56), 208
Hindenburg, Paul von (1847–1934), 255, 257, 260, 261, 273–7, 282, 283
Hippel, Theodor Gottlieb von (1775–1843), 171
Hitler, Adolf (1889–19), xi, 25, 137, 265–7, 272, 275–85
Hochkirch, battle (1758), 149

Hofer, Andreas (1767–1810), 169, 170
Hohenfriedberg, battle (1745), 147
Hohenlinden, battle (1800), 161
Hohenlohe, Chlodwig, Prince of (1819–1901), 241
Hohenstaufen dynasty, 9, 19, 24, 31, 36–52, 55, 58, 59, 61
Hohenzollern, principality, 191, 220, 226
Hohenzollern dynasty, 71, 115, 152, 154, 226, 227, 259
Holbein, Hans (1497/8–1543), 58
Holland, county, 51, 62, 74
Holstein, duchy, 37, 41, 54, 73, 105, 106, 178, 197, 198, 206, 215–17
Holstein, Friedrich von (1837–1909), 241, 242, 244, 247
Holstein-Glücksburg dynasty, 198, 215
Holstein-Gottorp dynasty, 119
Hood, Samuel, Viscount (1724–1816), 158
Hoover, Herbert (1874–), 275
Hrolf, D. of Normandy (911–32), 4
Hubertusburg, peace (1763), 149, 150
Hugenberg, Alfred, 252, 266, 276–8
Hugo Capet, D. of Francia (956), K. of France (987–96), 8, 14
Huguenots, 107, 134
Humboldt, Wilhelm von (1767–1835), 183, 189
Hungary, 8, 13, 15, 16, 21, 23, 49, 50, 59, 64, 71, 72, 75, 81, 83, 85, 92, 93, 97, 102, 117, 123, 124, 135–7, 141, 145, 157, 180, 199, 200, 202, 205, 208
Hus, John (1369–1415), 68, 69, 70, 103
Hussites, 69, 70, 83
Hyndford, John Carmichael, Earl of (1701–67), 146

Iceland, vii, 23
Iconium, battle (1189), 44
Illyria, 169
India, 247, 250, 258
Ingermanland, 107
Inn Quarter, 152, 170, 172
Innocent II, Pope (1130–43), 36
Innocent II, Pope (1198–1216), 46, 47
Innocent IV, Pope (1243–54), 50–2
Innocent XI (1611–89), Pope (1676), 136
Innsbruck, 90, 200
Investiture Struggle, 12, 26–36, 72
Iraq, 284
Ireland and Irish, 110, 126, 165
Irene-Maria (d. 1208), Q. of Philip (1197), 45, 46
Isabel (d. 1241), Q. of Frederick II (1235), 48
Isabel (1451–1504), Q. of Castile (1474), 81

INDEX

Isabella II (1830–1904), Q. of Spain (1833–68), 226
Istria, 160
Italy, 8, *et passim*
Ivan VI (1740–64), Tsar of Russia (1740–41), 145
Ivrea, margraviate, 8, 17

Jagellon dynasty, 81
James VI and I (1566–1625), K. of Scotland (1567) and England (1603), 102, 103, 119
James II (1633–1701), K. of England (1685–88), 139
James III (1688–1766), the Old Pretender, 139, 146
James (1610–82), D. of Courland (1639), 127
Jameson raid, 243
Jankau, battle (1645), 111
Japan, 244, 246, 249, 284
Jena, battle (1806), 130, 164, 168; university, 189, 190, 195
Jerome Bonaparte (1784–1860), K. of Westphalia (1807–13), 165, 166, 172
Jerusalem, 45, 48, 50
Jesuit Order, 97, 151, 207, 233
Joan (1479–1555), Q. of Philip I, 81
Joan d'Arc, the Maid of Orléans (1412–31), 70
Jobst (1375–1411), Mg. of Moravia, Elector of Brandenburg (1388), anti-King (1410), 68, 74
John XII, Pope (955–63; d. 964), 10, 11
John XIX, Pope (1024–32), 19, 22
John XXII (1249–1334), Pope (1316), 61, 62
John, Austrian Archduke (1782–1859), 169, 201
John, K. of England (1199–1216), 44, 46
John II (1319–64), K. of France (1350), 74
John II (1609–72), K. of Poland (1648–68), 131
John III Sobieski (1624–96), K. of Poland (1674), 136
John III (1537–92), K. of Sweden (1569), 107
John of Luxemburg (1296–1346), K. of Bohemia (1310), 61–64
John of Nepomuk (d. 1393), Saint (1729), 67
John Frederick (1503–54), Elector of Saxony (1532–47), 90
John Gratianus, *see* Gregory VI
John Sigmund (1572–1620), Elector of Brandenburg (1608), 101

Joseph I (1678–1711), Emperor (1705), 136, 139, 140, 144, 145
Joseph II (1741–90), Emperor (1765), 122, 125, 150–3, 157
Jülich, 66, 101, 102, 115, 130, 131, 174
Jutland, 8, 15, 106, 201, 216, 255

Kahlenberg, battle (1683), 10, 136
Kahr, Gustav von (1862–1934), 270, 283
Kalisz, 158, 171
Kant, Immanuel (1724–1804), 151, 171, 183, 278
Kapp, Wolfgang (1858–1922), 259, 270
Karelia, 107
Karlsbad, 189, 190
Karlsruhe, 186
Kaunitz, Wenzel Anton, Prince (1711–94), 148, 151
Kehl, 137
Keith, George, Earl Marischal (1693–1778), 126
Keith, James (1696–1758), 126, 149
Kesselsdorf, battle (1745), 147
Kiaochow, 246
Kiderlen-Wächter, Alfred von (1852–1912), 245, 250
Kiel, 217, 261
Kiev, 10, 33, 54
Klopstock, Friedrich (1724–1803), ix
Koch, Robert (1843–1910), 278
Kolin, battle (1757), 148
Königgrätz, 180, 218
Königsberg, 59, 139
Kosciuszko, Thaddäus (1746–1817), 159
Kossuth, Lajos (1802–94), 202
Kotzebue, Johann August (1761–1819), 189
Krefeld, 101, 149
Kremsier, 202
Kruger, Paulus (1825–1904), 243, 245
Krupp, Alfred (1812–87), 225, 266
Kühlmann, Richard von (1873–), 259
Kulm, 49
Kulturkampf, 185, 232, 233

Landau, 140, 172, 173
Langensalza, battle (1866), 218
Lansdowne, Henry, Marquess of (1845–1927), 244
Lassalle, Ferdinand (1825–64), 213
Latvia, 266
Lauenburg, duchy, 174, 216, 217
Lausanne, 275
Laxenburg, 123
League of Nations, xi, 274, 282, 284
Lech, 40, 54
Leghorn, 117
Legnano, battle (1176), 41

INDEX

Leibniz, Gottfried Wilhelm von (1646–1716), 120, 142
Leipzig, 25, 54, 60, 70, 94, 109, 141, 171
Leitha, river, 23, 181
Lenin, Vladimir Ilyitch (1870–1924), 265
Leo IX, Pope (1048–54), 22, 23
Leo XIII (1810–1903), Pope (1878), 233
Leoben, peace (1797), 160
Leopold I (1640–1705), Emperor (1658), 118, 120, 121, 132, 138, 139
Leopold II (1747–92), Emperor (1790), 125, 157, 158
Leopold V, D. of Austria (1177–94), 44
Leopold (1676–1747), Prince of Anhalt-Dessau (1693), 147
Leopold, Prince of Hohenzollern (1835–1905), 226, 227
Leslie, Alexander, Earl of Leven (1580–1661), 110
Lessing, Gotthold Ephraim (1729–81), ix, 154
Leuthen, battle (1757), 149
Levant, 126, 128
Lewis IV (1287–1347), D. of Bavaria (1294), King (1314), Emperor (1328), 56, 61–4, 67, 73, 99, 152
Lewis I, D. of Bavaria (1183–1231), 47
Lewis II (1845–86), K. of Bavaria (1864), 230
Lewis III (1845–1921), K. of Bavaria (1913–18), 233
Lichnowsky, Max, Prince (1860–1928), 244, 250
Liége, 44, 74
Liegnitz, battle (1241), 50
Liman von Sanders, Otto (1855–1929), 247
Limburg, 74, 178
Lincoln, Abraham (1809–65), President of U.S.A. (1861), 207
Linz, 146
Lisbon, 38
Lissa, battle (1866), 219
Lithuania, 59, 70, 259, 266
Liudolf, D. of Saxony (844–66), 10
Liudolf, D. of Swabia (950–54; d. 957), 10
Liutitzi, 17
Livonia, 49, 107, 141
Lloyd George, David (1863–), 245, 248
Locarno, pact (1925), 274, 282
Lochner, Stephen (d. 1451), 58
Lodomeria, 152
Lombard League, 39, 41, 42
Lombards (Longobards), 1, 3, 10, 14, 36
Lombardy, 1, 3, 4, 8–10, 27, 31, 33, 39, 41, 45, 48, 160, 172, 173, 181, 199, 210

London, 57, 66, 74, 96, 135, 140, 199, 244, 272
London, agreement (1887), 239; agreement (1914), 250; conference (1864), 216; conference (1867), 226; conference (1871), 229; peace (1518), 82; protocol (1850), 201, 206, 215, 216; treaty (1840), 197; truce (1848), 201
Lorraine, 4–6, 8, 10, 14, 20, 24, 29, 74, 91, 114, 120, 130, 138, 144, 145, 229, 230
Lothair of Supplinburg, D. of Saxony (1106), King (1125–37), Emperor (1133), 35–7
Lothair III, K. of France (954–86), 14
Loudon, Ernst Gideon von (1717–90), 126
Louis IV, K. of France (936–54), 8
Louis VII, K. of France (1137–80), 38, 39
Louis XI (1423–83), K. of France (1461), 74, 148
Louis XIV (1638–1715), K. of France (1643), 120, 124–7, 130, 133–40
Louis XV (1710–74), K. of France (1715), 144
Louis XVI (1754–93), K. of France (1774–92), 152, 158
Louis XVIII (1755–1824), K. of France (1814), 172, 173
Louis Philippe (1773–1850), K. of France (1830–48), 197, 199
Louis II (1506–26), K. of Bohemia and Hungary (1516), 81, 92
Louis William (1655–1707), Mg. of Baden (1770), 123, 136, 137
Louvois, Michel Le Tellier Marquis de (1641–91), 137
Lübeck, 37, 41, 48, 49, 54–8, 66, 67, 95, 96, 106, 162, 165, 192
Lucerne, 49, 73
Lucius III, Pope (1181–85), 42
Ludendorff, Erich (1865–1937), 245, 256–60, 270, 272
Lüneburg, see Brunswick-Lüneburg and Hanover
Lunéville, peace (1801), 161
Lusatia, 17, 21, 37, 111, 149
Luther, Martin (1483–1546), ix, 66, 83, 84, 135, 278
Lutheran Church, 84–7, 91, 97–101, 107, 112–14, 134, 135, 184
Lutter, battle (1626), 105
Lüttwitz, Walter von (1859–1942), 270
Lützen, battle (1632), 109
Luxemburg, viii, 19, 60, 64, 68, 74, 134, 178, 192, 226, 228
Lyons, 20, 50

INDEX

Maassen, Karl Georg (1769-1834), 191
Macaulay, Thomas Babington (1800-59), 154
Mackay, Donald, Lord Reay (1591-1649), 110
MacMahon, Patrick (1808-93), 228
Madrid, 109, 110, 139
Magdeburg, archbishopric, 8, 13, 16, 40, 115, 129
Magdeburg, city, 87, 108
Magna Carta (1215), 48, 281
Magyars, 6-8, 10, 49, 59, 92, 135, 136, 145, 157, 179-81, 202, 208, 211, 218, 249, 258
Main, river, 18, 66
Malplaquet, battle (1709), 139
Manchester school, 252
Manfred (1231-66), K. of Sicily (1258), 52
Manin, Daniele (1804-57), 182
Mann, Thomas (1875-), 154
Mannesmann steel works, 225, 248
Manteuffel, Edwin von (1809-85), 203, 206, 208, 209
Mantua, 170
Map, Walter (d. 1208), 38
Marengo, battle (1800), 161, 164
Marie-Antoinette (1755-93), Q. of Louis XVI (1770), 152
Marie-Louise (1797-1847), Empress of Napoleon I (1810), 11, 170
Maria Theresa (1717-80), Q. of Bohemia and Hungary (1740), 66, 144-51, 153
Marienburg, 49
Mark, 101, 102, 129, 132
Marlborough, John Churchill, Duke of (1650-1722), 124, 139, 140
Marne, battle (1914), 255
Marseille, 20
Marsilius of Padua (d. 1342/3), 62, 63
Martin V (1368-1431), Pope (1417), 68
Marx, Karl (1818-83), 199, 213
Mary (1457-82), Q. of Maximilian I (1477), 74
Mary I (1516-58), Q. of England (1553), 92
Matilda (d. 1167), Q. of Henry V (1114-25), Countess of Anjou (1137-51), 34
Matilda, Marchioness of Tuscany (d. 1115), 24, 29, 31-3, 35, 36, 41
Matilda (1156-89), Duchess of Henry the Lion (1168), 39
Matthias (1557-1619), Emperor (1612), 98, 102
Matthias Corvinus (1443-90), K. of Hungary (1458), 72, 75
Maurice (1521-53), Duke (1539) and Elector (1548) of Saxony, 90, 91, 94, 174

Maurice, Count Palatine (1620-52), 112
Max, Prince of Baden (1867-1929), 260, 261
Max Emanuel (1662-1726), Elector of Bavaria (1679), 125, 136, 138, 139, 142
Maximilian I (1459-1519), King (1483), Emperor (1493), 1, 52, 73-82, 121, 148
Maximilian II (1527-76), Emperor (1564), 97, 98
Maximilian I (1573-1651), Duke (1597) and Elector (1623) of Bavaria, 100-4, 108-12, 138
Maximilian I, Joseph (1756-1825), Count Palatine (1795), Elector (1799) and K. of Bavaria (1806), 160
Mayence, archbishopric, 7, 13, 14-16, 18-20, 35, 36, 39, 41, 44, 52, 67, 68, 78, 120, 121, 125, 127, 128, 138, 153, 158, 162
Mayence, city, 48, 54, 58, 158, 189
Mazarin, Jules (1602-61), 137
Mecklenburg, 10, 23, 38, 41, 66, 106, 109, 114, 121, 122, 129, 168, 171, 174, 192, 231
Medici dynasty, 144
Mediterranean, 1, 24, 45, 56, 66, 83, 192, 239, 247
Mehemed Ali (1769-1849), ruler of Egypt (1804), 197
Memel, city, 107, 129, 132, 174, 220
Memel, river, 1, 49, 114, 174
Merovingian dynasty, 3
Messina, 14
Metternich, Clemens, Prince (1773-1859), 170-4, 177, 180, 182-200 passim, 202, 208, 209
Metz, 91, 228-30
Meuse, river, 1, 4, 5, 40, 115
Michaelis, Georg (1857-1936), 258, 259
Michaelis, Johann David (1717-91), 122
Milan, 27, 36, 39, 42, 61, 80, 117, 138, 140
Militch of Kremsier, John (d. 1374), 69
Minden, bishopric, 115
Mirabeau, Honoré Gabriel, Count of (1749-91), 154
Misica I, D. of Poland (960-92), 15
Misnia, margraviate, 17, 37, 40, 45, 51, 60, 70, 71, 90
Modena, 161
Mohacs, battle (1526), 92
Mollwitz, battle (1741), 145
Moltke, Helmuth von (1800-91), 210, 216, 218-20, 223, 224, 227, 229, 239, 241
Mommsen, Theodor (1817-1903), 177, 252

Montenegro, 249
Montfort, De, 58
Montgelas, Maximilian, Count (1759–1838), 166
Moravia, 59, 60, 64, 68, 74, 135, 145, 162, 182, 202, 285
Morocco, 225, 247, 248
Mörs, county, 118
Motz, Friedrich Adolf von (1775–1830), 191
Moys, battle (1757), 149
Mozart, Wolfgang Amadeus (1756–91), 136
Mühlberg, battle (1547), 90, 106
Mulde, river, 40
Munich, 25, 41, 54, 100, 102, 108, 109, 125, 127, 142, 146, 153, 186, 265, 272, 285
Münster, 87, 100, 111, 112, 115, 117, 120, 124
Münster, Ernst, Count (1766–1839), 194
Murat, Joachim (1767–1815), Grand Duke of Berg (1806), K. of Naples (1808–14), 163
Mussolini, Benito (1883–), 284

Namur, 74
Nancy, battle (1477), 74
Nantes, Edict of (1685), 134
Naples, 44, 47, 61, 81, 117, 138, 140, 145, 165
Napoleon I (1769–1821), French Emperor (1804–15), ix, x, 11, 112, 149, 154, 156, 157, 160–74, 181
Napoleon III (1808–73), French Emperor (1852–70), 8, 208–10, 213, 215, 217–20, 226–8, 230
Narva, battle (1700), 141
Nassau, 60, 189, 192, 214, 219
National Assembly (1848), see Frankfort; (1919), see Weimar
National Liberal Party, 211, 224, 232–5, 239, 251–4, 256–8, 267, 281
National Socialist Party, xi, 184, 191, 265–7, 272, 274–85 *passim*
Nationalist Party, 266, 276–8, 283
Naumann, Friedrich (1860–1919), 192, 267
Netherlands, viii, 74, 80, 82, 86, 87, 91, 92, 96, 97, 101, 102, 104, 105, 113–15, 118, 120, 123, 127, 128, 133, 140, 142, 146, 147, 159, 165, 178, 192, 261, 284
Netherlands, Spanish (Austrian), 82, 111, 114, 117, 120, 128, 134, 138–40, 153, 157–60, 172; from 1830, see Belgium
Neuburg, County Palatine, 100–2, 120, 130

Neuchâtel, 118, 140, 163
New Guinea, 239
New York, 274
Nice, 20, 40
Nicholas I (1796–1855), Tsar of Russia (1825), 196, 206, 208
Nicholas II (1868–1918), Tsar of Russia (1894–1917), 242
Nicholas V, anti-pope (1328), 62
Niebuhr, Barthold (1776–1831), 168
Niemen, river, 159
Nijmegen, peace (1679), 121
Nikolsburg, peace (1866), 219
Nish, 137
Nördlingen, battle (1634), 110
Normandy, 4, 34
Normans, 4, 18, 21, 32, 34, 36, 41, 42, 44–6, 49
North Sea, 5, 49, 96, 106, 114, 192
Northern March, 37
Norway, vii, 3, 15, 57, 141, 174
Notke, Bernd (fl. 1471–95), 58
Novgorod, 57
Nuremberg, 25, 40, 57, 58, 71, 79, 85, 90, 109, 130, 160, 162
Nystadt, peace (1721), 141

Ockham, William of (d. 1349/50), 63
Oder, river, 115, 129, 141
Odo, Count of Champagne (d. 1037), 20
Oldenburg, 153, 174, 194
Oliva, 132
Olmütz (Olomuc), 15, 206, 207
Orange dynasty, 161, 194
Orkney islands, 23
Osnabrück, 111, 112, 115
Ostend, 117, 128, 145
Ostrogoths, 1, 3
Otto I, King (936–73), Emperor (962), vii, 6–14, 16, 19, 28, 35, 106, 163
Otto II, King (961), Emperor (967–83), 11, 13, 14
Otto III, King (983–1002), Emperor (996), 14–18
Otto IV (1182–1218), King (1198–1215), Emperor (1209), 46, 47, 51, 58
Otto, Count of Nordheim, D. of Bavaria (1061), and Saxony (1075; d. 1083), 30–2
Otto I of Wittelsbach, Count Palatine (1156), D. of Bavaria (1180–83), 42
Otto, Bp of Bamberg (1102–39), Saint (1189), 37
Otto, Bp of Freising (1137–58), 37
Otto VIII, Count Palatine (d. 1209), 46
Otto Heinrich (1502–59), Elector Palatine (1556), 100

INDEX

Ottokar II, K. of Bohemia (1253-78), 58, 59
Ottonian dynasty, 7-19, 27
Oudenaarde, battle (1708), 139
Oxenstierna, Axel, Count (1583-1654), 109, 111
Oxford, Robert Harley, Earl of (1661-1724), 140
Oxford University, 63

Palatinate, 68, 82, 97, 99, 100, 102-4, 111, 112, 114, 118, 124, 125, 137, 144, 146, 152, 160, 194, 205
Palatinate, Upper, 64, 66, 112
Palermo, 45
Palestine, 33, 37, 38, 44, 45, 48, 50, 247, 275, 284
Pallavicino, Giorgio Marchese (1796-1878), 182
Palmerston, Henry Temple, Viscount (1784-1865), 183, 197, 216
Pan-German League, 252, 253, 272
Panizzi, Antonio (1797-1879), 182
Papal State, 10, 140, 181, 228
Papen, Franz von (1879-), 275-7, 283
Paris, 4, 8, 14, 25, 74, 120, 158, 163, 170, 172, 173, 177, 209, 218, 228-30, 236
Parma, 117, 140, 146
Paschal II, Pope (1099-1118), 33-5
Paskievitch, Ivan Fedorovitch (1782-1856), 202
Passarovitz, peace (1718), 141
Passau, bishopric, 8, 15, 54
Passau, treaty (1552), 90, 91, 106
Paul (1754-1801), Tsar of Russia (1796), 160, 161
Pavia, 17, 83, 100
Peasants' War (1525), 69, 86, 87
Peene, river, 141
Pellico, Silvio (1789-1854), 182
Peloponnese, 137, 141
Pennsylvania, 127
Persia, 247
Peter I (1672-1725), Tsar of Russia (1682), 137, 141, 154
Peter III (1728-62), Tsar of Russia (1762), 119, 149
Peters, Carl (1856-1918), 252
Peterwardein, battle (1716), 141
Petrarch, Francesco (1304-74), 66
Philip (1178-1208), German King (1198), 45, 46, 58
Philip I (1342-1404), D. of Burgundy (1363), 74
Philip II (1396-1467), D. of Burgundy (1419), 74
Philip II Augustus, K. of France (1180-1223), 44, 46, 47

Philip IV (1268-1310), K. of France (1385), 9, 60
Philip (1504-67), Lg. of Hesse (1509), 87, 90
Philip I (1478-1506), K. of Castile (1504), 81
Philip II (1527-98), K. of Spain (1556), 82, 92
Philip V (1683-1746), K. of Spain (1700), 139
Philippines, 246
Philippsburg, 137
Piacenza, 117, 140, 146
Piccolomini, Octavio (1599-1656), 110, 111
Piedmont, see Savoy
Pillau, 107
Pillnitz, 158
Pisa, 18, 68
Pitt, William (1759-1806), 158-61
Pius II (1405-64), Pope (1458), 72
Po, river, 161
Podiebrad, George of (1420-71), K. of Bohemia (1458), 72
Podolia, 137
Poitou, 46
Poland, 13-18, 21, 23, 40, 49, 66, 70, 72, 73, 107, 108, 114, 115, 117, 118, 124, 129-32, 136, 137, 141, 144, 147, 151, 156-9, 164, 172, 173, 181, 202, 215, 221, 259, 268, 269, 271, 284, 285
Poles, in Austria and Prussia, 181-5, 194, 200, 232, 233, 236, 250
Poltava, battle (1709), 141
Pomerania, ix, 15, 37, 41, 64, 106, 108, 114, 115, 117, 118, 129-34, 141, 142, 152, 164, 174
Portugal, 81, 111, 152, 226
Posen, 158, 183-5, 196, 233
Potsdam, 134, 266
Pragmatic Sanction (1713), 128, 144-7
Prague, 13, 15, 59, 66, 69, 70, 103, 104, 111, 112, 115, 146, 148, 171, 219
Pressburg, 163, 218
Preuss, Hugo (1860-1925), 268
Princes' League (1785-90), 131, 153, 154, 157
Progressive Party, 212, 239, 252, 256-8, 267, 279
Prussia, dukedom, ix, 49, 59, 70, 72, 73, 107, 115, 117, 118, 129, 131, 132, 143, 149, 152, 164, 171, 183; kingdom and republic, 7, 9, 21, 73, 118, 122, 125, 126, 129, *et passim*
Prussia, South, 158, 165; West, 152, 171, 183
Prussians, 15, 49, 59

Puttkamer, Robert von (1828-1900), 240
Pyrenees, 4, 226; peace (1659), 114, 132, 138

Quedlinburg, 13
Quisling, Vidkund (1887-), 283

Radetzky, Joseph, Count (1766-1858), 171, 200, 208
Radowitz, Josef Maria von (1797-1853), 205, 206, 214
Rainald of Dassel, imperial Chancellor (1156-67) and Abp of Cologne (1159-67), 39, 41
Rainulf, Count of Aversa (d. 1044), 21
Raleigh, Sir Walter (1552-1618), 103
Ranke, Leopold von (1795-1886), 180
Rapallo, 271
Rastatt, congress (1797), 160, 161; peace (1714), 128, 140
Rathenau, Walter (1867-1922), 271, 273
Ratisbon, 25, 54, 106-8, 110, 113, 123, 161, 162, 214
Ravensberg, county, 102, 132
Reichenbach, 157, 158
Remscheid, 101
Rense, 64
Reuss-Gera, 224
Reuter, Fritz (1810-74), 190
Reval, 54
Rhenish Alliance (1654), 120, 123, 131
Rhenish Confederation (1806-13), x, 160, 163, 165-72, 191
Rhenish Town League (1254), 56, 57, 68, 73
Rhine, vii, 5, 54, 63, 66, 115, 124, 130, 136, 149, 157-61, 172, 174, 197
Rhineland, 31, 46, 51, 53, 55, 56, 95, 101, 114, 124, 159, 160, 166
Rhineland, Prussian province, x, 169, 174, 183-5, 187, 192, 196, 205, 217, 264, 271, 272, 274, 282, 284
Rhodes, Cecil (1853-1902), 244
Rhone, river, 40
Richard (d. 1272), Earl of Cornwall, German King (1257), 50, 58, 59
Richard I (1157-99), K. of England (1189), 44, 46, 77
Richard II (1367-1400), K. of England (1377-99), 57, 64, 66
Richelieu, Armand Jean Duplessis Duc de (1585-1642), 107, 108, 111
Richter, Eugen (1838-1906), 252
Rienzo, Cola di (d. 1354), 66
Riga, 49, 54
Rijswijk, peace (1697), 137
Robert Guiscard, Count of Apulia (1057-85), Duke (1059), 27, 28, 32

Robert II, K. of France (996-1031), 20
Roger II, D. of Apulia (1128), K. of Sicily (1130-54), 42
Röhm, Ernst (1887-1934), 283
Roman Catholic Church, 85-7, 90, 91, 96-103, 106-8, 114, 125, 135-7, 151, 162, 184, 185, 196, 197, 198, 252, 279
Rome, city, vii, 1, 4, 8, 9, 11, 13, 14, 16, 17, 22, 25, 28-35, 39, 61, 62, 64, 74, 83, 93, 104, 228
Röntgen, Wilhelm (1843-1923), 278
Roon, Albrecht von (1803-79), 212, 219, 223, 227
Rossano, battle (982), 14
Rossbach, battle (1757), 125, 149
Rossetti, Gabriele (1783-1854), 182
Rostock, 54
Rothschild, bankers, 102, 185
Rotteck, Karl von (1775-1840), 187
Rouen, 8
Rudolf I (1218-91), German King (1273), 58-60
Rudolf II (1552-1612), Emperor (1576), 96, 98, 101, 103
Rudolf III, K. of Burgundy (993-1032), 20
Rudolf IV (1339-65), Archduke of Austria (1358), 60, 64
Rudolf of Rheinfelden, D. of Swabia (1057), anti-king (1077-80), 30-2
Rügen, 114, 142, 174
Ruhr district, 101, 265, 270, 271
Rumania, 117, 141, 144, 208, 209, 226, 237, 249, 258, 259
Rumanians, 180
Rupert (1352-1410), Elector Palatine (1398), King (1400), 68, 73
Rupert (1481-1504), Count Palatine, 99
Rupert, Count Palatine (1619-82), 104, 112
Russia, 13, 33, 49, 50, 107, 108, 117-19, 122, 126, 129, 132, 137, 141, 142, 144, 145, 147-9, 151, 152, 158-62, 164, 165, 169-73, 183, 189, 197, 201, 202, 208, 209, 215, 219, 226, 228, 229, 236, 237, 239, 242, 244, 246, 248, 259, 264-6, 271, 284, 285
Ruthenes, 180, 181

Saale, river, 6
Saar territory, 134, 173
Saarlouis, 172
Sadowa, 218, 225
St Germain, peace (1679), 133
St Gothard pass, 49
St Helena, 173
St Petersburg, 126, 141, 151, 162
St Thomas, 127

Saladin, Sultan (1171-93), 44, 45
Saleph, river, 44
Salerno, 32
Salian dynasty, 19-36
Salic Law, 144, 195, 198
Salisbury, Robert, Marquess of (1830-1903), 239, 244
Salonika, 208
Salzburg, 16, 114, 125, 162, 170, 172
Sarajevo, 181, 250
Sardinia, 40, 117, 140, 146
Savoy, 8, 9, 71, 126, 137, 140, 166, 172, 173, 181, 199, 200, 209, 226
Saxe-Weimar, 153, 186, 188
Saxony, electorate, 52, 71
Saxony, kingdom and republic, 165, 172, 174, 191, 192, 194, 205, 214-16, 218, 219, 231, 254, 259, 270-2
Saxony (= Lower Saxony), dukedom, vii, ix, 4-8, 11, 13, 15-18, 23-5, 29-32, 34-7, 42, 48, 51, 53, 55, 56, 95, 100, 105, 106
Saxony (= Misnia), electorate, 84, 87, 90, 94, 99, 100, 103, 108, 109, 111, 114, 115, 118, 136, 141, 142, 144-50, 153, 164, 168
Scandinavia, vii, 1, 5, 15, 21, 23, 57, 66, 96, 102, 113, 161
Scharnhorst, Gerhard von (1755-1813), 168, 171, 183
Schaumburg-Lippe, 224, 231
Scheidemann, Philipp (1865-1939), 261
Scheldt, river, 4, 5
Schiller, Friedrich (1759-1805), ix, 110, 122
Schleicher, Kurt von (1882-1934), 275-7, 283
Schleiermacher, Friedrich (1768-1834), 190
Schlick, Kaspar, German Chancellor (1429-49), 72
Schlieffen, Alfred, Count (1833-1913), 255
Schlözer, August Ludwig von (1735-1809), 122
Schlüter, Andreas (1664-1714), 142
Schmalkalden, League of (1530-47), 87, 90, 93, 153
Schomberg, Frederick, Count of (1615-90), 126
Schönborn, Johann Philipp von (1605-73), Abp of Mayence (1647), 119-21, 123, 127, 138
Schönbrunn, treaty (1805), 162
Schonen, 57
Schurz, Carl (1829-1906), 207
Schwarzburg-Sondershausen, 191
Schwarzenberg, Felix, Prince of (1800-52), 202, 204-7, 209

Schwarzenberg, Karl, Prince (1771-1820), 170, 171
Schwerin, Kurt Christoph, Count of (1684-1757), 145, 148
Scotland and Scots, 110, 126, 147, 167
Sedan, 228, 259
Seine, river, 4, 156
Seljuks, 38, 44
Semmering pass, 66
Senlis, peace (1493), 80
Serbia, 71, 117, 141, 144, 180, 208, 237, 249
Sforza, Bianca Maria (1472-1511), Q. of Maximilian I (1493), 80
Shakespeare, William (1564-1616), 154
Sicily, 4, 18, 21, 24, 32, 42, 44-9, 52, 81, 117, 137, 140, 144, 145, 199
Sickingen, Franz von (1481-1523), 82
Sidon, 45
Sigismund (1368-1437), Elector of Brandenburg (1378), K. of Hungary (1382) and Bohemia (1419), German King (1410), Emperor (1433), 64, 68, 70-2
Sigismund III (1566-1632), K. of Poland (1587), K. of Sweden (1594-1604), 107
Silesia, x, 15, 23, 40, 50, 64, 66, 118, 130, 135, 145-7, 150, 205, 209, 264
Silvester I, Pope (314-35), 16
Silvester II, Pope (999-1003), 16
Silvester III, Pope (1045-46), 22
Simmern, County Palatine, 100
Sistova, 157
Skagen, Cape, 216
Slavonia, 137
Slavs, ix, 6, 7, 9, 10, 13-15, 17, 18, 23, 37, 40, 59, 70, 129, 180, 181, 285
Slesvig, city, 7; duchy, 73, 141, 197, 198, 201, 215-19, 250; march, 7, 8, 17, 21
Slesvig-Holstein, Prussian province, 192, 197, 198, 201, 215-19, 225, 264
Slovakia, 15, 180
Smith, Adam (1723-90), 167, 191
Smolensk, 49
Social-Democratic Party, 228, 232-5, 239, 251-8, 261, 267, 268, 274, 276, 279, 281
Socialists, Independent, 264, 265, 267
Solferino, 210
Solingen, 101
Sophia (1630-1714), Electress of Ernest Augustus of Hanover, 118
South-West Africa, 239, 253
Spain, 1, 3, 26, 51, 57, 80-3, 92, 95, 96, 98, 102, 103, 105-7, 110, 111, 113, 114, 120, 126, 127, 131, 132, 136, 138-40, 144, 145, 149, 159, 169, 173, 226, 228, 233, 239, 246, 248, 284

Spartacus League, 264
Spielberg, 182
Spires, 34, 46, 54, 58, 84
Spoleto, 4, 40
Stade, 96
Stadion, Philip, Count (1763-1824), 169, 170
Stanislas I Lesczynski (1677-1766), K. of Poland (1704-9, 1733-35), D. of Lorraine (1736), 141, 144
Stanislas II Poniatowski (1732-98), K. of Poland (1764-95), 151, 159
Stein, Karl Baron vom (1757-1831), 168, 170-2, 174, 183
Stephen IX, Pope (1057-58), 27
Stephen of Blois, K. of England (1135-54), 37
Stephen, K. of Hungary (997-1038), 15, 21, 23
Stephen Langton, Abp of Canterbury (1207-28), 46
Stettin, 115
Steuben, Friedrich Wilhelm von (1730-94), 152
Stinnes, Hugo (1870-1924), 270
Stockholm, peace (1720), 141
Stoss, Veit (1438-1533), 58
Strafford, Thomas Wentworth, Earl of (1593-1641), 213
Strafford, William, 94
Stralsund, 57, 106, 115
Strasbourg, 58, 98, 134, 137, 229
Strasser, Gregor (1892-1934), 276, 283
Stresa, 284
Stresemann, Gustav (1878-1929), 257, 267, 272-5
Struensee, Johann Friedrich (1731-72), 126
Stuttgart, 186, 205
Styria, 42, 44, 50, 59, 72, 75, 102
Suarez, Karl Gottlieb (1746-98), 150
Susa, peace (1629), 107
Sutri, synod (1046), 22
Svein, K. of Denmark (986-1014), 17
Svein, K. of Denmark (1047-76), 23
Swabia, vii, ix, 4, 9, 10, 19, 20, 24, 25, 30, 31, 36, 38, 40, 45, 53, 55, 56, 86, 87, 124, 160, 166, 220, 226
Swabian Town League, 57, 68, 73
Sweden, vii, 24, 57, 105, 107-15, 117-21, 123, 130, 131-4, 141, 142, 145, 148, 149, 165, 168, 171, 174
Switzerland, viii, 20, 50, 54, 60, 73, 74, 80, 87, 97, 114, 118, 161, 172, 229
Syria, 38, 44, 45, 247
Szlankamen, battle (1691), 137

Talleyrand, Charles Maurice, Prince (1754-1838), 161, 163, 169, 172, 177

Tancred of Lecce, K. of Sicily (1190-94), 44, 45
Tanganyika, 239
Tangier, 247
Tannenberg, battle (1410), 70
Tauroggen, 171
Tell, William, 60
Teschen, peace (1779), 152
Teutones, 1
Teutonic Order, 49, 59, 70, 72, 73
Theophano, Q. of Otto II (d. 991), 11, 14
Thiers, Adolphe (1797-1877), 197, 229
Thorn, 157, 158
Thuringia, vii, 18, 23, 30, 40, 46, 51, 60, 108, 126, 269-72
Thyssen, Fritz (1873-), 270
Tilly, Johann Tserclaes, Count (1559-1632), 103-5, 108
Tilsit, peace (1807), 165
Times, The, 195, 228, 229
Timisoara, 141
Tirpitz, Alfred von (1849-1930), 239, 243, 245, 250, 256, 257, 259
Tobago, 127
Togoland, 239
Tordesillas, treaty (1494), 81
Toul, bishopric, 22; city, 91
Toulon, 158, 159
Transvaal, 243
Transylvania, 49, 93, 136, 137
Trent, Council (1545-63), 97
Treves, archbishopric, 19, 20, 52, 60-2, 82, 120, 125, 153, 162, 174, 182
Trianon, 126
Trieste, 128, 169, 192, 220
Tunisia, 236
Turin, 139, 209
Turks and Turkey, 10, 71, 83, 85, 92, 93, 105, 109, 117, 123, 134-7, 141, 144, 151, 157, 197, 242, 247-9, 258
Tuscany, 40, 117, 140, 144, 161, 162, 200; *see also* Matilda, Marchioness
Tusculum, 44
Tyler, Wat (d. 1381), 69
Tyndale, William (d. 1536), 84
Tyrol, 62, 64, 75, 163, 169, 170, 172, 220

Uhland, Ludwig (1787-1862), 187, 205
Ulm, city, 57, 58, 162; treaty (1647), 111, 112
United States of America, 127, 152, 204, 207, 229, 246, 247, 255-8, 284
Urban II, Pope (1088-99), 32, 33
Urban III, Pope (1185-87), 42
Utrecht, peace (1713), 140

Valdemar IV, K. of Denmark (1340-75), 57

INDEX

Vandals, 1, 3
Venetia, 173, 181, 210, 217, 218, 220
Venezuela, 127
Venice, 41, 56, 68, 80, 126, 128, 136, 137, 141, 160
Verden, bishopric, 114, 142
Verdun, city, 91, 158; treaty (843), vii, 3
Verona, 61, 80
Versailles, 113, 115, 126, 136, 137, 142, 148, 197, 229, 230
Versailles, peace (1919), 130, 219, 269, 271, 273, 280, 282
Vicenza, 200
Victor II, Pope (1054-57), 23, 25
Victor Emmanuel II (1820-78), K. of Sardinia (1849) and Italy (1861), 226, 228
Victoria (1840-1901), German Empress (1888), 210, 229, 239, 240
Victoria (1819-1901), Q. of Gt Britain (1837), 195, 210, 217
Vienna, 10, 25, 54, 59, 66, 71, 75, 78, 85, 93, 108-10, 115, 117, 123, 126, 128, 134, 136, 138, 142, 145, 148, 163, 199, 200, 202, 203, 209, 211, 218, 228
Vienna, conference (1834), 195; congress (1813-14), 172-8; final act (1820), 190; peace (1809), 169; peace (1864), 216
Vienne, 35
Vikings, 6
Vilagos, 202
Villafranca, 210
Virchow, Rudolf (1821-1902), 252
Vischer, Friedrich Theodor (1807-87), 205, 231
Vischer, Peter (1455-1529), 58
Visconti, Matteo (1250-1322), Lord of Milan (1287), 61
Visigoths, 1, 3
Vistula, river, 49, 114
Vogtland, 40
Voltaire, François Marie Arouet (1694-1778), 154
Vosges, 236
Vossem, peace (1673), 133

Wagner, Richard (1813-83), 205, 230
Wagram, battle (1809), 169
Walachia, 141, 144
Waldeck, principality, 123, 224, 269
Waldeck, George Frederick, Count of (1620-92), 123, 131
Waldersee, Alfred, Count (1832-1904), 241
Wallenstein, Albrecht von (1583-1634), 24, 103-10
Walsingham, Francis (1530-90), 57
Warbeck, Perkin (1474-99), 80
Warsaw, 118, 131, 146, 159, 206
Warsaw, grand duchy, 165, 167, 170
Wartburg, 46, 84, 189
Washington, D.C., 256, 275
Washington, George (1732-99), President of U.S.A. (1789-97), 152
Waterloo, battle (1815), 173, 197
Weber, Wilhelm (1804-91), 195
Weimar, 25, 210, 266
Weimar, National Assembly (1919), 264, 266-9
Weimar Republic (1919-33), x, 25, 191, 260-77 *passim*
Weissenburg, battle (1870), 228
Wellington, Arthur Wellesley, Duke of (1769-1852), 173
Welser, Augsburg bankers, 95, 127
Wenceslaus I, D. of Bohemia (921-29), 7
Wends, 14, 15
Wenzel (1361-1419), King (1376-1400), 67, 68, 70
Wesel, 129
Weser, river, 114, 115
Westminster, treaty (1756), 148
Westphalia, 12, 42, 87, 100, 101, 112, 124, 164; peace (1648), 77, 96, 112-15, 122, 130, 135
Westphalia, kingdom, 165, 166, 172, 186
Westphalia, province, 174, 183, 185, 187
Wettin dynasty, 37, 51, 71, 76, 118, 151, 259
Wetzlar, 25, 153
Wibert, *see* Clement III
Widukind of Corvey (fl. 970), 7
Wieland, Christoph Martin (1733-1813), ix
William, Count of Holland, German King (1247-56), 51, 58
William V, Count of Aquitaine (990-1029), 20, 22, 24
William IV (1493-1550), D. of Bavaria (1508), 99
William V (1548-1626), D. of Bavaria (1579-97), 99
William (1806-84), D. of Brunswick (1830), 236
William I, D. of Normandy (1035), K. of England (1066-87), 27
William, English prince (1103-20), 34
William III (1650-1702), Dutch Stadholder (1672), K. of England (1689), 123, 126, 135, 137-9
William IV (1765-1837), K. of Gt Britain (1830), 178, 195
William I (1797-1888), K. of Prussia (1861) and German Emperor (1871), 196, 197, 199, 205, 206, 208, 210-12, 214, 217, 219, 227, 230, 234, 236, 237, 239, 240

William II (1859–1941), German Emperor (1888–1918), 24, 236, 240–61 *passim*
William, German Crown Prince (1882–), 257, 261
William II, K. of Sicily (1166–89), 42, 44
Willigis, Abp of Mayence (975–1011), 14
Wilson, Woodrow (1856–1924), 260, 269
Wimpheling, Jacob (1450–1528), 77
Winchester, 25
Windischgrätz, Alfred, Prince of (1787–1862), 200, 202, 208
Windsor, 244
Wismar, 114, 142
Wittelsbach dynasty, 42, 61–4, 99, 100, 112, 120, 121, 124, 125, 138, 144, 146, 152, 153, 265
Wittenberg, 83
Wolfenbüttel, *see* Brunswick-Wolfenbüttel
Wolff-Metternich, Paul, Count (1853–1934), 244
Wolfgang William (1578–1653), Count Palatine (1614), 101, 102
Wolsey, Thomas (1474–1530), 82
Worms, bishopric, 120
Worms, city, 29, 34, 54
Worms, concordat (1122), 35, 46; council (1076), 30; diet (1231), 48; diet (1495), 78, 79; diet (1521), 84, 85; diet (1557), 97

Wörth, battle (1870), 228
Wrangel, Ernst, Count (1784–1877), 201, 203
Württemberg, ix, 94, 120, 122, 153, 156, 161–3, 166, 168, 177, 186, 190, 191, 205, 206, 214, 218, 220, 254, 259
Würzburg, bishopric, 12, 120; city, 214; grand duchy, 172
Wycliffe, John (d. 1384), 69

Yorck, David, Count (1759–1830), 170, 171
Young, Owen (1874–), 274
Yugoslavs, 179–80

Zabern, 232, 250
Zanzibar, 239, 242
Zapolya, John (1487–1540), K. of Hungary (1526), 93
Zedlitz, Karl Abraham von (1731–93), 151
Zeeland, 74
Zenta, battle (1697), 137
Zeven, capitulation (1757), 149
Zinna, convention (1667), 95
Zorndorf, battle (1758), 149
Zürich, 49, 60, 73, 87, 97
Zutphen, 74
Zweibrücken, County Palatine, 100, 131, 153
Zwingli, Ulric (1484–1531), 87, 97

WITHDRAWN